Women, State, and Party in Eastern Europe

Women, State, and Party in Eastern Europe

Edited by Sharon L. Wolchik and Alfred G. Meyer

Durham 1985 *Duke University Press*

Printed in the United States of America
on acid-free paper ∞
Library of Congress Cataloging-in-Publication Data
appear on the last printed page of this book.

"The Rites of Women: Oral Poetry, Ideology, and the Socialization of Peasant Women in Contemporary Romania," by Gail Kligman, is a revised version of an article by the same title that appeared in the *Journal of American Folklore* 97 (1984): 167–88, and is being reprinted by the permission of the American Folklore Society.
Table 14.2, "Time spent on household tasks in Yugoslavia," in Susan Woodward's chapter, "The Rights of Women: Ideology, Policy, and Social Change in Yugoslavia," is drawn from Alexander Szalai, ed., *The Use of Time: Daily Activities of Urban Populations in Twelve Countries* (The Hague: Mouton, 1972), pp. 583–94. It is reprinted by the permission of Mouton Publishers.
Tables 9.4, "Specialists and intermediaries among Polish deputies by sex," and 9.5, "Men and women among specialists and intermediaries (Poland)," in Daniel Nelson's chapter, "Women in Local Communist Politics in Romania and Poland," are drawn from Krzysztof Jasiewicz, *Role Społeczne Radnych Wojewodzkick Rad Narodowych* (Wroclaw: Zakład Narodowy im. Ossolinskich, 1979), p. 67. They are reprinted with permission from Krzysztof Jasiewicz.

Contents

Tables and Figures

Tables

Figures

Acknowledgments

We would like to thank several organizations and individuals for their help with this project, including the Joint Committee on Eastern Europe of the American Council of Learned Societies and the Social Science Research Council; the Ford Foundation; and the International Research and Exchanges Board, which funded the conference; the authors of the papers in this volume; and the staff of the Institute for Sino-Soviet Studies. We are particularly grateful to Gail Warshofsky Lapidus for her help with the early stages of planning for the conference and to Carmen Barroso, Carlos Chagas Fund, Brazil; Jessie Bernard, Pennsylvania State University; Susan J. Carroll, Rutgers University; Walter D. Connor, Boston University; Drude Dahlerup, University of Aarhus, Denmark; Norton Dodge, St. Mary's College; Joan Ecklein, Boston State College; Jan Marie Fritz, Georgetown University; Christine Halkiotis, Ohio State University; Devaki Jain, Institute of Social Studies, New Delhi, India; Jane S. Jaquette, Occidental College; Lisa Kahn, Texas Southern University; Mary Kilbourne Matossian, University of Maryland; Krystyna Kraczuk, Research Institute of Contemporary Capitalism, Warsaw, Poland; Phyllis M. Palmer, The Women's Studies Program and Policy Center, George Washington University; Jean Quataert, University of Houston, Clearlake; Ellen Ross, Ramapo College; Virginia Sapiro, University of Wisconsin; and Richard Stites, Georgetown University. We are also indebted to Jane S. Jaquette, Phyllis Palmer, Virginia Sapiro, and several anonymous readers for their comments on earlier drafts of this manuscript. Phyllis Palmer deserves our special thanks for her help in linking our work to that of women's studies scholars.

We would like to thank Gaston J. Sigur, Director of the Institute for Sino-Soviet Studies, for his interest in and support of this project and Virginia R. Allen, former Special Assistant to the Dean for Women's Studies, and Mary P. Haney, former Coordinator of International Programs of the

Women's Studies Program, for their help in organizing the participation in the conference of representatives of governmental agencies and others interested in women's issues working in private organizations. Our thanks are also due Suzanne Stephenson, Executive Assistant at the Institute, for her help in organizing the conference and preparing the papers for publication, and Sheila Murphy, Dorothy Wedge, and Leila Sanders, also of the Institute for Sino-Soviet Studies, and Andrew Chance for their help in typing and organizing the papers and correspondence involved in the project. Bonnie Semilof, Patricia Willacker, Andrew Wedeman, David Joens, and Karen Cutliff also deserve thanks for their help in tracking down missing references and copyediting the papers that follow. Finally, we wish to thank our families and Candida Gargiulo for their help throughout this project.

Foreword

Ten years ago the comparative study of women was in its infancy. In politics, Maurice Duverger's *The Political Role of Women* was the only work to which the scholar could turn—a classic, insightful in many ways, but barely a beginning.

The changes in this field over this decade have been dramatic. Anthologies and monographs on the status of women now exist for every continent, and country studies have been given an immense anthropology, building on the painstaking assembly of data on women and work and on women in the family. Sociologists and historians have looked to political science, anthropology, and psychology for an understanding of how consciousness, ideology and participation have been changing the constraints under which women labor, raise families, and enter the public sphere.

Women, State, and Party in Eastern Europe is a significant addition to this literature, not merely because it fills a geographical gap in our knowledge, although that alone would be welcome. Nor is it useful solely because it discusses the status of women in countries where women have been rapidly and intentionally integrated into modern roles by administrative fiat under the aegis of a gender-egalitarian ideology, though such comparisons put North American and Western European experiences in a very different perspective.

This book is most valuable because it provides new data and new perspectives while confronting the major issues that feminist theory has raised about the origins of feminist change, the gap between symbolic action and reality for women, and the limits of change under current political arrangements.

The status of women in Eastern Europe varies widely due to differences in history, culture, the degree of modernization, and patterns of government intervention among the nations represented in this group. More importantly, the absence of women's movements in these countries that are independent of state policies and definitions of the ideal makes it difficult for these governments to change direction in response to the unintended consequences of their policies or to meet new needs as expressed by women themselves. Women are not empowered by this process. The fact that the state stands astride the path to women's emancipation may be a plus for women's material welfare, but it is ultimately politically alienating; the state "appropriates" what should be productive political labor by preempting it.

Thus the experience of Eastern European women illustrates, in part because government policies have gone much further than our current consensus in the West (excluding Scandinavia) will allow, the limits of government-sponsored change. It also proves beyond a shadow of a doubt that such sponsorship, though it makes a real difference, falls short of our vision. Comparing East and West forces us to think more clearly about our goals—and to realize that under the current terms of the social debate we are following principles that appear contradictory: equality for women *and* positive recognition of their special roles. This should not deter us. The best measure of women's power is not the consistency of its demands—that would better describe an abstract system of justice with women as its objects—but its ability to give access to individuals whose needs and goals may vary widely. This study helps clarify this issue and adds immeasurably to our understanding both of female realities and of the complexity of the task we have set for ourselves.

Jane S. Jaquette
Occidental College, Los Angeles
November 23, 1984

Sharon L. Wolchik

Introduction

This volume grew out of a series of papers prepared for a Conference on Changes in the Status of Women in Eastern Europe held at George Washington University, December 4–6, 1981, which the editors of this volume organized. Sponsored by the Institute for Sino-Soviet Studies with the cooperation of the Women's Studies Program and Policy Center of George Washington University, the conference was funded by the Joint Committee on Eastern Europe of the American Council of Learned Societies and Social Science Research Council with funds provided by the National Endowment for the Humanities and the Ford Foundation; the International Research and Exchanges Board; and the Ford Foundation. It brought together approximately twenty–five American and East European scholars who are specialists on various aspects of women's status in Eastern Europe. The revised and updated contributions of many of these scholars form the basis for this book. In addition, our discussions and the chapters to follow benefited from the comparative perspective and numerous useful insights and criticisms provided by the fourteen American, West European, and Asian scholars expert on women's roles in other parts of the world who also participated in the conference.

Our discussions, which centered on the topics reflected in the pages to follow, were directed toward several purposes. First, we wanted to compare notes about various aspects of women's status in different East European countries with an eye to identifying both commonalities and differences in their situations. As the essays to follow illustrate, Eastern Europe is an area of great diversity. It is currently defined as a region by political factors, but the countries in the region have historically differed from each other in many important respects, and many of these differences persist to the present day. Thus, we asked the question of how such factors as different levels of economic development, national traditions, and political histories influenced women's status, in particular countries and in the region as a whole.

We also were interested in how Marxist-Leninist ideology and a political structure in which the Communist party is the dominant if not sole political force (factors common throughout the region) affected women and policy toward women. Secondly, while our primary focus was on women in Eastern Europe, we also wanted to discuss how women's status in this region of the world compares to that of women elsewhere and what looking at women's roles in Eastern Europe can tell others who are interested in women's status in other world areas. Finally, by bringing together scholars working on various aspects of women's roles in different countries, we wanted to identify areas that needed additional research. The pages to follow reflect some of our conclusions.

The book to follow consists of five main parts, each of which is introduced in more detail in the body of the book. In Part I the editors discuss some of the factors that conditioned later efforts to change women's roles in Eastern Europe. Meyer analyzes the theoretical basis of support for women's equality found in Marxist theory and discusses the often uneasy relationship between Marxism and feminism in this part of the world and elsewhere. Wolchik's essay examines other factors that influence women's roles in Eastern Europe, including the precommunist situation; the political structure and organization of public life in communist states; and the general strategies of economic and political development that have left their mark on women's lives as well as men's. Part II, which deals with women's movements and policies that affected women in several countries in the precommunist period, provides more detailed historical data on women's status in a number of countries at different stages of economic development and with different traditions in regard to women's roles. It should thus allow the reader to come to some conclusions concerning the starting point for later efforts to change women's status; it also should provide a basis for judging the distinctiveness of the elite's approach to women's issues in the communist period. Parts III and IV focus on women as makers of and objects of public policy; they also highlight the relationship between women's roles in the public and private realm. The essays in Part III discuss women's relationship to political power at both the national and local level; they also provide information concerning elite efforts to increase women's political participation and data on women's participation in political activities that take place outside accepted political channels. In Part IV we look at women's roles in production and reproduction, as well as at the public policies that influence women's roles in both areas. The essays in this section highlight women's importance as economic and reproductive resources for the state in these countries. They also discuss the policies political leaders have enacted to facilitate women's performance of these functions and the sometimes unanticipated or contradictory results of these policies for women themselves as well as the political system. In Part V we return to the broader society and examine popular attitudes toward women and women's roles as these are reflected in survey research, folklore and ritual, and popular literature. The essays in this section, which deal explicitly with a theme that runs throughout the volume, demonstrate the intimate relationship between women's private and public roles and illustrate the impact that change, or lack of change, in the private sphere has on women's public roles. They also illustrate the continuing tendency for women to be defined primarily in terms of their private, or domestic, roles in these societies, despite the fact that they also typically work outside the home.

As the reader will note, this volume does not treat all East European countries equally. Certain countries, such as Czechoslovakia, Poland, Hungary, Yugoslavia, and Romania, are the subject of several essays while others, such as Albania and East Germany, receive less attention, and Bulgaria is dealt with explicitly only in the essay on social services. To a large extent this unevenness reflects the uneven state of scholarship on women's roles in particular East European countries. Thus, while we would have liked to include more explicit consideration of women's situation in Bulgaria, for example, we simply did not know of any scholar (outside those in Bulgaria) who has explored the subject in any depth. Similarly, while it might have been preferable in certain respects to discuss particular subjects across the area in a single essay, with few exceptions, scholarship on women in this part of the world reflects the same division by country or region as other scholarly work on East European subjects.

We attempted to deal with this problem in two ways. First, we encouraged our authors to discuss more than one case whenever possible. Thus, Mieczkowski's look at social services for women spans the area as a whole; Nelson's discussion of local level leaders examines women's roles in two countries with very different political regimes, Poland and Romania; Jancar's examination of women in dissent includes the Czech and Polish cases; and McIntyre's essay on demographic policies contrasts the Hungarian and Romanian experiences. In other cases, we selected a mix of typical and atypical cases. In those cases where a particular aspect of women's status had been examined in numerous countries by different scholars, we generally chose to include a case typical of trends and results across the area. In a few cases, however, we selected a country as the focus for discussion because we expected that certain facets of women's lives in that country might be atypical of the region due to particular aspects of the country's culture, level of economic development, or political structure, or because certain phenomena, while not found in the region as a whole, are nonetheless important in individual countries. Thus, in the historical section we sought to include a mix of countries at different stages of development and with different traditions in respect to women in order to see how these factors affected women's opportunities to organize and the status and activities of women in the precommunist period. We also included one essay that dealt with the activities of women who were members of an ethnic group that was a minority in the state. In the section dealing with women's political lives, we selected two countries in which there have been recent efforts to increase women's political visibility as the focus of discussion of women's roles in national level politics; although we anticipated that these efforts might be reflected in results atypical of the region as a whole, in fact women's political behavior in Romania and, to a lesser extent, Albania, appears to follow many of the same patterns found elsewhere in the region. Jancar's chapter on dissent discusses actions that are atypical within the region but extremely important in the countries studied. We have attempted, in our introductions to each section, as well as in the individual chapters, to address the issue of how general or representative the case being discussed is for the area as a whole. Where relevant, we also have indicated how the particular case or general East European pattern corresponds to women's situation elsewhere in the world.

Our decision to invite scholars from Poland, Hungary, and Yugoslavia was based on our judgment that the most sophisticated and innovative social science research on women has been conducted in those East European countries in the recent past. Their topics reflect their own research specializations as well as our efforts to balance the country coverage in particular sections.

The sources used by our authors are diverse and reflect both disciplinary predilections and, in some cases, the problems of access that plague Western scholars researching contemporary topics in Eastern Europe. Most of the chapters in this volume are based on a mix of aggregate data, including national and international statistical collections; official documents, including party and government statements, collections of laws, party congress documents, and reports of the women's organizations; and information in the popular and specialized press in these countries, including mass circulation newspapers, women's magazines, and specialized publications. They also typically draw on research conducted by scholars in Eastern Europe, as reported in books, articles in specialized journals, and published as well as unpublished, or limited circulation, research reports. In addition, some authors, particularly Kolsti in his discussion of women's political roles in Albania and Rosenberg in her analysis of attitudes toward women in the German Democratic Republic (GDR), used literature as a source of information. In most cases, the authors also benefited from firsthand observation and discussions with women, experts on women's issues, and officials responsible for policy areas that affect women during research in the countries involved. However, given the restrictions on empirical social science research by foreigners in all of these countries, most did not conduct systematic interviews with women or gather detailed oral histories.

Exceptions to this pattern include two of the contributions by East European scholars and the chapters by Kligman and Nelson. Thus, Renata Siemieńska's examination of popular attitudes toward women's roles in Poland is based on her own extensive survey research in Poland, while Kulcsár's discussion of women's economic roles draws on aggregate and attitudinal data collected by a research team of which she was a member in the Hungarian Central Statistical Office. Kligman's chapter on marriage rituals in Romania is based on observation at the village level as well as an analysis of collected *strigături*, or shouted verses. Nelson's examination of women's roles in local politics is also based on his own field research, in this case on interviews he conducted as part of a project on local level leaders in Romania and Poland.

The contributors to this volume discuss many of the same topics treated by western, and particularly American, women's studies scholars, although they often use different vocabularies and frameworks of analysis. Perhaps the most important of these is the centrality of the relationship between the private and public areas of life for women and the resulting need to analyze both areas. As the essays to follow illustrate, women continue to be defined in these, as well as in other, societies primarily in terms of their private roles. Life in the public sphere, on the other hand, continues to be organized according to patterns determined largely by the male experience, to women's disadvantage.[1] The East European experience is important in this respect, for it demonstrates the impossibility of equality for women without change in men's as well as women's private roles and the reorganization of life in the workplace and politics; it also illustrates the costs of such a reorganization.

Another often-examined topic dealt with in the chapters to follow is the frequently contradictory impact of modernization on women's status.[2] In the East European case, as in the Soviet Union, rapid industrialization was one of the main goals of the communist leaders who came to power after the Second World War, and the particular development strategy chosen has had a major influence on women's opportunities as well as standard of living. As in other parts of the world, economic development has had both positive and negative results for women in Eastern Europe. It also has had different impacts on different groups of women. The subordination of women's interests to "broader" issues by policymakers, political leaders, and many women themselves; the continued influence of patriarchal attitudes in certain areas of life, despite change in others; occupational segregation and other forms of continued inequality in the workplace; women's continued exclusion from the direct exercise of economic or political power; the double burden and its negative impact on women's economic advancement and political participation; the devaluation of activities that become known as "women's work," whether in the home or the paid economy; the deep resistance on the part of many men and women to actual equality for women; and the role of childrearing practices, the family, and the broader culture in perpetuating women's unequal status are other themes that those familiar with women's roles elsewhere will recognize in the discussions of women's roles in Eastern Europe that follow.[3]

At the same time, it is important for Western readers to keep the East European context of the following essays in mind, for this context conditions the meaning of the reality analyzed for those who live it as well as those who observe it. While East European women experience many of the same problems as women elsewhere, their evaluation of the importance of these problems as well as the opportunities they have to do something about them are in many cases very different from those of Western feminists.

The specific context also influences to some extent the topics discussed in this volume. In part because mass feminist movements do not exist in these countries, the nature of debate over women's issues and roles differs from that found in the United States and Western Europe. The reader will notice, for example, that beyond a discussion of the "medicalization" of reproduction in Czechoslovakia, we have not dealt explicitly with women's sexuality in this volume. This is largely because there is very little open discussion or debate on the topic in Eastern Europe. In Eastern Europe, as well as in the Soviet Union, it is not generally considered proper to discuss such issues in public. Nor is it considered proper, apparently, to discuss the issue of violence against women. Certain other topics of interest to Western feminists and scholars, such as formal recognition of equal rights for women, reform of language to remove its sexist elements, or the relationship between patriarchy and particular political systems, are also non-issues in Eastern Europe at present, either because they have been resolved or because they are considered too trivial or too controversial.

Although we did not begin with a common theoretical framework and although our authors used different approaches and types of information, several common themes emerge from the chapters to follow. First, as in other parts of the world, it is clear that women's contemporary roles and status are determined by the interplay of several factors, including the impact of state policies (both those consciously designed to affect women and those that unintentionally or only secondarily have such an impact, such as strategies for economic development, demographic and social policies, and educational or cultural policies) and popular attitudes and patterns of social interaction, which are in turn influenced by a country's history, as well as earlier forms of social, economic, political, religious, and family organization. Women's lives are also influenced by the political organization and political values of the societies in which they live. Taken together, these factors determine the structure of both the public and private aspects of women's lives; they condition the opportunities women have to enter the public sphere, as workers and citizens, and have a profound impact on the ways women, as well as men, live their private lives. The chapters to follow illustrate how these factors have influenced women's status in Eastern Europe; they also demonstrate how national peculiarities, as well as differences in levels of economic development, culture, religion, and social customs, have modified the impact of similar strategies of economic development, political change, and social transformation.

As the chapters to follow illustrate, women's lives in Eastern Europe reflect a blend of new and traditional elements. In some cases, communist leaders have been successful in challenging aspects of the precommunist culture and have altered men's and women's behaviors as well as attitudes. In other cases, elite efforts to change women's situation have encountered resistance or apathy on the part of large sectors of the population, and little change has occurred. In still others, communist leaders have not tried to change women's roles, but rather, as Kenneth Jowitt has argued is the case in other areas,[4] have sought to incorporate certain aspects of women's roles and attitudes with respect to women prevalent in the precommunist period into the new socialist value system. As several of the essays to follow illustrate, there are also important differences in the extent of change among different groups of women.

But, although the persistence of precommunist patterns of behavior and values, especially evident in behavior in the home, in all of these countries demonstrates the continued importance of informal patterns of social organization and traditional values in Eastern Europe, the institution of communist states in the region has had an impact on women's lives. Looking within the region at the pattern of changes in women's roles, it is tempting to conclude that political factors have been more important than others, including level of economic development, previous traditions in regard to women, and previous patterns of social and political organization, in determining women's roles. While there are important differences in women's roles in urban and rural areas and in different regions within particular countries, women's contemporary roles in different countries in Eastern Europe do not vary consistently by any of the factors noted above. Women in Czechoslovakia and East Germany, for example, do not differ markedly from those in Romania and Bulgaria in their access to higher education or representation among political leaders, and efforts to improve women's position or change their roles in certain areas of life, such as politics in the recent past, have been successful and energetic in some of the least as well as the most developed East European countries. Further, the pattern of change in women's roles has been the same across all countries of the region. Although there are differences within the region, there has been most change in women's educational access and employment patterns and far less change in women's role in the exercise of power or behavior in the family in all countries. This pattern is found as well in the two East European countries that differ most in terms of their institutional structures and relationships to the Soviet Union—Yugoslavia and Albania. It is also very similar to that found in women's roles in other communist countries, particularly the Soviet Union, which served as a model for efforts to change women's status in many of these countries.

The importance of political factors, including state policies as well as the particular pattern of organization and values of contemporary communist states, is also evident if we compare women's status in Eastern Europe with that of women in countries with other types of political systems. As several of the commentators familiar with women's roles in other areas of the world noted, compared to women in noncommunist, less developed countries, women in Eastern Europe have made a number of important gains. Thus, there is legal recognition of women's equality in all of these countries, and women have, formally, equal rights to education and careers. Communist leaders are also committed, at least on paper, to ease the conflict between women's domestic and work roles by providing public childcare and maternity leaves and improving services. In contrast to the situation in many parts of the world, women in all East European countries except Romania at present also have the right to control their own bodies, at least in terms of relatively unrestricted access to abortion. Although there are problems in all of these areas, there is no doubt that the advent of communist systems has had some positive results for women in these countries.

If we compare women's status in Eastern Europe with that of women in other developed Western countries, one of the main differences appears to be the timing of change in women's roles. Thus, while women's access to education and participation in paid employment outside the home are currently more similar to those of men in Eastern Europe than in the United States or most Western European countries, differences between the two groups of countries have narrowed in the last two decades.

From the perspective of Western feminists, perhaps the most striking difference in women's situation in these countries is the lack of feminist consciousness and feminist movements. Despite the many difficulties East European women face and despite their recognition, documented by social science research as well as evident in conversations with women themselves, of numerous problems, there has been very little interest in these countries in explicitly feminist issues. As Jancar notes in her discussion of Czech and Polish women in the opposition, this is also true among those women who are extremely critical of the system on other grounds. Rosenberg argues that there are currently feminist tendencies in literature in East Germany, but the East German case appears to be atypical in this regard. Only in Yugoslavia, where the limits of political debate and action are wider than elsewhere in the region, have groups of women who identify themselves as feminists formed outside the official women's organization, and, even in that country, their numbers appear to be small.

To some extent, the absence of feminist movements reflects the fact that the organizational principles of these political systems make it difficult if not impossible for all citizens to form independent organizations in these countries. It also may reflect the uneasy relationship between feminism and Marxism, particularly in its Leninist variant that is the official value system in these countries today. But the lack of interest in feminist issues also appears to be related to another distinctive aspect of women's contemporary situation in Eastern Europe compared to that of women in other relatively highly developed Western countries, and that is the fact that change in women's roles in these countries, to a larger extent than elsewhere, has been imposed on women from above rather than fought for or chosen by women themselves.

Although there are some distinctive features of women's status in Eastern Europe, it is the similarities in women's situation in this region of the world and elsewhere that are most noticeable. Thus, although women are more often employed and have had levels of educational access equal to those of men for a longer time in these countries than in the United States or Western Europe, they face many of the same problems in the area of work as women elsewhere and are by and large excluded from the direct exercise of political and economic power.[5] A detailed analysis of why this should be the case, despite the many important ways these countries differ from others, particularly in the political sense, is beyond the scope of this volume, but it is striking that political leaders in these as well as in most other countries, with the exception of Norway and Sweden, have done little to foster change in the roles of men and women in the domestic sphere. On the contrary, women's unpaid labor in the home has been an economic resource for communist leaders as well as others. One can argue, in fact, that the strategy of economic development chosen by leaders in Eastern Europe in the late 1940s, which emphasized rapid industrialization with a corresponding concentration of investment in heavy industry and neglect of the consumer sector, would have been difficult if not impossible to implement had political leaders and planners not been able to count on women both to increase the labor force and continue to provide the valuable services they contribute by their unpaid work at home. Thus, it is clear that the sexual division of labor, particularly in the home, has been one of the underpinnings of communist as well as other political and economic systems.

This consideration brings us back to the points raised at the beginning of this introduction. The chapters to follow illustrate the often uneven, sometimes contradictory changes that have taken place in women's roles since the institution of communist systems in Eastern Europe. By highlighting both the positive and negative aspects of these changes, they illustrate how factors such as political structure, ideology, and elite goals and policies interact with social customs, popular attitudes, and the actions of men and women in their everyday lives to influence women's opportunities and roles.

I

Conditioning Factors

1

Alfred G. Meyer

Feminism, Socialism, and Nationalism in Eastern Europe

The conference for which the contributions to this volume were written dealt with the relationship between Marxism and feminism in the part of Europe that since the end of World War II has come under communist rule. The many questions these contributions raise can be grouped under two main headings: first, what have the concerns of women been in Eastern Europe? Has there been a feminist movement, and what was its relationship to various other political movements—socialism, liberalism, and nationalism? Second, what have approximately forty years of East European socialism done for women? The space the conference gave to the second of these questions was disproportionately larger than that devoted to the nature of East European feminist movements; indeed, one of the most important topics belonging to the first topic was left out altogether, either because it was considered too complex to be fitted in or because the participants' acquaintance with it was taken for granted. This is the relationship between feminism and Marxism. In this chapter I examine this relationship, placing the problem into the East European context as much as possible. In doing this, I dwell on the differences between East European feminism and its counterparts farther west; in many cases my remarks take the form of raising questions for which as yet we do not have answers.

Marxism and Feminism: Theoretical Considerations

Women in the Western world who, for whatever reasons, became conscious of being oppressed have always been drawn to radical movements. That is only natural, because feminist consciousness itself is a protest against the prevailing order. The more patriarchal the relations in any society, the more revolutionary any feminist sentiment will seem. Consequently, feminists tend to identify with movements on the left, and in Europe they participated actively in every one of the many revolutions that have occurred since 1789. From early on they also participated in the socialist movement as journalists, agitators, and organizers of women workers. Most of the radical women from America and Western Europe with whose lives I am acquainted remained self-conscious feminists after joining male-dominated revolutionary or reform movements.

The lives of radical women are now being studied extensively, but we still do not know enough about the process by which they were radicalized. My impression is that a large number of feminists in radical movements came from upper classes and that many of them were endowed with outstanding intellectual and organizational talents. To be talented and female and a member of a privileged class can be very alienating because the talents are given no proper outlet, and thus the privileges easily appear empty or phony. If such gifted young ladies also receive a religious upbringing, which they then take seriously, Christian morality easily turns into a strong stimulus for social criticism. Almost every American or West European radical feminist of the nineteenth century with whose life I have become acquainted came into radical politics through the path of an earnest commitment to religion. This is true also of many Russian feminists, but whether it applies in Eastern Europe is still an unanswered question.

Radical movements in their turn have tended to be sympathetic to the cause of women and often have made women's emancipation part of their own programs. That is true of the most radical spokesmen of the French Revolution, such as Condorcet and von Hippel; it applies to such men as Godwin and John Stuart Mill and to some of the Utopian Socialists, particularly Fourier, whose strong endorsement of women's liberation Engels and Marx quoted with approval. In the case of Marxism, the relationship to the cause of women's emancipation is quite complex, however, and deserves to be explored in some detail.

As a protest movement, Marxism has been concerned with the alienation of labor, a process Marx and Engels traced back to the beginnings of human civilization but that they saw as being carried to extremes under capitalism. Marx and Engels regarded productive labor as the expression of the human essence. We are distinct from animals by being endowed with intelligence and purposiveness and, therefore, have the capability to re-create the world in our image by "appropriating" it. The human species does this by means of productive labor. But with the institution of private property in the means of production, labor is alienated because property enables its owners to exploit the labor of others by appropriating the products of their labor for the benefits of the privileged class. From a mode of self-actualization, productive labor thus turns into mere drudgery, an imposed and hateful activity. Capitalism, according to Marx, intensifies this alienation because it has converted all human relations into market relations and has thus transformed all human qualities and potentials, including talents, skills, and labor power, into commodities. We can regain our humanness only by abolishing this entire system and the institution of private property on which it is based.

For Marx and Engels the history of humanity is the story of how our species has struggled to secure the material means for survival and comfort. It is a tale of progress because it has involved steady improvement in the productive forces at the disposal of human beings. Human inventiveness, creativity, and ingenuity have been the driving forces of this history. All societies are primarily production mechanisms designed to maintain and develop all available productive forces and put them to use in productive processes. To accomplish this, all societies generate an elaborate system of institutions (property systems, laws, governments, mores, beliefs, kinship patterns, etc.) that form the "superstructure" in the Marxian scheme. The superstructure is particularly necessary since all but the most primitive societies are torn by conflict between the laboring and the privileged classes and would disintegrate if they were not held together by system-maintaining institutions. Yet while the superstructure is indispensable for holding class-divided societies together, it can do so only temporarily. By its very nature, the superstructrue is static; it seeks to fix relations as they are. Yet the productive forces develop all the time, and sooner or later they will find themselves cramped and confined by the superstructure, which will then function primarily as a device for maintaining the privileges of a ruling class that has become obsolete and dysfunctional. But no ruling class can maintain itself in power forever. The productive forces of society will sooner or later become strong enough to burst out of the confinement of oppressive institutions. The old system will be destroyed by the masses of those who perform the productive labor. They will seize control in a revolution and erect a new system appropriate to the new stage in the development of the productive forces.

While in previous historic eras this cycle then began anew, Marx and Engels expressed confidence that communism would be free from baneful contradictions. It would be a society without property and without classes; it would, therefore, be able to dispense with political authority, institutions of coercion, myths, thought control, and all kinds of social inequality. It would be based on genuine sharing of all benefits and burdens and on communal self-government. All this would be possible because capitalism, by accumulating unprecedented material wealth, had made abundance possible.

In the writings of Engels and Marx, capitalism indeed emerges as a social order that has liberated all human urges toward acquisition and accumulation of material wealth, thus unleashing and stimulating inventiveness and creativity on an unprecedented scale. Capitalism has accomplished this through the institution of private property, which thus is the quintessential reason for the success it has had in promoting the wealth of nations. Yet private property is also seen as the reason for the predicted failure of the system. For an economy based on private property operates under the laws of the market, first described by the theorists of free enterprise and later amended by Marx. Marx was convinced that the laws as he interpreted them proved the coming collapse of capitalism. Briefly—and in commonsense language—he argued that the system was operating under an intrinsic compulsion toward ever greater capital intensity, and this indeed was the secret of its ever increasing volumes of production. He believed, however, that the profitability of capitalist enterprises depended not on capital intensity but on labor intensity, so that the more material wealth the system amassed, the less capable would it be to make use of this wealth. Ultimately, therefore, capitalism would choke in its own abundance.

Moreover, not only was the system incapable of using its accumulated material wealth; it was equally unable to make use of the creative potential in its human beings. Ever-increasing numbers of people would be forcibly idled, competing fiercely with each other for a shrinking number of jobs; wages would be depressed; the misery of the working class would increase. Marx and Engels summarized their views of capitalism by stating that it was a system which accumulated great wealth and great poverty, either being the precondition of the other. From this observation it was only a short step for them to convince themselves that the working class would soon revolt against this inequitable system, that it would recognize private property in the means of production to be the key institution that had to be abolished. A proletarian revolution, followed by a brief period of proletarian dictatorship, would accomplish this task. By abolishing private property it would abolish class differences and create a social order worthy of human beings. The task that Marx and Engels set themselves as their lives' project was to prepare and mobilize the working class for this revolution.

Anyone looking for the place that women and women's concerns may have in this theory will find no more than the barest hints that Engels and Marx were aware of special concerns or grievances women might have, or (in the case of Marx) that they should even be regarded as having a function to fulfill in the economic and political life of society.[1]

In his fragmentary early essays that remained unpublished during his lifetime, Marx seems to echo Rousseau's view that to be human means being dependent on and complementary to others and that, therefore, the paradigmatic human relationship may be that between male and female. Heterosexual love, for Marx, is the model of a genuinely human social order. In cryptic but beautiful words he suggests that in the love between men and women, nature and humanity, biological drives and highest ethical commitment merge with each other. Private property, he and Engels pointed out repeatedly, corrodes this ideal relationship: in a market society, where everything we do is based on profit calculations, money acts as the universal pimp, converting all human character traits—bravery, beauty, talent, skill, persuasiveness, sexuality, etc.—into marketable commodities and all human relations—friendship, love, sexual intercourse, and marriage—into forms of prostitution.[2]

While in the writings of Marx this theme was not explored any further, Engels on several occasions took pains to emphasize that middle-class marriage was a species of prostitution since the woman bargains her sexuality for economic security. He expressed his awareness that women were oppressed in various ways: lucrative careers were closed to them; they were barred from participation in politial life; as wage workers they earned less than their male cohorts; the double standard in sexual morality imposed terrible hardship on them; and their intellects were crippled by miseducation. Both he and Marx echoed Fourier's radical feminist views, though in watered-down form. Fourier had argued that the emancipation of women was the chief cause of progress, while the oppression of women led to general social regression. In their joint work, *The Holy Family*, Marx and Engels modified this by declaring the emancipation of women to be the most natural *indicator* of general emancipation.[3]

Consequently, they took it for granted—though they did not express this in any of their writings—that under socialism women would enjoy equality with men in all areas of public life: equal status under the law, equal political rights, and full participation in economic life. This last point was crucial. Engels and all subsequent Marxist theorists have taken it for granted that the mobilization of all women for productive work outside the home would guarantee their emancipation. For once all able women were independent wage earners, they would be economically independent, hence free from oppression or domination by men, particularly if at the same time some traditional women's duties, such as housekeeping and childrearing, could be performed by public institutions or in cooperatives. Once these changes had occurred, marriage would cease functioning as an economic unit or as a publicly sanctioned institution regulating sexual intercourse and procreation. Mutual attraction would be the only reason for women and men to live together.[4]

In this general way, the Marxist movement was committed to declare the emancipation of women to be a part of its political program. August Bebel, who for several decades was the undisputed leader of the largest Marxist party (the Social Democratic party of Germany), gave emphasis to this commitment in his *Women and Socialism*, first published in 1879, a book that for many decades remained the only authoritative statement by a Marxist leader of the movement's attempt to speak for women. The endorsement it gave to attempts at mobilizing women for work in the party convinced many radical feminists that Marxian socialism was supporting them, and it attracted many women to the movement. Yet within the Marxist movement there were many leaders who did not share Bebel's views, and in practice women's issues remained, at best, a marginal concern. Many party activists, moreover, regarded women's grievances as a decidedly unwanted and disturbing side issue that would take attention away from the really important matter—the class struggle of the proletariat. Indeed, the general tendency among those who spoke for the movement was to argue that the only oppression that mattered was that of labor by capital, all other forms of oppression being seen as derivative. Thus, all inequities in society could be subsumed under the exploitation of the working class, and the party could, in general, subscribe to the simplistic view that women's emancipation would be an automatic consequence, a fringe benefit as it were, once socialism had replaced capitalism.[5]

As a consequence, Marxist parties did little more than make polite formal bows to women, tried indeed to mobilize them for party activity, but made very sure that women kept "their places" in the movement as auxiliaries to the male proletariat. Moreover, there were many prominent leaders who thought that even in this the party was going too far and that in fact there was no place in it for women. To some extent this was nothing else than a discrepancy between confessed theoretical beliefs and personal life-styles.

The patriarchal family life and convictions of Marx himself are well known—his regret for not having any sons, his preference for weakness and submissiveness in women, and his total unwillingness to allow his wife a role in his political work, even though she yearned to be accepted as a comrade-in-arms and repeatedly cursed the fate which condemned her to be a housekeeper.[6] Similar observations could be made about a very large number of prominent Marxists everywhere, who often did not take women any more seriously. Rosa Luxemburg's letters to her lover are one of many sources for this observation.[7]

Another issue which probably deserves more exploration is the persistence of what scholars now call proletarian antifeminism. While Engels had suggested that women would be liberated from dependency and oppression by engaging in wage labor, the average male worker in Europe and North America tended to demand the *elimination* of women from the industrial work force; agitation to this effect continued to be heard in the Marxist movement until the end of the nineteenth century and sometimes beyond that. Has it ever really been overcome? Did it move from party congresses to the trade union movement? Have Marxist parties made sustained efforts to combat it and, if so, under what circumstances? Here is an area in which much more work deserves to be done.

Further, many leaders of the Marxist movement were quite frank in stating their conviction that women, as a group, were more conservative, less militant, perhaps less courageous than men. Women clearly were regarded as a backward element within the proletariat who needed far more political education than the men. Women thus were treated with some of the same condescension with which society as a whole tended to treat them.

Today it must appear ludicrous to us to think that it might be possible to discuss the special concerns of women without bringing in all the troublesome questions about sexuality and women's right to control their own bodies. Yet the leaders of the Marxist movement around the turn of the century were products of the patriarchal Victorian culture prevalent at that time. They were ill-prepared, by and large, to address some of the issues of particular concern to women, especially matters related to sexuality, reproduction, the sexual division of labor, or patriarchalism itself. They had been brought up to regard these matters as indecent, hence unfit for public discussion. Some of them were concerned with the public image of Marxism and wished to avoid offending the citizenry. Working-class culture, at least in significant sections, was deeply committed to patriarchal family traditions, and the same can be said, as we have seen, for many of the leaders, beginning with Marx himself. All these factors made it easy for Marxist theorists to argue that women's issues were minor problems that the coming of socialism would solve automatically.

Despite these handicaps, radical women have joined the Marxist movement and become prominent in it. They came from various radical movements—from feminism, like Clara Zetkin; from Tolstoyan pacifism, like Krupskaia; from Christian orthodoxy, like Kollontai; or directly from early involvement in radical socialism, like Luxemburg.[9] It would be interesting to have more biographical information for their sisters in the Marxist parties of Eastern Europe or just to find out whether these outstanding female Marxist leaders had their equivalents in that part of the world. One thing is clear: once women were in the movement, they either had to play down or altogether forget whatever feminist ideas they had had before, or else they found themselves highly suspect, and many of them were eliminated from the Marxist movement in due course.

Those that stayed and tried to overcome the orthodox leaders' hostility to feminism found themselves denounced as Revisionists. They ought to be of particular interest to us because their attempt to merge Marxism with feminism makes them precursors of an ideological current that has gained strength in recent years. One might summarize it as an attempt to radicalize and humanize Marxism by feminizing it. Let me explain what I mean by offering a redefinition of Revisionism.

Revisionism is the term that was coined after Eduard Bernstein, around 1900, suggested that many of the ideas of Marxism as it was then understood were outdated or had been inane from the beginning, and that Marxist doctrine needed to be revised. It should also be brought in line with the reformist politics that the movement was then in fact pursuing. Bernstein questioned the philosophic foundations of what was then known as dialectical materialism; he questioned the theory of the inevitable breakdown of capitalism, and he also defined away the end goal, communism, as utopian. In effect, Bernsteinian revisionism can be defined as a *liberalization* of Marxism, i.e., as an attempt to bring it more in line with the nonrevolutionary practices of the socialist movement. This kind of revisionism became the ideology of democratic socialism.[10]

But there were people in the Marxist movement around the turn of the century who criticized Marxist theory and practice on different grounds. Their chief criticism was directed against the narrow orientation of the movement—its exclusive interest in securing power for the proletariat, its unicausal explanation of all ills as resulting from the exploitation of wage labor, its total unwillingness to join forces with other radical movements, and its unconcern for the many forms of alienation beyond the exploitation of labor that characterize modern industrial society, whether that be the plight of peasants, domestic servants, waitresses, or prostitutes; the insults to aesthetic sensibilities that come from the architecture of cities, the despoliation of nature, or the vulgarities of mass culture; the tortures inflicted on children by the educational system; or the sexual repression inflicted on all by patriarchal and puritanical traditions.

Many of these issues—prostitution, alcoholism, educational reform, cultural blight, sexual repression, and others—had been of direct concern to radical feminists; when feminists joined the Marxist movement, they often brought these issues with them, as part of their concern for the emancipation of women from all sorts of oppression. Some of them tried to bring an *awareness* of these and other modes of alienation into the Marxist movement and suggested that, as a liberational movement, Marxism ought to make these things matters of its own concern, since liberation, in order to be meaningful, must be total and comprehensive. They also tried to cure their male comrades of sexist attitudes and sexist language, an effort that was not much appreciated. Instead, they were criticized and called Revisionists for injecting allegedly extraneous issues into the cause of the proletariat. Yet one could argue that *their* Revisionism was by no means a liberalization of Marxism; it was, instead, an attempt to radicalize it, an attempt to save it from its own economic and proletarian tunnel vision.[11]

There is one other observation which is relevant to an understanding of Revisionism. Marxism around the turn of the century was undergoing subtle transformations from what it had been in the minds of Engels and Marx. In its "orthodox" form, that is in the form which it took on in the German party around the turn of the century, it had taken on the characteristics of the prevailing culture. These included the permeation of its philosophy with Darwinism and crude materialism and the acceptance by its aestheticists of standards based on Realism and Naturalism. If we try to generalize from these and similar observations, we might come to the conclusion that Marxism around the turn of the century partook generously of what might be called late Victorian or Edwardian culture. At the same time, if we examine the pattern of management in the German Social Democratic party, its style of leadership, its conception of the rights and duties of members, its general political outlook, we might want to say that Marxism in this particular party had taken on a specifically Prussian form. And since the German party set the tone for the international Marxist movement, I would be prepared to say that Marxism around the turn of the century represents a Prussianization of the movement and its ideology, just as after 1917 international Marxism was Russianized. All this, by the way, I mention only because it then becomes apparent that *Revisionism* was, among other things, an attempt to overcome both the Victorian and the Prussian elements in Marxism.

After 1917, of course, the center of gravity of revolutionary Marxism shifted East, to Moscow, and in its Leninist form Marxism became thoroughly Russianized. The conflict between orthodoxy and Revisionism, therefore, was no longer one between Prussian and, say, Fabian conceptions but between Russian and German ones, with German Marxism coming to be dubbed Revisionist. In the ensuing discussions it was natural, given their geographic location, that the Marxist parties of Eastern Europe should play a crucial role, both as mediators and as troublemakers. The Russian revolution of 1905 for the first time directed the attention of revolutionary Marxists to Russia as a potential model for the European movement. Rosa Luxemburg, for one, then began to urge the parties of the Second International to "start speaking Russian." At the same time other leaders, such as Martov and Dan, appalled at the direction that the Russian party seemed to be going, insisted that the Russian Marxist movement must "learn to speak German."[12] Similarly, after 1917, some Ukrainian communists, most notably Khvylovyi, insisted that the Ukraine, as an outpost of Western civilization inside a barbarian Russia, should seek to westernize the Russian revolution. These and many other examples suggest that within European Marxism a cultural conflict had developed which pitted Central European consciousness against a Russian spirit, and it is in the light of this culture conflict that the history of East European Marxism ought to be reexamined.

Cultural differences must be studied also with regard to the feminist movement. In every country women face different obstacles and have different opportunities. The American frontier woman, who in many respects was the recognized equal of the man, does not seem to have equivalents in Europe; neither does the radical abolitionist. Radical feminist agitation of the kind that led to the creation of the Women's Christian Temperance Union or the Salvation Army also remained almost exclusively an Anglo-American phenomenon. Nor has there been anything in Western Europe that was equivalent to the late nineteenth-century emancipated woman from Russia. From one country to another, feminist movements varied widely in political tactics, philosophic foundations, in the emphasis they gave to different issues, in the boldness with which they demanded sexual freedoms, and the like. Most important, for the context of this volume, not all radical feminists in the late nineteenth or early twentieth century turned to socialism. Nor did all radical women become feminists. In the Marxist movement, as I have suggested, some of the most prominent women chimed in with those who placed women's issues on the back burner and were at most "reluctant" feminists.[13] Meanwhile, radical women in Poland, the Czech Lands, Slovenia, or Ireland, that is, in countries where the principal popular cause was the fight against national oppression, tended to make this their main cause as well or to subordinate their concern with women's issues to the national struggle.[14] The papers printed in Part II of this volume illustrate this quite well. Meanwhile, the question whether radical socialism, in its Marxist or in any other form, was compatible with the vigorous pursuit of national liberation continued to be one of the most bitter disputes throughout Eastern Europe, which split nationalist as well as socialist movements.

Socialism and Women in Eastern Europe: The Results in Practice

Has socialism in its Eastern European form liberated women? Despite its inadequacies, orthodox Marxism has continued to attract radical women, and in times of revolution and civil war it has managed to mobilize them, by the millions, for active participation. In all communist revolutions, women have been so mobilized. They fought in the Russian Red Army and with Yugoslav partisans, in China, Vietnam, and Cuba, with a spirit of enthusiasm and a willingness for self-sacrifice equal to that of men. They may have been motivated by desperation when all institutions around them collapsed and survival was threatened; they may have been driven by millennial expectations and felt their service to be a liberation from old bondages. In the history of these revolutions their record is impressive.[15]

As the essays in this volume illustrate, communist regimes in Eastern Europe as elsewhere, immediately after coming to power, have recognized the services of women by enacting laws that made the status of women equal to that of men. Their leaders have always pointed to these laws and constitutional provisions with pride, and official doctrine in all societies governed by Marxist-Leninist parties has always stressed the recognition of the complete equality of the sexes. Every communist regime, furthermore, has made enormous efforts to draw women into the work force, to give them educational opportunities equal to those available for men, to open career lines for them which previously had been male preserves, and to encourage them to participate in public life, including party activities. All communist regimes have enacted laws or created institutions that are designed to reconcile participation in the work force with motherhood: paid maternity leave and day care centers are key measures in this category.

But, as the essays in this volume illustrate, the long-term results of these efforts are ambiguous. Seen from a feminist perspective, socialism does not seem to have done very much for women.

First, even when communist revolutions have mobilized women, the women have usually, though not always, remained an auxiliary force. If you look at the millions of women who served with Tito's partisans, you will notice that they were promoted to officer's rank far more slowly than men and that not a single one made it to general's rank. That seems to be the typical pattern. Moreover, in virtually all cases, the mobilization of women for revolution and civil war was followed by their demobilization once the crisis was over. Once times became more normal, gender differences reasserted themselves.

There are several reasons for this. One of them is the fact that women's needs are easily classed among consumer needs, and these, as we all know, are very low on the priority list of communist regimes. Investment and defense are the areas where resources are allocated, while consumers must tighten their belts. Hence the low quality or inadequate quantity of child-care and obstetric facilities, the inadequacies of welfare and pension payments, or the unavailability of birth control devices.

This last item leads to the observation that most political systems, including the socialist ones, regard demographic trends as an issue of public concern. Promotion or curbing of births has been official policy in communist countries, and that means that the people's freedom of decision in this matter has been severely restricted. Moreover, wherever pronatal policies were pursued, the painful dilemma arose for both the regimes and women, whether to opt for a career or for motherhood or whether to attempt the difficult task of combining the two.

According to Engels and Bebel, once women were fully mobilized into the work force and freed of economic dependency on male providers, the oppression of the female sex would be at an end, particularly if their recruitment into the work force were accompanied by an elimination of legal and political inequalities. These measures have been taken, but the hopes of the Marxist founding fathers have not been fulfilled. Instead, as the essays in this volume illustrate, the situation of women in the East European socialist countries is surprisingly analogous to that of their sisters in the capitalist West. Let me argue this in the most summary fashion by adducing the following generalizations, all of them amply supported by the essays in this volume.

1. An impressive proportion of women has indeed been drawn into the work force, and almost all lines of work, including many that had hitherto been the preserve of men, have been opened to them. But those working women who are married are saddled with the double burden of also having to do housework and child care, a burden all the more oppressive due to the relative scarcity of time- and labor-saving appliances, the inadequacy of food retail outlets, and the undeveloped state of the food packaging industry. Housework, in short, is an infinitely greater burden in most socialist countries than it is in the West.[16]

2. By and large, women still (or again) are concentrated in those lines of work that carry less prestige, less authority, and smaller wages. As in the West, certain lines of work have been "feminized" and thereby downgraded. Moreover, within specific professions in which women and men work together, promotion to positions of responsibility and authority goes disproportionately to men.

3. The political life of these countries similarly is dominated by men. The proportion of women in the various communist parties has remained small, and it decreases the closer one gets to the top of the hierarchy.[17]

4. Conversely, a socioeconomic analysis of communist systems reveals them to be bottom-heavy with women. Among people living below officially defined poverty lines in the Soviet Union and Eastern Europe, a rather heavy majority seems to be female; it consists of old-age pensioners, farm workers, and single mothers.

In short, socialist societies in their entirety and in their various subdivisions are hierarchies in which the proportion of men increases toward the top and that of women toward the bottom. One can explain this by the double burden, which leaves women less time and, therefore, makes them less eligible for elite positions; but one should also observe various kinds of evidence which suggest that many countries run by Marxist-Leninist parties have retained profoundly patriarchal attitudes and habits, so that the continued oppression of women would appear to be engrained in the traditional culture, which years or decades of socialist rule have not eliminated.

From the point of view of Western feminists, one of the most serious deficiencies in socialist countries is the inability of women to create autonomous organizations through which to advance or defend their interests. Of course, there is no group which is allowed to organize independently, so that women are no more discriminated against in this respect than anyone else. Nonetheless, it seems to me that they do have advocates; they have them in those institutions which function as advocates for other groups as well. I am talking about the party and more particularly about social scientists and other professionals, for instance, in medicine, who deal with women's issues and who at times do not hesitate to identify grievances and to propose reforms.

It will become clear from the present volume that such agitation has had some significant results, particularly in the German Democratic Republic (GDR), in which women have achieved somewhat greater advances and more equality in status, authority, and remuneration than in any other socialist country. The GDR is the country that was the most highly industrialized and modernized before it came under communist rule. In the recent past, political leaders also have made concerted efforts to improve women's position (or at least increase their visibility in public life) in Albania and Romania, which are among the least developed East European states.

When Western feminists look at Eastern Europe, they are tempted to argue that socialism has done little for women or even that if anything it has subjected them to heavier oppression than capitalism did in the past. Given the degree of equality achieved in the German Democratic Republic and the dramatic changes, despite continued inequality, in women's lives in Albania, this generalization obviously cannot be made. Or are these countries exceptions that confirm the rule? Western feminists are likely to argue that whatever equalities have been achieved have been handed down to the women by the male ruling elite in yet another exercise of patriarchalism. Rights graciously granted by an elite can be taken away. The only genuine liberation is self-liberation. But self-liberation of anyone in Eastern Europe seems impossible. Under communist rule autonomous organizations of any kind are regarded as a threat to the existing order and will be suppressed, just as Solidarity was suppressed in Poland.

Yet the very fact that an independent labor movement could arise and organize and gather millions of adherents for a few brief months should make us cautious in ruling out future spontaneous movements. Moreover, it may very well be a mistake to judge the success and failure, the strength and the weakness, of feminism in other countries by the same criteria that we use to assess political movements in our own culture. Occasionally, in the essays that follow this introduction, the reader gets hints that women in East European countries have ways of networking, of crying out in protest, and even of making their protests effective, or of asserting their own role and place in societal life, that do not fit our own political categories and expectations. If that could be shown to be the case, it would serve as a healthy warning to Western observers to be cautious in their eagerness to show their sisters in other cultures the way to emancipation.

Women's Inequality: Theoretical Roots

So far I have tried to show that there was a strong affinity between Marxism and feminism (even though that affinity had its limitations), but that from the point of view of women's equality, with several partial exceptions, socialism in Eastern Europe has done disappointingly little for the female gender. To be sure, the male portion of the population in Eastern Europe obviously is not satisfied either: citizenship rights in single-measures curb intellectual freedom for everyone; and economic austerity and scarcities hit all consumers with equal sharpness. Yet these societies are stratified with regard to authority, status, prestige, material benefits, and other criteria; while there are some women near the top of the societal pyramid, they are largely concentrated in the bottom layers.

The customary explanation of this, as I have noted earlier, is that women in Eastern Europe still carry the double burden of wage work and housework, that housework in these societies is by far more arduous and time-consuming than in the United States, and that, therefore, women are prevented from devoting much time to their professional careers or to activity in the party or other public organizations. Hence they are perpetually tired, underpaid, and underrepresented in positions of authority. This situation, it is often claimed, is perpetuated by the fact that women in these societies, in addition to being excluded from the direct exercise of power, are also unable to organize independently to pressure political leaders to change their policies to deal more effectively with the problems women face. But there is also a more theoretical reason for women's inequality in these societies. In this section I would like to examine this double burden through Marxist eyes in order to explain its persistence.

Let me begin by suggesting that the so-called double burden is in reality a triple burden. Women are wage earners; they do housework; and they carry out reproductive and childcare functions. Anyone reading Marxist writings on "the woman question," as it used to be called, will note that they tend to take the reproductive functions of women more or less for granted, even though, from Engels cn down, many writers at least took cognizance of them. In making this assertion I am arguing that even Engels or Bebel, who at least recognized that women labored under especially difficult conditions, let the *burdens*, the *labors*—to say nothing of the bloodletting—of reproduction go virtually unmentioned. Obviously they were aware of them, but they did not build them into their model of the social system.

Marx, Engels, and their disciples were interested in analyzing capitalism, and capitalism for them was the economic system based on the production of commodities. *Das Kapital* begins with a chapter on the commodity because for Marx it was the core phenomenon of the system. For this reason, the only labor that he regarded as relevant to his analysis was that labor which produced marketable commodities. I will come back to that observation because Marxist feminists in the last decade or two have made it central to their analysis of the double burden. Now, if indeed the only labor worth taking into consideration is that which produces marketable commodities, then this would exclude that labor from purview which is spent on human reproduction, however arduous and life-endangering it may be. Indeed, such an argument may well explain why neither Engels nor Marx accounted for that labor in their model of capitalism.

Yet it ought to be remembered that for them capitalism was that system which had converted human labor power and all human activities and potentials into commodities. Moreover, according to Marx, human labor power is that magic commodity which alone is capable of producing surplus value in the process of being used up. Thus human reproduction should have been recognized by Marx as commodity production and indeed as the production of the commodity most essential for the development of capitalism. Once this is recognized it becomes clearer that omitting human reproduction from the Marxist model of capitalism means omitting one of the core elements of the *economic* system, so that even in its own terms Marxism was grossly deficient in its failure to include human reproduction in its calculations.

Similarly it was deficient in its neglect of housework as an essential element of the capitalist economy. If human reproduction insures the steady replacement of worn-out or used-up labor power by providing new generations of workers, then housework must be recognized as labor that maintains existent labor power resources on a day-to-day basis. It too ought to have been part of Marxist theories concerning the replacement of resources; yet the founding fathers of Marxism did not build it into their theories.

The deficiencies noted above were recognized by a few feminists within the Marxist movement around the turn of the century; they began to raise demands for easing the lot of working wives and especially of working mothers, suggesting legislation that would give women workers pregnancy and maternity furloughs with pay and with guarantees of getting their old jobs back. Demands of this kind have become standard legislation in all socialist countries, as several chapters in the present book make clear. But let us note that these ideas concerning the need to protect mothers against the exhausting demands of wage work did not originate in Marxism but came, instead, from late nineteenth-century concerns with eugenics, with the need to perpetuate the white race, and from worry over growing infant mortality and declining birthrates. They were Darwinian and Nietzschean in origin, not Marxist. Feminists who raised these demands clearly recognized reproductive functions as an essential service women were rendering to society. For instance, in response to those who argued that women did not deserve voting rights because they did not serve in the armed forces—one of the standard arguments in favor of denying them the vote—some feminists objected that without women there would be no soldiers at all and that reproductive functions were just as life-endangering and self-sacrificial as frontline service.

As for housework, Marxists, beginning with Bebel and Engels, have always recognized it to be an extra burden on wage-earning women. They also acknowledged it to be boring and unrewarding work—an unmitigated curse from which women ought to be liberated. Indeed, according to orthodox Marxism the emancipation of women would be brought about by a twofold process that would entail freeing them from housework and mobilizing them for wage work or, to use the orthodox phrase, drawing them into the productive processes of society.[18] This phrase makes very clear that the theoreticians of the movement did not consider housework to be productive work. A number of Marxist feminists in recent years have dwelled on this implication in their writings. They have sought to explain the double burden by suggesting that capitalism rewards people only for that kind of labor which produces commodities, or exchange value. Household work, they argue, produces only use value, and use value does not become part of the capitalist economy; hence, the labor that goes into it cannot be rewarded.[19]

This line of analysis is reminiscent of Hegel's treatment of the working class. A keen observer of social relations in the early nineteenth century, Hegel was well aware of the working class and its conditions. In line with then prevalent liberal conceptions, he also regarded property as an essential precondition for citizenship. Indeed, he seems to have suggested that without property a person cannot be fully human. People without property, therefore, were not really members of what he called *bürgerliche Gesellschaft*, a term meaning both civil society and bourgeois society. Hence when Engels and Marx referred to the workers as in but not of society, they were merely paraphrasing Hegel's views.[20]

The liberal solution to propertylessness typically was to express the expectation that sooner or later those without property would be able to acquire property, be it because in some way or other the stereotypical bourgeois virtues would be instilled in them—frugality, thrift, love of work, foresight, and the like—or because, as the wealth of nations increased, some of it would trickle down to the poor. In short, classical liberalism purports to solve the problems of the working class by suggesting that they ought to turn into bourgeois. One might argue that classical Marxist ideas about women's emancipation are quite analogous: drawing women into the productive processes of society, mobilizing them for wage work, is tantamount to saying that their oppression will come to an end once they have become proletarians like their men. Of course, the ultimate Marxist solution is to do away with wage work altogether by eliminating class differences, and in the classical Marxist writings this is always regarded as an automatic solution to women's problems as well.

The contributions to this volume, however, make it quite clear that the elimination of private property in the means of production has not eliminated the oppression of women. They still carry the double or triple burden, and often it seems to be heavier than it is in Western countries. This suggests some deficiency in the classical Marxist explanation of women's oppression. There is, however, another term in the Marxist vocabulary that might, perhaps, provide a more adequate explanation.

In 1903, *Vorwärts* publishing house, the official publisher of the German Social Democratic party, printed a lengthy pamphlet by Lily Braun, *Die Frauen und die Politik* (Women and Politics), which was a manifesto to mobilize working-class women for active and militant work in the Marxist movement. In chapter two of this pamphlet Braun suggests that throughout the history of capitalism women have constituted the reserve army of labor to be mobilized for wage work whenever it suited the system and to be demobilized whenever they had become redundant. Technological progress, she argued, continually replaces men with machines, thus rendering numbers of workers superfluous. But, because work with machines differs from more primitive forms of labor that required strong muscles, technological innovation also makes it more and more possible to utilize the labor of women, thus making men doubly superfluous. As a result, wages are depressed because women have always been paid less than men; once women become available, men's wages also go down. Consequently, wives and daughters are increasingly *compelled* to seek wage work to keep the workers' families alive, which in turn depresses wages even more; meanwhile, women carry the double or triple burden of wage work, housework, and human reproduction. They receive payment only for their wage labor, and that in amounts way below minimum subsistence levels.[21]

What Braun implied, however, and quite rightly so, was that all three contributions are essential to the maintenance of the system and of society in general. The wage labor done by women is a source of profit; their housework is essential for the maintenance of the proletarian family; and their reproductive labor reproduces the available source of labor power.

In the writings of Marx the reserve army of labor is that portion of the proletariat that has been rendered redundant by technologial and managerial innovation, but Marx does not identify it any closer. It seems to me that Lily Braun has in fact identified the reserve army as consisting primarily of the female labor force. In doing so she has used Marx's term to show why the mobilization of women for wage work is essential to the preservation of the capitalist system: it is the existence of a reserve army carrying the triple burden that ensures recurrent profitability; it is specifically the female gender that pays for the success of capitalism.

The contributions to this volume suggest that in the historical era that Marxist-Leninist theory calls the building of socialism, the female gender has once again served as an essential part of the reserve army of labor, the triple burden carried by women in Eastern Europe being analogous to that carried by their proletarian sisters in the West two or three generations ago. This means that it is they who have carried perhaps the heaviest burden in their countries' efforts to industrialize and modernize, which in turn indicates that the concept of the industrial reserve army is not specific to free enterprise systems operating on the principle of profitability. It is applicable also to socialist society. One conclusion emerging from this is that relying on orthodox Marxist explanations of the double and triple burden limits our understanding of the reasons for the continued victimization of women and will also frustrate attempts to devise action programs for their emancipation. Above all, Marxist analysis, which forms the basis for understanding "the woman question" in Eastern Europe as in other communist countries, seems to neglect the possibility of the existence of patriarchal attitudes and a patriarchal culture in socialist societies, a culture that takes the inferiority of women for granted and ensures that they remain in but not of society.[22]

2

Sharon L. Wolchik

The Precommunist Legacy, Economic Development, Social Transformation, and Women's Roles in Eastern Europe

The status of women in contemporary Eastern Europe reflects the influence of Marxism-Leninism's support for female equality and the results of elite efforts to improve women's lives. But the outcome of these efforts has been influenced as well by the legacy of the precommunist period and by the broader strategies of economic development and social transformation communist leaders followed once they came to power in these societies. The first of these factors set the stage for later efforts to change women's status and determined the resources communist leaders could draw on as well as the strength of opposition to change in this area. Plans for economic development and social transformation, more than any abstract consideration of women's equality, have determined the concrete actions political leaders took to encourage change in women's status as well as the opportunities available to women to determine their own lives once communist elites came to power in Eastern Europe. The political structures communist leaders set up in these societies also have had an impact on the way women's issues have been treated in the region.

The pages to follow discuss these factors and outline the impact they have had on women's lives and on elite policies in regard to women in Eastern Europe. As they illustrate, there is a great deal of variation in Eastern Europe from one country to another in terms of the first factor, the precommunist legacy. The strategies of economic development and social transformation, as well as forms of political organization, adopted during the communist period, however, have been rather similar in most of the countries of the region. As a result, although certain aspects of women's lives in each of these countries reflect national differences dating from the precommunist period, the pattern of change in women's roles has been similar throughout the region.

The Legacy of the Precommunist Period

The East European countries (defined here as the German Democratic Republic, Czechoslovakia, Poland, Hungary, Romania, Bulgaria, Yugoslavia, and Albania) differed greatly prior to the establishment of communist systems in levels of economic development, social structure, religious and cultural traditions, and political culture and organization. They also differed from one another considerably in terms of women's status and the opportunities open to women to take part in activities outside the home.

The diversity in the area reflects the impact of different political histories, as well as the influence of geography, location, and size of nations. Occupying an area at the heart of Europe and for the most part consisting of small groups, the peoples of Eastern Europe often have been subject to foreign influence or outright domination. In addition, conflicts within nations or between nations made the area one of great political instability prior to the establishment of communist political systems.[1]

Of the East European states which were created as independent nation-states at the end of World War I, all but Czechoslovakia were overwhelmingly agrarian, economically backward countries. In all cases the leaders of the newly established states began programs to industrialize their countries, but these efforts were not particularly successful due to the impact of the world depression, as well as domestic inefficiencies and corruption. However, there was some variation within the region. Albania, Romania, and Bulgaria remained overwhelmingly agrarian countries, with 75 to 80 percent of the population dependent on agriculture in the 1930s.[2] Yugoslavia also remained a predominantly peasant society as World War II approached, although there were differences in the percentage of the population in agriculture and levels of development in different regions of the country.[3] Poland and Hungary, in which 59 percent and 52 percent of the population remained in agriculture in 1930, were still predominantly agrarian but somewhat more developed than the Balkans. But it was only in Czechoslovakia, where approximately 34 percent of the population remained in agriculture in 1930, and in what would later become East Germany that levels of economic development and the social structure approximated those found in the more developed West European countries.[4]

There were also substantial differences in forms of family organization in the region as well as in different parts of particular countries. To some extent these differences paralleled differences in levels of economic development, but there were also idiosyncratic variations seemingly unrelated to other indicators of modernization. Differences in this regard were most striking between the countries of the northern and central parts of the region and the Balkans. In the former, although there were variations in family size in urban and rural areas, the two-generation nuclear family had become the prevalent form of family organization in cities as well as in most of the countryside. Although sizable numbers of families continued to be three-generation, the dominant trend was toward a single-family household, with the possible addition of a widowed mother or mother-in-law.[5] In many, although by no means all, areas in the Balkans, the extended family system continued to exist until the eve of World War II. Under this system, the economic as well as personal lives of husband, wife, and children were closely intertwined with those of the husband's mother, father, and brothers and their families. Finally, in Albania and in certain of the Moslem areas of Yugoslavia, the clan continued to have an influence on family life during this period, and individual families were subject to the will of the ruling patriarch.[6]

There were corresponding differences in fertility levels in the region as well as within particular countries. In the late 1930s the East European countries fell into three groups in this respect. In the first, which included Czechoslovakia, Hungary, and Germany, birthrates were under twenty per thousand population and approximated those in northern European countries; in the second, which included Poland, Bulgaria, Romania, and Yugoslavia, birth rates ranged from 22.8 to 29.6 per 1,000; Albania alone fell in the third category, with 34.3 births per 1,000 population. Thus, there were nearly twice as many births per 1,000 population in Albania as in Czechoslovakia.[7]

There were also great differences in literacy rates and educational levels in the region. Whereas near-universal female as well as general literacy had been achieved in Czechoslovakia by 1921 and literacy rates in Hungary approximated those in the more developed West European countries by the early 1930s,[8] in the Balkans from one third to one half of the adult population remained illiterate at this time.[9] The problem was particularly acute in the case of women. From 43 to 56 percent of women were illiterate in Bulgaria, Romania, and Yugoslavia in the early to mid-1930s, and from 30 to 35 percent of women in the late 1940s and early 1950s.[10] The extent of female illiteracy in Albania during this period may be judged from the fact that over two-thirds of women nine years of age and older were illiterate in 1950.[11]

These differences were paralleled by the differences among countries in women's educational levels and access to secondary and higher education, although women's access to higher education, in particular, did not differ greatly in countries at different levels of economic development. In the late 1930s, for example, women's proportion of students in higher education was somewhat lower in Czechoslovakia (17.3 percent in 1936) and Hungary (14.7 percent in 1937) than in Bulgaria (22.7 percent in 1937), Yugoslavia

(23.3 percent in 1938), Romania (26.0 percent in 1938), or Poland (28.3 percent in 1937).[12] The Albanian situation is once again unique in this respect, as there were no institutions of higher education in Albania prior to World War II and only eighteen secondary schools in the entire country. Nonetheless, 25.1 percent (1,425 of 5,677) of secondary school students in 1938 were reportedly girls.[13]

The countries of Eastern Europe also differed considerably in terms of political organization and political culture in the precommunist period. Although the new nation-states created after World War I were all parliamentary democracies or constitutional monarchies at their outset, democratic government persisted until the eve of World War II only in Czechoslovakia. In all the other countries in the region the lack of the social requisites for democracy and the activities of extremist groups (particularly those on the right), coupled with the lack of real support for democracy on the part of the traditional elites and the absence of any experience with self-government by the masses, led to the restriction of civil liberties and eventually to the institution of authoritarian, nondemocratic governments dominated by coalitions of military men, traditional landowning elites, and representatives of the new industrial classes. As the interwar period progressed, the recurring crises and turmoil that resulted from domestic factors were compounded by the impact of the depression and led to increased penetration, both economic and political, by outside powers and persistent political instability. In this context the activities of political parties and social organizations were increasingly restricted or suspended entirely, and East European citizens had fewer and fewer opportunities to participate in political life.[14] Although women were enfranchised in 1919 in Czechoslovakia, Poland, and Germany, they received the right to vote only after World War II in the remaining countries in the region,[15] and in most countries their political opportunities were, in practice, quite limited throughout this period.

The chief exception to this pattern existed in Czechoslovakia. Although Czech and Slovak leaders faced many of the same problems as leaders in the other states of the region, democratic liberties and a representative government were preserved in Czechoslovakia until they were eliminated by outside actors. Thus, opportunities for participating in public life were greatest for women, as well as for men, in Czechoslovakia during this period.[16] In addition to the fact that a democratic government continued to exist in Czechoslovakia throughout the interwar period, citizens' opportunities for taking part in the broader life of the community also were enhanced by the tradition of organized community or group activity that, particularly in the more developed Czech Lands, dated to the middle of the nineteenth century.[17]

Authoritarian governments restricted citizens' opportunities to take a direct role in politics in much of the rest of the region, but citizens were active in small groups devoted to a variety of causes during the interwar period, including charitable and sports associations, educational or cultural societies, and national as well as religious organizations. Numerous self-help organizations and, in rural areas, peasant cooperatives also provided some opportunities for public activity.

Women's opportunities to participate in the activities of these organizations, as well as their general status in the precommunist period, varied greatly within the region and depended on the other factors discussed above. Whereas Czech women in particular enjoyed opportunities to take part in public life comparable to those of women in the more developed West European countries, women in Albania remained bound in a highly patriarchal, feudal society that granted them virtually no rights as individuals and, in all but the most urban areas of the country, kept them from leaving the privacy of their homes. Women's options were also limited in the other Balkan countries, particularly in rural areas. In what would become East Germany, women's opportunities to take part in public life or work outside the home were restricted by Nazi ideology (although Nazism's impact on women varied considerably), but had been comparable to those of women in the other developed countries of Western Europe in the pre-Nazi period. As the war put increased demands on German industry, work outside the home was presented as part of women's patriotic duty.[18] There were also substantial differences in the opportunities open to women of different classes and in urban and rural areas throughout the region.

The Communist Period: Political Change, Economic Development, and Social Transformation

Differences in women's status and other conditions during the precommunist period set the stage for later efforts on the part of communist leaders to change women's roles in Eastern Europe. However, despite continuing diversity in the region and certain features peculiar to particular countries, women's status today is in many respects similar in all of the countries of the area. In addition, the pattern of change in women's roles that has occurred since communist systems were established has been common throughout the region.[19]

In large part these similarities reflect the fact that, despite the important differences in precommunist conditions discussed above, communist elites adopted very similar political institutions as well as strategies for economic development and social transformation after coming to power. Further, in all cases efforts to promote women's equality, though initiated and supported by communist leaders, have been fairly low priority concerns throughout the communist era. As Lapidus has argued in the Soviet case,[20] policies toward women have been determined not so much by an abstract commitment to women's equality (although such a commitment formally exists in these countries) as by larger strategies of economic, political, and social development. At times, policies adopted to pursue these strategies have furthered women's equality. At others, and particularly in certain areas of life, policies adopted primarily to achieve higher priority economic or social goals have had negative implications for women in these societies.

Political change and the institutional framework

Upon coming to power in Eastern Europe, communist elites undertook a number of common policies designed to destroy the old social and political order and consolidate their power. For our purposes, the most important of these from a political perspective were the effective elimination of all organized political opposition and the consolidation of the Communist party as the chief, if not sole, political force in the country. Following Soviet practice, East European leaders used a number of measures, including social and economic policies as well as political changes, to eliminate the power bases of their opponents as well as the political power of any noncommunist groups. They also set up a new institutional system and political rituals designed to create new allegiances on the part of their populations. As in the policies they adopted in the economic and social spheres, East European leaders borrowed heavily from the Soviet Union and copied many features of the Soviet political institutions which existed at the time. Thus, although there has always been some variation in this respect within the region, the East European countries, with the exception of Yugoslavia, have very similar political structures.

In all East European countries including Yugoslavia, the Communist party is the only effective political party, and there is no legal opposition. Marxism-Leninism is the official ideology, although the degree to which this belief system influences policymakers or citizens is open to question in many of the countries in the region. The party reserves to itself the right to interpret the ideology, set national policy, and oversee its implementation. Furthermore, censorship of information exists in all countries. With the exception of Yugoslavia, the political systems of all the Eastern European countries are also highly centralized. Finally, in all but the Albanian, Yugoslav, and to a certain degree Romanian, cases, there is a special tie to the Soviet Union that determines the limits of political debate and change in these countries.[21]

The main exception to these regularities occurs in Yugoslavia. Although the Yugoslavs originally copied Soviet institutions and policies as faithfully as the other East European leaders, since 1948 they have developed an increasingly original brand of socialism that differs considerably in an institutional sense, as well as in the policies adopted, from that found in the other countries in the region. Thus, although the Communist party is still the dominant political force in Yugoslavia and political opposition is officially not allowed, the role of the party (known since 1952 as the League of Communists of Yugoslavia) is quite different from that of the communist parties in the Soviet Union and the other countries in the region. The political climate also allows much more open and far-ranging debate and discussion. In addition, the Yugoslav political system is decentralized, and the subnational units, particularly the republics, have a good deal of political as well as economic power. This decentralization is also evident in the economic sphere, where workers' self-management exists in the form of workers councils and enterprise autonomy. A final difference in the political realm is Yugoslavia's nonaligned, independent position in foreign policy.[22]

The features of the East European political systems discussed above structure the policy-making process and determine the options open to women to influence public policy and take part in politics. The dominance of the Communist party means, first of all, that women, as well as all other citizens, have fewer avenues to participate in politics or become part of the political elite than citizens in democratic political systems. As the section of this book on women's political roles illustrates, women who advance to elite positions in these societies are, like their male counterparts, dependent on party backing; given this fact, they appear unlikely to challenge existing views concerning women's roles in a fundamental way or press women's interests assertively in policy debates. The party's monopoly of power also means that efforts to influence public policy must be channeled through party bodies. Opportunities for political action are somewhat broader in Yugoslavia, but the party remains the most important political arena in that country as well.

In addition, debate on women's situation and action on issues that have an impact on women have been influenced by the fact that these are officially Marxist-Leninist states. The official ideology contains a formal commitment to women's equality. Although this commitment appears to have been less important than other considerations in determining concrete policy measures that affect women, it does to some extent benefit women, for it has supported certain changes to improve women's status, and it rules out certain policy options that might be considered if they did not so blatantly contradict the ideology. In addition, the fact that there is a single official value system has influenced the terms in which issues related to women, as well as other issues, must be discussed in these societies. In some respects, this framework for discussing women's issues has negative effects for women, for it means that only those solutions, approaches, and analyses compatible with Marxism-Leninism can be considered. Further, because the ideology does not admit that the interests of social groups will continue to conflict under socialism and, particularly in the past, has tied progress for all groups to the interests of the proletariat as a whole and the advance toward socialism, it typically has not been seen as legitimate to consider the needs of women separately from those of men or of society as a whole. This tendency was reflected in the distrust of feminism and feminist consciousness evident in the early Marxist movement, but it is also evident today in debates about women's issues.

Finally, as numerous analysts have noted,[23] the organizational principles of socialist society in Eastern Europe, as in the Soviet Union and other communist countries, mean that women have, in usual political times, very little opportunity to organize independently to define their own interests or pressure political leaders to take action on issues of concern to them. Women are sometimes able to work through existing groups, including the official women's organizations, to advocate women's interests, but they cannot go outside the established structures to set up autonomous groups independent of the political authorities.

Economic development, social transformation, and policies toward women

As part of their efforts to consolidate the new political system, communist leaders in Eastern Europe tried in the early post–World War II years to win women's allegiance and urged women to join the party and become involved in politics. As a result, large numbers of women, including peasant and rural women who previously had little awareness of the political world, came to take part in the political life of their countries, if only by being exposed to political information or as participants in elite-organized demonstrations and other activities designed to show support for the regime. But the main emphasis of work among women during this period was related not so much to political as to economic ends, and policies that affected women were determined largely by their relationship to economic goals.[24]

As in the political sphere, the new communist leaders in Eastern Europe also copied Soviet institutions and policies in the economy. In addition to nationalizing industry, attempting to collectivize agriculture, and setting up a system of central economic planning, they soon adopted ambitious industrialization plans designed to overcome the problems of economic backwardness. While there were some variations in individual countries, the basic elements of the development strategy were the same throughout the region and included rapid rates of projected growth, a very high rate of investment, and concentration on the development of heavy industry to the neglect of the consumer sector and agriculture. In addition, the plans for economic development also relied on a mass mobilization of all possible labor resources to compensate for scarce capital.[25]

Women were the chief remaining labor reserve and were encouraged to enter paid employment outside the home in all of these countries, although these efforts were less energetic, as well as less effective, in certain countries, such as Poland and Yugoslavia, particularly in the early post–World War II years. As in the Soviet Union, political leaders and activists whose task it was to work among women emphasized the importance of paid employment for women's emancipation and used a variety of financial and moral incentives to encourage women to see themselves as economic producers.[26]

This development strategy, adopted during the Stalinist period, did achieve some positive results in most East European countries, particularly through the 1960s. Thus, all nations, but particularly those which had been least developed at the start of the communist period, became more industrialized and less agrarian. Changes in this respect were most noticeable in the Balkans, where the proportion of the population dependent on agriculture dropped to 57.4 percent in Romania, 49.7 percent in Yugoslavia, and 44.9 percent in Bulgaria in 1965[27] and to 58.7 percent in Albania in 1960.[28] By the 1970s the agricultural population exceeded one-third of the total only in Albania (49.4 percent in 1973)[29] and Yugoslavia (34.0 percent in 1979).[30] These changes, which have been reflected in changes in the social structure, are also evident in educational levels and literacy rates. By the mid-1960s and early 1970s, for example, illiteracy among the population fifteen years of age and over was greater than 25 percent only in Yugoslavia[31] and Albania.[32]

These changes had many positive results for women. Campaigns to eliminate illiteracy and the expansion of educational opportunities opened the way for far greater numbers of women, as well as men, to obtain an education and gain new skills. Similarly, the adoption of ambitious plans for rapid industrialization created new demand for women workers and employees and undoubtedly helped overcome resistance to women's employment outside the home. In addition, many women, particularly those in rural areas and those in countries that were previously least developed, also experienced improvements in their standards of living.

There are limits to all of these benefits, however. As in other contexts, modernization in Eastern Europe also has had certain costs for women resulting from the destruction of traditional ways of life. In certain areas, industrialization appears to have eliminated some of women's earlier tools of influence without replacing them with forms appropriate to industrial society. Furthermore, as the essays in this volume, as well as the writings of other analysts, amply demonstrate, equal access to education does not necessarily mean that men and women will end up with the same skills. Nor does mobilization into the labor force automatically lead to equality for women in the area of work (in terms of exercise of power or income), increased influence in politics, or equality in the family. Given the one-sided emphasis on women's economic roles and the lack of change in the division of labor within the home, for many women in Eastern Europe entry into paid employment has led not to liberation but, as in other countries, to a double or triple burden.

Similarly, despite the improvement in the economic situation in the least developed countries, there are still substantial differences between the more and less developed countries in the region, differences that influence general standards of living and affect women in particular. In 1978, for example, GNP per capita in the GDR was estimated to be approximately eight times greater and GNP in Czechoslovakia was approximately six times greater than that in Albania. There was less difference in the rest of the region, but GNP per capita in the GDR (slightly higher than in Czechoslovakia) was still 1.6 times higher than GNP per capita in Poland and Hungary, 1.8 times higher than in Bulgaria, 2.4 times higher than in Yugoslavia, and 3.2 times higher than in Romania in 1978.[33] Thus, although women's roles have changed in similar ways throughout the area, their standards of living in different countries, and, in some cases, in different parts of the same country, may differ markedly.

Furthermore, in all countries in the region, with the partial exception of Yugoslavia, the strategy of economic development adopted by political leaders has led to a number of chronic economic problems, which have been reflected in poor services, inadequate housing, problems with the quality and availability of consumer goods, and sporadic shortages of food supplies. Women in particular have felt the burden of the investment patterns followed and the problems created, for despite their assumption of jobs outside the home, they continue to be responsible for caring for home and children and are expected to do so, by public authorities and planners as well as by their husbands and families, without substantial help from the state in the form of labor-saving devices and more adequate services or a redistribution of chores within the home.

In Yugoslavia, the country that diverged from the Soviet model most dramatically in economic as well as political terms, toleration of a large amount of private enterprise in the service sector, the different incentives operating under market socialism with its reliance on the profit motive, and the higher level of integration with Western economies have meant that certain of these problems have not been as severe in that country, at least until recently. However, regional disparities in living standards are still quite marked within the country.[34] In addition, Yugoslavia's decentralized market socialism has also led to a good deal of unemployment, which is higher among women than among men.[35]

The strategies of economic development and social transformation chosen by communist leaders in Eastern Europe, then, have had mixed results for women in economic terms. Elite efforts also have been more successful in transforming material aspects of society than values and attitudes. While there undoubtedly has been some change in this respect in particular countries, there is ample evidence that precommunist attitudes persist among many groups of the population in a variety of areas, including religious belief, attitudes toward nationalism and internationalism, aspirations for self and children, beliefs about the value of the individual versus the collective, and attitudes toward the political system.[36] The creation on a mass scale of "new socialist citizens" who have internalized the officially approved value system is a task for the future in most if not all of these societies. Traditional attitudes also continue to exist in regard to women and their proper roles among both party leaders and ordinary citizens.[37]

Finally, in all of the East European countries, the strategies of economic development and social transformation adopted have led to a number of unintended consequences and unforeseen results.[38] Two of these with particular implications for women are the impact of the development strategy on the demographic situation and the current economic crises most of these countries are experiencing.

Beginning in the early 1960s, many of the East European countries began to experience declines in their birthrates. In part, these decreases parallel the pattern that occurred in many Western countries as they became more industrialized. But in the East European countries, the drop in the rate of natural increase was greater than the level of development alone would suggest and reflected the particular features of the development strategy chosen, including the high rates of investment in heavy industry to the neglect of the consumer sector, housing shortages, the high cost of raising children, and the high employment rates of women in the main childbearing ages.[39] The decline in the birthrate has been of greatest concern to policy-makers in Czechoslovakia, Hungary, Romania, and the GDR, but political leaders in Poland and Bulgaria also have been alarmed by population trends since the 1960s.[40] Only in Albania, where the rate of natural increase and levels of population growth are still the highest in Europe, despite a marked decrease in the birthrate from the mid-1950s to the late 1970s, are trends different in this respect.[41]

Fearful of potential labor force shortages and other negative results of low birthrates, including aging of the population and, in Czechoslovakia, a potential upsetting of the ethnic balance, political leaders in a number of these states adopted aggressively pronatalist programs designed to increase the rate of reproduction. Those programs were accompanied in many cases by a shift in emphasis in the elite's orientation toward women's roles and issues. With the exception of those countries in which no pronatalist program has been adopted, policies toward women are now determined largely by their relationship to the demographic situation. The earlier emphasis on women's economic roles has thus given way to renewed focus on the importance of women's roles as mothers.

In many countries, investigation of the causes of the birthrate problem also led to a reopening of discussion, at least at the elite level, of women's issues after over a decade of official silence concerning women's problems. As a result, leaders of the official women's organizations and, occasionally, party leaders now describe women's situation more accurately and acknowledge remaining inequalities more openly than in the past. Social scientists and other specialists and professionals now also discuss and do research on a variety of issues related to women's status.[42]

As the chapters in Part IV illustrate, in some respects this new orientation has been beneficial for women, for it recognizes the contribution women make to society by bearing and raising children. In those countries in which this recognition has been accompanied by extensions of maternity leave and payments to women who stay home to care for small children, it also has been of help in a more practical sense, for it relieves women who choose to take advantage of such leaves of the need to juggle the competing demands of work and family while their children are infants. However, although these measures may thus aid certain women in coping with the demands they face in the short run, their impact on women's equality is problematic, for they may well reinforce old attitudes about separate roles for men and women and impede women's advancement in other areas of life.

More recently, women's status and policies that affect women have been influenced by the persistent and severe economic crisis that exists throughout the region. In part due to the chronic problems of centrally planned economies but also to the unanticipated impact of world economic trends, including high energy prices and economic recession in the West, the East European countries have entered a period of retrenchment and austerity in the economic sphere.[43] Concerned with saving scarce raw materials and conserving energy, reluctant or unable to turn any longer to the West for technology and loans, leaders in Eastern Europe have adopted economic plans designed to make more efficient use of domestic resources. For political leaders, the need to enact austerity measures poses clear political as well as economic problems. No longer able to satisfy the population's desires for a continuously increasing standard of living, they must find some other way of ensuring political allegiance or at least acquiescence.[44] The Polish events of 1980–81, in which economic hardship proved to be the catalyst for expressions of popular discontent with the system as a whole, are the clearest illustration of the potential political repercussions of economic problems in these countries. While a repetition of these events is not likely at present in any of the other countries of the region, the potential for political instability remains.

The era of austerity also has a number of additional implications for women and policies toward women in these societies. Coupled with the poor economic performance that preceded them, the austerity measures adopted in the recent past have led, in practical terms, to greater hardship in daily life: fewer consumer goods, shortages of food and basic supplies, longer lines, and fewer services. Since it is still women who are primarily responsible for running the household and caring for children, they undoubtedly feel these changes more on a day-to-day basis. In addition, in several countries the austerity programs have been accompanied by a decrease in spending on social services, as well as a reduction in the number of retail outlets.

Ironically enough, as Jancar suggests in her discussion of dissent in Czechoslovakia and Poland, it is quite likely that issues typically regarded as "women's" issues, such as food supplies and the availability of consumer goods, will be among the most important political issues of the next decade in Eastern Europe. But in the current economic climate there is little evidence that political leaders will pay particular attention to issues related to women's equality. Preoccupied with economic matters and the need to find a new formula to ensure political stability, it appears unlikely that East European leaders will initiate or even encourage any concerted attack on the remaining sources of women's inequality in these societies.

II

Women in the Precommunist Period

Sharon L. Wolchik

Introduction

Much of this volume deals with women's status in Eastern Europe during the communist period. But efforts to improve women's status predated the establishment of communist states in the region, and later efforts to change women's roles were influenced by conditions in the precommunist period, which determined the "starting point" for such efforts. As the chapters in this section illustrate, women activists used a variety of means and strategies to fight for legal recognition of the principle of women's equality and improvements in various aspects of women's lives prior to the institution of communist systems. Political leaders and party activists of a broad range of persuasions also sought to mobilize women and gain their support for partisan, national, or other objectives during this period.

The nature of the battles fought and the objectives of political leaders and women activists depended on such factors as the degree of freedom women already enjoyed to be active outside the home, general levels of literacy and education, the opportunities for open political organization and agitation, and the religious and other traditions of a society. Levels of economic development also had an influence on the strategies of women activists and political leaders in regard to women. Thus, as Johnson documents, in the Czech Lands, which were among the most economically advanced regions in the Austro-Hungarian Empire, women activists worked for access to medical education for Czech women in the last years of the Empire, in addition to participating in various organizations devoted to other causes. Women activists continued to work to improve women's situation during the interwar period, when Czechoslovakia and several other independent nation-states replaced the Empires that had ruled Eastern Europe prior to World War I. As Garver's essay demonstrates, women made measurable gains during the period of independence in Czechoslovakia. Although they were seldom elected to public office, Czech women in particular contributed to the public realm through their participation in political parties, women's and charitable organizations, and by their activities as outstanding individuals in many areas of life. They also organized independent women's groups to pursue a variety of aims and worked to remove the remaining inequalities in women's status. The activities of women in Czechoslovakia during this period were facilitated by the secularized culture, high general levels of literacy and education, and relatively open political climate that existed in that country, particularly in the Czech Lands, at this time. The situation was somewhat different in Slovakia, where the influence of the Catholic Church and the fact that Slovakia was a more agrarian, less literate region restricted women's opportunities to take part in public life to a greater degree.

Bohachevsky-Chomiak's discussion of the activities of Ukrainian women in Galicia and Reed's essay, which examines the efforts of Peasant and Communist party activists to mobilize women in Croatia, illustrate the very different conditions that prevailed in other parts of the region during this period. Working in what had been one of the more backward areas of the Austro-Hungarian Empire and was still an overwhelmingly peasant society, Ukrainian advocates of change in women's position focused on tasks that had more relevance for peasant women, such as improving the level of hygiene in the villages, encouraging women to learn new methods of preparing food and caring for their homes and children, and other practical measures designed to relieve peasant women of some of the more burdensome aspects of their daily lives. Despite the fact that Croatia was one of the more developed regions of Yugoslavia during the interwar period, activists from the Communist and Peasant parties faced conditions closer to those that prevailed among the Ukrainians in Galicia than those which existed in Czechoslovakia. As Reed documents, in these conditions efforts to mobilize peasant women were more successful when they drew on women's traditional tasks and interests than when they sought to radically change women's roles in the villages.

In both of these contexts, however, the women activists discussed avoided larger ideological questions and worked within the framework of existing institutions.[1] Although they did not challenge many aspects of women's traditional roles, including women's roles as wives and mothers, their activities nonetheless encountered opposition, as well as occasional support, from their male conationals. As the Ukrainian and Croatian cases illustrate, this opposition was particularly acute in less developed regions, where any change in women's status was perceived as threatening to traditional peasant values and life-styles.

Despite the different conditions that each of the following chapters discusses, there are a number of common themes which run through them all. First, they illustrate the tendency, which appears to occur in other situations and geographic contexts as well, for women's issues to be put at the bottom of the list of demands for change or social reform. Whether it be Ukrainian nationalists, members of the developing Czech national intelligentsia, Yugoslav communists, or members of the Croatian Peasant party, most of the political actors discussed in this section consistently put women's issues behind other, higher-priority goals. In many cases women activists in these and other groups concurred with this ranking and agreed with their male counterparts that national, class, or other social issues should take precedence. The tendency for women to see themselves as part of a larger community whose needs must come first is aptly summarized by Bohachevsky-Chomiak, who notes that Ukrainian women in Galicia felt their efforts to improve women's position could only be successful if the national cause triumphed. The experiences of East European women in this respect parallel those of women elsewhere, including American women in the labor movement, the civil rights movements, and other political organizations; women in Marxist parties and movements in Europe and elsewhere; and women in national and national liberation movements around the world.[2]

The chapters in this section also illustrate the tendency for activists attempting to mobilize women, who were for the most part men but in some cases women, to rely on certain existing conceptions of women's roles in their appeals to women. In their efforts to recruit women, Yugoslav Communist and Peasant party activists, as well as Ukrainian nationalists, frequently couched their appeals in terms of women's roles as mothers and caretakers, wives, and guardians of the home. Although members of these groups, as well as the Ukrainian women's activists Bohachevsky-Chomiak discusses, advocated change in women's roles, including greater access to education and more participation in the public life of the community, they sought to reassure women and, perhaps more importantly, men that these changes would not undermine women's traditional roles in the family. This was true not only in the more traditional societies of the region but also in more "modern" Czechoslovakia, a fact that demonstrates the similarity of certain popular notions concerning women's characteristics, traits, and calling in life, despite the substantial variation in the actual opportunities open to women and possibilities for engaging in atypical behavior within the region.

The essays to follow also highlight the factors that determine women's status in societies at various levels of industrialization and illustrate the impact development has on women's status. Although their activities were constrained by social prejudices and conventions that dictated a subordinate role for women, women in the peasant societies discussed in this volume did have certain forms of power and tools to gain respect. In some cases, as among the Ukrainian women in Galicia or Croatian peasant women, women's control over economic activities such as the production of eggs and milk, which were frequently the family's main source of cash, gave them a degree of power within the household. As in other parts of the world, development had ambiguous results for many women, particularly during its early stages. In addition to leading to the breakdown of traditional norms and a potential increase in violence against women, economic development eroded many of women's sources of power without giving them equal access to the new forms found in industrial societies.[3] Women and women's activists sometimes tried to mitigate these effects. As Bohachevsky-Chomiak's essay illustrates, although peasant women in particular were often the objects of others' attempts to change their views and lives, in some instances they also played a more active role in the process by establishing and taking part in women's and other community organizations.

Finally, the chapters to follow illustrate the different "starting points" for efforts to change women's status and direct women into new activities once communist states were established. As noted in chapter 2, women's status and popular attitudes concerning women differed considerably within the region at the start of the communist period. In certain states it was commonplace for women to receive higher education, work outside the home, and take part in the broader life of the community. In others women's opportunities were far more restricted. Throughout the region, however, later efforts to change women's status were conditioned by and to some extent could build upon earlier attempts to create new opportunities for women and harness women's energies to a variety of broader causes. These attempts in turn were influenced by the fact that, long before the communist period, most East European countries were societies in flux in which old patterns of behavior were being challenged, if not actually uprooted, by the effects of industrialization, political change, and foreign influence or intervention.

3

Karen Johnson Freeze

Medical Education for Women in Austria: A Study in the Politics of the Czech Women's Movement in the 1890s

Within the context of Europe between the two world wars, Czechoslovakia represented enlightenment, egalitarianism, and relatively equal rights for women.[1] Especially in the 1920s, when Czechoslovakia enjoyed a healthy economy while surrounding countries suffered from runaway inflation, women advanced in education, the professions, and politics. Having achieved the right to vote and equality before the law in 1918, they took steps to realize the benefits of these rights. Within a decade, they constituted 30 percent of the labor force and 25 percent of the university student body. Thus Czechoslovakia's record in the field of women's rights was better than that of most other European countries and certainly outshone that of the other successor states of the Habsburg monarchy. It may be surprising, therefore, to discover that although the Czech women's movement can trace its roots to the early 1800s, it began to flower only at the very end of the century.[2]

This chapter examines the emergence of that movement through a case study of its first cause célèbre: higher education for women. It focuses on how Czech women achieved entrance to medical education for all women of Austria and on why this achievement came nearly twenty years later than it did in most of Europe and the United States.

The setting of this story is unlike that of most others considered in this book: Bohemia by 1890 was by far the most highly developed region of what is now called Eastern Europe; it had less than 40 percent of the population on the land, a 90 percent literacy rate, and a culture highly secularized from the dual processes of modernization and religious conflict. Along these indices, Bohemia (unlike Slovakia) most resembled Western Europe, not the rest of the Habsburg monarchy. Yet in terms of a movement toward equality for women, in law or in practice, Bohemia (with the rest of Austria) was far behind these countries, which could boast articulate feminists such as Mary Wollstonecraft, George Eliot, Florence Nightingale, and Luise Otto-Peters, who became symbols of feminism from the mid-nineteenth century and even earlier in France, England, and Germany.[3] Where were Czech women during this period? Drawing upon a variety of sources, including the women's press, Czech and Austrian political journals, Reichsrat protocols, and memoirs, this chapter examines the Czech women's movement in the broader context of turn-of-the-century Austrian politics and suggests a rational explanation for this rather tardy development.[4]

The Problem: A Belated Women's Movement?

Czech women were first politicized during the Revolution of 1848, when they joined men on the barricades and articulated principles of equality between the sexes. After the Revolution failed, they—like the rest of society—lapsed into silence for over a decade.[5] With the gradual extension of civil rights in the Habsburg lands after 1860, women's organizations began to proliferate, but not until the 1890s did they become organized and vocal enough to attract public attention as a feminist movement, even in the fundamental sphere of education for women.

That Czech women waited so long to mobilize their efforts toward gaining access to professional education is puzzling. The demand for higher education had been a foremost component of women's movements throughout Europe and America for nearly half a century and had achieved considerable success.[6] Moreover, Czech national tradition emphasized the importance of education: Prague was the home of the first university in central Europe, established as Charles University in 1348. Seventeenth-century Czech exile Jan Amoš Komenský (or Comenius, as he is known in the history of European pedagogy) was the first educational reformer to declare in writing that both boys and girls should receive the same education in the same classroom.[7] And education was a focus of the Czech national movement. As a result, by 1869 all Czech children in the Czech Lands could go to Czech primary schools, and boys could attend Czech gymnasia, or academic secondary schools.[8]

Although Czech women's charitable organizations had zealously supported elementary education in the Czech language for both boys and girls, by 1890 they had managed to establish and sustain only three schools for girls over age fifteen: the City Higher School for Girls in Prague (1863),[9] the Girls' Pedagogical Institute (1869),[10] and the business and industrial courses for women first organized by the Women's Industrial and Commercial Training Association in 1871.[11] Indeed, interest in an academic education appeared slight. When a few Czech gymnasium professors announced the opening of a gymnasium for girls in 1868, only two prospective students came to register.[12] Economic conditions could be decisive too: hindered by the often prohibitive cost of obtaining a university education abroad, few Czech women elected to acquire privately the academic preparation they could not subsequently use. By 1890, only three women had done so, and one of these died before finishing her preparatory studies.

On the eve of the opening of the Czech University in 1882, Eliška Krásnohorská, the strategist and spiritual leader of the Czech women's campaign for higher education, lamented that most Czech women neither sought a higher education nor sympathized with those who did. But even if Czech women had wished to claim a place in the new Czech University, she noted, they could not, for they lacked the prerequisite: a gymnasium education.[13] By then Krásnohorská had resolved to remedy the situation, but by her own recollection she did not anticipate that it would be another eight years before women had their own gymnasium and fifteen before they would be admitted to the university—and then only to the faculty of philosophy. Entrance to medical study did not come until 1900 and to law only after the demise of the Habsburg monarchy in 1918.[14]

Why did Bohemia, the monarchy's most economically advanced province and one of Europe's most culturally developed regions, not produce a women's movement—Czech or German—comparable to that in other parts of Europe until after the turn of the century? Unlike women in the less developed parts of Austria and the rest of Europe, the Czechs were not hampered by widespread illiteracy or poverty. Nor were they hindered by a pervasive conservative view toward women—with *Kinder* in *Küche* and *Kirche*. Paradoxically, it is in Bohemia's advanced state of development, the egalitarian nature of Czech society itself, and the heritage of the Czech national movement that an explanation can be found.

Czech Women and Czech Nationalism

The Czech national movement began as a cultural renascence—the "awakening," as it was called—in the early nineteenth century. As a cultural movement it spread quickly, affecting an ever broader spectrum of the nation. Having lacked an indigenous nobility for two centuries, the Czechs sought leadership in the talents of compatriots from any social stratum—women as well as men. Like other small, modernizing nations in any period,[15] the Czechs could hardly afford to ignore half their human resources. From the earliest murmurings of the national awakening in the late eighteenth century, Czech women played an important role in the national endeavor. In traditional roles in charitable societies or alongside fathers, husbands, and sons, they were often heralded as yet another proof of the nation's wealth of talent.[16] Not a few achieved status and exercised leadership on their own; particularly in belles lettres, Czech women shone and were permitted to do so without hiding behind a masculine name. Božena Němcová (1820–62) was but the most illustrious of the early female literary figures and the first Czech woman publicly to proclaim herself a "feminist."[17]

In the maelstrom of the 1848 revolution, the Czech cultural awakening was transformed into a political movement for parity in language and autonomy in economic and political life. The movement accelerated after 1860 in concert with rapid social, economic, and political change throughout Bohemia. Since 1861, the national movement had been united behind the conservative Czech National party (Old Czech party), but by 1889 the seeds of pluralism, born of this social and economic development, were bearing fruit. The National Liberal (Young Czech) party won spectacular election victories in 1889 and 1891 and led the nation for the next few years.[18] National unity was already breaking down, however; with many fundamental rights already achieved for the nation as a whole, distinct social classes and interest groups were beginning to voice their special concerns. University students agitated in the Progressive student movement.[19] The Social Democrats, already articulating the grievances of the workers in the 1870s, emerged as an autonomous party in 1896, and several other incipient political parties that would be well established by the turn of the century were contributing to the increasing pluralization of political life.[20] In this rapidly changing situation, Czech women finally found their voice and led the women of Austria into the halls of academe.

Eliška Krásnohorská and Medical Education for Women

The right to medical education and the practice of medicine was a key focus of women's movements throughout Europe and America.[21] It was a particularly compelling demand not only because of women's supposed affinity, as mothers, for health care but because of its mass appeal. Women of all classes increasingly demanded women doctors, especially for obstetrics, gynecology, and pediatrics. For colonial rulers in cultures that forbade male doctors to examine female patients, the demand for women doctors took on a humanitarian aspect.[22] But medicine was a profession with a long tradition of male dominance, replete with as much superstition as science, and its practitioners were often loathe to share its secrets, even with one another.[23] Nevertheless, from 1844 to 1890, hundreds of women were granted the opportunity to study and practice medicine throughout the world—though not in Austria-Hungary.[24] Then in April 1890, Emperor Franz Josef permitted Rose Kerschbaumer, a Russian-born, Swiss-educated ophthalmologist, to open a clinic together with her husband in Salzburg.[25] That single measure unlocked the door to higher education for women in the Habsburg realm; this story tells how Czech women pushed that door open.

Eliška Krásnohorská (1847–1926) came to Prague in 1874 to edit the major women's journal, *Ženské listy* (Women's Gazette), published by the Women's Industrial and Commercial Training Association from 1873.[26] Progressively debilitated since childhood by rheumatoid arthritis, she had thrown herself into intellectual work at an early age. Although she had wanted a university education, her family could not afford to send her abroad. Under her editorship, *Ženské listy* became the main Czech source for information about the women's movement outside Austria. It tantalized readers with a picture of the opportunities for women to study and work in America and most of Europe, revealing that only Germany remained more intransigent than Austria in its opposition to women as university students and professionals.[27] The journal also sought to inspire readers with biographical sketches of women in various fields of endeavor throughout the world and gave particular prominence to women doctors.

Until the 1890s, only two women from the Habsburg lands (both Czechs) had earned degrees in medicine: Anna Bayerová (1852–1924) and Bohuslava Kecková (1854–1911), who graduated from Swiss universities in the early 1880s. But they had no hope of practicing their profession in Prague—or anywhere else in Austria; Bayerová established a private practice in Berne, and Kecková returned to Prague to work as a midwife.[28] In 1889 *Ženské listy* published an open letter to Bayerová, praising her achievement and wishing that she could be permitted to return home to practice among Czech women. The letter, signed by seven hundred women, reflected a new activism in the women's movement and the desire of many women for female doctors. It also foreshadowed a readiness among Czech women to carry their demand for women doctors further, to the Austrian Reichsrat.[29]

Polite Assault on Vienna

In February 1890 *Ženské listy* printed a petition to the Reichsrat for the admission of women to university education in the faculties of medicine and philosophy.[30] It was drafted by Krásnohorská and sponsored by the Czech Women's Industrial and Commercial Training Association, which had collected 4,810 signatures to accompany it. When Young Czech deputy Karel Adámek presented the petition to the Reichsrat assembly in March 1890, he met with a generally favorable response.[31] Many prominent Czech men and women supported it, as did the press, even most conservative papers. As a result,

Krásnohorská and colleagues had good reason to feel elated. Few suspected that the Reichsrat and Ministry of Education would take nearly a decade to approve their request.

This first petition, which pronounced women's higher education one of the "most noble and most just demands of the day," used several arguments in its effort to persuade the Reichsrat deputies that the position of women in the modern world had changed. For one thing, it noted, millions of women did not marry and find protection "at the home hearth"; even for those who did, an auxiliary income was often essential to the family budget in the economic situation of recent years.[32] But to earn that income, women could not remain content with traditional occupations in which they could not develop their talents. Rather, they should be free to choose any occupation, especially "two beautiful life tasks: the education of youth and the care of the sick." Seeking to strike a chord in traditional mentalities, the petition declared that the qualities that made women good mothers could make them not only good governesses and nurses, but also exemplary secondary school teachers and physicians. Yet, whereas almost every other enlightened state of Europe admitted women to university study, Austria did not even have a gymnasium for women.[33] The issue was a moral one, the petition added: it was simply wrong to deny women access to the "highest estate of mankind, knowledge . . . the province of the most perfect freedom."

Finally, the petition advanced practical, humanitarian arguments: women doctors were needed by "young girls and even wives" who "suffer in silence in such cases of illness in which natural shyness prevents them from entrusting themselves to a male doctor while help is still possible." Here the comparison was not only with the "civilized" European West, but with the East as well: "Even the subjugated women in eastern lands, in India, China, and Japan, have been given the possibility of consulting with women doctors, but with sorrow and indignation women in the highly educated center of Europe feel how very little their sense of decency and moral sensitivity is respected." The petition noted that women doctors had proven their worth "on the battlefields of the Russo-Turkish war, the military hospitals of bombarded Paris, in the suffering of the cholera epidemic in Italy, and in the dangers of the missionary stations in Asia and Africa." Indeed, it informed the deputies, women doctors had been practicing for forty-three years, and there were four thousand of them worldwide.

The Czech petition was radical neither in conception nor in rhetoric. It was, rather, a deliberate attempt to tap traditional values, to find strength in practical arguments, and to offer world experience in its own behalf. It concluded with the hope that the Austrian homeland, most especially Bohemia, would not be the last to give women "the most human of all human rights: the right to satisfy the longing for knowledge and the development of inborn spiritual and mental gifts." To that end it asked that women be permitted to pursue regular studies in the philosophy and medical faculties under the same conditions as men,[34] and that, after obtaining academic degrees, they be permitted to teach in secondary schools and practice medicine in all the lands of the monarchy.

Despite the evidence of public support for the petition at least in Bohemia, the Reichsrat deputies did nothing more than agree to insert the petition into the session's protocols.[35] Shortly afterward, two more petitions came from Bohemia to Vienna. One came from the Czech student organization, *Jungmann*, and another, with 723 signatures, from Pilsen.[36] In May, Ruthenian women from Galicia sent a similar petition, and six women's clubs in Vienna with a combined membership of 3,500 sent a jointly sponsored petition. All these petitions remained buried in the Reichsrat's school committee.[37]

Such legislative delays did not halt progress toward women's higher education altogether. In 1890 the most important government body was the Emperor, not the Reichsrat, and when Emperor Franz Josef made the decision in April to permit Rose Kerschbaumer to practice medicine in his realm, Krásnohorská knew she finally had the leverage to initiate a more pressing project and one that could be undertaken on a local level: a girls' gymnasium. Addressing the Prague City Council almost immediately, she announced her intentions and asked for the council's support. The council approved her proposal and eventually provided the school with rent-free space.[38]

Minerva: The First Women's Gymnasium in Central Europe

When subscribers opened *Ženské listy* for July 1890, they found a special insert announcing the birth of Minerva, a society for women's higher education just formed by the Women's Industrial and Commercial Training Association.[39] Not only that: Minerva was about to open a girls' gymnasium, the first in all central Europe. "Let it not be said of the Czechs that they are the first in words, but last in action . . . that they boast of their past, not caring about building an equally glorious future." The announcement, from Krásnohorská's pen, stated that the curriculum of the new gymnasium (soon to be called Minerva) had already been approved by the Bohemian Provincial School Board and invited girls over age fourteen to apply.[40] The case of Anna Honzáková (1875–1940), destined to be the first woman graduate of the Czech medical faculty, was typical. She had had to cancel her plans to study medicine abroad because of her father's death; for her Minerva meant a second chance.[41] Despite obstacles and public skepticism about the feasibility of opening the school so soon, Krásnohorská won the financial and moral support of prominent Czechs, and fifty-three girls entered their first semester at Minerva in the fall of 1890.[42]

Petitions from Below, Progress from Above

A few months after the *Minervistky* began to study Latin and Greek, Emperor Franz Josef took yet another step in their favor. At the request of Governor Kallay in Bosnia-Herzegovina, he agreed in April 1891 to send women doctors to serve the large population of Moslem women, whose religious laws forbade medical examination by men.[43] The first to go was a Czech, Anna Bayerová, who left her practice in Berne; frustrated by hostility among male doctors and administrators, however, she stayed only eleven months. Her replacement was her compatriot and former colleague Bohuslava Kecková, who stayed eighteen years.[44] Further petitions and signatures flowed into Vienna, and various groups at home (including the Progressive student movement) took a public stand for women's emancipation in education as well as in other realms.[45]

The issue came into public view again in the fall of 1891, as a newly elected Reichsrat met and began to debate budget questions, including a secondary school reform package.[46] Deputy Adámek, representing the Young Czechs, repeated the original petition he had presented in May of the previous year. Deputy Tomáš G. Masaryk (later to become the first president of independent Czechoslovakia) and Minister of Education Paul von Gautsch both spoke at length on the question of women's higher education.

Masaryk argued in favor of the petition with the traditional view: educated women would make better mothers. Turning to women's education in general, he suggested that private girls' schools be regulated—and supported—by the state.[47] Minister Gautsch declared that although there could be "no talk of complete equality for women at this time," the matter of women's professional education was important, especially for self-supporting women. His position was still cautious: even if women were capable of training as teachers or doctors, the major task must still be "to educate women so that they can educate their own children."[48] Since Gautsch did not reject the petition out of hand, *Ženské listy* interpreted his speech as favorable.[49]

On November 6, Deputy Adámek presented a new petition from Minerva that boasted of the uncompromising success its students had demonstrated at their examinations. It reminded the Reichsrat that these students would complete the equivalent of six years in a gymnasium by

1893 (and thereby be prepared to study pharmacy if they chose). Two years later, in 1895, they would be ready to take the *maturita* exam (*Maturitetsprüfung*) and enter any faculty at the university.[50] The petition urged the deputies to think ahead and have the doors of the university open when the women approached with diplomas in hand. Although one deputy during the ensuing debate called educated women a threat to the family and a crime against nature, such rhetoric was distinctly exceptional; even if the Reichsrat deputies were not yet ready for women's political emancipation, by now most could recognize their right to higher education. Still, they took no decisive steps to realize this right.[51]

Minerva's First Graduates

As the first Czech women gymnasium students completed their education, *Ženské listy* continued to agitate for women's rights to higher education, informing readers of the activities and achievements of women at home and abroad. Reflecting editor Krásnohorská's special interest, the journal brought detailed information on women doctors and especially praised the work of the Czech women doctors in Bosnia.[52]

In May 1895 Minerva produced its first sixteen graduates. They had been required to take their final examination not before their own teachers but at the boys' Czech Academic Gymnasium in Prague. There, one of the sixteen later recalled, the professors were indifferent, even "cold" to them —except for historian Zigmund Winter, who viewed their efforts and achievements sympathetically.[53]

At the graduation ceremony, Krásnohorská briefly summarized the history of the women's education movement, focusing upon the accomplishments of thousands of women doctors in America and elsewhere. Many had suffered prejudice, abandonment, and poverty before attaining their goal, she noted. Reiterating the story of Bayerová and Kecková, Krásnohorská praised Minerva for protecting its students from the trials of their predecessors. In her concluding remarks, she expressed pride in the graduates and hope for their future education.[54]

Yet the immediate prospects for the graduates were dim. Even after five years, the government still had not acted upon the many petitions to admit women into the universities of Austria. Ironically, the very fact that women were now technically qualified for university study seemed to arouse hostility and opposition hitherto not so visible.[55] In 1895 the male medical student society of the Czech University published a statement against admitting women. The argument was a common if indefensible one: for every job a women takes, a man will lose one—and thus not be able to get married and take care of an unemployed woman.[56] This vocal minority among Czech medical students also claimed that it was "unnatural" for women to want medical or other professional training, that women were "happiest being mothers." These students would continue to harass their women colleagues after the latter finally did gain entrance to the medical faculty.[57]

More disturbing was a ludicrous brochure published in 1895 by a high government health official and prominent surgeon at the University of Vienna, Czech-born Eduard Albert (*Die Frauen und das Studium der Medicin*).[58] Albert contended that all discoveries, inventions, and products in the world had been made by men, that women were but grown-up children, that their brains were smaller and inferior, and that they were interested only in having children and keeping their coiffures in order. For those who took emancipated American women as a model, he cited the report of an American psychiatrist that "one in three American women is insane." All this would have been amusing but for Albert's status. His brochure provoked replies from all over Europe by colleagues who professed embarrassment at such nonsense from the pen of a reputable scholar.[59]

Such fierce opposition was rather isolated, and in October qualified women were permitted to audit courses in medicine—not, however, at the Czech University of Prague. Although the philosophy faculty at the Czech University voted to admit women auditors, the medical faculty refused. Hence it was the German University—acting upon the advice of an anatomy professor who had worked with women medical students in Switzerland—that gave Czech women their first chance at formal medical study, if only as auditors.[60] Although the Czech medical professors reconsidered their decision only a semester later, the first class of three Czech women remained at the German University for two years, until the nationality conflicts among students in Prague made it impossible for them to stay.[61]

On the Eve of Success

While women waited for full rights as regular medical students, they witnessed progress in the right of women to practice medicine in Austria. The Ministry of Education decreed in 1896 that foreign-educated women doctors of Austrian birth could practice in their homeland if their diplomas were validated through examinations at Austrian universities.[62] Swiss-educated Baroness Possaner was the first to take advantage of this law, receiving a diploma by exam from the University of Vienna in April 1897.[63]

This explicit recognition of women doctors, though still encumbered with certain obstacles, encouraged the auditors in both Prague universities. Judging the mood of the imperial government in late 1896 to be susceptible to personal pressure, the director of Minerva went to Vienna with the next petition and presented it directly to Minister of Education Gautsch, who assured her that reforms would be forthcoming.[64] In March 1897, the Ministry opened regular study to women in the faculties of philosophy. *Ženské listy* praised Gautsch for his role in this decision and pointed out that the success of the women auditors no doubt had helped convince the ministry officials to approve the reform. The journal also optimistically voiced the expectation that a similar reform concerning the medical faculties would soon follow.[65]

Yet three more years passed before Vienna opened the medical faculties to women. The Reichsrat and Ministry returned petition after petition without action.[66] In part the problem was one of priorities: the government and politicians were preoccupied in the late 1890s with what they considered far more pressing matters, such as the inflammatory conflict between Germans and Czechs over language rights and the clamoring for universal male suffrage.

In the summer of 1899, after four years of auditing, the three Czech women aspirants to medical careers went to Vienna to present their request in person.[67] Although they were refused an audience with the Minister of Education, they did see a section chief of the Ministry, Wilhelm Hartel, a former gymnasium professor, who assured them that if the authorities had allowed them to audit so long, they would eventually let them finish properly.[68] A year later Hartel himself became Minister of Education, and on September 3, 1900, the Ministry approved a resolution permitting women to enter medical study as regular students with full rights to practice upon graduation. It also opened the study of pharmacy to women.[69]

Thus the persistent campaign led by Czech women resulted in victory for all Austrian women. To be sure, individual struggles remained; the pioneers had to pass special examinations to get credit for five years' auditing; they would also have difficulty obtaining hospital internships for practical training.[70] On March 16, 1902, Anna Honzáková became the first Czech —and the first Austrian—woman to receive an Austrian medical degree based exclusively on study in an Austrian university: the Charles-Ferdinand University of Prague.[71]

Now What? and So What?

Czech women—and most men—were jubilant over the achievement that Honzáková's graduation ceremony represented.[72] Yet 1902 was late indeed for such an event within the context of the European women's movement. Among western and central European countries, only German universities (with the exception of Baden) were slower in permitting women to study medicine.[73] But the late start of the Czech women cannot be attributed to lack of interest or to extreme hostility on the part of the male establishment. It was, on the contrary, a conscious political choice made by some women and an unconscious patriotic choice made by many more. Until the 1890s women—like workers and other groups—deferred their own special interests for the sake of the Czech national movement for language parity, cultural institutions, and political autonomy. During the nineteenth century many self-educated Czech women were active in public life, but with few exceptions their energies were devoted to those causes vital to the whole nation, not just to women.

When Czech women finally did make public their desire for professional education in medicine and the humanities, their timing was right and their strategies highly effective. By 1890 the leaders of the women's movement—especially Eliška Krásnohorská—had already made men and women alike aware that the Czechs lagged far behind most of Europe in the area of women's emancipation. Hence the near unanimity of support for the first petition for university admission merely reflected a consensus that indeed it was time for the Czech nation to catch up. Groups and political factions that a decade later would be irreconcilably in conflict could in 1890, on this issue, enthusiastically unite, offering money and signatures in support of future women university students.

Strategically, the campaign for women's education was pragmatic and moderate, even conservative, seeking support among both Czech nationalists and Austrian officials. Politically schooled in decades of work for the national cause, Czech women were extraordinarily effective when they turned to their own concerns. In their efforts to gain entrance to the university, they did not allow themselves to be distracted or deferred by the broader and more controversial issue of female suffrage, which would have alienated some of their supporters. Genuinely patriotic but also politically astute, Czech women were careful to exploit the myth of national unity still powerful in the early 1890s; when approaching skeptical Czech politicians, they stressed the contributions that educated women could make to the nation's welfare. Yet they were not chauvinistic; when their own Czech University's medical professors rejected them, they turned to the German University. For them the language issue was trivial next to their quest for knowledge. At higher levels, in Vienna, their approach characteristically featured arguments tailored toward Austrian politicians and bureaucrats—humanitarian, economic, and moral reasons for allowing women into the universities.[74]

In sum, the victory for Czech women in the medical profession, a crucial victory in the struggle for women's higher education throughout Austria, was the victory of a middle-class feminist movement that was moderate, pragmatic, and determined. Blessed with the extraordinary leadership of such women as Krásnohorská and with the support of many prominent intellectuals and politicians, it never turned to violence nor did it need to. Its results, nonetheless, were no less revolutionary than elsewhere in Europe, for the new status and new roles of women professionals in the twentieth century would have consequences far more complex than those anticipated by Czech women in the 1890s.[75]

4

Bruce M. Garver

Women in the First Czechoslovak Republic

In 1918 Czechs and Slovaks at home and abroad with the support of the Western Allies established the Czechoslovak Republic. In contrast to other newly independent states in Eastern Europe, it possessed an advanced industrial economy and maintained throughout the interwar period a democratic representative government. Despite this prosperity and political stability, Czechoslovakia also experienced internal social and nationality conflicts. And neither its arms nor its alliances with France and the Soviet Union saved it from destruction by the Nazis in 1938.

This chapter surveys the place, aspirations, and achievements of women in the Czechoslovak Republic, a subject seldom more than cursorily discussed in published scholarship.[1] Because Czech women were more numerous than Slovak or Sudeten German women and had more extensive and influential women's organizations, this chapter focuses on Czech women. After reviewing the situation of Czech and Slovak women up to 1918, it examines their social and economic status and education after that date and the extent to which the new Republic furthered their efforts to achieve equal opportunity with men. The chapter next discusses the organized activity of Czech and Slovak women to advance their own as well as class, occupational, and national interests. Finally, it considers why in the 1930s the pace of women's emancipation slowed and why the fate of Czech and Slovak women's movements remained so closely tied to that of the Czechoslovak Republic.

The Situation and Expectations of Czech and Slovak Women Prior to 1918

The status, organizations, and goals of Czech women during the late nineteenth and early twentieth centuries came to resemble those of women in industrialized European countries, as Czech women organized themselves in a predominantly upper middle-class feminist movement on the one hand and in groups of working-class women associated with Social Democracy on the other. Slovak women's associations reflected similar divisions but, like Slovak political parties, were much weaker than their Czech counterparts primarily because economic underdevelopment and severely restricted civil liberties obtained in the Hungarian half of the Dual Monarchy. The greater influence of Roman Catholicism among Slovaks than among Czechs also helped retard the emergence of any strong Slovak feminist movement before 1919. Up to that time neither Czech nor Slovak women had achieved prominence in politics comparable to that which they enjoyed in literature and the theater and were acquiring in journalism and primary education. In contrast to the difficulties women faced in more traditional, patriarchal societies, no evidence indicates that very many Czech or Slovak women in any strata of society experienced domestic violence.

No feminist movement, charitable association, or trade union embracing women of all nationalities, religions, and social classes emerged in Austria-Hungary or later in the Czechoslovak Republic. Rather, the division of women by nationality and within each nationality according to social status, occupation, or religion was reflected in the diversity of women's aims and organizations.

Czech and Slovak feminists, like turn-of-the-century feminists elsewhere, advocated that women be granted the same rights and obligations of citizenship as men with the exception of military service.[2] They recognized that the struggle for women's rights was but one manifestation of what Tocqueville called the inexorable advance of democracy and what among middle-class Czechs was a liberal, patriotic, anticlerical, and to a lesser degree egalitarian national movement. The predominantly middle-class men who had led the Czech national movement since 1848 were more hospitable than their German counterparts to participation by women in public life in part because they recognized that the Czechs as a national minority in an authoritarian monarchy could achieve cultural, political, and economic autonomy only by cultivating individual talent regardless of gender or class origin. Those who contended that women's emancipation was a necessary part of the struggle for national autonomy often drew parallels between Czech needs and experiences and those of the Finns, Serbs, and Norwegians. On the same grounds, Czech and Slovak women before and after 1918 usually subordinated specifically feminist to generally national goals, believing that economic and political autonomy was a prerequisite for women's as well as workers' emancipation. Moreover, most feminists, conscious of their political weakness, sought assistance from any political party that would support them. Though men led all parties, the more a party leaned to the left the more it usually advocated equal rights for women and encouraged women to seek party and public offices.

Most politically aware Czechs and Slovaks viewed the winning of national independence in 1918 as the crowning achievement of more than a century of national revival as well as the logical outcome of industrialization, universal education, and the gradual democratization of politics. Czech and Slovak women, whether Social Democratic or feminist in outlook, had every reason to expect that national independence followed by the land reform of 1919 and the extension of civil liberties and social welfare would provide favorable circumstances for the further advancement of women's rights despite the fact that the structure of the Czechoslovak economy and the relationships between social classes and nationalities had changed very little.[3] The World War had given hundreds of thousands of young women a taste of fiscal independence and, married or not, a disinclination to perpetuate all traditional relationships between the sexes. Women also expected that postwar economic growth and the expansion of public education, especially in Slovakia, would provide more jobs for them as well as men. Furthermore, land reform and the introduction of universal suffrage in local and district elections in 1919 completed the economic and political defeat of the predominantly German-speaking great landowners who had frequently blocked reform legislation in the provincial diets of the Dual Monarchy. Coincidentally, the defeat of the Imperial and Royal Army and the disintegration of the Habsburg civil bureaucracy in 1918 had eliminated the principal bastions of authoritarian male supremacy in the Czech Lands and Slovakia.

Czechoslovak independence resulted not only from the Western Allies' defeat of the Central Powers but from the efforts of a Czechoslovak revolutionary movement abroad and at home in which Czech and Slovak women had participated as propagandists, fund raisers, couriers, and political prisoners.[4] Because of this and the fact that they had shared the hardships of war, Czech and Slovak women had a strong moral claim to equality in the new Republic whose universal suffrage, representative government, and healthy economy gave them their best opportunity to date to try to overcome the remaining inequalities with men in employment and educational opportunities. Because these women recognized the fortuitous circumstances under which the Republic had been founded and took cognizance of its many enemies at home and abroad, they could not, as did British and American feminists, take the survival of representative government and national independence for granted. This fact, as much as the traditionally legal and nonviolent tactics of Czech and Slovak politics, explains why Czech and Slovak feminists so loyally upheld the Republic as they made the most of their new opportunities to advance women's emancipation and social reform.

The Social and Economic Status of Czech and Slovak Women after 1918

In the Czechoslovak Republic, where women always outnumbered men, the place of women in society changed little from 1918 to 1938, despite social change and economic growth that facilitated the entry of women into the professions and the industrial labor force. Most Czech and Slovak women continued to live in working-class or farming families, while a growing number and percentage entered the lower middle and upper middle classes. A women's social status was usually determined by that of her father or, if she were married, her husband. On nearly a million small to mid-sized farms, women labored in the fields as well as handling most domestic chores. Here and in producers' and consumers' cooperatives, the enormous contribution of women to agricultural prosperity was inadequately acknowledged and rewarded. Lower middle-class women, like women on farms, seldom became politically active, in part because they often worked full-time as partners of husbands in small businesses or as white-collar employees. The Czechoslovak industrial working class, second only to farm families in numbers, included homemaking wives of workers and the married and single women who comprised 34 percent of the industrial labor force in 1921. These women, like their husbands and male coworkers, usually voted Social Democratic or to a lesser extent Communist or National Socialist.[5]

In Czechoslovakia most upper middle-class and professional women, like most male national leaders, were civic-minded patriots who encouraged all citizens to adopt middle-class values. These women also practiced nonviolence and moderation in politics, often as members of a political party and of one or more feminist organizations like the Women's Industrial and Commercial Training Association (*Ženský výrobní spolek*), the oldest and most conservative such organization; the Central Association of Czech Women (*Ústřední spolek českých žen*) whose more militant program dated from the turn of the century; Minerva, an association primarily of professional women founded in 1895; or the League for the Defense of Motherhood (*Spolek pro ochranu mateřství*) that emphasized birth control, better personal hygiene, and better childcare.[6] Upper middle-class and professional women principally sought to alleviate the problems of working-class women through charitable work or improving public schools, public health, and labor regulation.

Devoutly Catholic women, more numerous in Moravia and Slovakia than in Bohemia, often placed Church interests before those of feminism or social class. Such women usually voted for clerical party candidates and participated in Catholic charitable and fraternal associations. Tens of thousands also found personal as well as spiritual fulfillment in religious orders for women.[7]

Studies about women in many societies in recent times indicate that women are usually more active in nonpartisan, community service or charitable associations, whether religious or secular, than in partisan political organizations. This was also the case in interwar Czechoslovakia with its strong YWCA, Red Cross, and religious charities, despite a higher degree of partisan political activity by women than in any other East European country.

In Czechoslovakia more than 80 percent of all women between the ages of thirty and fifty were married, and most had children, despite a birthrate that declined from the mid-1920s onward. Women's magazines and newspapers, regardless of political outlook, featured articles on homemaking, and Social Democratic papers, among others, emphasized how the eight-hour day would enable working women to devote more time to their families as well as to physical and intellectual self-improvement. Catholic publications celebrated women as nurturers and the family as a fundamental and divinely sanctioned social institution, while Agrarian journals not only hailed the family as the backbone of Czechoslovak agriculture but echoed liberal publicists in extolling the family as the primary incubator of national consciousness.

The stability of the Czech and Slovak family is evident in statistics on divorce and emigration as well as in the number and longevity of marriages. In Czechoslovakia, less than five percent of marriages ended in separation or divorce, with the typically less urbanized and more religious inhabitants of Moravia and Slovakia experiencing only one-third to two-fifths as much separation and divorce as did citizens in Bohemia.[8] Czechs emigrated almost exclusively in family units, and Slovaks, who less frequently did so, usually established close-knit families in the New World and sent back for relatives.[9]

Czechoslovak women, whether feminists or working-class advocates, concentrated primarily on obtaining for women the same advantages men enjoyed in wages and employment opportunities. To a lesser extent, they also tried to modify society's double standard for premarital and extramarital relations by insisting that men be held to the behavior expected of women. Like many feminists in the United States and Western Europe during this period, these women believed that their advocacy of women's rights would not weaken the family but rather would strengthen family ties by encouraging greater equality, harmony, and mutual respect in married life.

The productivity of Czechoslovak industry and agriculture during the 1920s that made Czechoslovakia the world's seventh largest industrial power augured well for future economic growth and helped maintain social peace but did not provide markedly higher wages for most Czechoslovak laborers and farmers, women or men. Women from working-class or poor farming families usually shared their husbands' and fathers' political views and believed that advocating greater job security, more equitable distribution of income, and government ownership of utilities and certain industries should take precedence over endorsing feminist goals that would primarily benefit bourgeois women.

As table 4.1 illustrates, women contributed greatly to the material prosperity of the Czechoslovak Republic. Women were a much larger part of the labor force in highly industrialized Bohemia and Moravia than in predominantly agrarian Slovakia. Table 4.1 very inadequately reveals the contribution of women to the high productivity of Czechoslovak agriculture, however, because it does not include among the gainfully employed all wives and daughters whose labor was essential to the success of family farms.

By helping to increase the prosperity and diversity of the Czechoslovak economy, women strengthened their still unrealized demand that they receive pay and opportunities for promotion equal to men's. The fact that the percentage of Czechoslovak women obtaining jobs through state employment agencies generally exceeded by 5 to 10 percent the percentage of men who did so indicates that these women probably had qualifications comparable to men and could often be hired less expensively. Statistics for 1929 and 1930 also reveal how the advent of the Great Depression simultaneously increased the number of men and women seeking jobs by more than 50 percent while diminishing the number of women receiving jobs more than the number of men.[10]

The increase of Czech and Slovak women in the national labor force as well as their growing political activism reflected the remarkable educational progress made by Czech women since 1869 and by Slovak women after 1918. The state-supported, free, and compulsory primary schools established in the Czech Lands in 1869 had educated two generations of literate men and women by 1918. At that time, Slovaks were generally less well-educated primarily because rural poverty, inadequate primary and secondary schools, and forced Magyarization had prevailed in prewar Hungary. During the 1920s in Czechoslovakia, 45 to 46 percent of students enrolled in school were girls. That Czechoslovak women by 1930 had received an elementary education comparable to men is clearly indicated by the fact that in Czechoslovakia 90.3 percent of women as opposed to 92.9 percent of men over age five were literate and by the fact that literacy among women was within

Table 4.1 Women in the Czechoslovak labor force in 1921 as (A) a percentage of all employees and (B) a percentage of all women employed

Category	Czecho-slovakia		Bohemia		Moravia-Silesia		Slovakia	
	(A)	(B)	(A)	(B)	(A)	(B)	(A)	(B)
Professions, public and civil service	29.0	4.1	29.5	4.2	33.8	4.5	23.0	3.5
Armed forces	0	0	0	0	0	0	0	0
Business, transport	21.0	6.4	22.3	7.4	22.1	6.0	14.4	4.1
Industry	21.0	23.7	23.5	29.3	18.7	21.4	13.0	9.6
Agriculture, forestry	31.9	38.6	36.1	31.6	37.9	40.9	23.3	57.0
Domestic, part-time	67.0	3.5	73.1	3.4	73.9	3.3	52.5	4.0
Other employment	62.3	23.7	61.6	24.1	62.6	23.9	65.8	21.8
	30.2	100.0	32.3	100.0	32.2	100.0	24.1	100.0

Source: Statistical Office of the Czechoslovak Republic, ed., *Manúel Statistique de la République Tchécoslovaque,* vol. 4 (Prague: State Statistical Office, 1932), pp. 11–14.

1 percent of that of men in all parts of the country except Slovakia and the Carpatho-Ukraine. In 1930 the percentage of literate women over age five was 96.5 in Bohemia, 95.3 in Moravia, and 79.0 in Slovakia.[11]

Throughout the 1920s Czechoslovak women also made great educational gains at the secondary and higher levels. In 1922, in response to the fact that women voted in numbers equal to men and that political parties advocating equality of opportunity controlled Parliament, the Ministry of Education and National Culture established equal access to and equal treatment for women in secondary schools, a reform viewed by its supporters and opponents as another step toward the democratization of society. Headed by veteran Social Democrat Gustav Habrman, the Ministry set high standards for all secondary schools, took over and funded many heretofore private boys' and girls' lycées, encouraged schools to adopt coeducation, and required that all state nonclassical secondary and specialized schools, whether coeducational or not, offer women the same choice of curricula as men.[12] By the 1930s the effects of increased coeducation or the equalization of curricula in the absence of coeducation were evident in the greater numbers of financially independent professional women whose views and expectations had begun to affect relations between the sexes in family as in public life.[13]

Women's utilization of these new opportunities in Czechoslovakia varied according to nationality as Czech women more often acquired higher education than German or Slovak women. At the Charles University in

Prague and the Masaryk University in Brno, Czech women comprised 24.7 percent and 17.5 percent of all full-time students in the academic years 1921–22 through 1927–28. By contrast, women were only 13.2 percent of the student body at the German University in Prague and 12.5 percent of the students at the Komenský University in Bratislava. Czechoslovak women in higher education usually studied the liberal and fine arts as opposed to business and engineering. In the two Czech and two German polytechnical schools of the Republic, women made up only 2 to 3 percent of the undergraduates; at the Czechoslovak Academy of Fine Arts, however, approximately 30 percent of full-time students were women.[14]

The primary avenues of professional advancement for Czech and Slovak women continued to be literature, journalism, and the performing arts, where, beginning with Romanticism and the National Revival, Czech and Slovak women of every generation had won renown. Among the many women who figured prominently in the cultural and intellectual life of the Republic, some, like the novelist Marie Majerová, used their public recognition to advocate feminist or other political goals. Additional public arenas in which women excelled were elementary and secondary education, social services, and, to a lesser extent, the learned professions and appointive and elective political office.[15] By contrast, very few women occupied managerial positions in commerce and industry. Several young women successfully competed with men in fields heretofore exclusively male like professional athletics and auto racing.[16] Within Protestantism and Judaism, women began to win appointment to lower-level lay offices, while the Roman Catholic Church continued to offer women opportunities for leadership in various religious orders.[17]

The entry of the first Czech women into the learned professions after 1902 was followed during the 1920s by an accelerated movement of Czech and Slovak women into the civil service, medicine, and university and lycée teaching, as the first generation of women professionals, now established in positions of influence, helped inspire and educate the second generation. Most of these women continued to help lead the feminist movement of the interwar years, thus demonstrating to younger women how professional achievement could increase one's effectiveness in public affairs. Though few in numbers, probably not more than ten thousand by 1938, these feminists served as role models to countless young women and encouraged professional women to assume greater responsibility for the education and welfare of rural and working-class women.[18]

Women in Czechoslovakia benefited not only from increased educational opportunities and civil liberties but from the ambitious program of industrial, social welfare, and public health legislation enacted by the Red-Green (Social Democratic, National Socialist, and Agrarian) coalition governments of the early 1920s with the support of women's and labor organizations and President T. G. Masaryk. Typical new laws that directly affected millions of Czechoslovak women were Law 91 of 1918 that instituted the eight-hour day and the forty-eight hour week, Law 29 of 1920 that regulated the circumstances and remuneration for dometic employment, and Law 420 of 1919 that tightened existing regulation of evening and overtime work and of labor by women and children.[19] Women as well as men viewed the eight-hour day not only as a means of strengthening the working-class family but as a necessary corollary to women's newly acquired right to vote in all elections. Workers of both sexes for the first time not only acquired a voice in local government but had time enough to serve as elected local officials.[20]

Establishment of the eight-hour day encouraged Parliament to enact laws to promote the more wholesome use of leisure time, especially those curbing prostitution and restricting the sale and consumption of alcoholic beverages. Czech and Slovak women's organizations, feminist and Social Democratic, had for several decades advocated such legislation to improve not only the status of women but the stability and prosperity of working-class families. Law 86 of 1922 prohibited the sale of alcoholic drinks except beer and wine to any person under eighteen and the latter beverages to anyone under sixteen. The Abstinence League (*Abstinentní svaz*) founded in 1920 with women among its leaders had, with the support of feminists and President Masaryk, encouraged passage of this law and complementary legislation that limited prostitution and facilitated the detection and treatment of venereal disease.[21]

Other laws that sought to improve family life were the series of six in 1919 that aimed at mitigating a severe postwar housing shortage by stimulating the construction of small apartments, primarily through subsidies to builders and guaranteed loans to purchasers. Additional social legislation that responded to demands of women included the establishment of national unemployment insurance in 1919 and its expansion in 1921–22 to give workers a small stipend in the event of layoffs and to provide assistance in obtaining other employment.[22] Broadening disability, accident, and health insurance for industrial workers and extending it for the first time to agricultural employees and domestic servants, many of whom were women, also helped diminish somewhat the harsh uncertainties of life for working-class families. Parliament's passage in October 1924 of Law 221 providing social security for workers completed five years of ambitious social legislation that advanced directly or indirectly the welfare of women as well as men.

The Organizations and Political Activity of Czech and Slovak Women

The Czechoslovak Republic advanced women's emancipation and social reform not only through universal suffrage and welfare legislation but through a prosperous economy and democratic representative institutions. Though in any national election only several dozen women ran for office and at most fifteen were elected, over 80 percent of Czechoslovak women exercised their right to vote. They voted in larger numbers than men but on most issues appeared to have voted no differently than men of comparable education and occupation.[23]

Women who rose to positions of leadership in Czechoslovak political parties were often those who after the turn of the century had worked on party or feminist journals or who had been among the first women to enter the learned professions. Other leaders, especially in the Social Democratic and Communist parties, were drawn from the intelligentsia and from the thousands of women who had served as rank and file members of trade unions or local party organizations. Even the split between the Social Democrats and Communists that weakened the Czechoslovak left in 1921 did not set back the increasing efforts of working-class women to obtain a greater share in party management and policymaking. Instead, these women were helped by the fact that the two parties competed to win their support much as the two factions of the unified party had done before 1921.[24]

The division of Czech and Slovak women between predominantly middle-class feminists on the one hand and working-class adherents of Social Democracy or Communism on the other persisted through the interwar years. Though Czech and Slovak women of different political persuasions often worked well together, no women's organizations ever became truly multinational in the sense of including German and Hungarian as well as Czech, Slovak, and Ukrainian women of differing ideological outlooks. To be sure, Czech and German Social Democratic women pursued common goals, and the Communist party united like-minded women regardless of nationality. But, on balance, allegiances to class, nationality, and religion usually outweighed any common interests women had on the basis of their gender.

From 1918 through 1938, the leftward orientation of Czechoslovak politics and of all but one national government—that of the clerical-Agrarian coalition from 1926 to 1929—also facilitated the advancement of women's rights and employment opportunities. All parties of the left had advocated women's emancipation since the prewar years and offered women the greatest possibilities for party leadership. The Agrarian party, a partner to every government of the Republic and dominated until 1938 by its more liberal elements, sought no specifically feminist goals but supported universal suffrage and most of the social welfare legislation of the early 1920s.[25] The comparative weakness of clerical and right-wing parties in Czechoslovakia, particularly in comparison to Germany and Austria, partly explains the willingness of Czech and Slovak Agrarians, among others, to enfranchise women without fear that either priest-confessors or husbands of reactionary views could sway the votes of enough women to tip the political balance against parties of the center and left.

Successful efforts to advance women's interests in Czechoslovakia also owed something to the fact that its principal founders and leaders, T. G. Masaryk and Edvard Beneš, were married to feminists and were themselves longtime advocates of women's emancipation. Their prewar speeches and publications reveal not only the fervor of this advocacy but the fact that they had committed themselves to this cause at a time when to do so was not politically expedient.[26] In this and other respects they were not typical Czech or Slovak men, but after 1918 so great was Masaryk's prestige and political influence that his and Beneš's encouragement of women in public life certainly facilitated the work of reform-minded feminists like Beneš's wife Hana and Masaryk's eldest daughter Alice.[27]

In trying to realize equality of opportunity with men, Czech and Slovak women during the 1920s and 1930s worked through various women's organizations, patriotic associations, and political parties in proportionately larger numbers than Sudeten German and Hungarian women. The coordinating body for fifty-three independent Czechoslovak women's organizations was the National Council of Women (*Ženská národní rada*), founded in 1922 and chaired through most of the next sixteen years by Františka Plamínková, who also served in Parliament as a senator representing the Czechoslovak National Socialist party. Like most of its constituent organizations, the council worked to enlarge women's rights and opportunities and was affiliated with the leading international women's associations.[28]

Czechoslovak women in the Social Democratic and Communist parties also maintained ties with women's associations in the Second International and Communist International, respectively. An outstanding Czechoslovak Social Democrat in this respect was Betty Karpíšková, delegate of her party to the Second Socialist International and principal organizer in Prague of the February 1934 meeting of the International Conference of Social Democratic Women.[29]

The variety of organizations available to Czech and Slovak women who wished to be active in public life is reflected in the number of Czech and Slovak newspapers and journals addressed primarily to women. These publications, which had first appeared during the last decades of the nineteenth century and generally adopted a more partisan political orientation after 1918, may be classified into six main categories: (1) liberal and patriotic journals addressed primarily to middle-class women; (2) the feminist and radical feminist press; (3) newspapers and periodicals addressed primarily to working-class women, almost exclusively Social Democratic before 1921 and thereafter Communist and National Socialist as well; (4) political or devotional publications of the Roman Catholic Church; (5) magazines and journals that emphasized either fashion or homemaking or both of these traditional interests of women; and (6) trade and professional journals, of which the most influential were those addressed to women teachers in elementary and secondary schools.[30] All women's periodicals aimed, to a greater or lesser degree, to broaden the outlook of women and encourage them to participate more fully in the political, intellectual, and cultural life of the Republic.[31]

The first periodical to speak for Czech women on public issues was the monthly *Ženské listy*, founded in 1873 by Eliška Krásnohorská, published by the Women's Industrial and Commercial Training Association and edited during the 1920s by Jindřiška Flajšhansová. With the Association's program for women's emancipation largely realized by 1922, the "Women's News" continued perspicaciously to discuss culture and politics and did not become the organ of any political party. Other feminist journals that retained their prewar outlook included *Ženský obzor* (The Woman's Horizon) and the more militant *Ženský svět* (Women's World), established in 1896 and published after 1900 by the Central Association of Czech Women under editor Terésa Nováková. Anna Ziegloserová, who edited the postwar *Ženský obzor*, and Milada Sísová, her counterpart at *Ženský svět*, both participated in politics, the former with the Czechoslovak National Socialists and the latter with the National Democrats. That the women's movement came late to Slovakia was indicated by the fact that the first exclusively Slovak women's journal, the fortnightly *Slovenská žena* (The Slovak Woman), began publication only in the spring of 1920.

The most far-reaching postwar change in Czechoslovak women's political journalism occurred when the Communists, in withdrawing from Social Democracy to form their own party in 1921, took over the Social Democratic *Žena* (The Woman) in Brno and *Ženský list* (The Woman's Paper) in Prague, transforming the former into *Komunistka* (The Communist Woman) and the latter into *Rozsévačka* (The Woman Sower).[32] To replace *Ženský list*, Czechoslovak Social Democrats enlarged their *Ženské noviny* (Women's News), "a political and economic weekly for women's education," edited by Betty Karpíšková. Czechoslovak National Socialists revived the prewar *Ženské snahy* (Women's Endeavors) and started several new periodicals.

Catholic religious orders and charities for women were complemented by magazines that sometimes expressed partisan political views. *Česká žena* (The Czech Woman), published by the Bishop of České Budějovice, had first appeared in 1909, but its counterpart in Brno, *Moravská žena* (The Moravian Woman), "a cultural and political weekly," dated from 1919. *Katolická učitelka* (The Catholic Woman Teacher), sponsored by the Archbishop of Olomouc and edited by Marie Šebiková, completed its eighth year in 1920 as the largest Catholic educational journal for women.

The large number of women active in the Sokol, the North Bohemian and Šumava National Unions, and other popular Czechoslovak patriotic and fraternal associations reflected the great extent to which men had welcomed the participation of women in work deemed essential to the national interest. In the 1920s these associations had female leaders as well, most notably Renata Fügnerová Tyršová, the grand lady of the Sokol, daughter of one of its founders and widow to the other. From its inception in 1862, the Sokol had included women among its members, albeit initially as members of auxiliary organizations. By the 1920s Czech and Slovak women were taking an active part in this and comparable patriotic gymnastics organizations that promoted national solidarity and physical and intellectual fitness, in 1922 constituting 29 percent of adult members in the Sokol and some 30 percent of such members in the Workers' Union (Svaz), the Workers' Federation (Federace), and the Catholic Eagle (Orel). The presence of girls among adolescent members of the Sokol and similar organizations in almost equal numbers and proportion to boys reflected the rapid movement and was a trend that augured well for the future of women's emancipation.[34]

Czech and Slovak women who entered politics usually joined one of the established political parties as well as various occupational and professional associations and feminist organizations. Proportionately more Czech than Sudeten German or Slovak women held elective and appointive political office or positions of responsibility within political parties.[35]

The Czechoslovak Social Democratic party and its German counterpart had since the 1880s supported women's suffrage and equality of opportunity. The former party and its trade unions primarily proposed legislation designed to improve wages, working conditions, and unemployment and disability benefits for both sexes but occasionally addressed issues of special concern to women. For example, of thirty-four desiderata that the Social Democratic unions presented to Parliament in 1929, none exclusively addressed women's interests, but all to some degree aimed to improve the lot of working-class men and women directly or indirectly.[36]

Of all parties in the Republic, the Czechoslovak and German Social Democrats, the Communists, and the Czechoslovak National Socialists gave women the most opportunities to run for public and party offices.[37] In 1926 Czechoslovak Social Democratic women held 103 party offices at the district and local levels in Bohemia compared to fourteen in Moravia and none in Slovakia. This party not only attracted able female leaders; it encouraged, as did its Communist and National Socialist rivals, participation by working-class women in party affairs. In the same year 17,518 women were party members, comprising 18 percent of all members, or 19 percent of members in Bohemia, 16 percent in Moravia, and 14 percent in Slovakia.[38]

The Czechoslovak National Socialist party also had long championed equal rights and public responsibilities for women as the Action Program of its Twelfth Party Congress of April 1931 indicates:

> From our philosophical convictions and our concepts of democracy, nationality, and socialism naturally arises our belief in the complete and valid equality between man and woman in family, political, economic, social, and cultural life. Accordingly . . . wages, salaries, and working conditions should no longer be established differently for women than for men nor should the legal order favor men over women. We gladly join in the struggle for women's rights and all that it necessitates in the reform of civil, criminal, and other law.[39]

This Action Program, designed by a commission of sixteen men and three women, reflected the party's ongoing efforts to extend social reform legislation and make higher culture and education accessible "to all citizens without regard for sex or socio-economic status" and thereby contribute to the "cultural and moral improvement of all citizens."[40] Františka Zeminová, a feminist and journalist, served as first vice-president of the party's Senate delegation during the 1930s. Another Senator, Františka Plamínková, had become the foremost woman of her party in public esteem and international recognition thanks to the extraordinary eloquence and administrative ability she demonstrated as an officer in various Czechoslovak and international women's organizations.[41]

The two Czechoslovak clerical parties did not include women among higher party officers or candidates for national public office and interpreted women's emancipation as well as the social question primarily in light of Pope Leo XIII's 1891 encyclical *Rerum novarum*. For example, in 1928 the Czechoslovak People's party asserted: "Higher than individual rights are the rights of the family and society, but of course only in the sense that within the family an individual's rights are protected just as society protects the natural rights of the family."[42]

The Czechoslovak People's party accepted not only republican institutions but the ambitious social and labor legislation of the early 1920s.[43]

The preoccupation of the tactically less flexible Slovak People's party with trying to enlarge Slovak political and cultural autonomy precluded its taking much interest in women aside from reaffirming their traditional place in the home.[44]

Czech National Democracy, successor to the prewar Young Czech party and State Rights Progressive party, obtained most of its women members from the latter organization which, unlike the Young Czechs, had endorsed some feminist objectives before the war. From 1919 to 1922 National Democracy had supported universal suffrage and equality before the law for women but had unsuccessfully opposed some legislation for social and educational reform. In this party of the upper middle-class and conservative intelligentsia, women as well as men advocated greater state concessions to industry in order to promote the economic development they believed necessary to maintain national security and the prosperity of all social classes.[45]

Despite the high level of political activism by women in Czechoslovakia, few were elected or appointed to public office. No women received any cabinet posts, and the highest party office held by a woman was that of vice-president of the Czechoslovak National Socialist party. In the lower house of Parliament, women in 1924 numbered twelve, or 4.1 percent of the 294 delegates; in 1930 there were ten women among three hundred delegates, or 3.3 percent of all representatives. The situation was similar in the upper house where women held three of 150, or 2 percent of the senatorial seats in 1924, and five, or 3.3 percent of these seats, in 1935 (see table 4.2).

Setbacks of the Czechoslovak Women's Movement in the 1930s

Why in the 1930s did progress toward equal opportunity slow down and Czechoslovak women's organizations experience a slight loss in national influence? First, advocacy of political and social reform by Czechoslovak women's associations and left-of-center political parties generally outpaced public opinion as the economy worsened and dangers from abroad began to mount. In addition, the two Czechoslovak parties with the largest popular vote and parliamentary representation, the Agrarians and the Social Democrats, believed, respectively, that further reforms should await improvement in agricultural conditions and that the woman question would be resolved only with resolution of the social question.

Second, the strength of nationality, religious, class, and occupational loyalties insured that no unified Czechoslovak women's movement would ever emerge despite many instances of successful cooperation among

Table 4.2 Representation of women by party in the lower house of the Czechoslovak parliament

Parties	Elections of 1924			Elections of 1930		
	Total Representation	Total Women	Percentage Women	Total Representation	Total Women	Percentage Women
cs. Social Democratic	52	2	3.8	43	1	2.3
cs. Agrarian	42	1	2.4	46	0	0
cs. National Socialist	27	3	11.1	32	3	9.4
Communist	27	1	3.7	30	3	10.0
National Democratic	22	2	9.1	14	1	7.1
cs. Peoples	20	1	5.0	25	0	0
Slovak Peoples	11	0	0	20	0	0
cs. Small Business	6	0	0	12	0	0
cs. Socialist Union	3	0	0	0	0	0
German Social Democratic	30	2	6.7	21	2	9.5
Other German parties	41	0	0	42	0	0
Hungarian parties	9	0	0	12	0	0
Unaffiliated Representatives	4	0	0	3	0	0
Total Delegates	294	12	4.1	300	10	3.3

Sources: *Ročenka Národního Shromáždění Republiky Československé 1923–24* (Prague: Archiv Národního Shromáždění, 1924), pp. 83–84; and *Poslanecká sněmovna ve III. volebním období* (Prague: Archiv Národního Shromáždění, 1930), pp. 68–82.

women of different nationalities. This division not only paralleled those in other advanced industrial countries but reflected the fact that no feminist goal was ever compelling enough to win support from all women or to persuade most women that their principal political allegiance should go to a unified movement for women's emancipation rather than to a state, class, nationality, or church.

Third, and perhaps most important, the Great Depression retarded the advance of Czechoslovak women toward equal opportunity in at least three ways. As in most industrial societies with increasing unemployment, the laying off of recently hired workers affected a higher percentage though not larger numbers of women than men. The shortage of capital, which occurred as a result of the Depression, affected government as well as business and individuals and led to cutbacks in many social services administered by or to women. In addition, the Depression so impressed unemployment and problems of economic recovery upon all citizens that specifically feminist goals appeared less urgent or worthy of support.

Fourth, and finally, Nazi Germany's rearmament and increasingly aggressive foreign policy after 1935 so gravely endangered Czechoslovak security that all other issues, including even economic recovery, began to pale by comparison. Moreover, leaders of Czechoslovak women's organizations saw in the victories of fascism and Nazism direct threats to the well-being and continued emancipation of women, given the great antipathy of those ideologies to women's demands for equality. These fears were well grounded, for the Nazis, after establishing the Protectorate of Bohemia and Moravia in 1939, destroyed all independent Czechoslovak political parties and feminist and workers' associations. The satellite Slovak Republic undertook the same task in Slovakia.

The Place of the Czechoslovak Republic in the History of Czech and Slovak Women

The influence of the Czechoslovak women's movement during the 1920s and 1930s is better measured by its many accomplishments than by the number of women involved in politics or the individual achievements of outstanding women in the arts and letters and learned professions. The establishment of equality before the law, the social and educational reforms of the early 1920s, improvements in the quality of family life, and a generally prosperous economy facilitated the advance of Czech and Slovak women toward equality of opportunity. The Great Depression retarded but did not stop this progress. So long as the Republic endured, the Czechoslovak women's movement could face the future with confidence. It is no coincidence that the Nazis who destroyed the Republic also dismantled its women's organizations and made martyrs of three of their leading representatives—Betty Karpíšková, Františka Plamínková, and Anna Ziegloserová.

The first twenty years of Czechoslovak independence were the halcyon days of Czechoslovak feminism, perhaps as much for opportunities offered and hopes engendered as for concrete achievements. In contrast to the Habsburgs, whom the Czechoslovak Republic supplanted, and the Nazis, who dismembered it, that Republic provided much greater independence and influence for feminist and working-class women's associations. Thus for many Czech and Slovak women as for many Czechoslovak citizens generally, the Republic has, as Václav Havel suggests, a lasting moral importance.[46] Despite its many shortcomings and the inability of Czech and Slovak feminists and working-class women to agree on a common program, many Czechs and Slovaks remember the Republic as the regime that provided both sexes with the greatest civil liberties and with many opportunities for careers open to talent. Though women were disappointed by continuing social inequality and the fact that they had achieved less professional advancement in the industry, law, and medicine than in education and the arts, many Czech and Slovak women retrospectively recognized the 1920s and 1930s to have been one of the happier times in their individual and collective experience.

5

Martha Bohachevsky-Chomiak

Ukrainian Feminism in Interwar Poland

This chapter examines the organization and activities of Ukrainian women in Poland between the two world wars and the manner in which broader political factors deflected these women from articulating an explicitly feminist position. The activities of these women were influenced by two important factors during this period. First, like numerous other groups, the Ukrainians in Poland found themselves to be minorities in states dominated by members of another ethnic group. This minority status colored the articulation of the goals of women activists and their relationships with their male conationals. In addition, the work of the women was also influenced by the fact that they lived in an overwhelmingly agrarian society where opportunities for economic and social advancement were limited. The pages to follow illustrate the manner in which women activists responded to both these factors in their efforts to improve women's status during this period. As they demonstrate, Ukrainian women in interwar Poland developed a type of practical feminism that does not fall within either the liberal or the socialist conception.

The Western Ukrainian women, who, as a result of the border shifts that occurred after World War I, found themselves in Poland, Czechoslovakia, and Romania developed very effective and highly pragmatic women's organizations.[1] Hindered by the prevailing political conditions from consolidating themselves into one organization until 1937, Ukrainian women nonetheless showed a remarkable degree of cohesion, cooperation, and tolerance in their work.

Both Eastern and Western Ukrainians had failed to preserve the independent sovereign states they had established after World War I. The Eastern Ukrainians, who had been under tsarist rule, had been instrumental in pressuring the Bolsheviks into creating a federal structure for the new political entity, the Union of the Soviet Socialist Republics. Many prominent Ukrainian women, predicting that the Ukrainizing course of the Bolsheviks was, at best, a temporary expedient, emigrated to Poland and Czechoslovakia. Sizable territories inhabited by Ukrainians, among them Volyn', Polissia, and parts of Pokuttia, passed from Russian to Polish domination.

Ukrainians in the former Austrian Province of Eastern Galicia hoped that the Allies would sanction the existence of a separate Western Ukrainian successor state. The Allies did not do so. Instead, they mandated Polish administration of Galicia (in March 1923), with provisions for broad cultural autonomy and political rights for the minorities living there. The other successor states also signed special clauses promising to honor the rights of minorities.

At the same time, Soviet Ukrainian women were pursuing policies aimed at modernization, equal rights, and industrialization. The actual impact of Soviet women upon Western Ukrainian women was negligible, since the political, social, and economic systems under which the Soviets were operating were not attractive to them. However, Western Ukrainian women followed with interest the achievements of Soviet women and with horror the manipulation of the whole society resulting in the collectivization of 1928, the political trials of 1930, the mass famine of 1933, and the mounting purges of the 1930s. The suppression of Ukrainian Communists was a prelude to the suppression of Ukrainian cultural activists, men and women alike.

Outside the Soviet Ukraine, the most compact groups of Ukrainians were those in Galicia and Volyn'. The defeats suffered by the Ukrainians in 1918 and 1919 did not chasten them. For the women, who had been pressuring for equality before the outbreak of the war, the defeat only underscored the absolute necessity of becoming involved in the process of nation-building. It was in Galicia that women's groups were strongest after 1884. Galicia was still predominantly rural, its school system underdeveloped, and opportunities for advancement severely limited. Since the 1870s, however, Ukrainians in this area had organized community and cooperative associations aimed at the dissemination of knowledge, self-help, and community service. Initially founded within the Ukrainian Catholic clergy, which had the option to be married, these organizations quickly incorporated the secular intelligentsia that emerged from both the clerical and peasant milieus. The women in the area, exhibiting all the characteristics of women of preindustrialized societies, were subordinate but somewhat autonomous and retained their individualistic status that the middle-class women had generally lost.

The first women's organizations in Galicia emerged among the women of the clergy. Through the 1880s and 1890s two separate tendencies were evident among women, with some interesting attempts at fusing the two. There were the philanthropic, church-oriented ladies' groups that edged into greater community involvement. There were also a number of women who espoused different variants of socialism, subordinated "women's issues" to those of social and political liberation, and created organizations of their own. The latter groups, composed mainly of young women students in turn drifted toward a progressive democratic nationalism without compromising their socialist ideals. But the high-handed, paternalistic treatment the women received from their male socialist colleagues predisposed them to accept a pragmatic, common sense feminism, devoid of the rhetoric of liberation, which had emerged among the society matrons who had also experienced condescending treatment by the males. During the war the two groups—the socialists and community matrons—began to inch closer to each other while working together in war relief committees. The Western Ukrainian women's movement, as it developed in the interwar years, was the result of the fusion of these organizations, reinforced by contacts both before and after World War I with politically active Eastern Ukrainian émigrés. The core of the movement was in Eastern Galicia in Poland, with similar organizations established in other areas.

At the time Poland numbered approximately 30 million people, of which one-third were not Poles. Ukrainians constituted about 15 percent of the population of Poland but were settled in areas in which the countryside was frequently solidly Ukrainian. The Ukrainians, therefore, did not see themselves as a minority in Poland, but as rightful residents of their own lands, which happened to be under Polish occupation. Although cities and towns were heterogeneous, composed of Jews, Poles, Ukrainians, Armenians and others, the villages were either Ukrainian or Polish, with the Ukrainian villages predominant.[2]

The Ukrainian Women's Movement: A Place in Society

The organization that de facto if not de jure grouped all Ukrainian women outside the Soviet Union was the *Soiuz Ukraiinok*, the Ukrainian Women's Union. Unlike other European women's movements, which were largely composed of middle-class women, the Ukrainian Women's Union had a mass membership in which all classes of the population participated. However, peasant women constituted the majority of the Union's members. The Union pursued moderate policies and had no rigid ideology. With few exceptions, Ukrainian women displayed little interest in theoretical analyses of feminism or women's role in society. Rather, as in other preindustrialized societies, the women responded to the needs of the population. As the Czech women's movement did at the turn of the century, the

Ukrainian women incorporated programs of self-improvement, community initiative, and attempts at modernization in a society where financial resources were limited. As the Poles had in the previous century, Ukrainians also stressed the final goal of national liberation, glorifying motherhood for its social role and not just for personal fulfillment. But Ukrainian women activists went beyond the Poles, both in their stress on women's autonomy and in the importance of the women's organization within the community as a whole. In this particular mix of pragmatism, modernization, policies to foster the care of mother and child, and efforts to promote individual and national liberation, the Western Ukrainian women's movement foreshadowed the contemporary movements of the women in the Third World.[3]

The Ukrainian Women's Union helped Ukrainian women to help themselves step into modernity and emerge as conscious, active, and political citizens of the Ukrainian community. Before the Union and its activities fell victim to the ravages of World War II, Ukrainian women had made a significant impact upon the lives of Ukrainians in Ukrainian territories and elsewhere. The women helped establish economic and cultural agencies that served as levers for the improvement of the quality of life of all Ukrainians. The Union also brought the Ukrainian cause into the international arena. It helped establish the Ukrainian Women's Union in other Ukrainian territories, and it was instrumental in the formation of the Ukrainian National Women's League of America in 1925 and other similar organizations of Ukrainian women in Europe and America.

The work of the Union can be divided into two parts. Between 1921 and 1930 its goals were centered on local economic and cultural achievements. The second phase, from 1931 to 1938, gave the movement high visibility and generated an interest in feminist issues. While its goals were still economic and cultural, the movement's second phase was geared toward the political and economic life of the Ukrainian people in Poland.

The Union was constituted at a formal congress of Ukrainian women in December 1921. By the 1930s its membership, mainly peasant, numbered between 50,000 and 100,000 women. The discrepancy in the estimate was due partly to the fact that the Poles prevented the consolidation of the Ukrainian women in the Polish state into one organization and partly to the overlapping membership of women in other community groups.[4] For Ukrainians, the Women's Union became one of the most effective organizations, along with the Enlightenment Society, the Society for the Promotion of the Native School, and the economic cooperatives that covered the Ukrainian areas with a network of local organizations and that had arisen when the area had been part of the Austrian Monarchy. One of the most important of these was the *Sil's'ky Hospodar* (Village Farmer), established originally in 1899, which had as its goal the dissemination of practical farming techniques among the peasants. Although not technically a cooperative, it promoted economic cooperation among the peasants, fostered the growth of the cooperative movement, and encouraged women to join.

Although the leaders of the Union were motivated by some feminist concerns, an open feminist statement was made only after the organization achieved mass membership since it was only then that most women realized their second-class status. Encouraged by a belief in patriotism and progress, the Union carried out policies that resulted in modernization and depended upon the consensus of the broad number of activists who helped initiate social and economic change among the masses. The Union defined itself by its work; its feminism was a feminism of operation, not a feminism of theory.

The leadership of the Women's Union was drawn from the Ukrainian Catholic clerical milieu and from the intelligentsia. The activists came from the women's clubs and from women who had worked in the temperance movement, public schools, and community enlightenment groups. The backbone of the organization was its largely peasant membership. Work centered on the local unit—the circle in the village and the branch, which coordinated the work of the circles, in the cities.

Some of the organization's circles were formally connected to the Enlightenment Society, since that was easier than getting the required special police permit necessary for the establishment of a new organization. Frequently the pastor's wives organized the peasant circles, which then were run by the peasant women themselves. On the whole, women of the middle class and the intelligentsia threw themselves wholeheartedly into the work of the Union. Many of them had grown up in the villages, some in clergy families that had moved through a number of villages, and most kept up ties with the village. In contrast to the earlier populist activity of the Ukrainian intelligentsia in the Russian Empire,[5] these women did not preach the gospel of revolution or abstract progress. Rather they stressed the need for organized forms of social activity and the establishment of economic and cultural agencies that could serve as levers for the advancement of the peasants and as concrete means of bettering their lives.

The main activists seem to have been women in their twenties and thirties, frequently the first generation to have formal secondary schooling. Their keen sense of duty toward the nation and the people was not due to any feelings of guilt vis-à-vis the peasants, since they could not consider themselves exploiters of the masses, but rather to a genuine, even somewhat romantic, dedication to the nation and the people. Yet their approach was very practical and pragmatic: let's help the peasants help themselves, and the whole nation will profit.[6]

The Polish government completely abrogated the promises it made to the minorities in 1934. By seeking to establish an exclusively Polish system of education and administration in Galicia, the government reversed the Austrian practice of granting some concessions to the local population. Ukrainians were frustrated by the slow and seemingly ineffectual nature of the parliamentary process in Poland. This frustration contributed to the growth of militant nationalism and the creation in January 1929 of the clandestine Organization of Ukrainian Nationalists. The growing international tension, the turn of the Polish republic to pseudo-fascist tendencies, and the unlimited reign of Stalinist terror in the Soviet Ukraine predisposed an increasing number of young Western Ukrainian women to espouse not so much the ideology as the ethos of extreme nationalism. The fact that the Union managed to remain independent of that growing current was a measure of its maturity and strength. Members of the Union, like the majority of Ukrainians in Poland, remained opposed to the extremist position on moral, political, and practical grounds. Rather than engage in militant nationalist activities, they continued to build a network of legal community organizations that contributed to the economic and cultural progress of the people. The Women's Union fit within this framework.

Women in the Economy

To a greater degree than in other nonsocialist states, the industry and economy of interwar Poland were in the hands of the government.[7] Since Ukrainians did not have a strong outside government to speak up in their behalf, the Polish government allocated little of the limited funds available to it for the needs of the Ukrainian population. Community action was thus the primary tool available to members of the Ukrainian community to deal with their problems. Continuing the process begun under the Austrians, the Ukrainians expanded their network of cooperatives. The Central Ukrainian Cooperative Union was reconstituted in 1921, the same year that saw the final establishment of the Women's Union. Its aim was to strengthen the economic position of the Ukrainians by making them less vulnerable to economic exploitation and less dependent upon non-Ukrainian merchants who were not interested in community causes. The slogan "buy from your own" was eminently patriotic and also made good economic sense, especially for the peasants who lost to the middleman both in selling their goods and in buying needed consumer products.

Without engaging in theoretical analyses of the relationship of feminism to the principles of economic cooperation, the Ukrainian women had plunged into cooperative ventures as a matter of necessity, years before the outbreak of World War I. Of equal importance was the fact that the cooperative could not do without the active collaboration of the women. Ukrainian men were not any more responsive to the needs of women than other men in patriarchal, agricultural, traditional, and Catholic societies. But the economics of the area forced the men to take notice of the women, since the products which Ukrainians in Galicia had for export (mainly eggs and butter) lay in the women's preserve of the household. It was in the interest of the cooperative, therefore, to have peasant women aware of belonging to an entity larger than the village to influence their choice to whom to sell—the cooperative or the private entrepreneur. Moreover, the village was the natural consumer for the cooperative, which could not compete with the established stores in towns.[8]

The modest beginnings of the village organizations can best be illustrated by the advice Olena Kysilevs'ka, a longtime women's activist and the editor of the influential magazine aimed primarily at the village women, *Zhinocha dolia* (Woman's Fate), offered in 1926 on organizing a women's group in the village. She described how to get the women together, where to meet, how to conduct a meeting and set up an agenda, what the functions of the officers were, and what the procedures of election were. The peasant women were encouraged to choose among themselves who would be responsible for keeping up with new developments in home maintenance, poultry raising, gardening, dairy production, farming, and health care. Others would be in charge of bringing the circle into broader Ukrainian ventures, while yet another member should be made responsible for keeping the circle informed about childrearing and education.

The women's organization facilitated exchange of useful information and organized specific activities. One of the most important of these was childcare. In addition to helping set up childcare centers, the Women's Union offered training in organizing childcare centers and setting up babysitting barter systems and information on the care of children. But the peasant mothers were repeatedly told not to overlook their own needs and welfare in their zeal in caring for their children.

The Union also ran various training courses for its members. Among the most popular were cooking and sewing courses, which not only helped vary the diet and dress of the peasants but taught them marketable skills. Teenage girls were also able to attend extended three-month courses in home economics. Special sessions and courses to train women to become village organizers for the Union included bookkeeping, economics, hygiene, and political information. Finally, the local circles helped women exchange household and cooking implements, plant cuttings, and dress patterns. These were used by peasants for home consumption and to make items for sale. All of these methods enabled the peasant women to develop self-confidence and interests outside the home, as well as a realization that their activities could influence events in the whole country.

The Women's Union also fostered women's economic activities. The Ukrainian Folk Art Cooperative (*Ukraiins'ke Narodne Mystetstvo*) a direct outgrowth of the Union, collected peasant handicrafts, marketed them, and helped develop a public taste for a highly original blend of folk art and modernism in furnishing and clothing. The work of this cooperative was particularly significant in the poor mountainous areas of the Carpathians. By 1934 the Union mandated that each branch have an economic/cooperative section and that a separate person in the village circles be in charge of matters dealing with the cooperative movement. Through its cooperative work the Union participated in the meetings of the International Women's Cooperative Guild.

Political Activism at Home

Politically, the Union sought to rally the Ukrainian political parties to one common cause. Repeatedly, the Union called for political unity and encouraged its members to be politically active. Although the Union maintained an all-national and supraparty stand, its leadership participated actively in the politics and party policies of the country.

The Ukrainians in Galicia boycotted the first elections to the Polish Parliament that were held before the Allied decision about Galicia was made known formally. In Volyn', the Ukrainians elected among others a woman activist, Halyna Levchanivs'ka, one of the two women in the entire Polish Senate of that session. An ardent Ukrainian patriot, she tried to speak in Ukrainian at the swearing-in ceremony. She also represented Ukrainians at a number of international gatherings.

The middle-of-the-road Ukrainian political parties established the Ukrainian National Democratic Alliance (UNDO), which sought to coordinate Ukrainian political activity in Poland. The Women's Union, especially the leadership in L'viv, participated actively in the UNDO. Olena Fedak Sheparovych served as the official liaison of the Union with the group. It was UNDO which coordinated Ukrainian participation in the elections of 1927–28 to the Polish Assembly. In those elections two other Ukrainian women were elected: Kysilevs'ka to the Senate and Milena Rudnyts'ka to the lower house, the *Sejm*. Both belonged to the moderate party.[10] The traditional foci of women's interest in the legislature—welfare and education—became matters of national importance for Ukrainians. The Polish population was unable to understand why Ukrainians resented the introduction of more Polish language schools in Galicia. Levchanivs'ka and Rudnyts'ka were teachers by profession. They spoke in the interest of the entire Ukrainian population in favor of education in Ukrainian. They also joined other Ukrainian deputies in defending Ukrainian students, who, as the Organization of Ukrainian Nationalists strengthened its influence upon young Ukrainians, openly defied Polish authorities. Rudnyts'ka was particularly articulate on these issues.

Getting the Message Across

The Union received international recognition and was instrumental in bringing the cause of Ukrainians to the international arena in the 1920s and the 1930s. For a time the women were members of the International Council of Women. They remained in the Women's International League for Peace and Freedom and in the International Woman Suffrage Alliance. Milena Rudnyts'ka, president of the Union from 1928 to 1939, was also the spokesperson for the Ukrainian Parliamentary Representation. She argued the Ukrainian cause in London, Geneva, Berlin, and Rome. The Union protested effectively the so-called "pacification" in Poland—a centrally organized pogrom against the Ukrainians in 1930—in which women and children were among the victims. Its protest against the artificial famine of 1933 in the Soviet Ukraine, in which from 6 to 10 million Ukrainians died, was equally dramatic although not as effective. The Union also protested the antifeminist policies of Nazi Germany, although its official delegate to the International Women's Congress in Zurich in 1937 was blocked from leaving the country by the Polish authorities. The Union also effectively withstood pressure from Ukrainian nationalists to espouse their ideology.[11]

In the interwar years Ukrainian women tried to expand the role of women in existing institutions without challenging the social institutions themselves. Maria Strutyns'ka, a writer and activist, argued that feminism strengthened motherhood. Rudnyts'ka pointed to the social importance of feminism for the entire Ukrainian community. Unlike their predecessors within the socialist framework who championed both social change and the cause of women, these women argued that the conscious cooperation of the women in community life was the sine qua non of national independence. When pressed, they took the broadest possible interpretation of feminism: "It is nothing else but the conscious participation of women in the creation of national culture . . . and in the creation of a state."[12]

The work of Olena Kysilevs'ka illustrates their pragmatic approach to feminism. Her journal, *Zhinocha Dolia* (Woman's Fate) served as a means of organizing women for over ten years. She headed the Organizational Committee of the Union for almost a decade and had lifelong experience in working with village women. Her brother, who had emigrated to the United States, supported the journal financially and wrote descriptions of the American way of life, which Kysilevs'ka adapted in articles for her readers. The journal avoided rhetoric and offered practical advice. Its treatment of feminism was for peasant consumption; issues were discussed and put into practical terms. Kysilevs'ka argued that only an intelligent and knowledgeable woman could help with modern farming. A more rational approach to farming, she reminded her readers—and listeners because the journal frequently was read out loud—was a matter of life or death since seasonal labor and emigration were no longer open to the peasants. A low standard of living—frequently a marginal existence—would be the lot of the peasants until a generation of Ukrainian mothers would raise their children more intelligently. Education was the means to a better life. She also argued that women must exercise their political rights, for no one else would pass legislation on their behalf. She stressed the importance of the family and the crucial role of women in it because of its interconnection with the broader society.[13]

Feminism and Nationalist Concerns in the Second Decade

The second decade of the Women's Union was marked by an increase in membership, the spread of the organization into the villages, and the growth of feminist and nationalist concerns. The quality of feminist writing rose, and the new women's newspaper, *Zhinka* (Woman), founded in 1935 and edited by Olena Fedak Sheparovych and later by Milena Rudnyts'ka, tackled issues of interest to educated women: expansion of job opportunities, job equality, career training, living alone, personal growth for mothers, sports, and travel. No longer were women activists content with working in the cooperative movement or in the schools; they wanted to know why women were underrepresented in the central community organizations of Ukrainians.

In articles and transparent fiction, women activists stressed positive role models and tried to instill a work ethic. Correspondence among the women was full of this type of encouragement. Their goal was the emergence of the modern Ukrainian woman, capable and willing to serve the nation intelligently and effectively. To that end, exercise, nutrition, an optimistic world view, care of oneself, festivities, public appearances, and discussions were advocated. To eradicate the sluggishness and drudgery of peasant life, the Days of the Peasant Women were organized. They featured mass demonstrations, marches, concerts, and exercises in which thousands of women took part.

Purely feminist concerns, however, could not constitute the prime interest of even the most dedicated Ukrainian feminists in the 1930s. Important as their concern with women's issues was, it was overridden by developments in the Soviet Ukraine: artificial famine, purges, collectivization, mass arrests, suicides, and executions. The encroachment of politics (in the broadest sense) was exemplified in the resolution adopted by the general meeting of the Women's Union held on May 9, 1933, in L'viv:

> The difficult and grave moment that the Ukrainian nation is undergoing demands from the Ukrainian women the greatest energy in work in all aspects of community life. The particularly difficult tasks facing the [Galician] women's organization necessitate full consolidation of women's forces, the unity and strengthening of internal discipline, and organization. Convinced of the important role that the Ukrainian woman is destined to play in the struggle of the Nation and in the creation of national culture, the meeting charges the Board to remain steadfast in its defense of the rights that belong to Ukrainian women within their own society.[14]

Specifically and realistically, the women decided to continue their actions in support of the cooperative movement, while at the same time initiating a program to preserve and foster folk art. In order to demonstrate the strength of Ukrainian women outside the Soviet Union, the Galician Women's Union held a congress for Ukrainian women in 1934 in Stanyslaviv (now Ivano-Frankivs'k). It marked the fiftieth anniversary of the first public demonstration of Ukrainian women, which had also been held in that Western city.

The event was well-publicized and well-attended. It was a rally of national spirit. Representatives of all non-Soviet Ukrainian women's organizations attended, as well as Mary Skipkins from the Women's International League for Peace and Freedom. Both peasant and intelligentsia women took part in the congress. The four-day program reflected the broad range of women's interests. Topics discussed, one per day, included "our past," the peasant woman, "let's create our own native culture," and the economy.

The resolutions passed by the congress on June 27, 1934, deplored the lack of autonomy and equality for women under the Soviet system and the precariousness of the Ukrainian position in general. Delegates to the congress also discussed the position of the Ukrainian community in Poland and other non-Soviet states, and made political, economic, and national statements about the situation at hand. They stressed the important role of the Ukrainian peasant women and the active participation of women in general in Ukrainian community affairs. Speakers at the conference denounced unethical methods of political struggle, the internal splintering of society, and internal bickering. They called for civic peace, moderation in press polemics, abolition of party strife, and religious toleration. While identifying with feminism, motherhood, and nation, they underscored the equal responsibility of men and women toward the next generation and demanded equal rights for men and women.[15] And for all their stress upon motherhood, the Ukrainian women staunchly protested the growing conservative and fascist trend to limit the functions of women to Mussolini's "make babies." Their definition of motherhood focused on the socializing role of the mother and the critical importance of that role to society. At the same time, they stressed the autonomy and the rights of each individual woman. This blending of various ideologies, while preserving their own identity as women, was an original characteristic of the activities of the interwar Western Ukrainian women activists.

The growing interest in ideological issues among the male intelligentsia in Western Ukraine in the interwar years contributed to an increased tension between Ukrainian men and the Women's Union. The women were still largely in the stage of self-containment characteristic of preindustrialized women. To be a woman, a housewife, a mother was to have status and a job. As any special interest group, the women wanted influence and increased opportunities, which they sought to gain through the Union on their own terms. The various men's organizations tried to sway the women to join their ideological camps.

The offensive against the Union came from four sources: the radicals, the Catholic intellectuals, the liberals, and the Organization of Ukrainian Nationalists. All four attacks were spearheaded by secularized male members of the intelligentsia, although there were women within the Union and outside it willing to support the men. Despite these attacks, the Union itself was able to maintain its integrity and autonomy and to enjoy the support of the peasant masses until the collapse of Poland and the outbreak of World War II.

The Ukrainian Radical Socialist party, supported by émigrés in Canada, the United States, and Western Europe, managed to convince a group of Union activists to establish a Socialist women's organization, the Union of Ukrainian Working Women, or The Women's Community (*Soiuz Ukraiins'kykh Pratsiuiuchykh Zhinok, Zhinocha Hromada*) in 1931. The Community totaled fewer than eight thousand women but did publish a newspaper. Immersed as they were in organic work and shocked by the terror in the Soviet Union, most Ukrainian women were unwilling to espouse a revolution. Nor were the socialist Ukrainian women willing to resurrect the highly original blend of feminism and radical socialism of Natalia Kobryns'ka, a prescient writer who in the 1890s warned that industrialized socialism without a specifically feminist input would lead to a double burden for women. Since she staunchly maintained her commitment to both feminism and socialism, she remained unacceptable to both women and socialists. After her death in 1920, Ukrainian women began to venerate her as a pioneer of the women's movement while the socialists immediately forgot her. The Community did not foster feminist concerns beyond the conventional women's issues typical in moderate socialist movements. And although it cooperated with the Women's Union, it engaged in rhetorical sallies against the "ladies" even in that Union.

It was the Catholic intelligentsia and not the Ukrainian Catholic or the Ukrainian Orthodox churches that challenged the Women's Union between 1933 and 1935. Ostensibly, they insisted upon changing the constitution to include a fundamentalist and irrelevant plank on the traditional roles of women and the importance of the church and ethical behavior. The most active men and women in these undertakings, which at times took a very bitter polemical note, were persons who entered (or married those who did) secular professions, often breaking a family tradition of priesthood. They were representatives of a new secular Catholic intelligentsia, as removed from the village as it was possible to be removed in Galicia.

The Union, which counted among its members both Catholics and Orthodox, as well as a few deists and agnostics, avoided a confessional declaration. But self-styled defenders of traditional morality, the family, and the sacredness of motherhood initiated a veritable smear campaign against the leadership of the Women's Union. Aided by a few zealous women and playing up to the historical connection between the manifestation of Western Ukrainian nationalism and the Ukrainian Catholic Church, these men lumped feminism with free love, seeking either to push the Union into an openly Catholic stand or to create rival Catholic organizations under the aegis of the Catholic Action, the secular organization formed to promote lay activism.[16] Religious ceremonies had always played an important public function for Ukrainians, and they continued to do so in the interwar years in Poland. The Women's Union, as other broad community organizations, cooperated with the church, although the church for the most part did not expect public expressions of support. On the contrary, in the few open discussions of the religious issue, the clerics, especially the monks, defended the important contributions women made to both the church and to society. Older women, especially wives of priests, were also very effective in diffusing the potential rift in the women's movement and bearing witness to the compatibility of family life with public work.

The liberal and the nationalist challenges dealt with the political aspirations of women and with the organizational integrity of the Women's Union. The conflict with the Ukrainian National Democratic Union, known as UNDO, the most popular political party in Galicia, to which Kysilevs'ka, Rudnyts'ka, Sheparovych, and other activists of the Union belonged, came to a head in 1935. The Union refused to support a new policy of accommodation with the Polish government. In return for the goodwill of Ukrainians, the Poles promised them a certain number of seats in the coming elections, as well as some other concessions. However, the Polish government reserved the right to approve the Ukrainian candidates. Rudnyts'ka, the Union's candidate, was rejected by the Poles. Citing undue interference in Ukrainian affairs, the Union boycotted the elections. Overriding the Union, the men from UNDO tried to find other women candidates to fill the Union's seat. The Women's Union was appalled at this male interference. In the end, not a single Ukrainian woman was elected in the parliamentary election.[17]

Within a few months, in 1936, the peasant cooperative in its effort to undercut the influence of the Women's Union in the villages persuaded Kysilevs'ka herself to head a newly established women's section of the *Sil's'ky Hospodar*. This strong organization threw its resources into the villages, where it seriously challenged the Union.[18]

Ideally, Western Ukrainian women activists wanted to influence the feuding Ukrainian parties to create a united front. Male Ukrainian politicians questioned the right of the Women's Union to take a stand on political issues since it was composed of women of different orientations. The women countered that, following this logic, the men had no right to speak in the name of the nation without asking for the views of the women.

The Organization of Ukrainian Nationalists, in addition to its clandestine activities, began to see itself as having a monopoly on Ukrainian patriotism. Although it enjoined its members to be courteous to women since they might bear their sons, the Nationalists did not develop an ideology for women. The creed of selfless dedication and patriotic voluntaristic activism, including terrorism and service to the beleaguered nation, they espoused found a responsive chord among younger Ukrainian women who felt they already had equality. An increasing number of branch chairpersons gravitated toward extreme nationalism, and many sought to spread these views in the villages. By 1937 there were attempts not only to take over individual branches but also to include a nationalist plank in the program of the Women's Union.

At the congress of the Union held on October 9, 1937, Ol'ha Hasyn of Stryj argued that feminism, a product of egotistical women, was destructive to the moral fiber of the nation. There was little support for this thinking among the participants. In contrast, Rudnyts'ka's scathing attack upon the antifeminism of all totalitarian and pseudo-fascist ideologies received a thunderous ovation.

Rudnyts'ka, supported by the majority of the members of the Women's

Union, was vocal in her opposition to the tactics of the nationalists. At this congress she repeated her denunciation of the Nationalists in the keynote address and noted that "Ukrainian women must also overcome attacks and barriers from some segments of their own society, especially from nationalist circles. . . . The Ukrainian women's movement demands from the woman active participation in the life of the nation and in this we differ in our understanding of the role of the woman from the fascist doctrine."[19]

As the internal and external political situation became threatening, the Women's Union played an even more open political role. The leadership became involved in a concerted effort of Ukrainian moderates to establish a coalition and signed an agreement reaching a consensus among influential Ukrainian periodical publications. The Polish government considered this action politically dangerous and suspended the Women's Union. On May 5, 1938, the Polish police, in a synchronized swoop, arrested all the heads of the branches of the Women's Union. Members of the Union immediately initiated the proceedings that led to the freeing of the arrested women within days and to the reestablishment of the Union three months later. The Ukrainian Women's Union, as a mass movement of Ukrainian women, survived only to fall victim to the new war. But it also paved the way for similar organizations of Ukrainian women in Europe and America.

Conclusion

Historically, women have not been accustomed to seeing themselves as part of a community, nor have they been socialized into articulating a theoretical construct for defining themselves and their work. In matters of theory they tended to defer to men, especially when it came to religious and political ideology and national aspirations. They readily adapted their organizations to voice or reflect rhetoric dominant in their societies. In this, Ukrainian women were no exception.

In their writing, speeches, and memoirs, the Ukrainian women discussed in this chapter stressed their patriotism. But the main focus of their activities was the modernization of the village, improvement of the quality of life, inclusion of women in politics, and the attempt to gain recognition for the economic value of the work women performed in the home and on the farm. Uncomfortable with the sexually liberationist tone of contemporary feminism, Ukrainian women activists concentrated on the value of motherhood and the rights of women in the family. They did not develop an ideology; they charted a course of action I have called "pragmatic feminism." The women who practiced it had just begun to explore theoretical issues of feminism. The Second World War not only destroyed the Ukrainian women's organization; it aborted the interest generated by the practice of women's activism among the Ukrainians in articulating a form of feminism that was not yet recognized.

6

Mary E. Reed

Peasant Women of Croatia in the Interwar Years

An examination of resistance movements throughout the world reveals the valuable contributions of women of various cultures to the battlefront and support services.[1] The case of the Yugoslav woman is no exception, and the success of the Communist revolution is due in large part to these women who played a major role in the Yugoslav National Liberation movement. One unusual aspect of the resistance in Croatia and other parts of Yugoslavia that experienced partisan activity was the vigorous participation of women from a particular social and economic group—the peasantry—which has often been assumed to be politically passive or at least incapable of sustained political organization. Like women in the Chinese revolution, Yugoslav women supplied the partisans with food and clothing, harvested crops, carried the wounded from the battlefield, and served as couriers, nurses, political officers, and fighters.[2]

As is true with most investigations of events affecting or shaped by peasants, sources are generally restricted to those outside this economic-social group. This is particularly true in Croatia and, indeed, throughout Yugoslavia, where peasants had little if any education in the period before World War II. Many peasants were illiterate, and the shortage or expense of writing materials and burden of other tasks were major obstacles to the recording of events and thoughts. Because of these factors, our knowledge of how peasant women reacted to events, their own efforts to improve or change their condition, and their attitude toward reformers in the villages must be construed mainly from the writings of others. A study of Croatian peasant women during this important period must necessarily rely to a great extent on the records generated by the political parties, organizations, and activists involved in village affairs or on materials generated from other observers. Even if the total picture of peasant women must remain incomplete, the existing documents suggest important changes. Moreover, the effect of these changes may help explain the sudden growth and strength of the peasant-based Anti-Fascist Front of Women and emergence of peasant women leaders and activists during World War II.

During this period the two dominant political parties, the Croatian Peasant party and the Communist party, sought to include peasant women and issues concerning these women into their party organizations and platforms. The Peasant party, founded in 1904, gained strong influence in the newly created Yugoslav nation after World War I. It promoted a strong nationalistic program and adopted a belligerent position toward the central government in Belgrade. The Communist party, created in 1919, at first posed a real threat to the nation's stability and was outlawed in 1920 after a show of electoral strength. Forced to work illegally, the Communist party suffered internal contentions over ideology and tactics with many leaders, including Tito, imprisoned for several years. However, the party was able to work through the legal front of the Independent Workers party, and it formed a very strong communist youth organization that had many young women among its members.[3]

Work with peasant women did not promise the same results as did work with the more openly disaffected working-class women or the articulate and more militant intellectual women. Nonetheless, work among village women remained an important focus for reformers of all persuasions, who after all could not forget that Yugoslavia was predominantly a peasant nation.

Neither the Croatian Peasant party nor, to a lesser extent, the Communist party was entirely successful in its efforts with peasant women. Each party, however, did create among village women the consciousness that others were sympathetic to their condition, that they did have a right to education, health care and legal protection, and that they could participate in an organization that actively sought to solve the woman's question.

In the struggle for political influence within Yugoslavia, the Peasant party and the Communist party turned a reforming and political eye toward the woman's question, a phrase used to refer to women's social, economic, legal, and political rights. Like the Communist party, the Peasant party's interest in peasant women included selfless and selfish motives. On the humanitarian level, the Peasant party—indeed all reformers for that matter—agreed that women were the most oppressed group within each ethnic, social, or economic category. From its moral-ideological perspective, the Peasant party perceived peasant women as the cornerstone of the harmonious and well-ordered peasant household. The well-being of the peasantry and the continuation of the "true" Croatian peasant nation rested on their alignment with this ideal. The Peasant party feared a disruption of its political-social model if peasant women should adopt more feminist ideals or become beguiled with the attractions of the modern world.

The practical, more purely political reasons for the Peasant party's interest in peasant women were equally important. From its political base in the countryside, the Peasant party needed the support and loyalty of peasant women. Even though women could not vote in national elections, they did belong to Peasant party delegations, participated in the Women's Branch of the party, and generally contributed to the success of the powerful economic cooperative, *Gospodarska Sloga* (Agricultural Harmony), and the cultural cooperative, *Seljačka Sloga* (Peasant Harmony). Moreover, peasant women held the key to needed health reforms in the villages because it was they who washed clothes and utensils, cooked, cleaned the house, and cared for the children. The peasant woman's acceptance of and use of good health and nutritional practices would also help reduce the high death rate among infants and women of childbearing age.

In its position toward peasant women, the Peasant party was both progressive and conservative. Party leaders adopted an ambitious and comprehensive program of practical reforms using the resources of their urban supporters. However, in insisting on traditional values and roles for peasant women, they ignored the frustrations and anxieties of modern life which weighed heavily upon these women. The peasant woman was trapped in the disintegration of the extended family structure, an agrarian depression, and the transition to a cash economy. Her desire for modern living conditions and education was not met by any economic or social reforms of consequence, leaving her with few alternatives.

The Communist party also demonstrated a contradictory position toward peasant women. To a greater extent than the leaders of the Peasant party, Communist leaders held an ideological commitment to the total equality of women. As a competitor with the more influential and larger Peasant party, the Communist party developed a plan for creating an organizational network in the villages, including peasant women as one group through which it could gather cadres. In this blueprint for political change, however, peasant women usually appeared as a low priority in a list including workers, intellectuals, and youth.

Despite the low priority of women and its own small organization, the Communist party's appeal for a complete break with the past and the creation of a cooperative, humane society provided the Communists and their supporters with an energy and force that the Peasant party could not match. This was especially true among the urban groups and young men and women. Until the mid-thirties, however, the Communist party made few inroads among the peasantry except tangentially through leftist publications and activists. Nor did the Communist party seem to have the resources to devote to organizational work in rural areas. Both peasant women and men distrusted the foreign, nonpeasant ideas of the Communists, particularly when their own Peasant party supported a successful version of agrarian socialism. The Communist party's interest in peasant women increased with the political crises of the 1930s and the need to create a national front among all nationally minded, nonfascist groups in Yugoslavia.

Like the Peasant party, the Communists feared the appearance of feminist ideas among its ranks of highly motivated and generally well-educated and youthful women.[4] In that sense the Communist party was conservative despite its modern conception of women in the factory and in politics. Although both parties wished to improve the physical and social conditions of peasant women and include them in their political organizations, they were ideologically opposed to the growth and development of women's organizations beyond the limits they had set. Moreover, both the Peasant party and the Communist party used their achievements among peasant women as valuable propaganda. The Peasant party organized large public demonstrations in the cities where the self-taught and activist peasant woman in the splendor of her national dress testified to the party's successes. The reports of these gatherings filled the pages of newspapers and magazines with compelling examples of the strength of the Peasant party in the villages.[5] The Communists used their women's magazines to expose the terrible working and living conditions of peasant women and to suggest progressive solutions. By placing these stories in a context of international politics and highlighting the achievements of peasant women in the Soviet Union, they provided a larger perspective than that of the Peasant party on women's conditions. Irrespective of the sincere or opportunistic nature of these reforming efforts, the appearance of teachers, doctors and nurses, theatrical groups, choral societies, and artists in the villages brought the idea of progress into the countryside. The attention directed to the education, maternal, and household functions of the peasant woman was important, for it increased her sense of worth. Even if this consciousness had just begun to surface and reforms remained rudimentary at the outbreak of war in 1941, the seeds had been sown for change.[6]

The Status of Peasant Women

In educating and organizing peasant women, activists had first to identify the issues and problems. The status of the peasant women who were the targets of these efforts differed considerably in the various regions of Yugoslavia. Perspectives on the woman's question thus varied from the image of the matriarchal and robust figure in the more Westernized areas of the country to the downtrodden peasant woman in the southern mountains carrying a heavy load on her back as the man rode ahead on a donkey.[7]

Although these disparate images make any generalizations impossible, most observers of conditions during those years agreed that the worst abuses occurred in the most backward and patriarchal parts of the country.[8] But abuses also occurred in those areas experiencing social and economic change, for, as in other contexts, modernization led to somewhat contradictory results for peasant women in Yugoslavia, and as old patterns of behavior and values were uprooted, violence against women appears to have increased in many areas. Some of the most lurid examples of women's sufferings centered on the two biological functions of pregnancy and childbirth.[9] Both parties decried the primitive conditions and abuses peasant women suffered, and both freely used the more sensational examples in their publications as a means of provoking public indignation. However, the evidence indicates that conditions varied considerably according to region with poverty the most significant factor.[10]

The abuses women suffered because of their weaker, subordinate positions were more traumatic than the demands of physical work and motherhood that were accepted as the lot of peasants and women. Activists in the village found that one of their first tasks was to convince peasant women of the harm in passively accepting their secondary position. The assertions from reformers, newspapers, and public figures that the peasant woman was not inferior but should be regarded with respect and admiration released an outpouring from village women. They described the acute mental anguish they endured in being treated as inferiors or, what was worse, in being ignored. The appeal of reformers to the peasant woman's need for dignity and self-respect created an irreversible momentum. Peasant women began to question and challenge their subordinate position more openly, and many younger or more independently minded women left the villages for the cities.

Despite the suffering peasant women endured because of male chauvinism, it cannot be assumed that it was a simple matter of the husband and father wishing to be master at the expense of the woman. Ignorance, superstition, and the tyranny of tradition directed the course of peasant life. On a practical level it was in the man's interest that his wife bear healthy children, that she survive to take care of them and be able to resume her duties in the house, and that life in the household be marked by understanding and harmony rather than conflict and bickering. In areas of Croatia where the old traditions governing behavior between men and women were collapsing, women suffered physical abuse and a loss of status, however limited that had been. Where peasant life had stabilized along more modern patterns, such as in Slovenia, women enjoyed more equality and independence.[11]

As the traditional, extended family shrank to a one-family household, peasants had to perform all the numerous and specialized functions associated with family, house, and fields. Instead of participating in a communal enterprise with its division of labor, peasant women assumed a greater variety and burden of tasks now that they alone were responsible for the home and children in addition to helping with work in the fields and livestock.[12] The contradictions between the peasant family's movement to greater independence and the peasant woman's loss of status in the family and village were remarkable in view of the fact that many peasant women headed households. *Ženski svijet* (Woman's World, a liberal woman's magazine) reported in May 1939 that in the area roughly equivalent to Croatia, one out of five agricultural households was directed by a woman, and 500,000 out of 880,000 women earned their own bread.[13]

Dissatisfaction with their social and economic conditions nudged peasant women from the passivity they had practiced when the walls of tradition seemed impervious.[14] They began to listen to political activists, attend meetings held in the villages and cities, and ask for help in learning to read and write. Not every peasant woman was receptive to change, of course, but sufficient numbers were to encourage reformers in their work and to establish a network of societies between the cities and villages. The contact between village and city women was not restricted to reformers coming into the villages. Many peasant women left the villages to find a better life and economic independence. Others, equally moved by the plight of the peasant woman, stayed in the countryside where they employed their considerable talents for public speaking and organizing. The women who stayed worked primarily within the Peasant party and maintained their loyalty to peasant societies. Some, like Mara Matočec, a peasant writer, were extremely gifted and popular. Many of those who left the villages came under the influence of the Communist party, including Kata Dumbović, one of the first women to become an official delegate of the Communist party in Zagreb, and Milka Kufrin, a member of the young Communists and later a Partisan fighter, who became a party official in the postwar government.

Part of the problem both the Peasant party and the Communist party faced in organizing village women in the interwar period lay in the inability or refusal of activists of either party to come to terms with the changing needs of peasant women during this period. Although the Peasant party offered more practical reforms than did the Communist party, it failed to define and articulate the deeper needs of women to find stability and protection in the modern world. Instead of rethinking the imposition of the double burden, the Peasant party cajoled women to stay within the traditional mold of the mother figure of the Croatian nation. Nor did it understand that peasant women were more vulnerable than peasant men if they could not find a spouse, that they were less able socially and psychologically to live independently in either the village or the city. The Peasant party did formulate the design of an urban-peasant exchange through the women's branch of its party, but the concept of a network of organizations directed by peasant women emerged only during the resistance and then through the efforts of the Communist party. The Communist party, in contrast, realized the importance of a village-based organization in the interwar years, but it was as unwilling and/or as unable as the Peasant party to conceive of a truly peasant and relatively independent organization of women. It did not have a specific plan for transforming peasant life, much less one for transforming the lives of peasant women. The party's efforts in organizing women in the villages were thwarted by the allegiance of the Croatian peasants to their own Peasant party, and by the Communists' glaring neglect of peasant women.

The Croatian Peasant Party and Its Moderate Reformers

Of the groups in Croatia who were interested in women's issues, the Peasant party had the largest organization and following and was very active in the villages during the interwar period. The ideas of Stjepan Radić (one of the Radić brothers who founded the party in 1904) strongly appealed to the peasants who believed that the Peasant party would solve their material and social problems. Unfortunately, Vladko Maček, who headed the party after Radić's assassination in 1928, lacked Radić's personal authority and commitment to peasant leadership. Maček allowed nonpeasants to take over the party with the result that many peasants began to perceive that the Peasant party had little interest in their affairs.[15] Many activists of peasant origin found that the Peasant party had little to offer and transferred their loyalties to the National Front or the Communist party during the more oppressive political climate of the 1930s and early 1940s.[16]

The Peasant party persistently followed a much more conservative course and attracted a less radical clientele. One of its leading heroines was Mara Matočec, apparently a widow with four children who farmed her land by herself. Described as the most popular woman in Croatia, Matočec wrote short stories and poems, organized plays that traveled to the villages, and gave lectures.[17] She also organized branches of *Seljačka Sloga* and urged Croatian peasants to preserve their peasant culture.

Although the Peasant party lost many younger and more vigorous recruits to the more radical worker and youth groups, it enjoyed a loyal following because of its peasant activists like Matočec and the willingness of its organizers to go into the villages and work with the peasants. As the leading political force in Croatia until World War II, the Peasant party owed its position primarily to its ingenuity and resourcefulness in organizing peasant cooperatives during the world depression.[18] The social cooperative, *Seljačka Sloga*, complemented these economic activities by promoting the healthiest and "purest" elements of Croatian peasant culture and improving living standards. In its adherence to the idea that peasant culture was superior, the Peasant party demonstrated a keen interest in the continuation of the folk arts in which peasant women had an essential role. The skills to produce these treasures of clothing, linens, and decorative woven materials are transmitted from mother to daughter. Without the mother's or village's insistence that the daughter learn these tedious and time-consuming crafts, their production would be threatened.

In addition to the fear of losing this material culture, the Peasant party was concerned with the disintegration of the village community. It realized that urban life regularly attracted the young and ablest peasants who were then vulnerable to "foreign" influences in the cities. On the most practical level, the Peasant party needed women to produce healthy offspring. The president of the women's branch of the party made this point in expressing the fear that the villages could lose their young generations by emigration to the cities or through the practice of abortion.[19] The party also realized that in order to maintain or increase village populations, the more glaring defects of peasant life would have to be corrected. Of all the activities intended to improve village life, the literacy campaigns proved to be the most stimulating for the peasant and the reformer. The appearance in the villages of women like Matočec, who was obviously a peasant and whose writings had been published, caused a great stir, especially, in Matočec's case, when her play, *Return to the Village*, was performed. The example of these self-educated, peasant women speaking, writing, and traveling among the villages encouraged other peasant women to learn to read and write. The fact that these peasant women reformers were denounced by the village clerics as tramps and by the local government officials as Communists gives us some idea of their influence.

Urbanites received the peasant women reformers with equal enthusiasm. Newspapers and magazine articles described with admiration the appearance of the self-taught peasant women who attended the large public meetings in Belgrade and Zagreb, outfitted in their peasant finery and speaking before an approving audience of their urban supporters. These women speaking in their native dialects captivated their listeners with stories of how they had taught themselves to read and write in secrecy, scraping letters on a stone and furtively following the lessons of their brothers.[20] Groups within the Peasant party generously supported the ABC (literacy) clubs in the villages. They solicited contributions of materials and funds and published the results of the campaigns in each district. The results of these efforts immensely increased the prestige of the Peasant party. For the newly literate peasant woman, the gift of reading raised the hope of a new life based on information from the outside world.[21]

Along with its literacy campaign, the Peasant party focused its attention on practical reforms. These efforts—although abruptly halted by the outbreak of war in 1941—did much to improve peasant life in the years immediately preceding the occupation. The village clinics, free medical examinations, new wells, and campaigns to keep farmyards clean of refuse relieved the villages of the worst sources of disease. The key to the success of these projects lay in the cooperative nature of each venture and the technical assistance from the outside. The appearance of men and women repairing roads and the formation of the first women's society, the Society of Progressive Homemakers, anticipated the work of the communist-directed Anti-Fascist Front of Women during the war.

At one organizational meeting of the Progressive Homemakers in 1939, a doctor from the Institute of Health explained how the new society could improve family harmony by teaching women how to maintain an orderly house, grow better vegetables, and increase the variety of meals. Other reforms were promised. A weaver would demonstrate a new loom; a gardener would show how to grow seedlings in a hothouse and also how to sell the produce; and a nurse would lecture on the proper care of children. These were not insignificant goals, and the enthusiasm with which peasant women joined the new society and elected officers convinced the organizers that this village could serve as an example to others.[22]

Literacy and practical reforms were popular and generally not controversial. Other issues were not as simple. The Peasant party hoped to raise the level of literacy and living conditions in the villages, give a nod to women's suffrage, and avoid the implications of social equality. In view of the Peasant party's own struggle with Belgrade for control of local government in Croatia, it could hardly remain mute on the issue of voting rights for women that other political parties and groups were promoting. The Peasant party's newspaper, *Seljačka misao* (Peasant Thoughts), acknowledged the importance of peasant women in the party's battle by stating that the Croatian peasant woman could not stand aside while the entire Croatian people fought for their own political freedom. Using an argument that the Communist party would make good use of later in its resistance propaganda, the article stressed that it was not true that women were not interested in politics.[23]

Despite this rhetoric, the Peasant party interpreted rights for women as harmonizing with the larger interests of the "true Croatian nation" against the antinational elements who exploited the peasants and working people. The party warned against those movements for women's voting rights that were centered in the middle and privileged classes and that lacked a proper nationalistic spirit. Although Radić had supported equality for all women, he argued that the interests of the peasant woman and the working woman should come first.[24]

Vladko Maček, as Radić's successor, not only affirmed that women were equal but argued that they possessed special qualities that men did not have. His statement, which was published in the woman's leftist magazine, *Žena danas* (Woman Today), explained that his reservation in granting women complete equality was based on the fear that politically active women might neglect their homes and children and become alienated from their natural duties and social responsibilities.[25] Maček revealed his perception of the ideal Croatian woman before a conference of *Seljačka Sloga* in 1939: "There is no home without a woman-mother. As is the woman and the mother, so is the home. With women in the house, happiness, peace, prosperity, and progress arrive. . . . The fate of the great collective of the homeland is in the hands or in the hearts of the true Croatian woman because the home is the first seed of the homeland."[26]

The Peasant party might equate the survival of Croatia with the position of women in the home, but it was not prepared to go beyond advocating women's suffrage, education and health reforms, and preservation of peasant folk art. Ten years earlier the president of the women's branch of the Peasant party, Pavla Balenović, had expressed her fear that women would become alienated from their natural duties. She argued, "Why should women look on with folded hands while men fight for the national ideals in order to achieve happiness for the household and for their children?" Balenović urged that this struggle should be extended to women wage earners, apprentices, and merchants.[27]

Another woman active in the Peasant party, Barica Miletić, used forceful images but was unable to define the exact nature of the struggle or the strategy of the combatants. In her article, "And Women Must Be Prepared," Miletić warned that "every woman who goes united into the struggle must be prepared for everything. Some of the enemies will be in the village, the elders, gentlemen clerics, and chauvinistic intellectuals who are opposed to women's suffrage." Miletić exhorted, "Do not whisper in the corner! Proclaim your pain publicly; tell them about your centuries of fear and suffering!" And when the fight comes, "Women will not stay at home, but together with the men will go into battle against the enemies who are guilty for all evils." The fruits of the battle, however, were as unclear as the nature of the conflict: "If we will travel the path of truth . . . we will come to the true objectives, and life for us will be more serene and more beautiful."[28]

Although they called women into the struggle for women's rights, the Peasant party activists dodged the more persistent problems of the peasant woman caught between two worlds. Radić had stated that all women were martyrs, and if they were mothers, then they were also saints. As peasant women faced the modern world, they desired less martyrdom and sainthood and more knowledge and assistance. One symbol of the conflict between the old and new worlds was the peasant national dress. Nada Sremec, a future activist of the Communist resistance, denounced the slavery of embroidery and lacemaking which threatened the eyesight and physical health of girls. Mara Matočec, alarmed by Sremec's two articles in Peasant party publications, thundered against the modern tendencies of devaluating these skills.[29]

The disagreement over national dress was symptomatic of a wider split between reformers within the Peasant party's circle and more progressive or radical women. The large public meetings in 1940 between rural and urban women, unlike previous ones, had significantly fewer urban participants. Did this poor attendance signify a declining interest among city women in the situation of women peasants? Perhaps Zagreb women had become weary of hearing the complaints of their peasant sisters. After all, city women also suffered from the economic depression and the double burden of home and wage work. The strikes and demonstrations of women in the factories were closer and more vigorous than the distant campaigns in the villages. Despite the efforts of the Peasant party to link urban and peasant women in a unified cause, the bonds were more of sympathy than of a common cause. Because of disparate interests and modes of struggle, many women eager for change and alienated from the traditional world the Peasant party wished to preserve sought reforms through the Communist party and its front organizations.

The Communist Party and Its Radical Reformers

The Peasant party and its reformers perceived that the village was a healthy environment for women, with a few modifications. It vigorously opposed displacing this keeper of the family hearth and peasant nation. The Communist party, however, proposed to use its peasant networks to recruit cadres critical of or opposed to this peasant ideology. Although peasant women might be good allies, the young or disaffected peasants who left the village or returned as teachers and professionals sympathetic to the Communists attracted the most attention from Communist activists. In addition, the party's illegal status and preoccupation with the industrial base of its political activities and its revolutionary plans limited the quantity and seriousness of its work in the villages.

Women from the villages who joined leftist organizations usually did so in the larger towns and cities where they made contact with organizers in the work place or the high schools and universities.[30] Because the party could not openly recruit members, it developed an underground network of activists who propagandized prospective members and infiltrated existing organizations. The goals of the small Communist party, however, consistently exceeded its means. This situation was particularly true in the party's work with women and more especially with peasant women. The increasing militancy of unorganized working-class women and the popularity of the Peasant party added to the pressures upon the Communist party to influence and recruit women into its ranks. In 1928 the party frankly admitted that the last ten years had not been fruitful in organizing women. Party leaders thought that all work with women should be the concern only of women in the party; at the same time, the party failed to adequately support and direct its own active cadre of women. As a remedy, the women's secretariat of the party adopted a plan for organizing peasant women through the Central Peasant Committee.[31]

The results were disappointing. At the party's 1934 National Conference, the Central Committee admitted that except in Slovenia, Serbia, and Dalmatia, it had achieved meager results in improving its work in the villages. *Proleter*, the party newspaper, delivered an unequivocal denouncement: "Communists have not realized the importance of winning over the peasantry to the side of the proletariat."[32]

After these rebukes, the party made some progress by embarking upon an intensive program of infiltrating women's organizations, such as the Democratic party's Peasant Circle and the urban-based women's cultural groups the party condemned as feministic. According to the official party interpretation, it gained some influence with Heart of Croatia, a woman's cooperative formed to raise the cultural level of the villages.[33]

The Communist party also faced competition in its efforts to gain the support of urban women during this period. As the Communist party dispatched its organizers into the villages, the Peasant party widened its influence in the urban areas by establishing branches of women sympathetic to peasant women. It also intensified its educational activities among peasant women, especially in the more backward areas.[34] In this competition for the hearts and minds of the Croatian peasant women, the Communist party's organizations worked from its urban bases in publishing women's magazines and infiltrating moderate women's groups in cities and in some villages. The young Communist women successfully used a national front strategy at meetings of urban women's groups by asking questions that indirectly condemned the present government and its economic system, and by including working-class and peasant women in the meetings.

Despite the Communist party's official interest in peasant women and the efforts of students to form their own national fronts with peasant women as important additions, the party designated the city as the appropriate battlefield for its interwar struggles. City streets provided a better forum than did village squares for demonstrations against fascism, for women's right to vote, and for equal pay for equal work. In addition, the peasant women with the greatest potential for organizational work usually left the villages to join leftist groups in the towns and cities. To most observers the peasant woman was passive and uninterested in the issues which involved her city sisters.[35]

It may be that the peasant woman's lack of commitment to either the Communist or the feminist movements demonstrated more than apathy. The party had shown its peripheral and somewhat opportunistic interest in her welfare, and the philanthropic interest of the bourgeois women's societies could not have genuinely inspired many peasant women. Because peasant women did participate in the activities of the Peasant party, their alienation from other movements may have reflected a disinterest in urban problems and a disinclination to be manipulated by outsiders. Nor did the peasant woman perceive her position as inherently inferior to that of women working for wages. On the contrary, many peasant women believed their lives, despite difficulties and hardships, were preferable to the lot of the poor working women in the cities.[36]

The young Vida Tomšič (who is still an active Party member) delivered an official indictment of the Communist party's efforts to gain women's support at the Fifth Conference of the Croatian Communist party in November 1940. Tomšič charged that even as women were becoming more important to the party because of the economic dislocations of the war, work with women still remained one of the weakest points in the party's program. After emphasizing the needs of all women, Tomšič addressed those of peasant women: "Up to now we have left peasant women on their own as well as vulnerable to the influences of various middle-class organizations that have proliferated in the villages." Why had the party achieved so little success in the villages? Tomšič offered one explanation: "The real truth is that work in the village is more painstaking and requires more patience and persistence than any other kind of work, which is exactly why we must give it special consideration."[37]

According to Tomšič, another reason for the party's failure to make many inroads among peasant women lay in the fact that direct actions had proved to be the best means of recruiting and training women, as well as of identifying the best activists. Village women were effectively isolated from this type of movement.

As long as political confrontations remained an urban phenomenon and an essential strategy of the Communist party, the Communists could do little more than regret their weak position in the villages. It was only during World War II that the party succeeded in reaching large numbers of peasant women. The war and the resistance of 1941–45 against the occupiers and the Croatian fascists transplanted both the political issues and the activists to the villages. As a result, the Communist party finally achieved its national front of peasant and worker, and peasant women were motivated and directed to participate in the construction of a new society.

During the resistance and the subsequent construction of the new socialist Yugoslavia, peasant women profitably used their interwar experiences. The Peasant party, and to a lesser extent the Communist party, had prepared them to cooperate with reformers from outside the villages and to think in terms of a larger community and a larger purpose. In the National Liberation Struggle, peasant women achieved an independence and influence they had not known before nor would enjoy after 1945. Even though their assistance to the partisans was indispensable to the final victory, however, peasant women still remained the tools by which others achieved their political objectives.

Conclusions

Both the Peasant party and the Communist party attempted to increase their support among peasant women in Croatia in the period between the two world wars. Although their appeals and methods of organization differed to some extent, their approach to peasant women shared certain characteristics. Activists in both parties were sincerely interested in improving conditions for peasant women, but the political leadership also saw women as important resources to be mobilized for broader party purposes during this period. In both cases, party leaders and activists attempted to reach women by speaking to their everyday needs, while at the same time linking them to larger national political causes. Both groups of activists encountered problems in accommodating their plans for peasant women to the actual conditions of peasant life in the villages and in incorporating the actions of peasant women themselves into their activities. In addition, both the Peasant party and the Communist party rejected the possibility of a separate women's movement within their ranks. Both conservative and radical reformers declared their fear of feminism as either endangering the foundation of the idealized peasant nation or weakening the larger revolutionary movement. It must be noted that many, if not most, women within the two parties accepted this viewpoint.

The activities of these parties and peasant women during the interwar years also demonstrate the difficulty of organizing a group on the basis of its sex. Although urban women were sympathetic toward peasant women, diverse interests and culture prevented the formation of a unified woman's front or movement. Even many of the activists in the professional and highly disciplined Communist party who had peasant roots could not be persuaded or directed to overcome their biases toward organizational work with peasant women. This problem persisted during the resistance, even though most barriers between rural and urban women were surmounted. Nonetheless, the examples of city women taking active roles in listening to and assisting their sisters in the villages initiated lines of communication that Tito's fighters and activists would consolidate into a lifeline of supplies, medical assistance, and soldiers.

The efforts to organize Croatian peasant women also eloquently demonstrated the capacity of uneducated people to accept change and take a leadership role in the activities of a broader political group if they perceive a common link to that group. In the interwar years, the Peasant party represented this bond of purpose and interest. In the resistance the bond was transferred, in many instances, to the National Liberation Front and the Communists. Just as peasant women testified before the spring of 1941 how the Peasant party had opened their eyes to their true worth, so, too, did peasant women in the newspapers of the Anti-Fascist Front of Women published during the Resistance thank their "own National Liberation Struggle" and the Communist party for "teaching them about their rights."

Although the reformers of both parties did not succeed in radically transforming conditions for village women, enough solid work had been accomplished to raise expectations among peasant women for a more fruitful and independent life. The disappearance of the Peasant party during the war meant that it was the Communist party that reaped the benefits of peasant women's activism, for these women played a vital role in the resistance that ultimately led to a communist victory in Yugoslavia. The Communist party, in turn, was able to build on this foundation in its efforts to change women's status in socialist Yugoslavia.

III

Women and Politics

Sharon L. Wolchik

Introduction

The lives of men and women are influenced in important ways by their relationship to politics as both creators of and objects of public policy in all political systems. The impact of the public sphere on private lives and opportunities is particularly great in communist states, given the nature of these political systems and the large role that the Communist party plays in determining not only political events but economic as well as social policy. The chapters in this section look at how women relate to the political system in several East European countries. Focusing on different aspects of women's political roles in particular countries, they demonstrate that there is some variation in women's role in the exercise of political power according to the country, level of activity, and type of political organization or activity considered. However, they also lead to a number of common conclusions and illustrate trends that appear to be common to the region as a whole.

First, it is clear that women in Eastern Europe, as in most countries, play a relatively small role in the direct exercise of political power. Despite changes in other aspects of women's lives, politics remains largely a male preserve in these countries. Further, as in other political systems, women's representation among political leaders decreases as we get closer to the seat of real power.[1] At the same time, women are fairly well represented among governmental leaders, particularly at the local level. Although local governments in these societies have limited discretion and relatively little power, they do have jurisdiction over many matters, such as social services and retail hours, which have an impact on day-to-day life in their area. This fact, coupled with the restricted access that most citizens, men and women, have to the exercise of power at higher levels in communist countries, means that women do have at least the opportunity to have a say on many issues that have a direct bearing on their daily lives. Furthermore, as the papers by Kolsti, who looks at women's representation in the top political elite in Albania, and Fischer, who examines efforts to increase women's political visibility in Romania, indicate, there is some variation in women's political roles at higher levels within the region. In both of these cases, although women's representation in the top party elite is still far from equal to that of men, there are more women in positions of power than elsewhere in the region.

These cases raise a number of interesting questions, for they demonstrate that communist leaders, when they want to, can increase the number of women in the effective elites. The question remains, however, why communist leaders have tried to do this in certain countries but not in others. The Albanian and Romanian experiences suggest that communist leaders will make such efforts when increased political visibility for women coincides with other goals: in the Albanian case, the effort to promote a cultural revolution among the population as a whole and in the Romanian case, the campaign to increase the birthrate. Concern with the demographic situation, as well as the increased visibility of women's issues as the result of International Women's Year, appear to have been behind similar, though less dramatic, efforts to increase women's representation in the top party elite in Czechoslovakia and Hungary in the mid-1970s.

The Albanian and Romanian cases also raise the question of how powerful women who hold top political positions in these societies really are. What is the basis of their power, and how does their influence compare to that of men? Are the differences in the social backgrounds, previous experiences, and extent of influence of men and women leaders found in other parts of the world[2] also evident in Eastern Europe? Kolsti's discussion of the Albanian case provides us with contradictory evidence on these points. On the one hand, it is clear that the women selected by the party leadership to occupy top positions as part of their campaign to increase women's visibility in Albanian society were for the most part seasoned activists who had long records of participating in public affairs at the direction of the party. At the same time, with few exceptions, the women chosen were either closely related to men in the top political leadership or closely connected to women who were, although Kolsti argues that these connections were less important in the cases of the younger women leaders chosen more recently. The women elevated to the Romanian political elite included, in addition to the top party leader's wife, several of her close associates, and the daughter of the top party leader, Ludmila Zhivkova, was the single most influential woman in Bulgarian political circles until her death in 1981. These trends, which do not, however, appear to be as evident in the other countries in the region, suggest that the tendency for women to exercise power largely through their family connections[3] may also exist in present-day Eastern Europe. Jancar's examination of women's participation in opposition movements in Czechoslovakia and Poland indicates that family connections also may be an important factor in leading women to become active in the opposition in Eastern Europe. Particularly in the case of Czechoslovakia, many of the women most active in dissent in the recent past have been the wives or daughters of prominent dissidents or political prisoners.

The social backgrounds, previous political experiences, and paths to the top of women leaders who are not related to powerful men also often differ from those of their male counterparts. Fischer's and Kolsti's essays, as well as other studies of women in the region, demonstrate that, with few exceptions, women selected for positions of political leadership in these countries have had less experience in the political-administrative apparatus of either party or government than their male counterparts. Nelson finds similar differences in the occupational backgrounds of men and women in local political elites in Romania and Poland.[4]

How do these differences affect women's attitudes, behavior, and success once they are part of the political leadership at either the national or local level? The essays to follow do not answer this question definitively, but they do include information that allows us to speculate about the extent of women's influence at various levels and women's political style. At the national level Kolsti's and Fischer's essays suggest that, with the exception of those women related to top political leaders, most women elevated to top political positions in communist countries are less powerful than their male counterparts. They are also less likely to be assigned to work in important areas and typically do not remain in their positions as long as men. Women in local elites in Romania and Poland are also channeled into or choose different areas of concentration than men, a factor Nelson links to women's limited upward mobility within the elite. It is unclear, however, whether the concentration of women leaders' activities in certain areas is the result of administrative assignment, a reflection of differences in men's and women's political orientations and policy concerns, or a combination of both.

Jancar suggests that women in Eastern Europe may also have a distinctive political style, at least when in the opposition. She finds that women activists in Poland prefer nonhierarchical, less organized means of protest than men and suggests that women in the opposition in Czechoslovakia base their opposition to the current political system on different grounds than do men. But differences in men's and women's political concerns and style, to the extent that they exist more generally, have not been reflected in the development of specifically feminist orientations on the part of large numbers of women or the emergence of mass feminist movements.[5] In part, of course, this can be explained by the inability of men or women to organize independently and the factors that work against recognition of the special needs or rights of any group apart from society as a whole in communist societies. As Jancar's essay illustrates, official support for women's emancipation, coupled with personal experience with some of the unresolved problems resulting from the elite's approach to women's issues, also may diminish women's interest in feminism in Eastern Europe, for the goal of women's equality has become identified with the existing regime.

These issues are related to another issue the chapters to follow do not treat explicitly, but one that is at the heart of any discussion of political activism in communist states: the meaning of public life and participation in politics in these countries. The authors of the papers in this section concur with other analysts of women's political behavior in these societies that women in general appear to be less interested than men in political affairs (defined here as officially sanctioned, formal political activity) and somewhat less active at the mass level in activities other than voting. In democratic societies, differences between the sexes in this regard have been traced in part to the fact that women traditionally have had fewer of the skills needed to take part in politics than men and, due to family obligations, less interest in or time to be active politically. As more women receive higher education and work outside the home in these societies, differences between men and women in political interest and activism at the mass level decrease and, in fact, in several Western countries are presently negligible or non-existent.[6] But, at higher levels of activism, it is clear that a number of barriers, including differences in men's and women's private or family responsibilities, male opposition to sharing real power with women, and political practices and recruitment patterns geared to male experiences that make it difficult or impossible for women to succeed, still hinder women from entering or advancing in political careers.

Many of the same factors limit women's possibilities in the political realm, particularly at higher levels, in Eastern Europe. But it is also possible that another factor may be operating to limit women's political activism in communist countries, and that is the meaning of citizen participation in these political systems. Although we can only speculate on the impact of this factor, it may be that women are either less committed than men to the goals of communist states or less interested in the side benefits political activism brings than most men in these societies. We do not have enough information to judge the extent to which women are more conservative than men, less influenced by communist ideals, or more influenced by religious traditions in Eastern Europe. But there is considerable reason to suspect that they are less interested in the nonpolitical benefits, such as career advancement, of political activism in these states. Because, as the studies in Part IV illustrate, women less often advance to leading economic positions and may in fact be less interested than men in advancing to such positions (in large part because of their family roles), they may also have less need than men to join the Communist party or show a high degree of interest in political affairs. It is also possible, given the mobilized character of much citizen activism at the mass level in these societies, that women use their primary responsibility for home and children as an excuse for not being as active as men are required to be.[7]

A final question that the chapters to follow raise is what difference, if any, it makes that women are largely excluded from the exercise of political power and what differences, if any, occur if there are more or fewer women in the political elites of particular countries. In Romania and Albania increases in the number of women in the top elites were accompanied by campaigns to improve the status of women in other areas, but both steps clearly occurred not as the result of any action by women or women leaders, but because the top elite perceived both to be necessary and useful for other purposes. In the other countries of the region, there is little indication that variation in the degree of women's representation in political positions makes much difference. Political leaders have given increased attention to women's issues in the last decade in several of the other states of the region as well as in the Romanian and Albanian cases examined here. In some cases, this has been coupled with an institutionalization of a certain degree of representation for women in the top party as well as governmental elite.[8] But there is little indication that those elites in which there are somewhat more women pay more attention to women's issues. In part, this may reflect the fact that the women elevated to top positions, while they differ from their colleagues in terms of previous experiences and social backgrounds, generally do not have an independent power base but are rather greatly dependent on the Communist party for their current positions and the factors that work to limit the expression of group interests in communist societies. But it may also reflect the fact that there are few women in absolute terms even in those elites in which they are best represented[9] and the pressures to conform that operate in any elite group.

At the same time, the small number of women in all the elites in the region may well have negative consequences for women's status in other areas. Due to restrictions on social science research in those countries and the more controlled nature of political life, we have little direct evidence about the extent to which women leaders or women in general have different policy preferences than men. But, although we do not have sources such as those available to study the actions and impact of women involved in policy-making in Western countries,[10] it is clear that policy is made in all of the countries of the region by leadership groups that are heavily dominated by males. In this situation, and given the prohibitions on independent political organization in these states, there are few direct ways for women's views to be considered in the making of public policy. It is possible that women's political demands and policy preferences reach political leaders through informal channels not accessible to outside researchers or, indirectly, through the actions of male activists, channels of communication within the family, the many policy-related activities of specialists, professionals, and bureaucrats, or the results of survey research. But, as the sections to follow illustrate, in this situation, women's specific needs are often overlooked by policymakers.

7

Mary Ellen Fischer

Women in Romanian Politics: Elena Ceaușescu, Pronatalism, and the Promotion of Women

During the last decade, and especially since 1979, there has been considerable stress in Romania on the promotion of women into positions of greater economic and political responsibility. This policy has coincided with the elevation of Elena Ceaușescu, wife of President and party leader Nicolae Ceaușescu, to a position of political prominence and the development of a cult surrounding her person and activities similar to the cult of personality that has been created around her husband. It also has been introduced despite the continued enforcement of pronatalist laws that mitigate *against* increased activity and responsibility of women outside the home. This study first examines the origins and flavor of the "Elena cult" in an effort to explain the intense popular reaction against her and describes the reasoning behind the pronatalism and the campaign to promote women. It then contrasts the traditional pattern of women's participation in Romanian politics with post-1979 policies and concludes with a discussion of the implications of these contradictory policies for the future status of Romanian women. These implications are not favorable, since resentment against Elena Ceaușescu personally and against the pronatalist policies associated with her husband's rule may extend to other policies adopted during this period, including efforts to increase women's visibility and representation in top positions.

The Cult

The Romanian political system in the last decade has been dominated by a cult of personality.[1] Nicolae Ceaușescu has become the omniscient, omnipotent, and infallible leader of the Romanian nation. He is the brilliant interpreter of Marxism-Leninism, the hardworking communist who rose from poverty to party leadership, and the stately symbol of Romanian sovereignty in dealings with foreign heads of state, royal or revolutionary.

Many of Ceauşescu's relatives hold high political office, but the cult—that is, the image of public recognition and adulation created by the Romanian press—extends only to his wife, Elena Ceauşescu. She is his constant companion on official and unofficial occasions. She presides with him at party and state ceremonies, travels with him inside the country and abroad, and even holds formal positions directly below him in the political hierarchy.

Elena Ceauşescu is not a popular personality within Romania. She does not project the practical competence and concern of an Eleanor Roosevelt or the mystical charm and beauty of an Eva Perón. Despite the praise heaped upon her by the Romanian press, few Romanians seem to regard her as an ideal example of Romanian womanhood.[2] Rather, she is widely resented (like many political wives) as the undeserving recipient of such praise. Her husband, it is assumed, at least *earned* his high office, rising to the pinnacle of power through hard work and political skill. She, on the other hand, is regarded as merely the beneficiary of his generosity and, indeed, as an unjustified intruder on the Romanian political scene. Her unpopularity is intensified by pronatalist measures introduced in 1966, the year after her husband became party leader. Abortions, contraceptive devices, and divorces were suddenly outlawed in an effort to increase population growth, and Romanians then and now blame these policies on Elena Ceauşescu. This tendency to blame the "wife" instead of the leader is found in other political systems as well.[3]

Although Elena Ceauşescu was active in the Romanian Communist party (RCP) in the 1930s, there is little record of political activity on her part until the early 1960s.[4] By then she had three children and a doctorate and was secretary of the Party Committee at the Bucharest Institute of Chemical Research. After her husband was elected First Secretary in 1965, she became a member of the National Council on Scientific Research and eventually of its Bureau, and in 1968 joined the Bucharest Municipal Party Committee. Her public prominence began in 1971, and thereafter her offices proliferated. She was elected a full member of the RCP Central Committee in 1972, and the next year a full member of its Executive Committee; in 1977 she became the only woman ever to serve on the Bureau of the Executive Committee; and in 1979 she was named president of the National Council on Science and Technology with ministerial status. In 1980 she became one of three first vice-presidents of the Council of Ministers, directly below her husband in the state hierarchy.

Until 1971 she had appeared in public with her husband only on occasions when the Romanian leaders were hosting foreign dignitaries and their wives in Bucharest or returning such visits abroad.[5] However, in June 1971 changes began. The Ceauşescus went to China, and although she was still defined as his wife (*soţie*), Elena Ceauşescu was much more prominently featured in photographs of the visit than had previously been customary in the Romanian press. In early July she began to achieve a separate political identity. At a meeting of a national commission on economic forecasting, *Scînteia* (the party newspaper) showed her seated among the other members and listed her alphabetically as "doctor-engineer, and director of the Central Institute of Chemical Research." Later that month she broke precedent by publicly accompanying President Ceauşescu on a working tour inside Romania, to the Constanţa shipyards. By then she was a completely different woman, stylishly dressed and elegantly coiffed. In August she reviewed the fleet with him at Mangalia and took part in several other visits inside the country.[6] So far, in all joint appearances, she still was described as his "wife."

A new development occurred on the Romanian national holiday, August 23, 1971, when Elena Ceauşescu appeared on the reviewing stand for the first time, the only woman, beside her husband at the center of attention. The October 4 issue of *Scînteia* raised her status further: on Harvest Day, at a mass meeting in the *Piaţa Obor* in Bucharest, Nicolae Ceauşescu was accompanied by "comrade Elena Ceauşescu," at last a *tovaraşă* (comrade) rather than a *soţie* (wife).[7]

In the late 1970s the worship paid her by the Romanian press almost came to equal that of her husband. Her birthday is now an occasion for public rejoicing, although her age is not announced. The day was first revealed in January 1979, and the coverage was so extensive that it may have been her sixtieth birthday. She was praised for forty years of revolutionary activity, and the celebrations occupied the front page of *Scînteia* for two successive days. A long poem under a picture of her and her husband described them as "two communist hearts under the great Romanian flag" who were wished a happy life "enveloped forever in the love of the entire people." In 1980 the day was ignored, possibly in conformity with the usual Romanian practice of celebrating only the decade year of officials' birthdays. But in 1981 *Scînteia* greeted the occasion with a drawing of Elena Ceauşescu, smilingly receiving dozens of bouquets of flowers from a crowd of children surrounding her, and a poem entitled "Homage" ending as follows:

> *To the first woman of the country, the homage of the entire country,*
> *As star stands beside star in the eternal arch of heaven,*
> *Beside the Great Man (*Marele Bărbat*) she watches over*
> *Romania's path to glory.*

On International Women's Day in 1982, reports of the occasion rejoiced in the presence of "comrade academician doctor engineer Elena Ceauşescu, outstanding activist of party and state, eminent personage of Romanian and international science."[8]

Nicolae Ceauşescu's image is also quite ostentatious. He is portrayed as a symbol of royalty, sworn into office as president every five years in a ceremony more like a coronation than an inauguration, transported in a fleet of Mercedes or in a helicopter, and given a series of palaces (including the fairy tale Peleş) in which to live. Yet he is also portrayed as the industrious, self-sacrificing revolutionary, who rose to prominence despite the adversity of his youth—a socialist Horatio Alger. His wife is given revolutionary credentials as a former communist militant and textile worker. But his revolutionary activities and imprisonment in the 1930s are well-documented; her present extravagance is well-documented. The somewhat contradictory image of king and revolutionary projected for Nicolae Ceauşescu is paralleled by his wife's dual roles of consort and scientist. However, there is less balance in her case. She appears more clearly the extravagant queen with no positive personal features to endear her to the Romanian masses. It is little wonder that she is widely disliked.

Population Growth

This dislike is intensified by a number of measures taken in the mid-1960s to increase population growth, measures widely attributed in Romania to Elena Ceauşescu's influence. In fact, she has not played a major role in advocating such measures, so their attribution to her may be quite unfair. But pronatalism is without doubt a prominent feature of her husband's rule. When he came to power in 1965, the annual rate of population increase had reached a postwar low of 0.6 percent; Romania faced a potential labor shortage that endangered the party's long term plans for economic development.[9] In an effort to raise the birth rate, the communist leadership in October 1966 made abortions and divorces almost impossible to obtain and increased taxes on childless adults, married or unmarried. An intense press campaign encouraged people to have more children. *Scînteia* published articles on the pleasures of maternity, with many pictures of angelic, smiling children.[10] These measures had an immediate effect, as the population growth rate almost doubled during the next year. However, Romanians soon developed ways to reduce the effects of the new laws, and after the initial jump the birth rate declined to 18.2 live births per thousand inhabitants in 1973 (the comparable figures for 1966, 1967, 1979, and 1983 were 14.3, 27.4, 18.5, and 14.3). In contrast to leaders in several other East European countries, Romanian leaders have made only limited use of "positive" pronatalist incentives. Cash payments to parents are low compared to those given elsewhere in the region, maternity leave is "the shortest of any country in Central or Eastern Europe," and by 1974 kindergarten places for children aged three to six were available to "only about 42 percent of eligible children."[11] It is not surprising that Elena Ceauşescu has derived little popularity from the pronatalist policies associated with her.

Nicolae Ceauşescu and the Promotion of Women

The pronatalist campaign of the 1960s had been precipitated by a *potential* labor shortage. In 1973, however, an *immediate* need for workers produced a new emphasis: women in the labor force. Prior to this time, the Romanian Communist party had been less successful than most East European regimes in drawing women into the labor force, particularly in urban areas.[12] In June 1973 the Central Committee (CC) called for the more widespread employment of women and explicitly acknowledged that the party had to give them access to more prestigious and remunerative positions in order to attract them to the labor force.[13]

This recognition that special measures must be taken to assure equal opportunities for women in access to jobs and promotions was not completely new to regime rhetoric under Ceauşescu. At the Ninth Party Congress in 1965, Ceauşescu had merely mentioned women along with the nationalities as examples of minority groups whose recruitment into the party must be encouraged.[14] However, within a year the promotion of women had become a strong priority,[15] and in June 1966 a National Conference of Women was held, at which Ceauşescu praised women for their contributions to revolutionary and economic activity. He revealed his priorities by his stress on their current economic role, urban and rural, and insisted that they must "get jobs corresponding to their abilities." He promised to develop the "production of household appliances and utensils and ready-cooked foods" to facilitate housework and create "better conditions" for women's participation in the social-political life of the country.[16] In 1966 Ceauşescu did not see the sharing of household duties with men as the key to liberating women from such tasks. Rather, like leaders in most communist states, he assumed that socialist production would ease the lot of women by providing machines and communal facilities.

In the same speech Ceauşescu hinted at the pronatalist measures to be taken that autumn: "Measures are being examined," he warned, "to defend the integrity of families . . . and . . . increase the birthrate." The family, he declared, must be strengthened; the full equality of women is closely tied to "the durability of families" and "a high moral attitude in family life."[17] The unpopular pronatalist laws introduced in October 1966 were thus associated not only with the need to increase population growth, but also with the goal of female equality and so with the later campaign to promote women. In 1966 Ceauşescu chose to increase the population (the *potential* labor force). Indeed, from 1965 to 1969 there was no perceptible increase in the political role of women in the party. The proportion of women party members did rise slightly from 21 to 22.77 percent, but women's share of Central Committee members actually dropped.[18]

There was rhetorical support for women's equality in the years from 1969 to 1973. For example, in his report to the Tenth Party Congress in 1969, Ceauşescu recognized the difficulties confronting women in the economy: "It is not fair that, in enterprises in which ninety percent of the employees are women, all, or nearly all the managers and chiefs should be men. It is also unfair that in the agricultural cooperatives, where most of those who work are women, the chairmen, the brigadiers, the bookkeepers —in other words, those who are sheltered from work—so to speak—should also be men."[19] This analysis is reminiscent of Khrushchev's complaint that in agriculture it was women who did the work and men who directed them.[20] And just the year before in a talk at the Bucharest Garment and Knitwear Factory, Ceauşescu had complained that, although 80 percent of the personnel were women, it was the men who had been recommended for and hence were receiving the medals he was handing out.[21] But it was not until the CC plenum of June 1973 that a major campaign to promote women was introduced.

Ceauşescu's speech at that plenum is crucial to an understanding of his attitude toward the role of women in Romania. He asserted that women are citizens, like everyone else, not a special category; they are not "different" in their political or intellectual capacity. Women have proven themselves, he declared, in revolutionary activity, in science, in production. Women, he asserted, are capable of any effort and so must be allowed to contribute fully to society. Ceauşescu's view of any citizen, any worker, any professional, is instrumental: all should contribute to the Romanian nation. So women must contribute fully by working in the economy and also by fulfilling their other social role: giving birth to, raising, and educating the children of the socialist nation.[22]

Ceauşescu also recognized that women must be rewarded for their contributions and allowed to advance on an equal basis with men. At the plenum in 1973, he complained that not enough women had been promoted, that there were no women secretaries of the party county committees, no women on the Executive Committee, and very few on the Central Committee. The party must correct the situation, he declared, but in addition women themselves have to assert their rights and act more aggressively in order to achieve promotion. And he continued to view childcare and food preparation as problems to be solved by communal services: increasing the number of nurseries, kindergartens, and catering (fast food) shops, rather than adjusting gender roles.

Since the immediate result of Ceauşescu's criticism was the promotion of his wife to the Party Executive Committee, many Romanians concluded that this goal in 1973 was not really the promotion of all women but only of Elena Ceauşescu. This assumption was apparently confirmed when pronatalism continued and the stress on promoting women disappeared. A campaign against illegal abortions began in August 1973, and the Ministry of Health that autumn adopted a number of measures to increase the birthrate.[23] Women's representation among political leaders did increase to some extent, as the number of women in the Central Committee rose from six to ten in 1974 and the number of candidates from five to twenty-four (see table 7.1). The proportion of women in the party continued to grow slowly but steadily over the next few years. But, except for Elena Ceauşescu's election to the Bureau of the Executive Committee in January 1977, other top-level promotions of women did not occur until 1979.[24]

Women's Political Roles

The impact of the campaign to promote women has been most evident in the political arena. The Romanian political system is dominated by a highly centralized party that controls the society more tightly than any other regime in Eastern Europe, with the possible exception of Albania. As a result, it has been possible for the party leadership to set quotas regarding the promotion of women and get immediate and visible results. There are, however, disadvantages; for example, there are no independent women's organizations to influence or react to policy, and the arbitrary methods used often provoke resentment instead of changing attitudes.

Even under Ceauşescu, political participation of women in Romania has followed a pattern familiar to students of comparative politics both inside and outside the Soviet bloc.[25] First, the proportion of women varies inversely with the power of the political body or position. Second, women are concentrated in certain sectors where they are assumed to have special competence: health, education, light industry, and consumer goods. In Romania women are also regarded as a separate group in society that needs special political protection due to inherent disadvantages. In the case of minority nationalities, for example, the disadvantage is linguistic, and their culture must be protected by special privileges. In the case of women the disadvantage is physical, and they must be protected by special laws that strengthen the family and limit their access to certain types of labor. In order to demonstrate that their interests are being protected, women, like the national minorities, must be guaranteed participation in those political bodies that are meant to be representative, if only symbolically, of the

Table 7.1 Women on the Central Committee of the Romanian Communist Party

	Female full members	Female candidate members	Total female members	Percentage of women reelected at next congress	Percentage of all members reelected at next congress
1948	5 (12%)	2 (13%)	7 (13%)	43	61
1955	3 (5%)	4 (11%)	7 (7%)	57	73
1960	5 (6%)	2 (6%)	7 (6%)	57	84
1965	4 (3%)	5 (7%)	9 (5%)	44	68
1969	6 (4%)	5 (4%)	11 (4%)	45	65
1974	10 (5%)	24 (15%)	34 (9%)	68	52
1979	48 (20%)	52 (32%)	100 (25%)	54	53
1984	53 (20%)	73 40%)	1.26 (28%)	—	—

Sources: Compiled from lists published by *Scînteia* immediately following each Congress.

entire society: the People's Councils or local government bodies, and the Grand National Assembly or national legislature.

Before 1973 the only exception to this pattern was Ana Pauker, one of the most powerful leaders of the Romanian Communist party from 1944 to 1952. Pauker was unique in Romanian politics: a woman who exerted power directly rather than through a male "protector,"[26] she gained her position in the party through her own revolutionary activity. She also administered sectors outside the traditional areas of "female" responsibility, including the Ministry of Foreign Affairs, party recruitment, cadre policy, and the campaign to collectivize agriculture.

Since the downfall of Ana Pauker, only Elena Ceauşescu has risen to the highest party body, the Bureau of the Political Executive Committee (PEC).[27] From 1973 to 1979, she and Lina Ciobanu were the only women to be full members of the PEC.[28] Suddenly, at the Twelfth Party Congress in November 1979, nine more women were added to this important body, five as full members and four as candidates.[29] Unfortunately, this improvement in women's representation occurred just when the Bureau began to replace the PEC as the center of power—when the PEC shifted from being a decisive to a symbolic political body.[30] And, despite the campaign to promote women, there have been none (except Ana Pauker and, briefly in 1984, Lina Ciobanu) among the Central Committee secretaries, those powerful individuals directly administering the various sectors of the economy and society.

Women have been slightly better represented at the next level of the party hierarchy, the Central Committee. In the 1940s there were a small number of women prominent in the party, and at the first Congress of the

Romanian Workers' party in 1948, women made up 13 percent of the new Central Committee. The proportion then dropped off to about 5 percent until Ceauşescu's affirmative action campaign began in 1973. Thereafter, the number of women Central Committee members started to rise, and the increase in 1979 was quite sharp (see table 7.1). The pattern at first followed the Soviet model (although the Romanian percentages were slightly higher):[31] the early prominence of a few women, the subsequent reduction in female participation, and the continued low proportion of female Central Committee members. Other communist states also introduced campaigns to promote women in the 1970s,[32] but the dramatic changes of 1979 are unique to Romania and characteristic of Ceauşescu's sudden enthusiasms and drastic approach to solving problems.

The occupational distribution of women members of the Central Committee demonstrates that these individuals comprise the political elite among Romanian women (see table 7.2). The breakdown shows that, as in other political systems, the proportion of women in high economic and political posts is inversely related to the power of the office and directly related to distance from the capital city. The highest party positions are filled completely by males, as are most of those in the Central Committee apparatus in Bucharest. Even at the level of county first secretary, the crucial local position equivalent to the Soviet *obkom* first secretary, the forty posts had always been filled by males until 1979 when two women joined this elite stratum, Alexandrina Găinuşe in Bacău and Letiţia Ionaş in Sălaj.[33]

The 1979 campaign to promote women also led to their retention in the Central Committee. For the first time at the 1979 Congress a higher proportion of women than men were reelected to the new Central Committee (see table 7.1). Always before the turnover rate had been much higher for women. Sharon Wolchik has found a higher turnover rate for women than for men characteristic of the political leadership in many East European countries and suggests that selection criteria are less stringent for women, leading to shorter tenure.[34] This seems to be the case in the Romanian Central Committee, as a comparison of posts held by male and female Central Committee members reveals (see table 7.2). Males hold the higher and intermediate party positions, but among the full Central Committee members there are more women with posts at the local party level.[35] This may indicate a sex quota imposed for the Twelfth Party Congress when exactly 20 percent of the PEC and the same proportion of full Central Committee members were women. To achieve that proportion in both bodies, less experienced women may have been promoted over male colleagues, the latter moving only to the candidate state in the Central Committee where indeed almost all local party officials are male. If true, this

Table 7.2 Occupations of male and female members
1979 Romanian Communist Party Central Committee (CC)

	Full members				Candidate members			
	Male	Female	Total		Male	Female	Total	
Party								
Central Committee secretaries	9	0	9		0	0	0	
Other high party	2	0	2		0	0	0	
CC apparatus	7*	1	8		4	0	4	
County first secretaries	38	2	40		0	0	0	
Local party officials	8	10	18		13	5	18	
Union of Communist Youth	0	0	0		2	1	3	
			77	(32%)			25	(15%)
State								
Ministers or equivalent	30	4	34		1	0	1	
Other high state	23	6	29		25	2	27	
First vice-chairperson, county people's council	4	0	4		2	0	2	
Other local officials	4	11	15		6	8	14	
			82	(33%)			44	(27%)
Military	9	0	9	(4%)	8	0	8	(5%)
Education, science, culture	22	2	24	(10%)	19	5	24	(15%)
Production								
Director, heavy industry	17	0	17		3	1	4	
Director, light industry	2	2	4		2	2	4	
Director, agriculture	5	0	5		3	0	3	
			26	(10%)			11	(7%)
Worker	0	0	0		0	1	1	
Unknown	17	10	27	(11%)	23	27	50	(31%)
	197	48	245		111	52	163	

Sources: Information compiled from *Scînteia*.
*This is an estimate. Officials who disappear from public view but remain on the Central Committee tend to be employed in the CC apparatus (where positions are not announced). Several years later they reappear in another post.

could result in resentment and weak performance and contribute to low retention of females in the future.[36]

There is, I would suggest, yet another reason for the high turnover of Romanian women: the symbolic nature of their participation in the political process. They are present in the Central Committee in Romania and in other East European countries for the same reason as the national minorities (or directors of factories or collective farms): to demonstrate the democratic nature of the party, its representation of all groups in society. Turnover can be higher among women since many individuals are there not because of their personal power or specific position, but because they fill a particular demographic quota: the individual can be dropped as long as the replacement fits the same category.[37] This is clearly the case in the Grand National Assembly, as we shall see below; it has also been true in the Central Committee, even though that body is not meant to be representative of more than the elite strata of Romanian society.[38]

Women Central Committee members drawn from the state apparatus also tend to come from local levels, although there are more women in top positions in this less powerful hierarchy. Military representatives on the Central Committee are exclusively male, and even the "education, science, and culture" category is almost all male despite the many women working in the latter areas.[39] Similar trends exist in agriculture and in other areas of production: comparatively few women Central Committee members are directors, and those who are work mainly in light industry.

The pattern of women's political participation in party bodies is also visible in Romanian legislatures where again the number of women seems to vary inversely with the power of the organ.[40] In addition, there seem to be more women holding positions in the less powerful state hierarchy than in the party (compare tables 7.1 and 7.3, for example). Women delegates to the Grand National Assembly, like women Central Committee members, are clustered in lower posts and in certain sectors of activity. As table 7.4 illustrates, most delegates to the 1980 Grand National Assembly who hold high positions in party and state, as well as the top local positions, are male. Women tend to hold supportive posts at the local level. Women directly involved in production are almost all in light industry or agriculture and are less likely than their male colleagues to hold the position of director.[41] However, the increase in the number of women in the 1980 elections was dramatic: they went from fifty to 120 (14.3 percent to 32.5 percent), and they held more important posts in the state hierarchy. In addition, table 7.5, which compares the jobs of the fifty female delegates elected in 1975 with those of the 120 in 1980, indicates that their status as well as their numbers may be increasing.

A final characteristic of the political participation of women in Romania

Table 7.3 Female membership in the Romanian Grand National Assembly

Year elected	Total delegates	Female delegates	Female percentage
1948*	414	30	7.5
1952	423	72	17.0
1957	437	74	16.9
1961	465	81	17.4
1965	465	71	15.3
1969	465	68	14.6
1975	349	50	14.3
1980	369	120	32.5

Sources: Compiled from election reports in *Scînteia*.
*The 1948 elections were not yet completely controlled by the Romanian Workers' party; nine opposition delegates managed to win seats.

is also reinforced by data on the Grand National Assembly: their status as a protected "minority." Until the elections of 1975 the RCP carefully controlled the nomination process and nominated one candidate for each electoral district. The results of the election could therefore be predicted in terms of individual winners and the proportion of various demographic groups (such as the minority nationalities). In 1975 and 1980, however, some of the districts ran multicandidate elections; two, sometimes three, candidates competed for the same seat.[42] In 1975, for example, 139 of 349 seats (40 percent) were contested. No top official at the central or local level faced an opponent. Those with competition were instead local residents working in industry, agriculture, or other economic sectors, who faced opponents with the same occupation. In this way, the correct occupational balance was maintained among the winners.

But not only did teachers face teachers and directors of collective farms face other directors of collective farms: Hungarians faced Hungarians, Germans faced Germans, and women faced women. In other words, those individuals important to the party faced no opposition. Those who simply filled occupational or demographic categories ran against other candidates who filled similar categories. And while 40 percent of all seats were contested, 76 percent of the women candidates and only 28 percent of the male candidates were opposed.[43] The elections of 1980 showed a similar pattern (see table 7.6). While five times as many males were given uncontested seats, there were almost as many females as males in two-candidate contests and more females in three-candidate races.[44] Men continued to dominate the Grand National Assembly in 1980, and most women once

Table 7.4 Positions of delegates in the 1980 Grand National Assembly

	Total	Males	Females
Party			
Central Committee secretariat	8	8	0
High party officials	6	6	0
Central Committee apparatus	7	6	1
County first secretaries	40	38	2
Local party officials	51	9	42
Union of Communist Youth	8	3	5
State			
Ministers	34	29	5
High state officials	35	27	8
County first vice-chairpersons	3	3	0
Local state officials	6	1	5
Military	12	12	0
Education, science, culture	64	46	18
Production			
Directors			
Heavy industry	38	37	1
Light industry	12	4	8
Agriculture	27	17	10
Others			
Heavy industry	7	4	3
Light industry	10	0	10
Agriculture	1	0	1

Sources: Compiled from information given by *Scînteia*.

again ran as part of a demographic category. However, while in 1975 only thirteen women were important enough to run unopposed, five years later that number had increased to thirty-one. Again the direction of change appears to be positive.

There have also been gains for women at the top of the state hierarchy, in the Council of Ministers. In March 1975 the president of the National Women's Council (NWC) was given ministerial status, and so Lina Ciobanu became the first woman to serve on the Council of Ministers in almost twenty years.[45] She was already a member of the Political Executive Committee and in September 1975 became Minister of Light Industry while continuing as head of the National Women's Committee. The close connection between women and light industry was thus institutionalized. In

Table 7.5 Positions of women delegates elected to the Grand National Assembly in 1975 and 1980

	1975	1980
Party		
Central Committee secretariat	0	0
High party officials	0	0
Central Committee apparatus	0	1
County first secretaries	0	2
Local party officials	11	42
Union of Communist Youth	2	5
State		
Ministers	0	5
High state officials	5	8
County first vice-chairpersons	0	0
Local state officials	4	6
Education, science, culture	12	18
Production		
Directors		
Heavy industry	0	1
Light industry	5	8
Agriculture	5	10
Others		
Heavy industry	0	3
Light industry	6	10
Agriculture	0	1
	50	120

Sources: Compiled from information given by *Scînteia*.

June 1976 Ciobanu was joined on the Council of Ministers by Suzana Gâdea,[46] who served as Minister of Education and Instruction until 1979. Before 1979 the few women ministers (except for Ana Pauker) supervised traditionally female sectors: the NWC, light industry, culture, and education.

In June 1979 Elena Ceaușescu was elected president of the National Council for Science and Technology and as such became a member of the Council of Ministers. In August, Aneta Spornic[47] became Minister of Education and Instruction; Suzana Gâdea retained her ministerial status as head of the Council on Socialist Culture and Education, and Ciobanu continued as Minister of Light Industry. In March 1980 Elena Ceaușescu was elected first vice-president (there are three first vice-presidents) of the Council of

Table 7.6 1980 Multi-candidate elections to the Grand National Assembly

	Male	Female	Total
Candidates	367	231	598
Delegates elected	249	120	369
Percentage of candidates elected	67.8	52.0	61.7
One-candidate races	148	31	179
Two-candidate races	75	67	142
Three-candidate races	14	15	29
Male/female two-candidate races			9*
Male/female three-candidate races			10**
Total districts/total delegates			369

Sources: Information compiled from *Scînteia*.
*In the nine two-candidate races where a male and female ran against each other, seven males won.
**In the ten three-candidate races involving males and females, five males and five females won.

Ministers, Cornelia Filipaş[48] was made a vice-president (one of nine), and Ana Mureşan[49] became Minister of Internal Trade. There are just over fifty individuals on the Council of Ministers, so the female share of six is not impressive; with the exception of Elena Ceauşescu the women are all in traditionally female sectors. Nevertheless, there does seem to be a heightened consciousness of the need to promote women and some progress in doing so.[50]

Conclusions

The political participation of Romanian women follows patterns visible in other political systems. The number of women varies inversely with power and proximity to Bucharest. Women in Romania are clustered in certain economic sectors, especially light industry, agriculture, education, and culture, and the careers of those women who have reached high office clearly reflect this sectoral concentration. In spite of this traditional background, the cult of Elena Ceauşescu has been accompanied by high-level promotions of women in the last decade and particularly since 1979.

Full equality for women in political and economic life is not a new theme in the Marxist literature of communist systems. Lenin, for example, recognized that women must be included in the revolutionary struggle. They were needed to make the revolution and later to build socialism, and they would be liberated along with men from economic oppression. Like leaders in other East European countries, Ceauşescu is following very closely in Lenin's path. His views on women expressed at the June 1973 plenum coincide quite closely with those of the early Bolsheviks. But, as Gail W. Lapidus has noted, the Bolsheviks assumed that "the economic independence of women would guarantee . . . equality, outside marriage as within it." Women would be rescued from housework and childcare by "a reallocation of familial and societal functions . . . from the individual household to the social collective."[51] In the Soviet case, the priorities of industrialization and the opposition and hostility of men proved disastrous to the cause of female equality at all levels, but especially at lower levels.[52] In Romania also, the focus on developing heavy industry has taken priority over the provision of communal facilities or even a variety of consumer products to ease the individual burden of household work.[53] Romanian women must work side by side with men in the economy and take care of home and children, often by telephone. At the same time, they are prevented from legal access to effective methods of contraception.

The triple burden of job, home, and children makes it impossible for most Romanian women to devote the time and attention to their careers that would be necessary for promotion to the top of the economic or political ladder. To achieve full productivity from the women, Ceauşescu would have to eliminate the triple burden by providing communal eating and childcare facilities of quality comparable to home care. He would thereby achieve the Bolshevik dream of shifting housework and childcare from the individual household to the social collective, but the accomplishment would require a huge investment of economic resources. The only alternative to such an investment would be a reorientation of gender roles that would equalize reponsibilities in the home as they are equalized in the workplace. But Ceauşescu has not publicly recognized this second alternative.

Under the most ideal economic and social conditions, women start from a disadvantaged position due to their extra family responsibilities. In the factory, office, agricultural collective, or school they are faced by angry or indifferent male rivals who are not happy to relinquish their assumed superiority. Special measures to enforce equality bring anger, resentment, and hostility on the part of the formerly advantaged, whether that group is defined by race, nationality, or gender. In Romania, policies encouraging the promotion of women work under extra disadvantages: not only are they implemented arbitrarily and by force, but they are also associated with the unpopular image of Elena Ceauşescu and the equally unpopular pronatalist measures introduced in 1966.

The promotion of women is being required by the Romanian Communist party because women are needed in the labor force. But such coercion from above need not produce the attitudinal change necessary to achieve equality either in the home or at work. One analyst has concluded: "The East European experience tells us little about the degree to which directed social change can influence behavior in the family, because the elites have simply not used their considerable tools for socialization and influence to promote change in this area."[54] So far the Romanian elite fits this pattern: Ceauşescu has not sought to alter roles within the family. He wants women to participate more fully in the economy and, at the same time, to produce more children, goals that are contradictory unless a reorientation of gender roles occurs. Ceauşescu has demonstrated a strong commitment to the promotion of women and, while it is too soon to evaluate the long-term success of the program, there is always the possibility that he will attempt to ensure its success by imposing changes in the sexual division of labor within the family. He has certainly not hesitated to invade the privacy of the family with pronatalist laws.[55] Should he decide to promote change in gender roles, the Romanian experience could provide a test of the degree to which a political regime can influence behavior in the family. More likely, however, given Ceauşescu's past pronouncements, the Romanian elite will continue to fit the East European pattern and not attempt to bring about such a reorientation.

The Romanian Communist party may continue to impose improvements in the political and economic status of women, and the gains of 1979 may be consolidated or even increased in the next few years. Even so, the long-term prospects for women's equality in Romania are not good. Ceauşescu is given to drastic but brief campaigns, and his stress on promoting women could shift tomorrow, especially if the Romanian economy were to achieve the desired transition from extensive to intensive development. Such a transition would raise labor productivity, ease the labor shortage, and reduce the need for women in the economy. However, even without such a shift, it is all too likely that the association of women's equality with Elena Ceauşescu will bring the demise of the former with the latter. Once Nicolae Ceauşescu leaves the scene, this policy so closely associated associated with his wife may very well be denounced (like Khrushchev's harebrained schemes) or, at best, allowed by his successors to wither away.

8

John Kolsti

From Courtyard to Cabinet: The Political Emergence of Albanian Women

Ever since the Albanian government launched its cultural revolution in the mid-1960s the question of women's rights inside Albania has been linked to the survival of the present government of Albania and, to some extent, to the survival of the Albanian nation. That nation, as wall posters stress, is one that must use its own resources to break the blockade imposed on it by reactionaries and revisionists from without. It is one that must destroy from within, once and for all, the vestiges of centuries-long oppression and exploitation, visible reminders of which remain the abandoned churches and mosques that once hopelessly divided the Albanians socially and culturally, preventing the establishment of an ethnic Albanian state in the Balkans.

Five centuries of Turkish rule proved disastrous for the Albanians. In the sixteenth and seventeenth centuries mass conversions to Islam placed Albanians culturally as well as economically and politically on the periphery of the Ottoman Empire. Moslems along the lower Volga and in Central Asia similarly found themselves at the edge of first the Ottoman Empire and then the Russian Empire. The Moslem population of the Soviet Union has not been immune to the changes "from above" faced by Moslem Albanians, particularly women, in their forced entry into the twentieth century.[1] At the turn of the twentieth century, Albania emerged as Europe's only Moslem nation, 53 percent of the population belonging to the Sunni sect, 20 percent to the Bektashi. Among the Sunnis in North Albania and Kosovë (Yugoslavia) lived Albanian Roman Catholics (10 percent of the population), still considered the most traditional as well as backward elements in a mountainous area dominated by clan loyalties. In South Albania and parts of Epirus (Greece), 17 percent of the population was Greek Orthodox. It was in Greek schools and academies that Albania's first educated elites emerged. The schools were a window to the West not only for Orthodox Albanians, but also for their Bektashi neighbors who have been called by one Albanian scholar Albania's "Crypto-Christians."[2] It must be understood, however, that the language of instruction in Albania, wherever it existed, was Greek, Turkish, Serbian, or even Italian. Instruction in Albanian by the priests and hoxhas was forbidden by both the Porte and the Patriarch in Constantinople. It is not surprising, then, that the churches and mosques conveniently served the government in the mid-1960s as symbols of a political and economic system that supported and condoned Albania's backwardness, which was reflected in the position of women in the Albanian provinces in European Turkey and in King Zog's Albania in the 1930s.

All the symbols, the present leadership stresses, were transplanted to Albanian territory, at times violently assimilating converts to the different faiths. This made it all the easier for the government to proclaim Albania officially an atheist state in a drive to break the bonds that had helped enslave Albanian women. Albania's only internationally recognized writer, Ismail Kadare, in an early novel written in the 1960s, has one of his characters express her feelings about the past in these words: "Hundreds of rifles guard over these bonds. Some of us had been bought for cash, some had been exchanged for cows, sheep, horses, sacks of corn, and even for sheep dogs. We were one herd exchanged for another herd, the only difference being that we wore no bells around our necks."[3]

Those bonds, vestiges of a patriarchal social structure that had all but disappeared from most of European Turkey by the end of the nineteenth century, were finally broken or seriously weakened by the events of World War II. Before women volunteered in large numbers to swell partisan units in the field, they had had no voice whatsoever in Albanian political life. The war in effect produced a revolution from above in Albanian society, one in which prominent roles were played, at least on the surface, by a handful of women. It was only in the 1960s, however, that the revolution in Albanian society took on the character of a mass movement—to a great extent a women's movement—from below. The political turmoil that followed in the mid-1970s would reveal to what extent this revolution, which in theory was linked by the party to the problem of women's rights, had any real force. This chapter examines the political roles assigned to women in the 1970s and attempts to determine to what extent the rising stars of the party have progressed beyond the role model function a few women had performed in the new government before the social upheavals of the late 1960s.

Vito Kapo, the president of the Union of Albanian Women and the wife of the number three man in the party hierarchy, signaled that sweeping changes were about to take place in the party and in the government in a speech delivered in 1973. The most revolutionary elements in Albanian society were no longer to be neglected: "Proceeding from the fact that those who have been the most oppressed and subjected to the greatest suffering are the most revolutionary and progressive elements par excellence, it is easy to understand that women in general, and Albanian women in particular, who have suffered the most, who have been exploited the most, who have been in the past the most oppressed and deprived, are the most revolutionary elements in our socialist society."[4]

Vito Kapo's remarks, it is interesting to note, came three years after her husband, Hysni Kapo, could still point his finger at the "Anatolians" in the party and the government (conservative elements in the apparat) who seemed unaffected by the drive launched by Enver Hoxha and his number two man, Mehmet Shehu, to undo once and for all the injustices and humiliation Albanian women had suffered during the Ottoman period and under a Mat chieftain, Ahmed Bey Zogu, who proclaimed himself king of the Albanians in 1928.[5] Zog for the most part continued the legacy of five centuries of Ottoman rule that crippled the process of nation-building among the Albanians. Given the low educational and cultural level of the majority of the partisan brigades that eventually seized power in Albania in 1944, then, it came as no surprise that Hysni Kapo could find reflected in the party and government attitudes toward women deeply rooted in Albanian society as a whole, which was only a generation removed from its Ottoman and Zogist past.

The cultural revolution of the mid-1960s and the rise of women in the 1970s to posts in the cabinet and politburo were directed by Hoxha, Shehu, and Kapo, whose wives may or may not have been instrumental in their linking the survival of the Marxist-Leninist state in Albania to the question of women's rights. The leadership of the party, predominantly Tosk (i.e., from South Albania), saw itself as a continuation of the (Tosk-dominated) intellectual and cultural "Awakening" of the Albanians in the 1870s and 1880s that eventually helped rid the country of its Anatolian oppressors. But Albania's more recent generation of intellectuals-turned-revolutionaries fully realized that approximately 10 percent of its modern-day "Awakeners" were women. It was these women, Geg as well as Tosk, Moslem as well as Christian, educated as well as illiterate, who between 1939 and 1945 began to break the lashes that through the centuries of abuse had enabled the family patriarchs to reduce them to political and social nonentities.[6]

The Legacy

An understanding of the impact of five centuries of Turkish domination, which were followed by fifteen years of Zog's misgovernment, is essential to appreciate the scope of the economic, social, and political upheavals that affected the lives of Albanian women between 1939, when Zog fled the country, and 1945. Five hundred years of Ottoman rule, in the opinion of one academician in Tiranë, had condemned Albanian women to a lot more "gloomy and deplorable" than that of their counterparts in non-Moslem provinces of European Turkey, to say nothing of the rest of Eastern Europe.[7] As the power of the Porte weakened, the only Moslem-dominated ethnic group in the Balkans found itself increasingly at the mercy of its neighbors, all of whom could rally around their own national Orthodox churches, and all of whom had reasons of their own to settle accounts with an Albania they identified with Islamic terror, not with an Albania whose Christian minority, particularly the Roman Catholics of the Highlands (and Kosovë), was nearly isolated from the rest of Europe. This isolation, marked by the lack of any educational system provided in the vernacular, fell harshest, without question, on Albanian women, Christian and Moslem alike.

Albanian women were victims of a patriarchal society in widespread areas unaffected by the growth of towns and the spread of schools and immune to edicts or reforms originating in Istanbul or (after 1920) even in Tiranë, the capital of the new Albanian state. It was a society that could treat women as little more than sheep to be sold or bartered in the interest of the extended family or clan, and one that regarded women as social dangers or imbeciles,[8] ideas reinforced by Old Testament proverbs as well as the Qumran Shari'a introduced from Asia. Christian priests and Moslem hoxhas alike could quote scripture to justify their support of all pervasive customs among the Albanians codified in one district by a Dukagjin chieftain on the eve of the Ottoman invasion. The Law of Lekë, in the eyes of Albania's present leaders, sanctioned certain practices that, with the overthrow of the old order, had to pass from accepted custom and be considered crimes, owing to the social threat they represented, crimes such as infant betrothal, marriage by purchase, marriage under compulsion, and polygamous marriages that were to be consecrated by the Shari'a.[9] In effect, the religious institutions inside Albania, two Christian and two Moslem, either produced women as faceless as the impressionistic icons and frescoes on the walls of its churches or obliterated the faces completely, either by plastering and painting over the images in the new mosques or covering them with the veil—a practice that did not escape Christian women in some Albanian districts. In other words, the religious communities that owed allegiance to the Pope, the Patriarch, or the Porte and that hopelessly divided Albanians culturally and socially failed to improve the lot of women whose only release inside their own subculture, it appears, was expressed in a literature that remained unofficial in the Ottoman period, namely, in Albanian oral tradition.

Within the confines of their "white towers," the formula used in their ballads and lyric songs for the fortress-like dwellings in Albanian villages, women developed their own styles of expression that satisfied both artistic and emotional needs, given the unlucky lot handed them by a male-dominated society. Even a woman's dowry would ever remind her of her real worth whenever she recalled the lash rope and bullet presented by her father to her in-laws, among whom life was to be endured. These gifts to her father's *miq*, friends or in-laws, reminded the bride (she might be called bride the rest of her life by her in-laws or husband) that the *miq* had the right to beat her, or kill her if need be, if she did not submit to them. Ismail Kadare, in the novel referred to above, focused on this particular custom-crime when he described the appearance of the bride's father, a man of the old school, at his daughter's wedding, one she had arranged herself without his blessing.

Given the symbols of the lash rope and the bullet, it comes as no surprise that the richest and most lyrical genre of Albanian oral tradition was connected with the wedding ritual. Some songs, understandably, acquired an almost funereal flavor. At the same time, however, the songs and rituals revolving around the "death" of a daughter or sister provided women with a way to direct their fear or anger at the system that humiliated them.

The nonritual, narrative genres of Albanian folklore, on the other hand, present in rare instances a totally different picture or symbol of a woman, namely, one who dominates the course of events rather than one victimized by them. It is the image of the warrior maiden who quite literally casts off her womanish ways and dons the dress of a warrior. In tales of this type the warrior maiden exhibits traits totally lacking in the greatest heroes of the tradition.[10] That one such heroine, Fatima, could enter the fantasy world of Balkan (Moslem) epics is not too surprising, given the fact that the storytelling in this case reflected a reality in Albanian life: women could leave their courtyards, the "white towers," to serve as fighters. But this accepted way out of the confines of the home came at the expense of their identity as women.

Education, or the lack of any formal education, also served to restrict the movement of Albanian women, further reinforcing the Ottoman legacy that fell harshly on them. Women were excluded from Albania's first schools, which were established in North Albania by priests trained in Italy in the sixteenth and seventeenth centuries. Even the establishment of a few Albanian schools operated by foreign missionary societies at the turn of the twentieth century did not alter the fact that the language of instruction in schools in the Albanian provinces in European Turkey was, with only a few sporadic exceptions, Italian, Serbian, Bulgarian, Turkish, or Greek. The educational system, such as it was, only further removed the possibility of any intellectual stimulation among Albanian women who remained, especially in the more inaccessible mountain districts, practically imprisoned by the walls surrounding their own courtyards.

However, it should be noted that the first rays of the European Enlightenment did reach a few women in 1891 when the country's first school for girls was opened.[11] By that time, Albania's "Awakeners" had begun to publish materials, even literary works, in their own publishing houses outside Turkey. It was an American-sponsored missionary school that first gave Albanian women a chance to leave their family situations without having to lose their identities by becoming warriors or even nuns. Almost twenty years after the founding of the School for Girls in Korçë in South Albania, Albanian women for the first time organized a society, the main purpose of which was to press for the education of women.

These initial breakthroughs made for and by a handful of women, important as they were, came at a time when Ottoman rule was about to end violently. The Balkan Wars, World War I, and the political turmoil of the early 1920s seriously disrupted the progress toward the enlightenment, if not the emancipation, of women that had recently been realized. The lot of women inside Albania (and in Kosovë) for the most part remained unchanged in the 1920s and 1930s. Women, the overwhelming majority of whom remained illiterate, scarcely enjoyed any rights at all but were still regarded as a commodity in the hands of males in much of the country.

The Point of No Return

Zog's flight from Albania in 1939, the annexation of the country by Mussolini, German occupation, armed uprisings, the settling of accounts by political groups, and finally the emergence of the Albanian Communist party were events that led to fundamental changes in the lives of Albanian women. The party first gave Albanian women the right to vote during the war. Since 1945 they have also had the chance to participate in the building of the new political structure that surfaced out of the ruins of the war. In the 1950s and 1960s Hoxha continued to draw women out of their traditional roles. He justified gains made by women, especially in education, not only on the basis of the party's Marxist-Leninist-Stalinist principles, but also on the obvious historical fact that women had earned these rights in the war with their blood. No one in the country, and in the party that was a reflection of the society that produced it, could indeed deny their claim *liftuam dhe fituam* (we fought and we won).[12] In time of need they had won respect for their intellectual as well as physical capabilities. The Age of Fatima had come to a fitting end for Albanian women.

The war years had witnessed the first defection on a mass scale of

Albanian women from their families. Over six thousand, or approximately one-tenth, of the troops under Enver Hoxha were women. The majority of these women, to be sure, had received little formal education before the war. Most also had had little experience outside the economy of the household or extended family. Strong opposition to their breaking of traditional family ties came, not surprisingly, from all four major religious communities. The all-pervasive influence of the clergy was dwelt on at length by partisan women recalling the war years long after the fighting had ended.[13] Their remarks provide a glimpse of the strong puritanical streak that contributed to the unprecedented growth of a countrywide nationalistic women's movement during the final years of the war.

The second congress of this mass movement was held in 1946. Its name was changed from the Anti-Fascist Women of Albania to the Union of Albanian Women. Enver Hoxha's wife, Nexhmije, was elected president of the organization. From the very beginning the Union functioned as one of the party's most effective propagandistic wings, reaching as it did into all the administrative districts of the country and every level of a society whose traditional values and economic structure, such as it was, were undergoing rapid change. All three wives of the country's top leadership, Hoxha, Shehu, and Kapo, exploited their privileged positions in the party to gain what political influence they wielded in the postwar period. Putting their educational backgrounds to good use, however, they were in a position to serve as excellent role models for women just at the time the impact of a national educational system based on the Soviet model began achieving unprecedented results. By their involvement in public affairs—to say nothing of their proximity to political power—Nexhmije Hoxha, Fiqrete Shehu, and Vito Kapo added new dimensions to the image of women operating with authority in what still remained very strongly a man's world. The message they spread through the schools and the women's organizations was clear: modern-day Albanian heroines would have to reach for the same educational goals and technical skills their male counterparts were now required by the state to develop. The Union of Albanian Women, in effect, continued on a mass scale what a few educated women had set in motion between 1891 and 1946.

The Cultural Revolution

Two of the "old guards" of the Union concentrated their efforts on the country's educational system, serving on various national committees on education. One, Fiqrete Shehu, headed the V. I. Lenin Party School; the other, Nexhmije Hoxha, served as the director of the Institute of Marxist-Leninist Studies. In the 1950s and 1960s both could take justifiable pride in the fact that more and more of the graduates entering the labor force or continuing their education were women. A major social question became not the education of women but their emancipation. Given the public roles played by Nexhmije Hoxha, Fiqrete Shehu, and Vito Kapo, as well as their personal accomplishments and proximity to power, it is safe to assume they had some influence on the decision of their husbands to link the ultimate success of the socialist revolution in Albania to the problems of women's emancipation. These decisions culminated in Enver Hoxha's speech of Feburary 6, 1967, which signaled the new roles women would perform in a society they would help shape and preserve. These three women in particular, and the Union of Albanian Women in general, since the 1960s helped the leadership of the party "exercise political and ideological control over all sections of the community by propagating its special kind of Marxist-Leninist ideology and seeing that its policies were carried out."[14] Vito Kapo was thus correct in her estimation of the revolutionary role educated generations of Albanian women would play in the political and economic life of the country.

The political roles assumed by women during the war years would expand dramatically in the 1960s, when the party and state hierarchy would be able to tap for leadership posts individuals who would have been considered nonentities some thirty years earlier. Changes in the lives of women affected by the war were overshadowed by the first tangible results of job options and career opportunities made available through the schools and the country's first state university in Tiranë. That these changes and the cultural revolution in the 1960s failed to generate any serious opposition from the more conservative elements inside the country, particularly in the remote districts of North Albania, owed much to the indoctrination of Albania's first generations of schoolchildren and the spread of literacy throughout even the most backward regions.[15] But in some areas, once too remote even for the Porte to control effectively, the secularization of church property, particularly the schools, was not enough to silence the group still considered dangerous because of its links to the Vatican. In some instances the destruction of the local religious intelligentsia had to be carried out with death sentences as well as imprisonment. The policy of the government, which in 1967 officially proclaimed Albania an atheist state and outlawed religious practices,[16] succeeded in part because the targets of its campaign, or terror, had been held up as visible reminders of centuries of national humiliation. Agitprop teams sent out from the growing industrial and educational centers that were beginning to attract women from different parts of the country played no small role in the government's drive to sever the religious and social bonds that restricted Albanian women most of all. A point of no return was finally reached by Albanian women as a result of the cultural revolution of the 1960s.

Progress made by Albanian women in the 1950s and 1960s came at the expense of individuals, male and female alike, who were critical of Hoxha's internal policies, which reflected his diplomatic shifts away from Tito's Yugoslavia and post-Stalinist Russia. One woman, Liri Gega, was executed in 1956, and another, Liri Belishova, was removed from power in 1960 for her alleged involvement in a Soviet plot to overthrow Hoxha.

Ideological obedience, to be sure, also was expected from the men and women graduating from schools and institutes and joining the rank-and-file members of the party and the ministries. The mass printing of books for use in the schools in the postwar period made the work of the party all the easier. By the late 1950s publishing activity in the country had surpassed the publication of all books in Albanian between 1555 and 1945.[17] Teachers now armed with books could promote the policies of the government far more effectively than Zog's gendarmes who operated in a country almost devoid of schools. The correct ideological line reached every pupil not only in textbooks printed in Tiranë but also in the new postwar literature. Partisan heroines and women helping to build a socialist homeland, ever confronting the Canon, the Law of Lekë, clearly linked the survival of the nation to the question of the emancipation of women in the minds of their young audience. Albania's social revolution would, they showed, overcome centuries of stagnation. The implications of Hoxha's unprecedented speech of February 6, 1967, were described as follows by Kadare in his best-known novel, *The General of the Dead Army*:

> Albania is being shaken up. The mountains are squaring their shoulders. Do you know what that means? The mountains want to shake the Canon, the old prejudices and superstitions, off their backs. This requires a gigantic effort. The Canon is tough and nearly as old as the mountains. At times you can't tell where the mountains end and where the Canon begins. They are entangled and have penetrated each other. It is easier to budge huge rocks than old customs. Nevertheless, the impossible is happening.[18]

A basic question remains to be answered, however. Given the mass exodus of women from their villages during the war and their passage through the Soviet-model school system following the war and the break with Tito, what new roles were they to play in the expanding economic sectors opening up to them and in the party itself? The turmoil of the mid-1970s would show how well the leadership of the party could deal with opponents to change in the status of women in Albania, reactionaries who would allow the revolution to mark time by allowing women to lag behind.[19]

The New Albanian Woman

An examination of the People's Socialist Republic of Albania in the 1970s reveals a country light-years away socially, economically, and politically from the turbulent provinces of the Ottoman Empire and the land ruled by Ahmed Bey Zogu. The intense, even radical process of modernization that has transformed Europe's "Dark Hole"[20] into an industrial-agricultural state attempting to meet its domestic needs "using it own resources," in the words of Hoxha, has profoundly changed the lives of its citizens. These changes have indeed affected most that segment of the population that, before 1939, had barely ventured away from the home. The effects of modernization and the building of a new industrial base witnessed the addition to the country's labor force of over one-half of the population. The liberation of women from the economy, if not always the tyranny, of the home meant liberating them into the public sectors of the national economy. They participated directly in the drive toward urbanization and the transformation of the old towns and marketplaces into regional industrial and agricultural centers. The contribution of women to these processes was both encouraged and increasingly made possible by the establishment of social services, such as nurseries and day-care needs.[21] The breaking down of traditional family and behavior patterns related to the raising of children made available the option of continuing education for some women even after they had found employment outside the home. Evening schools and correspondence courses, available to villager and city dweller alike, further helped reduce the differences in educational opportunities that had developed since the 1920s between regions. The spread of schools and institutes into rural and even mountainous areas and the close proximity and availability of advanced degree programs in the major industrial and agricultural centers of the country meant that access to cultural, economic, and political organizations above the local and even district levels had reached women (as well as men) in all parts of the country. Thus, where Zog had failed to consolidate his power in a traditional, illiterate, and for the most part impoverished society, Hoxha and the party he headed within a single generation had propelled those Albanians loyal to it on a course that increasingly demanded the active participation of all its citizens, male and female alike, in the new socialist society that was being created. That the party succeeded at all in pushing forward Albania's cultural "leap forward" was proof enough of Hoxha's radical, but hardly "fossilized," government.[22]

Albanian publications focus attention on these developments with fairly impressive statistics. Women's access to education at all levels has improved greatly, to be sure, in the other countries of Eastern Europe, but that access was nowhere more limited than in Albania before 1957, the year Albania's first university was established. In 1977–78, for example, Albanian statistics show that of the 94,422 workers enrolled in schools of various types both in rural and urban areas, 40 percent were women.[23] The 56,238 women attending secondary schools were almost 56,000 more than were enrolled at the end of Zog's brief rule.[24] In 1938 no women were studying in what vocational schools there were. In 1977 nearly 23,000 women were enrolled in such schools.[25] The social and psychological distances they had traveled to get there speak louder than their number. All in all, 47 percent of Albania's school population were women in 1978; 44 percent of those in advanced programs were women.[26] Other statistics frequently quoted clearly point to advances women have made as a direct result of their educational levels in production and management roles in agriculture and industry and in some fields dominated by women, such as education and textiles.[27]

Interestingly enough, as in other East European countries, advances made by women in the Communist party itself in fact lagged behind the changes taking place elsewhere. But from 1967 to 1976 party membership in Albania for women more than doubled (from 12 percent to 27 percent), as did the percentage of women deputies elected to the People's Assembly (from 16 to 33 percent).[28] Hoxha's speech, clearly, was beginning to have its desired effect among loyal party members. The question of the emancipation of women assumed very practical implications in the mid-1970s. Between 1973 and 1976 upheavals in the country's power structure, particularly in the cultural, military, and economic sectors, resulted in changes that involved ever-growing numbers of professionally trained women at the lowest levels of the ministries affected. The political turmoil prompting these changes also propelled a few women, whose loyalty to the party or to factions in the party did not escape the attention of Hoxha and Shehu (and their wives) in Tiranë, to the top of the party and state structure. The significance of this new wave of leaders produced by the purges of the mid-1970s is evident if one keeps in mind the first hesitant steps taken just a decade earlier by women's agitprop teams. Party members had to cope with a new reality, namely, the decision of Hoxha, Shehu, and Kapo to elevate women who would help guarantee the "steel-like ideological and organizational unity of the party" to the highest national as well as district-level positions of political influence.

The crackdown against intellectualism, "opportunism," technocratism, and elitism fell first where there would be the weakest threat to those at the top, that is, in education. The Minister of Education, Fadil Paçrami, was one of the first alleged to have joined the "traitor groups" that were beginning to be exposed publicly in 1973. He was replaced by a woman,[29] as were some of the others who lost their positions in the mid-1970s. The careers of three women in particular mark a clear departure from past heroine images.

The one woman whose achievements are perhaps most familiar to Albania's new reading public and television audience is Themi Thomai, a personality connected with the government's successful efforts to turn once malarial lowlands into the nation's breadbasket. As the head of a major agricultural cooperative in the district of Lushnje, she attracted the attention of the leader of the party, who held the Këmishtaj cooperative up as a model to be emulated in the fertile, but not expansive, lowland areas. Her successes in agriculture were not only publicly recognized but also officially rewarded: in April 1976 she was appointed Minister of Agriculture. In taking her seat on the Council of Ministers she completed her rapid rise to the highest organ of the central government. In November of the same year she was elected to the party's Central Committee, joining two other women there who had been appointed candidate members of the Central Committee five years earlier.

One of these women, Lenka Çuko, also came from Lushnje in south central Albania. Her political credentials were more impressive than those of Thomai. In October 1974 she was elected to the People's Assembly; she also was appointed to its Commission on Foreign Affairs, on which Nexhmije Hoxha served. In November 1976 she was elevated to the country's politburo as an alternate member. In Lenka Çuko's case, party loyalty and administrative competence resulted in promotions unusual for women in communist states. She learned well the lessons stressed by the directors of Tiranë's Institute for Marxist-Leninist Studies and the Lenin Higher Party School during the turmoil of the mid-1970s.

Both party and personal connections, to be sure, remained a fact of life in Albania in this period. The sudden rise to prominence of yet another personality about whom relatively little is known further illustrates the importance of these connections. In April 1976, along with Thomai, Tefta Cami was appointed to the Council of Ministers when she became Minister of Education and Culture. In November of the same year she was elected to the party's Central Committee. Her political background, unlike Thomai's, was rather extensive. In 1972, just two months after her rise to the party's Central Committee as a candidate member, Cami was named party committee secretary in the district of Berat in central Albania. Two years later, we find, she was elected to the People's Assembly from the district of Dibër, which is located along the sensitive Yugoslav border.[30] In 1974, when she was placed on the Commission for Education and Culture, she came into direct contact with Fiqrete Shehu who then served as head of the commission. Cami, then, like Çuko, through personal contacts made at district as well as state levels, had by 1976 established strong links to the top leadership of the government. Her close relationship to Fiqrete Shehu in particular helps explain her sudden rise to the Council of Ministers after the fall of Paçrami. In November of the same year Cami, like Thomai, was elected to the Central Committee of the party.

The rapid rise to power of two of the women just mentioned, namely Çuko and Cami, may be tracked primarily along a political course, one no doubt shaken by Mehmet Shehu's "suicide." That of the third rising star, Themi Thomai, stems for the most part from her operation of the Këmishtaj agricultural cooperative, which still remains a favorite showpiece of the government. In the case of all three women, however, one fact is worthy of special note: their achievements came as the result of their own training and professional experience, not that of their husbands. Their achievements were realized in part because of connections inside the party and loyalty to its top leadership, but professional competence was now also required.

The three women we have drawn attention to belong to the class of '76, the class Vito Kapo just three years earlier had hinted was already well on its way to entering the mainstream of political life in Albania. By 1979 the number of women on the Central Committee of the Albanian Party of Labor had in fact tripled since 1967.[31] At this point not much is known of the women who have assumed managerial responsibilities in various economic sectors, like Thomai, or who have begun their rise through party ranks. Nor do we know very much about the extent to which the greater visibility women have achieved in national politics as the result of the party's explicit campaign to increase the number of women in prominent positions has been accompanied by an increase in women's role in politics at lower levels or the extent of popular support for leadership efforts to change women's roles. Given the progress made by women in Albania over the last fifteen years, however, it seems unlikely that further efforts to emancipate them—that is, integrate them into the labor force and the party—will not continue under Hoxha's successor, Ramiz Alia.

The outcome of these efforts will depend, no doubt, on how the country as a whole copes with its internal as well as external problems. It will also depend on whether the gains women have made in terms of greater visibility in national political positions are reflected at lower levels, the extent to which the population supports the changes mandated by the party, and, a factor that the leadership in Albania has not addressed in any systematic way, the extent to which women's new opportunities in the economy, education, and politics are reflected in change in the sexual division of labor in the family.

Conclusion

To sum up, then, we may say that the decade 1945–55 witnessed the first steps Albanian women took to emancipate themselves from the disastrous (as all Albanians see it) legacy of Ottoman abuse and Zogist neglect. They left their courtyards now not to fight but to receive an education. By the 1960s the new State University in Tiranë stood as a symbol of how far the country itself had progressed from the time when the missionary schools in the 1890s had first made Albanian books available to Albanian children. The decade 1966–76 marked the rise of professionally trained Albanian women in the country's power structure. Regardless of how much power they actually have—something that is impossible to determine from the outside looking in—it seems safe to conclude that with the passing of Kapo and Shehu and Hoxha, women in the party and state bureaucracies will owe their promotions more to professional experience and competence and less to family connections or clan allegiances, already a thing of the past.

Clearly, many inequalities continue to exist in Albania. Women's influx into the labor force has not led to the elimination of all barriers to equality in the workplace. Nor does it appear to have been reflected in any significant change in the division of duties within the home. In overall terms, the number of women in positions of political responsibility still is fairly small, and the characteristics of women who have achieved leadership positions, as well as their areas of specialization, do not differ greatly from those of women in similar positions in other communist states. At the same time, considering their position in Albania in the precommunist period, the gains they have made are impressive. Albanian women, within the framework of a rigid Stalinist state, have come a long way from managing their households and from struggling to preserve in their own subculture their identities as human beings. To come as far as they have, it is worth remembering, the Islamic world they had been born into had to be destroyed.

9

Daniel N. Nelson

Women in Local Communist Politics in Romania and Poland

Studies of women's political roles in many societies have concluded that women are less politically active than men.[1] Although higher educational levels close the gap between the sexes regarding their concern for and interest in politics, it remains generally true that women are less likely than men to enter "fully into the political realm."[2] Such an assessment is valid as well in Eastern Europe and the Soviet Union. Notwithstanding encouragement of female participation in principle by ruling Communist parties, data at the national level indicate that women are not politically emancipated in Eastern Europe; they constitute, at most, 30 percent of Communist party membership, while one in four or five Central Committee members or governmental ministers may be a woman. Even after the purposeful recruitment of women into the Romanian Central Committee during the 1970s, for example, a six-fold increase brought their presence in the Central Committee to just 24.5 percent.[3]

To let our judgments rest on such aggregate portraits of communist systems would be inadequate because, despite limitations on the entry of women into the national political elite, women in communist countries, as well as in other political systems, appear to be more active at lower levels of politics.[4] In both community politics and workplace governance in communist states, women are believed to have greater participatory roles. Because women appear to play a larger role at lower levels of the political system and because the forms and extent of local activity can enlarge our knowledge of the relationship between regimes and citizens, I examine the political roles of women at subnational levels. My data and examples are drawn from Poland and Romania—cases with historical, cultural, and socioeconomic distinctions such that one can regard generalizations drawn from their experience with some confidence. In the pages to follow I discuss both how and to what extent women are active in the local political life of communist states, as well as what explains that degree and kind of activity.

The Forms and Extent of Women's Political Activity at the Local Level in Communist States

Before examining women's political activities, it is important to understand the nature of citizen involvement in general in communist states. Political behavior can be autonomous, brought about by coercion, or produced by means of deception. When someone engages in political activity such as voting, attending a rally, etc., one might distinguish among the origins of such behavior following a typology proposed by Vernon Aspaturian. Arguing that a generic term such as "involvement" avoids biases of the West toward autonomy of action, Aspaturian suggests that mobilized involvement and manipulated involvement are most characteristic of communist states. Participatory involvement, while not excluded from communist systems, is less frequent.[5]

Participatory activity[6] thus denotes autonomous behavior—i.e., that which is not produced by environmental pressures—being performed by highly involved citizens. Participants, following such a denotation, have entered the political realm of their own volition and with a sense of efficacy. Manipulated activity is deceived behavior being performed by a citizen artificially involved whose autonomy has been compromised by falsely being convinced that his or her behavior has systemic importance. Mobilized activity is coerced behavior performed by citizens who are involved little or not at all in such behavior but who nevertheless obey when told to vote, join organizations, attend meetings, etc., because of actual or threatened coercion.

It is thus accurate but too simple to say that men dominate political activity in Eastern Europe and the USSR, since the kinds of political behavior women engage in will vary. If one can identify a higher proportion of involved, autonomous behavior among politically active women in some areas or times than others, we need to account for these differences.

Between 1973 and 1979 I had several opportunities to conduct in-depth interviews with local-level political actors in Romania and Poland. In previous reports on this research,[7] I have referred to samples without distinguishing subjects by gender. For the purposes of this paper, I have tabulated the number of women in local politics with whom I spoke during three periods of research (see table 9.1). Most of these individuals were selected because of their status as deputies to a people's council (*consiliul popular* or *rada narodowe*). Although randomness was compromised by many factors,[8] I am satisfied that I spoke with women who were distributed over a wide range of educational, career, age, and other variables.

The presence of women in local communist politics has increased sub-

Table 9.1 Distribution of interviews with politically active women in Poland and Romania

Level[a]	1973 Romania[b]	1977 Poland[c]	1978 Romania[d]	Totals by level
Judeţ/Województwo (county/province)	14	3	12	29
Municipiu and Oraş/Miast (city and towns)	25	11	13	49
Comuna/gmina (commune)	14	5	7	26
Totals (by year)	53	19	32	104

Source: Author's interviews, 1973, 1977, 1978.
a. Some individuals hold posts at more than one level.
b. Interviews conducted in Timiş, Cluj, Braşov, and Iaşi judeţe.
c. These interviews did not consist solely of deputies but also individuals in local administration; they were conducted in and near Warsaw, Cracow, and Poznań.
d. Some of the 32 individuals in the 1978 Romania sample were the same individuals interviewed in 1973. In this table, therefore, they are counted twice in the Totals by level column.

stantially since the early post-World War II period in both Romania and Poland. As late as 1958 in Poland, for example, women held fewer than 6 percent of all people's council seats and fewer than 2 percent of the subnational leadership posts. At that time the most advantageous environments for women's political activity appeared to be in urban settlements or quarters and urban districts (the former typically constituting new suburban apartment developments). A decade later those figures had changed considerably, such that almost 19 percent of council seats and about one in twenty presidia posts were filled by women. The rural communes (*gromady*), however, brought the mean down, whereas urban settings continued to exhibit higher levels of female political activity (e.g., 28.5 percent of members of councils in cities with provincial status, such as Łódź, Cracow, etc., were women).[9] By 1977, one *osiedle* (urban settlement) outside Poznan had a council in which women constituted 40 percent of the membership,[10] and more than a quarter of all people's councils members in Poland were women.

But in Poland, the distribution continues to be skewed in two principal directions. Women's political activity (as indicated in people's council data) is higher in cities and suburbs; it is also higher in less important roles (i.e., outside leadership positions). Female political activity does not, then, vary merely with how local the setting, since Polish communes exhibited the smallest proportion of council seats and leadership roles filled by women. Within the narrow confines of urban neighborhoods, however, women were not active.

Romania also shows an increase in the proportion of council seats held by women but does not exhibit such a dramatic urban-rural cleavage in women's political activity. As with Romanian Communist party (RCP) membership, central decisions mandated an increase in seats held by women during the 1970s. Each election raised somewhat the percent of women in councils at all levels. In Judeţul Timiş, for example, the 1977 elections uniformly raised by several percentage points the proportion of women in councils throughout that country vis-à-vis the 1975 election (overall from a mean of about 29.8 percent to just above 32 percent).[11] Nevertheless, Romanian rural communes do not exhibit lower percentages of council seats held by women, in contrast to Poland. In a highly urbanized county such as Cluj, for example, women held slightly *lower* proportions of council seats in municipalities and towns than in communes in 1969 (about 30 percent to 31 percent, respectively).[12] The *judeţ*-level council, i.e., the highest level of local assembly, was 25.6 percent female. Almost a decade, and several local elections later, women occupied 27 percent of *judeţ* seats and about a third of urban-based constituencies, while over 38 percent of commune deputies were women.

These contrasts between Romania and Poland may be attributable to the predominant authority of Catholicism in the Polish countryside, which may encourage women to remain outside the political realm due to familial values. Perhaps the demand for additional labor sources in Romania, drawing heavily on rural women, necessitates greater presence in communal organs. Put simply, however, women have more opportunities to become politically active in Polish urban environments but slightly less in Romanian cities and towns than in rural areas. In both cases the proportion of council seats held by women has increased over time (a change beginning somewhat earlier in Poland than in Romania), but such an increase is of uniform cross-nationally or internally.

As tables 9.2 and 9.3 illustrate, women in local politics in Romania are well-educated and rather young relative to men.[13] Overall, male deputies more often have only elementary (through eighth grade) education, but about the same proportion have university training as women. The ages of women in people's councils are also generally lower—or were, at least, in past years. The experience and educational levels of Romanian women in national-level roles has also risen, as discussed by Mary Ellen Fischer in this volume.

These Romanian data parallel the American finding that women active in local politics are well-educated, differentiated from the general popula-

Table 9.2 Education levels of politically active Romanian women and men in people's councils (in percentages)

	1973 sample		1978 sample		Cumulative	
	Men $N=145$	Women $N=53$	Men $N=57$	Women $N=32$	Men $N=202$	Women $N=85$
University degree or some university	34	30	35	47	35	36
Complete secondary or some secondary (lyceum)	44	58	46	50	44	55
Complete primary (şcoala generala)	22	11	19	3	21	8

Source: Author's interviews, 1973 and 1978.

tion in that regard much more so than are male political activists.[14] In the smaller Polish sample, women were also well-educated, as almost half had university degrees. (These interviews, however, included local administrators as well and are therefore not directly comparable.)

Such political actors among women are not, by any means, less qualified as a group in educational terms than men. With the advantages of relative youth and high educational levels, there appear few reasons for women not to have an equal chance for leadership posts and broad responsibilities. But the roles women fill in local politics remain, in several crucial respects, unequal.

Women in political life also clearly tend to be recruited for different reasons than men. While men are recruited due to their important socioeconomic roles, women are much more likely than men to have socioeconomic backgrounds outside the bureaucratic-managerial elite. One Polish sociologist has identified two categories among people's council members (*radni*): the *specjalisci* (specialists) and the *posrednicy* (intermediaries). Specialists are defined as: "deputies whose professional skills . . . have been confirmed by holding managerial posts (at the time of election). These managerial posts include . . . director (*kierownik*) of an independent unit, vice director of a *powiat*-level institution or director of a *województwo*-level institution. Also included are members of professions, scientific workers, officers of the Polish Army and citizen's militia. Completed higher education (*wykształcenie wyzsze*) was an additional condition for deputies' inclusion in this category."[15]

"Intermediates" are defined as: "individuals who do not hold any manage-

Table 9.3 Ages of politically active Romanian women and men in people's councils (in percentages)

	1973 sample		1978 sample		Cumulative	
	Men $N=145$	Women $N=53$	Men $N=57$	Women $N=32$	Men $N=202$	Women $N=85$
65 years and over	5	0	7	3	6	1
46 through 64 years	42	30	47	31	44	31
31 through 45 years	45	58	37	53	43	57
30 and under	8	11	9	13	8	12

Source: Author's interviews, 1973 and 1978.

rial posts, and those who hold managerial posts at a level not higher than basic (e.g., foreman in a factory) . . . these deputies usually are not highly competent, and by their presence in the council assure the desired configuration of characteristics. . . ."[16] In the research that led to such typologies, almost 2,200 deputies were surveyed of whom 74 percent were men and about 26 percent women (which was very close to the national mean among councils in urban *powiats*—the pre-1972 subdivision of provinces).[17] As table 9.4 indicates, women are underrepresented among specialists (only 15 percent) relative to the proportion of deputies sampled who were female and overrepresented in the category of intermediaries (32 percent).

Another way to consider the same data, of course, is to look at the percentage of both men and women deputies who fall into the specialist and intermediary categories. As table 9.5 illustrates, 19 percent of male deputies are specialists following the above-cited definitions, whereas only 10 percent of women in councils can be so classified. Once again, women are seen to be underrepresented. This perspective, which controls for the proportion of women among all deputies, suggests that the rate of specialists among female deputies is about one in ten, whereas for men the rate is doubled (almost two in ten). As discussed below, these data also point to the much higher proportion of men than women in councils who enter the top leadership at the local level.

For the Romanian case, I had noted a similar dichotomy on the basis of 1973 research on people's council deputies, referring to categories of deputies who were "the needed" and "fillers." The former constitute, in my view, people who are in the councils "primarily as a recognition of their positions in state organs or in their careers. . . . These are the educated, the expert and the loyal; managing and directing developmental/modernization efforts, their integration into local political institutions is essential."[18]

Table 9.4 Specialists and intermediaries among Polish deputies by sex (in percentages)

Sex	Specialists $N=371$	Intermediaries $N=893$	All deputies $N=2{,}195$
Male	85	68	74
Female	15	32	26

Source: Krzysztof Jasiewicz, *Role Społeczne Radnych Wojewodzkich Rad Narodowych* (Wrocław: Zakład Narodowy im. Ossolinskich, 1979), p. 67.

Fillers, by contrast, are "needed by the local political elite as a group but not as individuals. Abstractly, they partly fulfill a requirement of governments everywhere—to legitimize rule through representation of a broad popular base."[19] Of the women deputies interviewed, who constituted 28 percent of the sample, I found that about a fourth could be classified as needed or elites by my definition (see table 9.6), although the proportion varied considerably among *județe*. A much higher proportion of male deputies interviewed were elites or needed. Both men and women in this sample, of course, were drawn disproportionately from these upper echelons since the sample was skewed toward municipalities. At first glance, this might suggest that there are more opportunities for entry into political activity by professional and managerial women in Romania than in Poland (compared to the 10 to 11 percent of female deputies who are specialists and leaders in the Jasiewicz sample). Again, however, these results may be biased due to an urban overrepresentation in the sample. I think that the differences between Poland and Romania are, in fact, not as large as these samples would indicate; if Romanian people's councils are an arena for more activity by professional women than are Polish councils, the difference is likely to be marginal at best.

Women, then, are less often than men political activists because of their prior demonstration of competence or managerial experience. This seems to imply a pervasive, unstated expectation that women in political life are there, as Jasiewicz said, to "assure the desired configuration of characteristics" and, hence, to "legitimize rule through representation of a broad popular base."[20] Despite relatively high educational levels, women who enter local political life have not had the same degree of managerial and professional experience as have men. In the 1973 Romanian sample, for instance, 30 percent of the female deputies interviewed had university education (incomplete or complete), but only a fourth could be called needed by virtue of their previous or current careers. That both of these percentages are probably higher than the population of deputies, of course,

Table 9.5 Men and women among specialists and intermediaries (Poland) (in percentages)

Category	Men N=1,630	Women N=565	All deputies N=2,195
Leaders*	5	1	4
Specialists	19	10	17
Intermediaries	37	50	41
Others**	39	39	39

Source: Adapted by the author from Jasiewicz, p. 67.
*Members, People's Council presidium.
**See Jasiewicz's comments (p. 64) regarding deputies who fit into neither specialist nor intermediary category.

does not alter their relationship—that high educational achievement has not translated into socioeconomic roles similar to those of men or equal types of activity in local politics. Such a fundamental inequality vis-à-vis men is as persistent and pervasive in Romania as in Poland. It is, moreover, an inequality apparent also in the United States where women in political life typically have differed from their male colleagues in terms of social background characteristics and, therefore, fill lesser roles in legislatures, etc., and at higher levels of politics in Eastern Europe.[21]

That women, more than men, tend to be fillers in local councils does not mean that they *cannot* be participatory activists, but it will be distinctly harder. People whom I identified as fillers were recruited because their presence was useful, not because their participation was needed. But the performance of certain tasks as a deputy—committee work, constituency services, etc.—offers the potential for a filler (in the eyes of those in whose jurisdiction that post is found) to be a participant. Recruitment in the status of a filler does not condemn a woman solely to manipulated or mobilized forms of political activism—but those are precisely the expectations of persons (most likely males) who control recruitment for local assembly seats. Politically savvy women in communist states, however, may utilize such expectations of males in order to conceal the forms and extent of their participatory activism. A female deputy in Braşov who was a persuasive and efficient advocate for her constituency, for example, had held no managerial post and was given no high-level responsibility in the local council or party. She had been, I am certain, recruited because the people's council composition required a younger woman with complete higher education who taught school. As a deputy, however, she took initiatives to improve her constituency's neighborhood and utilized intelligence mixed with

Table 9.6 Elites, needed, and fillers among male and female Romanian People's Council deputies (in percentages)

	Men			Women		
	Elites + needed		Fillers	Elites + needed		Fillers
N=37		N=27			N=10	
Timiş	44		56	20		80
N=47		N=33			N=14	
Cluj	33		67	21		79
N=50		N=40			N=10	
Braşov	37		63	20		80
N=64		N=45			N=19	
Iaşi	36		64	32		68
Cumulative	37		63	25		75

Source: Author's judgments based upon interviews, 1973.

charm to get quick action on requests by citizens in her district.

In general, however, once they have entered into the political life of their community, town, or province, the roles played by women in local Polish and Romanian politics are limited vertically and horizontally. As in other political systems, women have proportionately fewer opportunities to rise in the local political hierarchy; they also are concentrated in a more narrow spectrum of duties.[22]

Among the roles in people's councils, a deputy can be a member of a standing commission, a chairman of a standing commission, a member of the executive committee, or a member of the permanent bureau. The latter role (member, permanent bureau) is reserved for local party elites, who are also in the executive committee, and some of the needed (specialist) deputies. Those specialists and others of similar background typically will chair standing commissions. All ordinary deputies are in a standing commission, membership in which connotes no special status. Of forty-two local members of permanent bureaus (the highest local government organ in Romania) interviewed in 1973, however, only two were women. Among other female activists interviewed (those in table 9.1), only five were members of council executive committees and only a few were either presidents or vice-presidents of standing commissions.[23] As noted earlier, electoral law changes reduced the number of deputies overall in Romania, and greater emphasis was placed on increasing the proportion of women on state and party bodies. After the elections of 1975 and 1977, the proportion of women among people's council executive committee and local party committee members apparently rose to about 25 percent nationwide.[24] In 1979 women became first secretaries in two *judeţe*, and the Ceauşescu regime's efforts to raise women's representation at upper echelons of national government were generally mirrored at the local level.

However, it does not appear that top local leadership roles (i.e., members of party bureaus and permanent bureaus of people's councils) are filled by women proportionately more often now than a decade ago. Indeed, one negative way in which to view such changes is exemplified by a hypothetical case based on the Romanian system. If there are more activist women now than there were ten years ago in local political life, the proportion of those activists who are tapped for leadership posts will have improved little and could actually have declined, given the smaller size of the councils and the continued overrepresentation of males generally. A male deputy in the late 1970s, then, was slightly *more* likely to have an opportunity for leadership duties than earlier, notwithstanding the greater proportion of women in the council as a whole. Local organs can be expected to exhibit similar trends. Were this circumstance to persist, the vertical mobility of female activists would have increased little or not at all as the result of or despite the greater proportion of women in local political life.

Perhaps more noteworthy, however, are horizontal restrictions on the breadth of responsibilities for women. In this respect, the experiences of women in local-level elites in Romania and Poland resemble those of women leaders in the United States and Western Europe.[25] As at the national level in Romania and other East European countries, women are most frequently assigned roles in one of several arenas—education, culture, or light industry. That women in Eastern Europe (and the Soviet Union) constitute the vast majority of those employed in such fields as education and textile manufacturing, for example, is an official rationale for such assignments. The uniformity with which such responsibilities are given to women, however, is striking. In the Romanian and Polish samples cited earlier, for instance, almost half of over one hundred individuals had primary responsibilities in education, culture, or local commerce.[26] This horizontal limitation on female political activity is also evident in the standing commission assignments for people's council deputies that appear to exhibit the same tendency. Recalling that women constituted perhaps 30 percent of most of Romanian people's councils, women deputies are heavily overrepresented (more than 50 percent of the members) in commissions concerning education, culture, and sport and somewhat overrepresented (31 to 50 percent) on commissions dealing with local industry and community services, health, labor, and social insurance. Women were underrepresented (fewer than 30 percent) in standing commissions such as budgeting and finance, construction, planning and roads, juridical-administrative, and agriculture and animal husbandry.[27]

Fully developed explanations for differences between women's political activity in Romania and Poland are, for now, beyond the reach of available data. I think it warranted, however, to expect that urban-rural differences in the political activity of Polish women could be explained in large part on the basis of cultural variables (the church) and economic necessity (the private ownership of agriculture in Poland, which means that more women in rural areas must contend full-time with household tasks, childrearing, and agricultural labor). That a *judeţ* such as Iaşi may exhibit a higher degree of needed (or specialist) backgrounds among women who are political activists perhaps can be explained on the basis of that region's rapid socioeconomic change.[28] It is at least plausible to expect that high rates of socioeconomic change would relate to needs for greater activity in local government by the professional and managerial stratum, regardless of gender. Simply put, rapidly escalating needs for expertise in regions where relatively little of it has existed in the past may increase the opportunity for and the necessity of recruitment of specialist women.

The forms and extent of women's political activity in local communist politics nevertheless have some generalizable characteristics. Despite rising educational levels, women were denied for many years even a modest presence in local political life. In Poland during the 1960s and in Romania during the following decade, the proportion of people's council deputy and local party committee posts held by women increased, trends evident in central party and state organs as well. But women who enter local political life in both systems continue, to a greater extent than men, to be intermediaries or fillers (not specialist/needed). And, once active, women enter into the local leadership stratum relatively less frequently (although this, too, has changed to the benefit of women during the 1960s in Poland and the 1970s in Romania). Responsibilities assigned to women, whether in the leadership stratum or not, have been weighted toward arenas traditionally defined as women's issues such as education and culture or economic concerns related to industries in which female employees dominate (light industry).

Involvement and Autonomy in the Political Activity of Women

Thus far, I have not discussed either the psychological or environmental dimensions of women's political activity. To what degree is local-level political activity among women in communist systems autonomous? To what degree, that is, is women's behavior in local political life characterized by the psychological involvement of those who are active?

Answers to these difficult questions must be indirect and tentative—

indirect because data are not available with which to test the subjective orientations of women regarding their political roles per se and tentative because the longitudinal and cross-national inferences that we *can* make are very restricted. As noted above, women who enter local politics in Poland and Romania are, more often than men, regarded by those who control recruitment as fillers or intermediaries. This finding raises the suspicion that those who determine who will be nominees for local political roles do not seek women who will be motivated to participate autonomously. That does not deny, of course, that some women are participatory activists at the local level. Neither do such data mean that other women who enter as manipulated activists could not, once in the political realm, undertake other roles of their own volition with deeply felt convictions. But the recruitment to and replenishment of local political roles reveals systemic biases across nations against women likely to be most capable of participating fully, i.e., women who have already demonstrated such capacity in professional or managerial roles.

Some women have entered political life without enthusiasm, primarily because environmental circumstances left them little choice. Even women with specialist backgrounds can be mobilized into political activity—the school director, enterprise accountant, or physician who because of her professional or managerial post in a community is nominated by the party's front organization to be a deputy, is elected, and is then made chairperson of a people's council standing commission. But in the same years I have interviewed such individuals, I have also met women for whom political activity is a long-term concern entered into out of deep personal commitment.[29] Although I cannot be precise about such judgments, it seems likely that a higher proportion of the needed women deputies have such commitments and exhibit more lengthy involvement in politics, while very few of the fillers are likely to view political activity as a long-term concern.

A recitation of individual cases, however, is less persuasive than are data regarding women's participation in enterprise governance. Studies of this issue in Eastern Europe indicate that women are much less likely than men to make complaints in the workplace; they also less often express dissatisfaction, have a greater inclination to conform, and are more concerned than men about relations with colleagues and bosses.[30] As in the United States, it seems likely that the explanation for such findings must combine socialization and structural variables.

Deferential attitudes regarding governance at the workplace appear to be related to stronger commitments among women than men to familial and parental obligations. Although women are motivated by material rewards at the workplace as are men, many East European women regard the primary duty or obligation of women as that of motherhood and wife, with obligations of one's profession and of citizenship lower.[31] Such attitudes may reflect the impact of socialization to women's roles and the view that the exercise of authority is primarily a male prerogative.

Socialization to more general female roles also appears to be a strong impediment to autonomous political action on the part of women in Eastern Europe as well as in the United States, for it may lead women to defer to men in political life as well as in the workplace. Given the view in East European cultures that politics and, particularly, the exercise of authority are unfeminine activities, East European women are less likely than men to have obtained the necessary skills to be efficacious political actors. The impact of socialization is further reinforced in Eastern Europe by the recruitment patterns already discussed that channel women, more than men, into filler roles in local politics.

Deference is not, of course, a quality simply measured. There may be several types of deference tapped by questions addressing women in the community or workplace—deference that deceives superiors (usually men) and thereby manipulates them, deference that is task, time, or locale-specific (outside of which, the subject will evince little or no deference), and deference that exhibits subservience. I label these, respectively, as (1) offensive deference, (2) defensive deference, and (3) submissive deference.

In all cases, deference is an attitude whereby decisions and choices are left to others, i.e., superiors. Translated into the political arena, offensive deference could be invoked by a woman who in local politics is a participatory activist. The mobilized activist might utilize defensive deference; brought into an environment where she is uncertain by a sense of coercion, she defers to authorities while in that activity but in no other behavior. A manipulated activist, because of the deception that brought her into the political realm, might not recognize the utility of offensive or defensive deference and may, indeed, submit entirely to prevailing authority.

The relationship of East European women to authority found in studies at the workplace may well be linked to the distribution of their political activity among participatory, manipulated, and mobilized types. Were such defensive and submissive attitudes of deference and familial orientations transferred directly into the political realm, one could expect women more than men to be susceptible to mobilization and/or manipulation. The transfer is not, of course, direct since the subset of women engaged in political life is substantially better educated than the population of women (as are the male political activists). Education may mitigate any views and values prevalent among women in the workforce that might lead them to be less participatory in enterprise governance, although data reported by Jerry Hough imply that this effect of education is not as great for women as it is for men in the Soviet case.[32] But it would be erroneous, in any case, to presume that such deferential attitudes can be erased entirely by education or political activity itself. The socialization of women, which insists that they defer to men in political life, is mitigated but not eliminated by education and training. As in the United States, an important barrier to women engaging in political activity "is their own perceptions about what they should and should not be doing in politics."[33]

Issue Orientations

In Eastern Europe women and men seem to give different priorities to public issues. Neither gender exhibits (at least as expressed to researchers) broadly distributed concerns. Romanian and Polish activists (people's council deputies) interviewed during the 1970s were asked, for example, "What are the most important problems facing your community in the next one to three years?" (see table 9.7). Women most frequently cited education, housing, and provisioning. Although men also frequently cited such problem areas, they outscored women in responses focused on industrial development, transportation, the pursuit of developmental plans, agriculture mechanization, and a few other items. Women were almost always the only activists to mention childcare and community aesthetics.[34]

Evidence from other communist countries also leads one to suspect that political concerns vary by gender. Years ago, for example, Inkeles and Geiger found that only a small proportion (5 percent) of signed letters published in Soviet newspapers were signed by women exclusively, while men (alone or with male cosigners) were responsible for 89 percent of letters. Moreover, a majority of the female-signed letters pertained to consumer items and public services "with which women are most intimately involved in their daily lives."[35] By the mid-1970s, women were somewhat more frequent writers, but they still concentrated on a narrow band of socioeconomic topics.[36]

From such results, one cannot infer necessarily that the issue orientations of all politically active people differ by gender or that the male and female populations as a whole would reflect those priorities. One could argue, for example, that women leaders are assigned responsibilities at the local level in part on the basis of their ability or willingness to fit into the expectations of those having the *nomenklatura* (the power of assignment and dismissal) for the post. The restrictions on women's free time *because* of domestic responsibilities also have been found to restrict the breadth and intensity of their political concerns.[37]

There is a rich literature debating the genesis of such differences between the political interest and activism of men and women in the United States.[38]

Table 9.7 Views on "What are the most important problems in your community—next 1–3 years?" (in percentages)

	N=232* Men	N=104* Women
Economic[a]	22	13
Quality of life[b]	34	46
Education	23	28
General development/modernization[c]	18	10
Other[d]	2	3
	99%	100%

*Romanian samples from 1973 and 1978 combined with 1977 Polish interviews.
a. Economic answers included those focused on agriculture or industry.
b. Quality of life answers included those focused on public services, housing, provisioning, health and sanitation, roads and transportation, and urban planning.
c. General development/modernization answers were those that used such terms without offering a specific substantive area.
d. Other includes finance, parks, democratization, day-care centers, etc.

There are also several possible explanations of these differences in Eastern Europe and the Soviet Union. These indicators may suggest that women are more concerned with the most immediate social and economic problems—where one works, where one shops, and where one lives—whereas men tend to have a different set of priorities. Such a portrait might be construed as a kind of parochialism among women who are engaged in local political activity in communist states arising from socialization or the continued differences in men's and women's domestic roles. Alternatively, it is possible that women choose to place emphasis on issues in which they think their individual and collective influence can be maximized.

The same kind of data also suggests that there are certain structural explanations for these differences. There appears to be a concerted bias against women entering local state organs compared to workers' councils and against women writing about certain topics to newspapers. Similarly, responses by women to questions about problem areas can also be a reflection of systemic biases institutionalized by the procedures of recruitment into local politics. Until more data allow testing of these explanations, we must remain uncertain about these inferences. Whether one explains these data by a socialization or situational/structural model, however, it is clear that men and women play different roles in communist political life.

Conclusion

The presence of women has increased in the local political life of communist states, although there are differences across nations in the timing of this increase and within nations in its extent at different levels. But a rising proportion of well-educated and youthful women in local state and party organs has not meant increased access to leadership posts relative to male activists, equal recruitment from managerial and professional career backgrounds, or broadly distributed responsibilities. Although women's participation in mobilized and/or manipulated political activity increasingly has been sought during the past decade and a half in Poland and Romania, women in local communist politics apparently face continued systemic obstacles to autonomous or participatory activism. These systemic biases, including lesser recruitment of professional women, limited committee specialization in people's councils, and lower rates of entry into local leadership posts, may help to produce the lower involvement and autonomy of politically active women. At the very least, the perpetuation of systemic obstacles to equal political participatory activity by women is reinforced by what appears to be greater deference toward authority on the part of women and issue orientations among women that differ considerably from those of men who are activists.

Women in Poland and Romania, then, have a higher rate of political activity than they did fifteen or twenty years ago. But, as at the national level, being a women in local communist politics appears not to imply equal participation. Surely, neither Poland nor Romania are, themselves, typical of all communist states in that regard. The fact that women's political activities at the local level are similar in these two countries, however, despite the important differences in their histories, culture, levels of socioeconomic development, and linkage to Soviet foreign policy, suggests that women's roles in local politics also may be similar in other East European countries.

10

Barbara W. Jancar

Women in the Opposition in Poland and Czechoslovakia in the 1970s

The 1970s witnessed the expansion of women's involvement in opposition activity throughout the Soviet bloc. In the Soviet Union women have been active in religious and human rights opposition movements since the sixties, and the last decade has seen the development of a Western-type feminist movement. In Eastern Europe, on the other hand, the participation of women in opposition has been more typical of the seventies.

Nowhere does the emergence of the woman opposition activist seem more pronounced than in Poland and Czechoslovakia. One reason may be that it is only in these two East European nations that an identifiable movement for human, civil, and political rights has developed.[1] Opposition in East Germany, Hungary, and Romania, for example, has so far been either the passive variant, an attitude of mind and behavior manifested by the population at large, or confined essentially to the cultural sphere.[2] It has also been largely individual. By contrast, the Polish and Czechoslovak oppositions have possessed leadership, platform, and diversified membership.

Polish opposition dates back to the first days of Communist rule. However, the trade union Solidarity is better understood as an outgrowth of the intellectual and worker oppositions of the seventies: the spontaneous mass strikes of 1971 and 1976, the more eclectic underground trade union movement, and several opposition organizations. The most influential of these before the emergence of Solidarity was the Committee for the Defense of the Workers (KOR). After the signing of the Gdańsk Agreements of August 31, 1980, Solidarity rapidly grew into a movement comprising virtually all of the Polish adult industrial labor force. In 1981 the movement held an organizing conference at which it elected a national executive council and decided on a national federal structure.

The Charter 77 movement in Czechoslovakia has its origins in the opposition generated by the Soviet invasion of 1968 and the suppression of the "Prague Spring" reform movement, euphemistically called "normalization." Many intellectuals and party members purged for their part in 1968 saw in the official signing of the Helsinki Agreements on Human Rights a way to influence the regime to modify "normalization." The first Charter 77 document, published by these disaffected individuals in January, 1977, called upon the Czechoslovak government to live up to the commitments made in signing the agreements. The movement quickly spread to other segments of the population and now numbers over a thousand signers. Charter 77 was severely repressed by the regime, and in 1978 the Committee for the Defense of the Unjustly Persecuted (VONS) came into being to defend the Charter signers victimized by the authorities. Charter 77 has developed what is best described as a two-tiered system of leadership, a collective of spokespersons to promote communication among the Charter signers and a triumvirate of three spokesperson-signatories who sign all the documents and make public statements in the name of the movement.

By contrasting the varied manifestations of women's participation in Solidarity and Charter 77, this chapter advances several generalizations as to why women became involved (*engagées*) more openly in the opposition of the seventies and suggests several types of activity that appear to be identifiable as specific attributes of women's participation. The first section of the study examines three dimensions of women's opposition activity, the characteristics of women opposition activists, and the modes of operation used by women in opposition. The last section explores some possible reasons for women's emergence in the activist role.

The Nature of Women's Participation in the Opposition Movements

A comparison of women's participation in Charter 77 and the Polish opposition movements immediately suggests the distinction between the mass character of the Polish opposition and the more eclectic composition of Charter 77. We have no hard data on the number of women in the Solidarity rank-and-file prior to the imposition of martial law in December 1981, but informed sources indicate that their representation was proportional to the presence of women in the work force, or around 50 percent. However, as one rose in the Solidarity hierarchy, the number diminished. Only 7.8 percent (sixty-nine) of the 881 delegates to the Solidarity Congress were women, while there was only one woman in the National Executive Council elected in the fall of 1981. By comparison, the proportion of women elected to the Central Committee of the Polish United Workers party (PUWP) in the summer of 1981 fell to 7.5 percent from 10.5 percent

Table 10.1 Occupational composition of KOR by order of frequency and by gender

Occupation	Males	Females
Historian	5	—
Writer	5	1
Scientist	4	—
Social scientist	4	—
Lawyer	3	2
Priest	3	—
Linguist	2	—
Actress	—	1
High school principal	1	—
Journalist	1	—
Student	1	—
Unidentified	1	—
Total	30	4

Source: Radio Free Europe Research, *Background Report/284* (October 6, 1981), mimeographed, pp. 7–10.

in 1980, although the first and only woman to be a member of the party presidium was also a member of Solidarity.[3] Nor did Polish women take a leading role in KOR. Of the thirty-four members listed in the organization when it disbanded in the fall of 1980, only four were women. These data suggest that in neither the official nor opposition organizations were women elected to leadership positions consonant with the size of their representation.[4]

In terms of age and occupation, opposition women intellectuals appear to share the same characteristics as their male counterparts, although they tend to be slightly younger and have less diverse occupations. In KOR, for example, one of the four women was born in prewar Poland, compared to fifteen of the thirty men (see table 10.1).

By contrast, the occupations of the working women strikers differ substantially from those of men, a consequence of the much-publicized phenomenon of the feminization of job categories throughout Eastern Europe. Although women do work in the Baltic shipyards, they have emerged as a significant opposition group in the textile mills and shoe factories, where they predominate.

Two final categories of women deserve mention in the Polish framework: the students and the teachers. While there are no data on the numbers of women involved in the 1980–81 student strikes or in the Teachers' Union, there must have been many since women represent 100 percent of the elementary teaching staff and a sizable proportion of secondary school personnel and are about equally represented in the student population.[5] In one reported instance, a woman served as spokesperson for the student strikers.[6]

The role of women in Charter 77 in Czechoslovakia differs from that of Polish women in KOR in both the rank and file and the leadership. Like KOR, Charter 77 is primarily an intellectual organization. However, women constitute around 21 percent of the total number of signers and are much better represented at the higher levels of the organization than Polish women were in either KOR or Solidarity. Of those who added their signature to Charter 77 in the first weeks of its existence, 23 percent were women.[7]

In the Charter's two-tiered system of governance four women were listed among the seventeen individuals identified as being members of the first-tier general spokesperson group in May 1980. Initially the three spokesperson-signers were men. However, when playwright Václav Havel withdrew in the fall of 1977, singer Marta Kubišová took his place. Havel replaced her in the fall of 1978, when she had to resign because of ill health connected with expecting a child.[8] Since that time a woman has generally been among the three spokesperson-signatories. In May 1980 two were identified as women.[9] In the annual 1984 turnover the new triumvirate included one woman, Jana Sternová, among the appointed trio.[10]

The fact that women have been willing to assume such highly visible and risk-filled positions in Charter 77 is in itself remarkable. Equally significant is what appears to be a Charter policy of giving women permanent representation at the highest leadership level. The fact that these positions are not elected but appointed suggests that opposition women may fare better outside the electoral process.

In terms of age and occupation, Charter 77 female signatories are similar to their male counterparts. However, there are some gender-related differences. Essentially women may be divided into three types: wives of persecuted ex-party members, intellectuals involved in the Prague Spring, and new Charter signers; female ex-party members; and frustrated artists, office, professional, and blue-collar workers.

Foremost in the category of wives is Josefa Slánská, the wife of Rudolf Slánský, the General Secretary of the Czechoslovak Communist party (KSČ), who was a victim of the 1950s purges. Slánská was one of the leading forces behind the manifesto. Other wives include Olga Havlová, wife of Václav Havel and codefendant in the trial of the eighteen in Prague (see below); Jiřina Mašinová, wife of the 1968 intellectual and writer Pavel Kohout; and Zuzana Dienstbierová and Dr. Libuše Šilhánová, wives of prominent human rights activists. Both Dienstbierová and Šilhánová lost their jobs as a result of their Charter 77 activities.[11]

Table 10.2 Occupations by frequency of women who added their names publicly to Charter 77, February 1, 1977

Occupation	Number
Office worker (*uřednice*)	7
Housewife	5
Journalist	5
Worker	5
Librarian	4
Nurse	2
Painter	2
Teacher	2
Technical worker	2
Chemist	1
Creative artist	1
Educator	1
Engineer-sociologist	1
Faculty fellow	1
Gardener	1
Hairdresser	1
Interpreter	1
Pensioner	1
Physician	1
Political worker	1
Psychologist	1
Service worker	1
Student	1
Writer	1
Total	49

Source: Charter 77, Document No. 5. "The Addition of the Names of Citizens Who Agreed that Their Names Be Made Public to the List of Those Who Signed Charter 77." Jiří Hájek, February 1, 1977.

Leading women among ex-party members include former postwar party presidium member Marie Švermová, member of the KSČ Central Committee (fall 1968–69) Jiřina Zelenková, and head of the Federal Council on Church Affairs (1969) Erika Kadlečová.

The occupations of women in the third category are primarily intellectual (see table 10.2). But office workers and housewives head the list in frequency, and blue-collar workers were as numerous as women journalists. The widely different occupations indicate the degree to which Charter 77 has provoked a response among women, especially in the Czech Lands.

The Czechoslovak government has not discriminated in its persecution of men and women. All of the more than three hundred persons who signed the manifesto in January 1977 were summoned for cross examination as witnesses for a criminal case of subversion of the Republic. Women as well as men have been subject to house searches and job loss. Document No. 6 of the Charter gives three instances of women listed as having "endangered their health or having bodily harm come to them" as a result of signing the manifesto.[12]

More recently three women figured prominently in the so-called trial of eighteen Czechoslovak human rightists. These were sociologist Jiřina Siklová, Olga Havlová, and writer Eva Kantůrková, who was provisionally freed on March 22, 1982. The blanket accusation was "ideological diversion." A fourth woman, 21-year-old Czech student Lenka Cvricková, was arrested in Feburary 1981 and sentenced in August of that year to an eight-month prison term.[13]

One of the most inhumane cases of treatment reported is that of typist Drahomira Sinoglová, who was sentenced in September 1980 for subversion. Since she was expecting, her sentence was deferred until her child was six months old. In March 1982 she was taken to prison, although she was again pregnant.[14]

The above review of the data is far from complete. Nevertheless, it is sufficient to indicate that women are involved in the opposition movement in both countries in significant proportions. Given the freer conditions for public expression existing in Poland prior to December 1981, participation, particularly of working women, has been more widespread in Poland than in Czechoslovakia. However, there has been some involvement by Czech working women. As regards farm women, there has been no information on the participation of women in Rural Solidarity, and so far, farmers generally have stayed aloof from Charter 77. In addition, there has been significantly less participation of Slovak men and women in Charter 77.

Women's Mode of Participation in the Opposition

The major difference in modes of participation between the Polish and Czech oppositions is obvious: in Poland, the opposition for both men and women acquired a mass character, in Czechoslovakia, it is more individual. Once that distinction is made, the question becomes whether one can distinguish a specifically female style of participation in either the Czech or Polish movements. The evidence suggests the emergence of three such styles.

The first relates to the Polish situation and may be described as marginality of participation. At the onset of the strike in Gdańsk in August

1980, one of the strikers' principal demands was the return of Anna Walentinowicz to work. She had been fired as a result of her activities in the former illegal trade union movement. The government permitted Ms. Walentinowicz to return to work, where she immediately took an active part in events, becoming one of the two women members of the Interfactory Strike Committee Presidium. She was also one of the signers of the Gdańsk Agreements on August 31. Despite this activity, however, she was not given a mandate as a delegate to the regional Gdańsk trade union conference in the fall of 1981. Her local chapter decided not to send her. At the conference there was some embarrassment at her failure to be elected, and one member suggested she be given the right to vote anyway. Ms. Walentinowicz refused, saying the decision in her case was made by majority vote in her chapter, and she did not want to make an issue of it.[15] The paradox suggested earlier finds substantiation here. As a self-selected member of the trade union movement, Ms. Walentinowicz played a significant role, but she failed to pass the test of free elections. No similar incident is reported in the case of men.

The second example of marginality of female participation also occurred within the Gdańsk regional organization. The second woman member of the original Interfactory Strike Committee Presidium was Joanna Duda Gwiazda, a shipping engineer and wife of Andrej Gwiazda, a strike leader second in popularity only to Lech Wałęsa. Ms. Gwiazda's name is on the list of presidium members in the first issue of *Solidarność* of August 23, 1980. Her name does not appear among the signers of the Gdańsk Agreements. In its place is her husband's signature.

Alina Pieńkowska was the other woman signer of the Gdańsk Agreements. At the regional conference she refused to be a candidate for membership on the regional board or a delegate to the national congress. Her name was left on the list anyway, and eventually she was elected to the regional board. Joanna Gwiazda ran for election to both the regional board and national congress. Like Pieńkowska, she was elected to the regional board but failed to be elected as a delegate to the national congress.

The electoral fortunes of these two women may in part be explained by factional politics within Solidarity. At the regional conference the struggle for leadership between Wałęsa and Gwiazda came out in the open. Both women supported Gwiazda. Gwiazda apparently had strong regional support, but the trade union desired a united delegation to the national congress and elected primarily supporters of Wałęsa. The failure of the women to be elected delegates at the national level thus does not imply sex discrimination as much as the normal working of partisan politics.

However, the issue between Gwiazda and Wałęsa sheds some light on Ms. Pieńkowska's and Ms. Gwiazda's understanding of participation.

Gwiazda apparently was in favor of greater regional autonomy within a loosely federated trade union organization. Wałęsa, for his part, desired coordination and control of the movement from a center that would be elected but that could call the regional unions to responsibility. In addition, there was some disagreement on the electoral process with Gwiazda favoring a less formal and Wałęsa a more formal one. In their selection of a leader, it would be difficult for the two women to separate personal loyalty from preference for a leader's politics. In this case, Gwiazda's opinion represented a less structured, more decentralized variant than Wałęsa's.

The politics behind the unsuccessful elections of Ms. Gwiazda and Ms. Pieńkowska lead directly to the second mode of participation in opposition evidenced by Polish women: the unstructured strike. On February 11, 1971, just when the Gierek leadership thought that the worst of the 1970–71 strikes were over in Poland, 10,000 predominantly women workers in the textile factories at Łódź went on strike over new work norms and food prices. Accounts of the strike are slim, but one fact stands out. The women did not choose delegates to represent them with the government. Thus, when the Polish premier visited Łódź in order to talk directly with the strikers, there was no one with whom he could negotiate. Instead, he was confronted with angry demands from the floor. Absence of representatives made communication impossible. The premier returned to Warsaw, and on February 15 the government announced that it would cancel the December rise in food prices and increase wages as the strikers demanded.[16] The Łódź strike method without representation forced the regime to change its mind.

In 1981 we have a similar phenomenon appearing in the women's hunger march in September and later in the massive food strike in Zyrardów, where reportedly 12,000 women staged a factory sit-in. Once again the women had no representation and, in the words of *The New York Times*, "seemed to have little idea of how to run a strike." But the strike method had its effect. Initially, the government said the strike was political in nature, so the women could not receive their strike pay of 50 percent of their regular wages. The government subsequently backed down and said the strike was economic. Despite lack of representation, the women drew up a list of sixteen demands, which they forwarded to the authorities.[17] Whether their disorganization was consciously planned or not, their actions suggest that they were highly capable of united, purposeful, and successful behavior. The unstructured strike seems a particularly Polish phenomenon in post–World War II Eastern Europe and specifically a women's weapon. The rules of the male power struggle call for hierarchy and organization. In the contest between Gwiazda and Wałęsa, Wałęsa won. But the Polish women's experience indicates that disorganization has its own rewards.

The third mode of participation that seems to be more typically female is what might be termed the symbolic use of women, particularly those who have been victims of injustice, as advocates. Poland provides cases in point. One of KOR's best-known spokespersons was actress Halina Mikołajska. Another KOR member, Anna Kowalska, was one of those who spoke out strongly on behalf of the workers in prison in August 1980.[18] But the symbolic use of women seems particularly characteristic of Charter 77.

First, we refer again to what might be described as the apparent institutionalization of women's participation in the trio of individuals designated spokesperson-signatories. Second, although space does not permit a listing of many instances of women's appeals for justice, both to the Czechoslovak and the international community, these appeals have been numerous in both the Czech Lands and Slovakia.[19] At the Third Congress of Slovak Writers in 1977, Slovak author Hana Ponická demanded a moment of silence for the Slovak writers who "lead their lives in our midst or more precisely away from us but around us. . . . Ours is a moral suffering, stemming from moral conflicts," she asserted. But she was sure "that the wrongs will be rectified and the conflicts solved," despite the loss to the national literature of writers who had been silenced.[20]

Actress Vlasta Chramostová's letter to Western intellectuals dated March 1, 1977, universalizes the theme of moral suffering. "Without any explanation, without any chance to defend myself," she writes, "I am prevented from working . . . I have come to realize that one can no longer consider human rights to be safe-guarded, wherever in the world it may be, if they are only conceded as a privilege . . . as a bribe for unconditional servitude, as a reward for uncritical consent." She urges the West to raise its voice for the legalization of Charter 77.[21]

One of the immediate concerns which had sparked Charter 77 was the Czechoslovak regime's crackdown on rock music performances. Pop singer Marta Kubišová used her international reputation to exhort young pop singers in all the countries that had signed the Helsinki Agreement "to act as long as there is time. If you allow justice to merge with lawlessness, then no one will be able to hear us any more."[22]

The common element in the above citations is their high emotional content, the personal appeal to the heart as well as to reason. Both the Polish and Czech oppositions have had powerful male spokesmen, such as KOR spokesmen Adam Michnik and Jacek Kuron, and Václav Havel and Zdeněk Mlynář in Charter 77. But a careful reading of their statements suggests a more intellectually oriented approach, an attempt to analyze, to objectify.[23]

Thus, women in opposition appear more marginal to the organizational structure of opposition movements, with visibility in leadership positions depending on male endorsement. Where structures and organization are not primary issues, as in Charter 77 or in the Polish strikes, women have demonstrated their ability both individually and on a mass basis to profit from an unstructured situation and, in the case of Poland, to force the government to accede to their demands. Finally, in their role of symbolic advocates of the opposition platform, women's appeal has been more immediately personal, addressed to the heart.

Women's Issues in the Opposition

In both the Polish and Czechoslovak situations the larger issues of social reform and human rights have taken precedence over special interest demands. What is significant in both cases is the degree to which women's concerns have been integrated into the general issues and indeed seen as basic components of the social problem.

The opposition platforms

Solidarity and Charter 77 alike have given women's issues a place in their priority list of problems facing the two societies. Document No. 7 of Charter 77 criticizing the violation of social rights in Czechoslovakia refers directly to the hardships women face. Women work, the document asserts, not because they desire a fuller life, but out of economic pressure, because the husband's wage would not assure a decent life for the family. Hence, the full employment of women is not a sign of increasing equality, but an indication of their increased dependence. The situation is aggravated by the regime's "systematic disregard" for services which would lighten women's load and by the rising cost of living.[24]

The demands generated by the Polish movement were less sweeping in their criticism but more focused. Three of the twenty-one demands put forward by the Gdańsk Interfactory Strike Committee in August 1980 related directly to women. These were increasing the number of places in nursery schools for children of working mothers, the introduction of a three-year paid maternity leave, and shortening the waiting period for housing.[25] The Solidarity statutes make more explicit the workers' interest in these issues. Paragraph 6, article 4 of the statutes gives as a union objective "the strengthening of the family, as well as family life."[26]

Clearly, Solidarity's position on women's issues is far more conservative than Charter 77's critique. The statutes in particular suggest that the Polish worker is not concerned with women's problems in and of themselves but with their impact on family life.[27] One is tempted to attribute this conservatism to the Polish religious culture and the influence of the Catholic Church. However, a second factor may be the rapid postwar growth of the Polish working class and its relatively recent separation from village life.

The Polish government's reply to the union's demands is worth noting. In the period between August 1980 and December 1981, three responses may be identified. The first was the announcement on September 24, 1980, of an increase of 400 złotys in grants to young married couples and to students. A day later the Labor and Social Affairs Committee of the national legislature made a statement that factory social funds should not be used for financing extraneous activities and that rules governing allocation of factory housing funds should be simplified to ensure that all the funds available were fully exploited.[28] Finally, at a January 1981 meeting attended by the then State Council Chairman Jabłoński, the Polish Women's Council issued a statement that women employed in the socialized sector of the economy should receive wages and benefits commensurate to their qualifications and equal to those of men.[29] Thus, while the premartial law government did nothing concrete in the area of solving the women's problems identified by Solidarity, it indicated an awareness of the issues and made motions to consider them seriously. Since it moved with deliberate slowness in the fulfillment of all parts of the union's demands, one cannot consider its failure to be more aggressive on women's issues an indication of discrimination or downplaying of the problems. So far the martial law regime and its successor have not taken any action on women's issues.

Women's Initiatives in the Opposition

In assessing the direct influence of women's activities on the opposition platforms, one must once again distinguish between the mass Polish movement and the more individual character of Charter 77. The Radio Free Europe chronology of Polish events between July 1980 and July 1981 makes at least thirty-eight references to incidents where women were explicitly involved or their involvement was suggested because of the nature of the incident, such as the student strikes, or the meeting of the Polish Teachers' Union. Women have borne the brunt of the difficult circumstances brought about by the worsening Polish economic crisis. In 1971 the Łódź women strikers refused to listen to the government representatives and rudely shouted, "Give us bread!" At Zyrardów in 1981 all but two of the sixteen demands sent by the strikers to the authorities reportedly involved improving the food supply.[30] As Document No. 7 of Charter 77 makes clear, obtaining life's basic staples is the central concern of most families in every communist country. Even in countries that are better supplied, the assortment of staples varies from week to week, from day to day, so that the anxious shopper never knows when she sees one product whether she will find it again the next day, next week, or even next year. Polish women forced back price increases in food in 1971. The improvement of the food supply was among the twenty-one original demands at Gdańsk. When the government proved unable to satisfy the demand, Polish women again took action to publicize their concerns.

Because of the more intellectual and elite character of Charter 77, Czechoslovak women human rights activists have shown particular initiative in exploring women's problems from a personal standpoint. A few examples will indicate the content of these initiatives.

Helena Klímová has written a thoughtful discussion of why and when a person should sacrifice his or her life and family to a cause that sheds light on the kinds of hesitations and anxieties women experience when they first come into contact with the opposition movement.[31] The anguish, misgivings, yet total support given by a wife to a husband or a mother to a child who has chosen the opposition are all present in this poignant distillation of feeling. Sacrifice, for Klímová, is a voluntary action. In traditional feminine style, the rightness of one's action is to be judged not on the basis of objective rationality but on one's capacity for love.

A second example that deserves mention is the book entitled *Twelve Women in Prague*, written by Eva Kantůrková, one of the codefendants in the trial of the eighteen mentioned earlier in this chapter. The book was published in Paris in 1981.[32] As the French reviewer noted, "a book by a woman about twelve other women that does not raise feminist issues is in itself a rare thing." In the words of Kantůrková, "feminism has been eradicated in our society by having been brutally transformed into a new form of woman's slavery: obligatory work. Thus, if in Czechoslovakia there is one thing that a woman wishes to obtain for herself, it is to recover her undistorted feminine essence rather than to promote herself."[33]

Twelve Women in Prague provides insight into women's approach to being in opposition. The twelve are women interviewed by Kantůrková concerning their views on Charter 77, the effect of opposition on their families, their personal careers, and personal development. All are intellectuals, artists, or wives of dissidents who have been sent to prison. Each became a Chartist by personal decision. In signing Charter 77, they entered the "community of the excluded." They automatically lost their well-paying jobs and became subject to police harassment and brutality. Their children were excluded from university and victimized at school. Prison casts a terrifying shadow over each interview. Yet the community of the excluded does not represent a group of browbeaten women. Each one tells a story of coming alive, of finding a sense of purpose in life, of having more friends than ever before, of "having enlarged her human experience." Each one speaks of the need of doing "the little thing" to transform society from relations based on authority and fear to a society based on love. And each one rejects all ideologies to talk of social reform in terms of changing the human heart. Kantůrková insists that her aim is not feminist. She chose women subjects because "women have so little sense of abstraction that ideas and reflection do not risk detaching them from the world as it really is. In telling me their life stories, my friends have told me something basic about our world."[34]

The book is subtly profeminist, although it fails to address any of the feminist issues raised in the West. It is profeminist in its conviction that only women can give an accurate picture of the real world. Women are more compassionate, more loving, more tolerant. Yet the author categorically refuses to question her subjects on problems such as women's dual burden of home and work, equal pay, and women's status in communist societies. The book suggests that women in opposition develop self-awareness, identity, a sense of community not experienced when they toed the line "vis-à-vis the rules of the game." Kantůrková does not share with us her views on the official vision of equality because that vision for her has little or no connection with what the women she knows are experiencing in opposition.

This line of thinking might denote an absence of feminist awareness like that in Western societies where women's second-class status is seen as a product of a male-dominated social system. In *Twelve Women in Prague*, women's slavery is linked to men's slavery (the husbands in prison); both sexes are the victims of the rule of an all-powerful bureaucracy. To quote Libuše Šilhánová, "The world of Kafka and Orwell long ago ceased to be literary fiction, absurdity. Reality is absurd, and it does not only menace us, but the whole world."[35] Dana Němcová expresses the same idea a little differently: "It's a question of young people who have experienced manipulation in place of natural development from their childhood up."[36]

Kantůrková's book is a graphic illustration of why women in officially approved women's organizations and women in opposition in the communist countries have failed so far to develop what might be termed "socialist feminism."[37] For the first group, the communist vision of equality has been realized. In the second, the perception that men and women are linked in similar oppression makes it difficult to conceive of women's liberation independently of men's liberation from the same system. Kantůrková's book suggests that women dissidents, at least in Czechoslovakia, find the universalist concepts of human rights and human liberty more relevant to their circumstances than the ideas of Western feminists.[38]

The final example is that of Lenka Cvrcková, mentioned earlier. This 21-

year-old student traveled to Poland in August 1980 and became involved in the Polish student movement. During the massive student strikes in Łódź in January and February 1981 she edited the student periodical, *Strike*. She was detained in Poland, because her visa had allegedly expired, and handed over to the Czechoslovak border authorities. At her trial the charges against her were subverting the Republic and harming the state of the world socialist order.[39] In contrast to the two previous subjects, Ms. Cvrcková's initiative is along more conventional opposition activist lines. However, her action is significant as concrete evidence of the extent of communication existing between the Polish and Czech opposition.[40] More important for our purposes, Ms. Cvrcková suggests the kind of commitment young Czech women can give to the human rights cause wherever it may be at issue.

Factors Influencing Women's Participation in the Activist Movement

Women appear to participate in the opposition in Poland and Czechoslovakia for a wide variety of reasons. Primary among these would seem to be personal considerations, the nature of the issues, and the crisis of "goulash communism."

Women in Poland and Czechoslovakia have become increasingly frustrated in the procurement of the basic means of survival: shelter, food, clothing. In all these areas, supply and distribution have improved only modestly in the postwar years, as every woman knows. In Poland the shortages started to become more evident after the OPEC price increases in 1974, although OPEC's impact was not fully felt until 1976. The situation deteriorated until in 1980 there were probably few women in the country who did not have to do daily battle in consumer lines for the material survival of their families. The early seventies were a fairly prosperous time in Czechoslovakia, the reward for submission to normalization. But from 1975 on, Czechoslovakia slid steadily into economic crisis. According to economists, the situation is all the more serious because the government is no longer at liberty to take from the consumer to give to capital investment.[41]

What I am suggesting is that women who become involved in the opposition do so because the economic and social problems exposed by the opposition now pervade every facet of their daily lives. Where women are less active, as in Slovakia and the Czechoslovak countryside, the effects of the economic situation have been cushioned. One of the consequences of normalization was a heightened effort to equalize the economic disparities between the Czech Lands and Slovakia. Slovakia has benefited in recent years from an influx of capital; new construction and new industry are visible everywhere. By contrast, the industrial towns of Bohemia, with some exceptions, look depressed and in need of renewal. In addition, Slovakia imports food and staples from Hungary. The general perception is that Slovaks have an easier time and experience less control than do the Czechs.

On the personal intellectual level, women appear to join the opposition because regime oppression has affected their private lives through a member of the family or because of job loss or loss of educational opportunities for themselves or their families. Since 1968 student unrest in Poland has challenged the official policies of enforced curriculum, compulsory language training, and administrative selection of students for higher education primarily on the basis of their privileged relationship to the party. The closing of educational doors to some 300,000 children of nonconformists between 1969 and 1976 in Czechoslovakia was an important factor in the formation of the Charter 77 movement.[42] Among the women directly affected by such policies, which virtually preclude upward mobility and a higher standard of living, was Dr. Libuše Šilhánová.

A final personal factor for entering the opposition that has found expression particularly among Czech women is the loss of self-worth. Film actress Vera Chytilová's letter to Dr. Husák is a case in point. After describing her inability to find work or to be employed in a profession where she has achieved international recognition she ends her letter, "What . . . am I to do? What am I to say to my friends, both at home and abroad . . . ?"[43] Speaking out against job loss and making a public stand in opposition ends the uncertainty and confusion about personal ability. In many cases, participation in the opposition reinforces the activists' sense of personal worth, as indicated in *Twelve Women in Prague*.

Consideration of personal motivations for women entering the opposition leads directly to the second group of factors, the nature of issues raised by the Polish and Czechoslovak oppositions. Both Charter 77 and Solidarity categorically denied any interest in playing the role of political parties. The Charter 77 manifesto specifically states that it is not an organization and the Charter has no rules or formal membership. Solidarity's statutes also stated that the union did not aspire to be a political party even though the union's increasing political role was one of the primary reasons given for the imposition of martial law. Neither movement openly sought to overthrow the government or install a new political leader. Rather, both protested their adherence to the laws of the land and insisted that their main object was to see that the government adhered to them.

Women appear to prefer to downplay the political and emphasize human and social rights. Kantůrková assumes that the defense of human rights is a "natural thing" for women. The strikers in Zyrardów told reporters that although the government thought their strike was political, it was not. All they wanted was food. It is not clear from the documents whether women in the opposition realized that their stance on a social right was essentially a political position, challenging the existing political system. However, the influx of women into the Polish and Czech oppositions in the 1970s suggests that women most probably feel more comfortable identifying with human rights issues that bear directly on their immediate situation rather than with the more abstract reformist-revisionist concepts of previous dissent platforms.

A second aspect of the nature of the current issues is the linking up of human rights both with traditional nationalism and with the modern politics of nonviolence. Czechoslovakia's current economic and social conditions are not seen by the population as a product of Czechoslovak mistakes but the result of the reimposition of Soviet power. Thus, to be in opposition to current regime policies is to be for one's country and against foreign domination. The same attitude is even more pervasive in Poland.[44] While it cannot be argued that women are more nationalistic than men, the family has been the main carrier of national tradition. Women play a principal role in the transmission of national values from one generation to the next and thus may enter more readily into a movement with a strong nationalist posture. Nonviolence is a modern political tactic which has shown its efficacy in such diverse countries as India and the United States. Although women have repeatedly demonstrated their capacity for violence in the service of a political cause, nonviolence is a participatory mode of action more accommodating of the conservative passive female self-image.[45]

Finally, the participation of women in the 1970s Polish and Czechoslovak opposition may be viewed as a product of the crisis of the 1960s "goulash communism." In a letter to Gustav Husák, Václav Havel states the matter plainly: "By nailing a man's whole attention to the floor of his mere consumer interest, [the government hopes] to render him incapable of appreciating the ever-increasing degree of his spiritual, political, and moral degradation."[46] To paraphrase Havel, the emergence of Solidarity may be described as the direct consequence of the effort of the Polish government "to imprison" the Polish worker "within the wretched range of parts he can perform as a consumer because of the limitations of a centrally directed market."

The failure of official consumerism appears to have been particularly effective in politicizing women. Women everywhere tend to be the most ardent consumers, hence their mobilization in Poland in defense of their interests. However, the remedy for consumer failure in Poland as in Czechoslovakia increasingly has been perceived in terms of the guarantee of the human right to a free and open society. Of lesser importance, but still a factor, has been goulash communism's failure to improve substantially women's condition in society. The dual burden has become a blatant problem in all the communist countries, while women's lower wage scale, the feminization of jobs, and women's low participation in high administrative and political positions have been the subject of both official and opposition criticism. Charter 77's Document No. 7 makes the linkage clear: the opposition of women is seen in the failure of the Czechoslovak government to provide adequate services and adequate pay to lighten women's burden or to promote greater equality for women in society.

Conclusions

In summation, the woman in opposition in both Poland and Czechoslovakia in the recent past has come from a variety of occupations and had a variety of skills. In Poland she associated herself with the mass workers' reform movement, while in Czechoslovakia her activity has been more individual. In Poland she was underrepresented in reform leadership circles; in Czechoslovakia she may be highly visible in leading opposition roles. Her mode of participation includes a certain instability of performance as political and personal demands intrude upon her public role. She probably favors unstructured, open, and more democratic styles of participation rather than the traditional organized hierarchies. In her role of spokesperson she tends to make symbolic emotional appeals rather than rational-functional demands. Essentially her concerns are centered on the basic issues of social and economic rights, and she is not likely to be interested in Western-type feminist issues. She has been as likely as her male counterpart to risk official persecution.

This chapter suggests that a distinctive female oppositionist style has emerged in the Polish and Czech opposition. Whether this style is a momentary phenomenon or is capable of becoming generalized over all of Eastern Europe will depend on the availability of the conditions that produced it: an organized opposition, the human rights issue, the national issue, the possibility of a successful outcome to nonviolent action, and the continued imposition of narrow parameters for legitimate political activity. For a little over a year nonviolent, essentially disciplined action by a surprisingly unified nation in Poland encouraged the hope that such behavior could initiate solutions to the economic and social ills plaguing the East European countries. The imposition of martial law clearly demonstrated that there could be no solutions without the restoration of national and individual freedoms. If economic and consumer failure spawned the human rights issue, then December 1981 converted it into one of the most urgent items on the East European political agenda. In Poland and Czechoslovakia all the conditions necessary for the perpetuation of a female oppositionist style continue to obtain, with the exception of the success of nonviolence. In Poland, therefore, we may expect that women will now have recourse to the more individual female style.

In the rest of Eastern Europe the development of an organized opposition movement remains problematic for the reasons advanced at the beginning of this chapter. In the event that organization occurs, then I would anticipate that women would first become involved along the individual female pattern noted in KOR and Charter 77. The mass, nonviolent participation of women in East European opposition would appear to depend, as it did in Poland, upon the degree to which the economic and political crisis in a particular country escapes the ability of the national regime to manage it.

IV

Women and Work: Production and Reproduction

Sharon L. Wolchik

Introduction

One of the clearest changes in women's roles in Eastern Europe since the institution of communist systems has been women's influx into paid employment outside the home. Encouraged by a variety of financial as well as moral incentives, many East European women responded to the urging of political leaders and policymakers and entered the labor force. At the same time, they retained their earlier roles as childbearers and continue to be responsible for much of the work done in the home. As in other industrialized societies, the demands of women's roles in these areas often conflict with each other. The chapters in this section examine the changes that have occurred in women's roles as economic producers and in the family; they also discuss the public policies political leaders have enacted to facilitate these changes and some of the consequences, anticipated and unexpected, of these policies for women and for policymakers. As they illustrate, women's roles in the economy are closely linked to their roles in the home and family.

Discussing a process that has occurred in the other countries of the region as well, Kulcsár, Mežnarić, Volgyes, and Woodward document the substantial increase in women's labor force participation in Hungary and Yugoslavia and point out the progress women have made in entering new occupations and professions. As they note, women's employment has become an accepted part of life in Eastern Europe, and many women clearly define themselves at least in part by reference to their roles in the economy.

The essays in this section, however, also discuss the barriers to equality that continue to exist in the workplace in all of these countries. Although larger numbers of women entered the labor force sooner in most East European countries than in the United States or most West European countries, East European women face many of the same problems in the area of work as women in countries where women's employment outside the home is either less widespread or more recent. Despite the fact that women have increased their educational qualifications and now are employed in a somewhat broader range of occupations, East European women continue to fare less well than men in the economy and more often end up at the bottom. Lower pay, lower social mobility, occupational segregation, and women's concentration in occupations that have lower prestige as well as lower pay are patterns that those familiar with women's roles in other countries will recognize, as is women's exclusion from most leading economic positions.[1]

As Volgyes documents in his discussion of women's economic roles in Hungary, women also are more likely than men to end up in poverty. Noting that most analyses have focused on women professionals or others who are relatively well-off in the present system, Volgyes reminds us that the poor, in these societies as well as in many others, are predominantly women and children. Echoing a theme common to other investigations of women's work roles in Eastern Europe and the Soviet Union,[2] his essay and Woodward's chapter demonstrate the different impact social change and public policies have on different groups of women.

In Eastern Europe as in other parts of the world, many of the difficulties women encounter in the economic sphere stem from the fact that the demands of the work world conflict with those of the home. As Woodward notes in her discussion of the Yugoslav case, state policies have had an impact on family organization and women's roles within the family in Eastern Europe. Paradoxically, however, many of the changes that have occurred in the function of the family in Yugoslav society have increased rather than reduced women's domestic responsibilities. As the essays of Woodward and Kulcsár, as well as those in Part V, illustrate, changes in men's and women's behavior in the family have not kept pace with changes in women's labor force participation, and it is clearly women who bear the brunt of the often discussed "double burden" of work outside and in the home in these as well as other societies.[3]

As the chapters in this section illustrate, women's roles in production and reproduction have been influenced in these societies as in others by the interaction of elite values, concrete policy measures, patterns of economic, family, and social organization, and popular values and attitudes. The support for women's equality found in Marxist-Leninist ideology undoubtedly had some influence on the approach communist leaders took to women's issues in Eastern Europe. As McIntyre and Woodward note, measures granting women legal equality, efforts to reduce the most abusive practices in regard to women in the family, and support for women's right to seek employment predated the need for their labor created by the adoption of ambitious industrialization plans in many East European countries as well as in the Soviet Union.

However, as Mežnarić notes in her discussion of women's employment in Slovenia, Yugoslavia's most developed republic, there is frequently a discrepancy between the official view of women's position in these societies (which she refers to as the legitimating ideology) and women's actual situation. Further, if one looks at the concrete measures political leaders have adopted in regard to women, many appear to have been determined largely by consideration of other goals rather than by the ideological commitment to women's equality. As in other political systems, that is, issues related to women's status have not been top priority concerns, and policies that affect women frequently have been adopted out of expediency or because they are useful for very different purposes. In the early communist period, policymakers in Eastern Europe focused primarily on women's roles as economic producers; in recent years, they have seen women primarily as reproductive resources in most countries of the region.[4]

But, although one can discern certain emphases in the approach of political leaders to women's issues and although the main emphasis of this approach has changed over time, it is also clear that the policies that have an impact on women are not a coherent set of measures. As Lapidus has noted in discussing the Soviet case,[5] the numerous public policies that affect women are prepared and administered by many different party and government bodies and are not seen as part of an overall policy program. The inconsistent and sometimes contradictory outcomes that result from this fact are compounded by the discrepancy that often exists between the intent of official policies and the actual outcome of policy measures when they are put into practice at the local or factory level. In part for this reason, certain measures adopted by political leaders in Eastern Europe have had unexpected or unanticipated consequences for both women and policymakers.

As McIntyre notes, it is difficult to judge the results of policies that affect women in Eastern Europe objectively. One's evaluation of the impact of particular policies may vary depending on whether one judges the outcome from the perspective of how the situation compares to the elite's abstract commitment to women's equality, progress compared to women's situation in the past, or women's situation in Eastern Europe compared to that of women in other societies. How individual women evaluate policies that affect them is particularly difficult for outside observers to judge, but it is also difficult for social scientists within Eastern Europe.

The chapters to follow approach these issues from different perspectives and come to different conclusions concerning the impact of public policies on women's lives. Mieczkowski, in his discussion of social services in the region, identifies childcare facilities, health care (particularly pre- and postnatal care), and various social payments, including maternity leave payments, as policies that have been beneficial to women. However, he also argues that the impact of other policy measures, including economic development strategies that led to the neglect of the consumer sector, constitute social "disservices" for women because women feel the adverse effects of these policies more strongly than men. Heitlinger also is critical of the process of becoming a mother in Czechoslovakia. Documenting the way in which the process of giving birth has become dominated by the medical profession, she notes that many of the measures women in the West fought for and obtained to give them more control over the birth and postpartum experience, such as the presence of husbands or coaches during prepared childbirth and rooming-in, are not generally available in Czechoslovakia.

McIntyre, in his examination of pronatalist policies in Romania and Hungary, points out the variation in the elites' approaches to the birthrate problem in Eastern Europe. Noting the negative effects that the Romanian strategy, which relies heavily on the prohibition of contraception and abortion, has had on women's right to control their own bodies as well as health, he stresses the benefits pronatalist policies have brought women in Hungary. Referring specifically to the extended maternity leaves, guaranteed return to jobs, and allowances paid to women who stay at home to care for small children, he argues that the socialist countries that have followed the Hungarian strategy have gone further than any except certain of the Scandinavian countries in dealing with the strains women who choose to be mothers face at this time of their lives. At the same time, however, his essay clearly demonstrates that policymakers in Eastern Europe continue to see the issue as a woman's problem, for there has been no concerted attempt to encourage young men to play a greater role in the care of children or to alter the work world to take the needs of men as well as women with small children into account.

As the essays in this section demonstrate, many East European leaders continue to define women primarily in terms of their roles within the family. And the family itself tends to be defined in traditional terms. In contrast to the early postrevolutionary period in the Soviet Union, when there was a good deal of experimentation with a variety of family forms and living arrangements,[6] East European leaders have accepted the nuclear family as the basic form of family organization from the beginning of the communist period. Echoing what was by then the Soviet view, they declared that the nuclear family was the foundation of socialist as well as capitalist society, and as such, the proper setting for the birth and rearing of children.

Reality, in the form of high divorce rates and the increasing numbers of single women who have and raise children by themselves, conflicts with the official picture of what constitutes a family in these societies. In recent years policymakers in some of these countries in fact have been encouraging single women to bear rather than abort their children, and maternity benefits are somewhat more generous for women who have children alone. But, as the essays by Mieczkowski, Heitlinger, and Volgyes illustrate, these provisions are generally inadequate, as are government attempts to deal with the problems that cause strains in family and marital relationships. Despite evidence of the need to do so, there also has been very little effort, at the elite level or among women themselves, to "rethink" the family, as has occurred among feminist scholars in the West,[7] by questioning its value to individuals, reconceptualizing what constitutes a "family," or challenging common assumptions about the proper roles of individuals within a family.

It is also clear that women continue to be seen largely as the objects of public policy rather than its creators in Eastern Europe. Although women's desires are sometimes taken into account by policymakers in formulating policy alternatives, women do not have systematic input into the making of many of the decisions that affect them in these societies. Far more open discussion of problematic aspects of women's situation is possible now than in the 1950s, but women continue to be seen primarily as resources to be mobilized or channeled in directions determined by political leaders and economic planners.

The impact of this orientation, evident in the economic sphere, is particularly noticeable in the area of reproduction, where political leaders have not hesitated to intervene in and, in some cases, markedly restrict women's freedom of choice. These restrictions have been most severe in Romania, where, as McIntyre's essay documents, political leaders in the late 1960s outlawed contraception and abortion virtually overnight and made divorce extremely difficult to obtain. But levels of knowledge about and use of contraception are very low in most countries of the region, and access to abortion also has been restricted somewhat in many in the past fifteen years. As Heitlinger notes, care of women's bodies increasingly has come to be seen as the responsibility of medical professionals, and in contrast to the situation in the United States and many West European countries, there are no independent women's groups to challenge this domination.

In this situation, it is perhaps not surprising that the efforts made to reconcile women's various roles remain problematic from the perspective of both women and policymakers in Eastern Europe. The current approach to accommodating women's childbearing roles, chiefly by means of extended maternity leaves and guaranteed return to jobs, has created numerous problems for economic planners and factory managers, particularly in branches of the economy with heavily female labor forces. In addition, while the current emphasis on women's maternal roles may be beneficial in economic terms in the long run, it at least temporarily increases the labor shortage in many of these countries. From women's perspective, the measures adopted to increase the birthrate may help certain women deal with the conflicting demands they face in the short run. But because they do not really address the issue of men's and women's unequal roles in the family but may in fact reinforce the notion that the home and children are women's responsibilities alone, such measures run the risk of perpetuating women's unequal situation outside the home.

The remaining inequalities women in Eastern Europe experience in the workplace, then, illustrate the difficulties women will continue to face as long as there is little change in the sexual division of labor within the home and little effort to restructure the work environment to reflect the patterns of women's, as well as men's, experiences. At the same time, the East European experience in this regard illustrates the magnitude of the task that will be involved in making these adjustments, for it suggests that efforts to alleviate the conflict between women's domestic and economic roles will not be successful as long as reproduction, childrearing, and organizing the day-to-day existence of family members continue to be seen solely or even primarily as "women's work."

11

Rózsa Kulcsár

The Socioeconomic Conditions of Women in Hungary

During the last three decades the living conditions of women in Hungary underwent fundamental changes. Traditional discrimination—the result of a long historical process—came to an end or if it was not completely eliminated at least decreased. Change in women's situation occurred not only in statistically verifiable areas such as women's participation in education, professional training, and socioeconomic activity, but also in areas that are difficult to quantify, such as the vanishing of prejudice against women, the higher regard for women's maternal roles, the division of labor within the family, and the availability and use of leisure.

This chapter deals only with quantifiable information characterizing the socioeconomic situation of women. The indicators I use are listed neither in order of importance nor with the aim of completeness. The factors I examine include women's place in the social division of labor and regional differences in this regard, women's status and position in the work world, women's educational levels, and women's earnings. I also discuss women's social mobility. Finally, I examine the time budgets of women, a factor that influences women's living conditions and opportunities for the use of leisure. Let me state from the outset that it would be difficult to investigate any of these indicators of women's status in isolation; for instance, social mobility is clearly a function of educational level, and geographic location influences occupation. This again affects earnings, living conditions, and ways of life.

Economic Activity

Women's occupations became important in determining their status when an increasing number of them began to participate in socially organized work and choose gainful employment at a younger age. Previously,

Table 11.1 Distribution of the population in the productive ages by economic activity and gender (Hungary)

Economic Activity	Percentage distribution Men 15–59 Years Old			Women 15–54 Years Old		
	1960	1970	1980	1960	1970	1980
Active earners	92.1	87.3	87.5	49.9	63.7	70.8
Inactive earners	1.2	2.9	5.3	0.7	6.1	12.3
Pensioners and others	(1.2)	(2.9)	(5.3)	(0.7)	(1.3)	(2.8)
Persons on childcare leave	—	—	(0.0)	—	(4.8)	(9.5)
Dependents	6.7	9.8	7.2	49.4	30.2	16.9
Pupils or students	(5.7)	(8.6)	(6.2)	(3.6)	(6.9)	(6.0)
Others	(1.0)	(1.2)	(1.0)	(45.8)	(23.3)	(10.9)
Total	100.0	100.0	100.0	100.0	100.0	100.0

Source: *1980. évi Népszámlálás. Részletes adatok a 2%-os képviseleti minta alapján* (Population Census in 1980. Full Particulars of the 2 percent Representative Sample) (Budapest: Központi Statisztikai Hivatal, 1980), p. 36.

women's social position (and with it their way of life) was determined by the social position of the head of the family, i.e., the husband or the father. Since a large proportion of women have become active earners and have a disposable income of their own, the social position and way of life and even the "prestige" of families are increasingly influenced by the occupation of women as well.

The fundamental difference between men's and women's employment in Hungary today is not quantitative but qualitative. About two-thirds of all women of productive age work outside the home and have earnings of their own. Approximately 83 percent of the female age groups between fifteen and fifty-four years, compared to 93 percent of men between fifteen and fifty-nine, are earners. The rate of earners includes the active as well as the so-called inactive earners, i.e., those who are pensioners or those living on childcare allowances. Forty-three percent of the active earners are women (see table 11.1).

One reason for the qualitative differences in men's and women's employment is that large masses of women have taken up socially organized work more recently than men. This fact is reflected in their occupational status. The average time of service of women employees in socialist industry, for example, lags behind the respective figures for men by two to seven years. In addition, as table 11.2 illustrates, many women in both white-collar and manual occupations have low qualifications.

Table 11.2 Distribution of active earners by characteristics of activity, staff group, and gender in Hungary (in percentages)

Characteristics of the activity and staff group	1970		1980	
	Men	Women	Men	Women
Skilled workers	34.1	8.9	43.5	11.1
Semiskilled workers	22.8	27.1	22.4	33.3
Unskilled workers	19.5	24.1	9.7	10.8
Helping family members in agricultural cooperatives	0.2	4.5	0.1	2.3
Manual occupations total	76.6	64.6	75.7	57.5
Nonmanual occupations	20.3	31.9	21.6	39.4
Those with the highest educational level	(6.0)	(3.7)	(8.7)	(7.7)
Self-employed workers and helping family members	3.1	3.5	2.7	3.1
Total	100.0	100.0	100.0	100.0

Source: 1980. évi Nepszámlálás. *Részletes adatok a 2%-os képviseleti minta alapján* (Population Census in 1980. Full Particulars of the 2 percent Representative Sample) (Budapest: Központi Statisztikai Hivatal, 1980), p. 95.

The basis for the extensive economic development that occurred in Hungary following World War II was provided, for the most part, by unskilled female labor. Not only younger single women, but also formerly dependent older women took up work outside the home. For the latter especially, socially organized work meant a tremendous change in their way of life. Because they had no skills, older women could perform only unskilled and semiskilled work. The results of sample surveys show that the share of unskilled women is higher in the older age groups. The 1980 census found similar results, as 51 percent of unskilled and semiskilled working women were over forty while only 14 percent were younger than twenty-five. Thirty-one percent of skilled working women were under twenty-five, while only 26 percent were over forty.

In professions where large numbers of women were able to find employment, the share of men gradually decreased. As women entered the field, the prestige associated with that profession plummeted, and typically "female professions" developed. On the other hand there are also professions that women have been compelled to relinquish. These occupations are so-called men's occupations; although the work itself could be performed by women with similar efficiency, it is not entrusted to them. The usual argument in such cases is that women are physically unable to perform hard work. However, in agriculture, hard manual work is traditionally performed by women. Similarly, the work performed in cotton mills or spinneries can hardly be considered easy, and the majority of workers there are women. And is the work of a machine operator, which is dominated by men, really hard manual work? Yet the proportion of women is low in this profession.

It can hardly be asserted that women generally are working under better working conditions than men. Considering the work schedules of the workers employed in socialist industry in Hungary, it becomes evident that the number of women working different shifts exceeds the number of men (49 percent of women, compared to 43 percent of men in 1979). A government regulation specified that the working conditions for women working on the night shift should be improved and that night-shift employment of mothers with many children should be reduced. This regulation mainly applies to industrial branches employing large masses of women, such as light industry and within light industry to the textile industry, where the proportion of women working different shifts is the greatest.

Occupational status plays an important role in determining an individual's social position in Hungary as well as in other developed societies. The place an individual occupies within the occupational hierarchy also strongly influences earnings and living conditions. Women in Hungary, as elsewhere in the region, generally have lower occupational status and less power and authority (see table 11.3). One of the causes for this is the fact that the number of women university graduates is much lower than that of men. However, lack of appropriate qualifications is not the sole reason why men are more easily assigned to leading posts, and there are many reasons why women do not and cannot become qualified.

The Hungarian government attaches increasing importance to the idea that in filling vacancies for responsible positions women should not be at a disadvantage. Special attention is paid to this in branches where the majority of employees are women (for instance, in education, public health, and domestic trade).

The activity of women is much more influenced by regional origin than that of men. Since women are generally less qualified, the additional handicap of being in rural areas where jobs are scarce makes it more difficult for women to find jobs. Employment opportunities are harder to find in rural areas; since the choice is more limited, most women remain in their original agricultural occupations.

In the more industrialized areas male labor is easily absorbed by the growing demands of agriculture, which with mechanization includes nonfield labor. Opportunities are open to men to find white-collar work without leaving the rural environment. As a recent study notes, "Agricul-

Table 11.3 Proportion of women in leading positions in Hungary (in percentages)

	Proportion of women among employed persons		
Occupation	1960	1970	1980
Managers of enterprises, directors of institutions	7.4	6.4	12.1
Directors of cooperatives	2.4	2.9	5.6
Leaders in public administration	8.1	11.8	19.6
Leaders in municipal administration	12.5	15.3	29.1
Technical managers, chief engineers, works managers	1.7	4.2	3.1
Financial managers, business executives	21.0	33.8	40.9

Source: *1980. évi Népszámlálás. Foglalkozási adatok. I.* (Population Census. Data on the Occupations) (Budapest: Központi Statisztikai Hivatal, 1981), vol. 22, data calculated from the table on p. 76.

ture becomes increasingly mechanized; modern technology as well as chemicals, herbicides, and pesticides are widely used. The women, however, are kept out of this transformation, without any chance to participate in modern production processes. Rather, women remain confined to hard manual work performed under severe conditions in branches of production where work processes are not yet mechanized."[1] Thus, there are increasing differences between men and women in agriculture compared to earlier periods when agricultural work was performed jointly using traditional means and techniques. In order to stop increasing differences or to reduce them, a government decree of 1970 ordered that in regional planning, industrial development activity concentrate in areas where employment opportunities for women were not yet ensured. However, it will require a long time for the desired effects to materialize. Until then, women either will continue to perform traditional activities in the countryside or not engage in paid employment (see table 11.4 for information concerning differences in the earner/dependent ratios between towns and villages).

Along with the occupational differences that developed as a result of regional differences, there is the problem of commuting. A commuting villager works and lives in two different milieus. Differences originating from two ways of life produce conflict. The first induces the commuter villager to change, the second to remain the same. Commuting is less impor-

Table 11.4 Distribution of the female population by activity and settlement in Hungary (in percentages)

	1960			1970			1980		
Areas	Earners	Dependents	Total	Earners	Dependents	Total	Earners	Dependents	Total
Budapest	55.7	44.3	100.0	71.3	28.7	100.0	75.2	24.8	100.0
Towns	36.6	63.4	100.0	54.4	45.6	100.0	62.9	37.1	100.0
Villages	30.8	69.2	100.0	45.1	54.9	100.0	59.5	40.5	100.0

Source: *1980. évi Népszámlálás. Foglalkozási adatok. I.* (Population Census in 1980. Data on the Occupations. I.) (Budapest: Központi Statisztikai Hivatal, 1981), p. 57.

tant for women than men because the majority of women do not commute to work (see table 11.5).

The share of the population that constitutes the labor reserve is continuing to decrease in Hungary, not only in the case of men but also among women. Long-term forecasts indicate that an increase in the number of male workers cannot be counted upon. Thus, a certain proportion of the vacancies must be filled by female labor. Female labor reserves have also decreased, however. Consequently, the development of the qualitative features of female labor power deserves attention in order to continue the supply of qualified personnel needed in the economy.

Educational Levels and Qualifications

The educational level of the population has undergone important changes in Hungary. Statistical data regarding the level of education and school enrollment ratios of new pupils are encouraging. Women's educational levels also have increased, although the educational level of women still lags behind that of men. There are also considerable differences as far as certain types of schools are concerned. The same proportion of women and men has finished primary school, but among university or academy graduates men are in the majority (see table 11.6).

In the area of higher education men's and women's chances of being enrolled are equal. Half of the students admitted to institutions of higher education currently are women. One can project that in thirty to forty years the number of women reaching the highest educational level will be equal to the number of men.

The core of the problem, however, is not access to education but the fact that men and women differ greatly in their skills and professions. This is due to the unequal enrollment by gender in vocational training. The differentiation starts as early as the end of primary school. Students going

Table 11.5 Commuters by gender in Hungary

Year	Commuters as a percentage of active earners	
	Men	Women
1960	16.9	7.0
1970	24.6	13.4
1979	24.9	15.3

Source: *A naponta ingázók adatai. 1979. január 1. Összefoglaló eredmények* (Data on Daily Commuters, January 1, 1979) (Budapest: Központi Statisztikai Hivatal, 1980), p. 10.

on to secondary schools show significant differentiation by gender. In general education secondary schools where the emphasis is on the humanities, the proportion of girls is rather high (65 percent at the beginning of the school year 1979–80), but in vocational secondary schools and in vocational training, it is lower. In vocational training the proportion of girls amounted to only 31 percent in the school year 1979–80. In addition, the distribution by professions chosen was unequal. The majority of girls are being prepared for the commercial professions and are choosing textile and wearing apparel trades, while their number in the traditional industrial occupations is rather low. This pattern is the consequence of the conventional labeling of trades as either "male" or "female." The work of a machine operator is by no means more difficult than that of a textile worker. Yet women are the minority in the former and the majority in the latter. In higher education similar discrepancies are to be found in certain fields. Women willingly choose teaching careers; they prefer philosophical and economic curricula. In comparison, women's proportion in engineering colleges and in courses of veterinary science and natural sciences is low.

The differences in qualifications between men and women naturally result in different structures of employment. In the long run, these differences contribute to the formation of different views and ways of life. Schooling, therefore, is a decisive factor in changing the roles of women.

Statistical data cannot reveal whether women are interested in continuing their studies as adults. Is it the burdens of housekeeping that keep them back from the opportunities mentioned or do they really prefer to assume the maternal role rather than a career? Whatever their choices, in further developing the educational system, the government is committed to paying increasing attention to the situation of women and the burdens weighing on them in order to promote their participation in continuing education.

Table 11.6 The distribution of the population seven years of age and older by highest educational level and gender in Hungary (in percentages)

	Primary school grades completed				Where qualification obtained			
	0	1–5	6–7	8	Vocational training and special secondary school	Grammar school	Higher education	Total
					Men			
1960	3.5	27.4	39.2	20.5	—	6.2	3.2	100.0
1970	2.1	20.0	29.3	26.6	7.5	9.9	4.6	100.0
1980	1.7	16.0	19.5	28.3	14.5	13.7	6.3	100.0
					Women			
1960	4.4	27.3	40.6	22.4	—	4.4	0.9	100.0
1970	2.7	20.4	33.7	29.5	2.3	9.5	1.9	100.0
1980	2.2	16.5	25.7	31.3	5.3	14.9	4.1	100.0

Source: *1980. évi Népszámlálás. Demográfiai adatok* (Population Census in 1980. Demographical Data), vol. 21 (Budapest: Központi Statisztikai Hivatal, 1980), p. 52.

Earnings

Independent earnings are one of the most important factors determining the position of women within the family and society. Where husband and wife are both breadwinners, women are less compelled to play a secondary role in the family since they can no longer be considered dependents. Equal wages for women and men are stipulated in Hungary by party and government decrees, for political as well as economic reasons. In practice, however, women do not receive the same wages as men.

There are many reasons why women earn less. The majority of jobs with higher wages (either because they require higher qualifications or because they are physically heavy and/or detrimental to health) are done for the most part by men. Job longevity for women is generally shorter because of repeated interruptions (pregnancy, childbirth, childcare); moreover, women have less opportunity to increase work intensity (undertaking less overtime work on account of their household duties after work time) than male workers in the same jobs (see table 11.7). There are cases, however, where no quantifiable explanations for the differences between the earnings of women and men can be found. In nonmanual occupations the main reason for the differential is the fact that women are less numerous in managerial positions and that the majority can find employment only in lower-paying occupations.

Table 11.7 Average monthly earnings of employed women as a percentage of the average monthly earnings of men in Hungary

Occupation	1972	1977
Managers	77.4	82.9
Managerial personnel	72.7	76.3
Top-level specialists	80.0	82.9
Medium-level specialists	75.6	80.9
Low-level specialists	76.8	77.1
Secretarial personnel	70.7	82.1
All nonmanuals	62.1	65.8
Skilled workers	72.0	72.5
Semiskilled workers	72.3	74.3
Unskilled workers	68.7	75.0
All nonagricultural manuals	67.5	68.4
Agricultural manual workers	70.8	83.5
Total	69.1	71.2

Source: "A keresetek szinvonala, szóródása és kapcsolata a családi jövedelemmel 1972 és 1977 években" (The Level and Dispersion of Earnings and Their Connection with the Income of Households) (Budapest: Statisztikai Idöszaki Közlemények), *Statisztikai Hivatal,* vol. 487, 1981, pp. 40–43.

According to a government decree, managers of enterprises and directors of institutions and cooperatives are responsible for carrying out the constitutional principle according to which women should receive equal pay for equal work performed within the same enterprise or institution. However, ensuring an equitable wage system is not only an entrepreneurial task. The creation of a financial basis for it is a matter of public policy. In addition, it rests with the family to ensure equal conditions for its members to obtain suitable qualifications and employment as well as to create conditions for an equitable sharing of burdens.

Social Mobility

When considering the factors influencing the living conditions of women, it is necessary to investigate the changes that have taken place in their social status. In addition to original social background, the life of an individual is also influenced by the changes that take place during that life. Surveys of social mobility show, however, that the influence of social background is different for women and men.

Earlier, social mobility for women simply meant that former dependents became active earners. As a matter of fact, this is the phase of the social

Table 11.8 Women's social group in 1973 compared to the social group of their fathers when they were 14–18 years old (Hungary)

Social group of the fathers when registered persons were 14–18 years old	Social group: Managers intellectuals	Other nonmanuals	Crafts-persons
		Percentage distribution	
Managerial, intellectuals	20.1	40.7	0.6
Other nonmanuals	8.5	43.1	0.8
Craftspersons	3.4	24.6	2.2
Skilled workers	4.1	32.4	0.7
Semiskilled workers	2.1	21.5	0.9
Unskilled workers	1.3	16.8	0.8
Agricultural manuals	0.9	8.0	0.7
Other (or father died earlier)	2.6	15.8	1.2
Total	3.0	18.5	0.9
		Percentage distribution	
Managerial, intellectuals	20.3	6.5	2.1
Other nonmanuals	18.8	15.1	5.7
Craftspersons	7.9	9.0	16.0
Skilled workers	17.4	22.0	10.3
Semiskilled workers	6.9	11.6	9.8
Unskilled workers	2.6	5.4	5.1
Agricultural manuals	12.6	17.5	30.9
Other (or father died earlier)	13.5	12.9	20.1
Total	100.00	100.0	100.0

Source: *Tärsadalmi mobilitás* (Social Mobility) (Budapest: Központi Statisztikai Hivatal, 1981), calculated data.

stratification process where the greatest changes occur in living conditions. Getting away from the family environment, changing the dull, indivisible full day of housework for a working place, and dividing the daily program between worktime and leisure have meant great changes in the life of a woman. The new schedule, the increased income, and having one's own profession mean a qualitative change, but finding a job has other indirect effects and may affect the number of children in the family as well as the woman's health (greater weariness, greater stress, etc.). Conversely, the number of children may result in differences even within the same social stratum and on the same income level. The way of life of a mother of many children differs markedly from that of a childless woman, and different social strata have different fertility behaviors. Higher social groups have of the registered women in 1973

Skilled	Semiskilled Workers	Unskilled	Agricultural manuals	Other	Dependents	Total
by social group of the father						
3.4	4.5	1.6	0.6	0.6	27.9	100.0
6.9	7.7	4.0	2.6	0.7	25.7	100.0
8.5	14.7	11.8	10.6	1.0	23.2	100.0
11.9	16.0	7.4	4.4	1.3	21.8	100.0
7.5	21.0	12.0	13.1	1.5	20.4	100.0
7.6	22.6	12.4	11.5	0.8	26.2	100.0
4.1	12.9	9.8	40.7	0.8	22.1	100.0
5.6	15.1	12.0	22.7	0.9	24.1	100.0
6.3	14.6	9.7	23.3	0.8	22.9	100.0
by social group of the women						
1.6	0.9	0.5	0.1	2.0	3.6	3.0
7.1	3.4	2.7	0.7	5.0	7.3	6.5
9.0	6.9	8.2	3.1	7.0	6.8	6.7
23.6	13.8	9.6	2.4	17.1	11.9	12.5
11.8	14.3	12.2	5.5	15.6	8.8	9.9
7.2	9.2	7.6	2.9	5.0	6.8	5.9
26.3	35.9	40.6	70.6	33.7	39.0	40.4
13.4	15.6	18.6	14.7	14.6	15.8	15.1
100.0	100.0	100.0	100.0	100.0	100.0	100.0

lower fertility, and the fertility behavior of women entering these groups slowly accommodates itself to the habits of the social strata in question. Change in the number of children desired in a family also creates new habits and opportunities.

There have always been significant differences between the social stratification patterns of men and women both before and after World War II in Hungary, and to some extent these differences still exist today. In earlier times women moved almost exclusively toward unskilled manual and nonmanual occupations while men had greater opportunities to enter intellectual occupations and become skilled workers. As noted earlier, this tendency is to some extent explained by the large masses of older, unskilled housewives who became active earners. As a result of the steady rise in

Table 11.9 Social origin of Hungarian managerial personnel and intellectuals (in percentages)

Social group of origin	1962–64 Men	1962–64 Women	1973 Men	1973 Women
Managerial personnel and intellectuals	16.1	28.3	16.1	18.4
Other nonmanuals	15.7	22.0	16.6	18.1
Craftspersons and retail traders	15.0	19.2	11.9	15.8
Skilled workers	17.1	6.7	17.4	15.8
Other workers	10.3	9.7	9.0	9.8
Peasants	24.3	14.1	24.6	17.6
Other and unknown	1.5	—	4.4	4.5
Total	100.0	100.0	100.0	100.0

Source: *Az 1973. évi társadalmi mobilitás vizsgálati eredményei* (Results of the Social Mobility Survey in 1973) (Budapest: Központi Statisztikai Hivatal, 1975), p. 4.
Note: The social status of the registered person was compared to the status of the father in 1938, since data referring to 1962–64 were available only in this manner.

educational levels, women becoming active earners at a younger age now stand nearer to the educational level of men; consequently, they are able to enter more qualified occupations.

Although the main directions of women's social mobility have conserved many traditional features, improvements are being made. Consequently, in a couple of decades, when women will have overcome the present lag, both in the number of employees and in their occupational structure, there probably will not be important differences between men and women in stratification patterns. Today, however, differences persist. Some social strata are relatively less open to women, so that in certain social groups women are not as heterogeneous from the point of view of origin as men (see tables 11.8 and 11.9).

The differences between men and women are obvious here. Women of intellectual origin have remained in greater proportion in their fathers' social group while daughters of manual workers have chosen to a lesser extent white-collar occupations (see table 11.10). By 1973 the situation had changed, but as far as social mobility is concerned, women are more inclined to display the characteristics of a closed group than men. The situation is similar in the case of women in manual occupations.

There was a sudden rise in women's social mobility in the last decade, when daughters of manual workers went into managerial and intellectual jobs in increasing proportions, while women of peasant origin held a greater share among skilled and semiskilled workers. As in the first period

Table 11.10 Persons of peasant origin among nonagricultural manuals in Hungary (in percentages)

	1962–64		1973	
	Men	Women	Men	Women
Among skilled workers (men and women)	41.5	32.4	45.1	38.4
Among semiskilled workers (men and women)	61.1	43.7	58.7	49.2
Among unskilled workers (men and women)	68.3	54.2	60.2	51.3

Source: *Az 1973. évi társadalmi mobilitás vizsgálati eredményei* (Results of the Social Mobility Survey in 1973) (Budapest: Központi Statisztikai Hivatal, 1975), p. 5.
Note: The social status of men and women was compared to the status of the father in 1938, since data referring to 1962–64 were available only in this manner.

after the liberation, when sons of manual workers (mainly skilled workers) started to enter the managerial and intellectual strata, now the daughters of manual workers have started to do the same. The situation was similar with the children of peasants: in the beginning only the sons chose nonagricultural, nonmanual occupations; later on, the daughters also were oriented in the same direction.

The effect of social mobility on life-styles differs from the younger to the older generation. Since social stratification was of less importance forty to fifty years ago than it is now, women belonging to older age groups are less mobile. In addition, in certain strata they form more closed and homogeneous groups than the members of younger age groups. Daughters of manual workers had at that time more difficulties in getting into nonmanual strata, since they had less chance to obtain secondary or higher education than the daughters of intellectuals. Today social stratification exerts greater influence on life-style. Nonetheless, in the case of large-scale inflow to a given stratum, the former style of life of the new entrants influences the way of life and behavior of that social stratum.

The social mobility of individuals in Hungary is expected to be still more independent of the social position of parents in the future. This means that social stratification should be influenced only by the person's qualification and educational level, by individual motivation, and by socioeconomic needs. One could say that conditions in Hungary are close to the realization of this goal since the mechanisms for that are rather efficient.

However, it is not sufficient to forecast or extrapolate the trends in stratification patterns on the basis of social origin alone. Forecasts should instead be interested in the future results of present policies and in how they can modify or influence social mobility in the future.

Table 11.11 Daily time schedule expressed in minutes on an average day according to economic activity and gender (Hungary)

Activities 1
Gainful occupation and productive activity
1. Main occupation
2. Intellectual extra work
3. Nonagricultural manual extra work
4. Agricultural manual work as supplementary income
Travel between the workplace and the dwelling
5. By foot or private vehicle
6. By means of local mass transit
7. By long-distance mass transit
Household and maintenance work
8. Cooking, serving, washing up
9. Tidying up the flat, courtyard, pavement
10. Heating
11. Carrying water
12. Washing, ironing, mending, sewing
13. Preparing or repairing household equipment, maintaining vehicles
14. Upkeep of buildings, construction, enlargement
15. Other work performed in the household
Purchase of goods and services
16. Purchase of goods
17. Use of services
18. Administration
Personal physiological needs
19. Sleep
20. Hygienics, dressing
21. Meals, eating, drinking, coffee drinking
22. Rest, recuperating from illness
Care and education of children
23. Care of children
24. Storytelling, playing with, and teaching children
Social life, communal activities
25. Talks and consultation
26. Entertainment of guests
27. Collective entertainment, dance, play
28. Unpaid work
29. Other communal activities

Men				Women			
Active earner 2	Inactive earner 3	Dependent 4	Total 5	Active earner 6	Inactive earner 7	Dependent 8	Total 9
341	59	85	279	259	42	28	171
1	—	1	1	1	—	—	1
2	4	3	3	1	1	—	1
58	105	19	64	50	46	69	53
6	1	1	5	3	1	—	2
3	1	1	3	2	—	1	1
1	—	—	1	—	—	—	—
11	23	7	13	106	138	136	118
12	23	10	14	48	64	59	53
8	18	3	9	3	5	6	4
1	2	1	1	1	1	2	1
1	3	3	2	44	51	50	46
10	3	6	8	—	—	—	—
15	11	9	14	3	3	4	3
16	34	8	19	6	13	13	9
7	16	6	9	18	24	19	19
3	5	1	4	5	6	4	5
1	1	1	1	1	—	1	1
482	566	527	496	488	545	541	512
56	47	50	54	52	45	45	49
77	89	72	79	73	82	82	77
28	83	16	37	22	55	48	33
6	3	3	5	16	36	12	19
7	5	4	7	6	12	6	7
23	39	25	26	19	28	29	23
14	15	14	14	15	19	16	16
6	7	11	6	2	2	2	2
2	1	3	2	1	—	1	1
2	2	2	2	2	5	3	3

Table 11.11 (continued)

Activities 1
Learning and other intellectual activities
30. Participation in lessons and lectures
31. Private studies, self-education
Cultural and entertaining activities
32. Reading newspapers and periodicals
33. Reading books (without learning purposes)
34. Listening to the radio (as exclusive activity)
35. Watching TV (as exclusive activity)
36. Listening to a tape recorder or record player
37. Traditional needlework
38. Hobbies, other entertainment
Visits to cultural and entertainment institutions
39. Cinema
40. Theatre, concerts
41. Expositions, museums, other programs
42. Sporting events
Outdoor activities, gymnastics
43. Walking, window-shopping, sightseeing
44. Excursions, open-air bathing, sports, other activities
Travel (aside from commuting between workplace and residence)
45. By foot and by private vehicle
46. By means of local mass transit
47. By means of long-distance mass transit
Other activities
48. Religious activity
49. Consumption of alcohol, pub-crawling
50. Other and unknown activities
Total

Source: Rudolf Andorka and Béla Falussy, "A magyar társadalom életmódja az 1976–1977. évi felvétel alapján" (The Way of Life of Hungarian Society on the Basis of the Survey in 1976–1977), *Statisztikai Szemle* 1980, vols. 8–9–10, pp. 828–42; 949–71.

Time Budgets

Both the amount of leisure time available and the way people use it influence life-styles. Having less leisure means having less spare time at one's disposal. In such situations people either renounce certain activities or

Men				Women			
Active earner 2	Inactive earner 3	Dependent 4	Total 5	Active earner 6	Inactive earner 7	Dependent 8	Total 9
3	—	154	10	2	1	38	9
8	1	74	10	5	2	22	8
18	33	8	20	7	11	8	8
13	26	27	16	11	14	15	12
5	16	5	7	2	6	5	3
86	105	88	89	75	92	78	79
2	—	11	2	1	—	2	1
—	—	1	—	13	22	18	15
7	9	13	7	3	3	3	3
4	1	19	4	2	1	3	2
1	—	1	1	1	—	1	1
1	—	1	1	—	—	1	1
1	1	1	1	—	—	—	—
7	19	15	10	7	13	8	8
8	5	33	9	4	3	7	4
41	33	50	40	32	30	33	32
14	10	22	14	16	10	9	13
12	4	21	11	9	4	8	8
—	2	—	1	1	2	1	1
6	7	2	6	—	—	—	—
3	2	2	3	2	2	3	2
1,440	1,440	1,440	1,440	1,440	1,440	1,440	1,440

decrease the time to be spent on these activities. According to a number of foreign investigations, women in Hungary are rather badly off from the point of view of leisure.

This conclusion is confirmed by Hungarian studies. The results of a time budget survey done in 1976–77 show that the fixed-time engage-

Table 11.12 Average time spent on housekeeping work by socio-professional groups, 1976–1977 (Hungary)

Socioprofessional group	Men (hours:minutes)	Women (hours:minutes)	Ratio of coefficients showing time spent on housekeeping: women/men
Managerial	1:25	3:13	2.3
Intellectuals	1:20	2:57	2.2
Other white collar	1:35	3:14	2.0
Skilled workers	1:34	3:38	2.3
Semiskilled workers	1:27	3:57	2.7
Unskilled workers	1:16	4:10	3.4
Plant growers	1:03	3:57	2.7
Stockbreeders	1:03	3:57	3.7
Agricultural self-employed workers and helping family members	1:08	5:34	4.9
Nonagricultural self-employed workers and helping family members	1:12	5:05	4.2
Inactive earners	2:19	5:05	2.2
Dependents	0:55	4:54	5.3
Total	1:26	4:19	3.0

Source: Andorka and Falussy, pp. 828–42; 949–71.

ment of women (time spent on the main occupation, other gainful occupations, housework, and travel together) is approximately half an hour longer than that of men; hence, their leisure time is shorter (see table 11.11). The span of this fixed-time activity shows, of course, differences according to social strata. The heaviest burden weighs on the agricultural workers; they are followed by the nonagricultural skilled workers, while intellectuals are in the most favorable position in this respect.

Women's time constraints have undergone no substantial changes in the last ten years. Although they spent less time on housekeeping activities, the time spent on gainful occupations increased. As table 11.12 indicates, women are spending substantially more time on housekeeping activities than men in all occupational groups.

Not every kind of household work falls entirely to the lot of women. Washing, ironing, sewing, and mending are exclusively duties of women; women also play a larger part in cooking and cleaning. Men participate intensively in shopping and heating. The burden of childrearing weighs for the most part on women, who, according to survey results, spend twice as much time on these activities as men, with variations depending on social group, age, and the number of children. There are considerable differences between urban women and rural women concerning time spent on housekeeping. Urban women generally spend half as much time on housework as rural women.

However, the leisure of women in all groups is less than that of men. Even in the intellectuals' group, where continuing education, learning, and reading are of greater importance, women spend less time on cultural activities than men. In social groups with a lower educational level, the situation is still worse.

What is the minimal span of time to be spent on rest, sleep, and regeneration, allowing us to perform our daily work without excessive strain? Are there differences between the needs of men and women in this respect? The opinion is widely held that women sleep less and not as deeply as men do (all women, not only mothers of small children). This may be simply their response to necessity since women must utilize spare time more efficiently in order to fulfill their manifold duties. If so, it would call for even more rest and relaxation. Unfortunately, the two aspects exclude each other. If someone does not spare either time or effort to work a "second shift" in the household, will that person be exhausted sooner? Or is it otherwise? The average life span of women is higher than that of men. What is the connection, if any, between the way of life and longevity?

Better utilization of leisure time by women is an important aim of social policy in Hungary. The state also assumes something of the burdens of the household insofar as it is anxious to improve the qualitative and quantitative level of housekeeping services available. This depends, however, not on intentions only, but much more on economic considerations.

This chapter has discussed features of the socioeconomic situation of women in Hungary. This situation is influenced also by nonquantifiable (or difficult to quantify) factors. Options as well as motivations are strongly influenced by such factors. It is thus necessary to clarify the motives and the scale of values that, under identical conditions, help form different styles of living. In the future, international comparisons would be useful in order to sort out the aspects of women's situation that are specific to Hungary from general characteristics which also manifest themselves in other countries.

12

Silva Mežnarić

Theory and Reality: The Status of Employed Women in Yugoslavia

Legitimacy

Theories legitimating the status of women in Yugoslavia generally are related to critical theory about the role of self-managed society in the process of women's and men's emancipation. As V. Tomšič, one of the outstanding figures in the field of legitimative concepts on the emancipation of women in Yugoslavia, writes, equality of the sexes in Yugoslavia was based on the laws governing social development as ascertained by Marxism: the equalization of sexes by law is not enough to eliminate women's subordinate position in society and the family. Legal equality only opens the way to discovering the real nature of women's subjugation. As Tomšič notes, the first prerequisite for the emancipation of women would be the reintroduction of women's work in public activities, and this requires the elimination of the individual family. Tomšič also argues that the emancipation of women and the full equality of sexes are related to the development of production relations on the basis of *social ownership* and the development of a political system in which the state, instead of being an instrument of rule, would become an instrument wielded by the working people to change social relations and achieve basic human rights. In such a situation, contradictions between individual and social interests and needs will be overcome in labor and in self-management. New human values will come into being. Further, the inclusion of women in productive labor outside of the family household and the abolition of private ownership will bring about a transformation of family relationships leading to the disappearance of the family as an economic unit and will make way for the socialization of household and family functions. In socialist, transformed society, the roles of men and women must become more and more identical. Differences in employment should not depend on gender but on knowledge, natural abilities, and inclinations.[1]

Consequently, Tomšič argues, the emancipation of women is the result of socialist revolution and social construction—it is inexorable. But neither socialist revolution nor the construction of a socialist society are uncontrolled processes. The development of socialism implies a conscious control over the processes of certain social transformations. The affirmation of women as equal, creative personalities requires change in marriage and family relations. Women, together with progressive and revolutionary men, must be the factor of change. The struggle for such profound social change is part of the struggle of the working class for the emancipation of labor, for control over the entire system of social reproduction by working people. This is why there can be no question of a struggle between women and men. Scientific socialism warns against sidetracking the struggle into a battle between the sexes. Thus, the struggle for the realization of equality between men and women, the struggle for changing their consciousness, is not so much the struggle for "equal rights" but rather for the emancipation of man and his labor. It is taking place in all areas, from the economy and politics to the areas of culture, science, and ethics.[2]

These passages from Tomšič's book *Woman in the Development of Socialist Self-managing Yugoslavia* illustrate the main characteristics of legitimative emancipatory rhetoric in postwar Yugoslavia. They also demonstrate the confusion of what "is" and what "ought" to be, which, in Yugoslav doctrines of emancipation and discussions of the status of women, leads to the characteristic error of utopian and dogmatic social thought: the confusion of legitimations with the real attributes of concrete social institutions.

Through the erratic operation of self-fulfilling prophecies, this idealistic idiom concerning the status and emancipation of women in Yugoslavia stands for reality. Thus, in Yugoslav political and scientific discussion the preponderant paradigm is of an "emancipated" yet still traditional woman, one who is equal in all her rights and duties to men within the self-managed political sphere. According to this image, a woman is able to act according to her political and self-managerial attributes and is paid the same amount of money for the same job as a man. Research on the status of women, especially employed women, gives us some notions about what is actually going on in the real processes of social life. In order to describe these processes as they actually exist apart from the idealistic idiom, we designed a study of the status of employed women in the most developed socialist republic in Yugoslavia, Slovenia. The pages to follow present some of the results of this research.

Attributes of Reality

The research that served as the basis of this essay was originally not aimed at exploring the status of women workers in the economy of

Slovenia. We overlooked the sex structure of individual economic activities even when the sampling was done. When the data processing yielded the first results, however, we were surprised at the extent to which they spoke "of sexes." The data suddenly revealed that hidden behind the apparently logical and well-known disparities in the skill pattern of individual jobs and tasks there lies a disparity known all over the world: the results of discrimination in job accessibility—discrimination based on gender.

Slovenia is the most advanced republic in Yugoslavia. It also is the republic with the highest levels of women's education and employment. Here the work of women outside of their households has had the longest tradition; the proportion of women in the total number of the employed is the highest in Yugoslavia and one of the highest in Europe (44.3 percent). Approximately 57 percent of all women between the ages of fifteen and fifty-nine are employed, half of them in the social sector.[3] The enrollment of girls in secondary schools equals that of boys (girls are 49.9 percent of students in secondary schools), and their orientation to various types of training and education is much more favorable than it was ten years ago, particularly in the increasing numbers of girls in technical schools.[4] The educational structure of women workers in Slovenia does not, except in two groups, differ significantly from the educational structure of employed men.[5] In the self-management organs of organizations of associated labor, women make up 30.3 percent of the members of executive bodies, yet they are only 7.7 percent of the members of all managerial (individual or collegial) organs.[6]

Where are Slovene women employed? As in numerous socialist countries, women are mainly employed in the less accumulative, labor-intensive branches, that is, in the branches depending on the intensive employment of "cheap" labor—women and immigrants from other republics to Slovenia. These are the electronics and textile industries, tobacco production and processing, catering, and tourism, etc.[7] Two principal questions are consequently raised: first, from the development point of view, is the concentraton of almost half of all employed women in certain nonaccumulative branches justifiable? Second, from the human point of view, is it justifiable that in self-managed socialism one part of producers pool their labor in activities in which they can hardly reproduce at a subsistence level?

Both questions are closely interrelated. It is unfortunately difficult to find an adequate, scientifically sustained answer to the first one, since the subject of the "female labor market" has been neglected and left to daily political practice. The second question has been discussed more frequently by political scientists, sociologists, and economists. Our own research work provided the premises for a discussion of the status of the woman worker in associated labor in the Slovene economy. We dealt with the following issues: How is the status of the woman worker treated by Yugoslav sociological and economic theory and by political practice? How is the problem viewed in our research, and what conclusions may be drawn from the results of the inquiry? What recommendations can be given to trade unions and to other political actors for the development of Yugoslav self-managing society in the forthcoming period?

One of our main conclusions was that in employment policy, the "male society" persists. What do we mean by "male society"? Does it mean that in associated labor there is still a reluctance to employ women for responsible jobs? As one analyst noted, "By its historical heritage and by the actual situation in social life, our society is a typically 'male' one. This is manifested for example in politics: since the war, the presence of women in political life has declined. But we are a 'male' society even when it comes to science, to cultural creation."[8]

Such is the assessment of sociologist and political scientist Stipe Suvar in his analysis of social self-management. Speaking of the role of women in associated labor, other sociologists, publicists, and politicians use even harsher words. The status of women is described as "occupational segregation,"[9] as a status "determined by discriminatory criteria and procedures,"[10] as "derived discrimination,"[11] as "negative selection,"[12] as influenced by "sectarianism" and "conservative views, antagonistic to socialism and self-management."[13]

According to Tomšič, old views on the reproduction of "women's" occupations persist not only because such occupations are thought to be easier for women or more convenient to accommodate motherhood but also because they are considered to be closer to the nature of women, who already performed similar work within the family and the household.[14] "Convenience" here means that women are thought to be better at, and traditionally oriented to, modern industrial weaving, tobacco picking and processing, crop processing, the garment industry, and, of course, the modern equivalent of the minute medieval embroidery—the production and assembly of "chips," the "white," "brown," and other electronics.

When discussing "derived discrimination" in the employment of women, S. Letica writes: "The conventional theoretical stereotypes of poor pay for women's work call for more serious theoretical consideration. There is in fact no discrimination against women by the distribution policy. The illusion that it exists results from the fact that women are in a disadvantageous position when it comes to career choice and that employment policy discriminates against them. Their employment in the economically 'inferior' organizations of associated labor preconditions the derived discrimination in distribution policy."[15] Sociologist Katarina Prpić discusses another problem and defines "negative selection" in the employment of women as "the phenomenon and act of preference for certain socio-demographic and social categories of job seekers . . . negative selection in the employment of women therefore embraces the acts of preference for male labor by the employers—organizations of associated labor."[16]

Are the qualifications of the female labor force so much different from the qualifications of men that women are justifiably employed in lower-paid jobs? The data indicate that 36 percent of all employed women compared to 23.4 percent of men occupy jobs that require unskilled or semi-skilled labor, i.e., narrowly specialized low-profile labor; 72 percent of lower jobs, of the "other" (unspecified) work—administrative work, switchboard operation, cleaning, and the like—are performed by women. All in all, we find that 44.5 percent of employed women and 25.4 percent of employed men work in occupations of this type. The unequal sex structure is particularly noticeable at the conveyor belt; here in 69 percent of cases the work is done by women. This fact, together with the information discussed above, gives rise to the following conclusion: "direct production" and "direct administration" in the economy of Slovenia rests largely upon employed women.

In order to establish clearly whether employed men and women in our samples differ from each other in terms of their qualifications for the work they perform, we gave full consideration to the aspect of gender. It became clear that more women than men are overqualified for the work they perform. Thus, for example, some women with university education perform jobs of the lowest value (2.5 percent), which men do not do at all. Even more interesting is the distribution of typical "lower valued" jobs by gender and qualification. Our research shows that the idea that administrative, "easier," and "leisurely" jobs are mainly done by women does not quite hold water; almost 39 percent of all men employed in such jobs (watchmen, operators, messengers, administrative staff, etc.) are skilled or highly skilled, which partly speaks about who is more "on the run" from production into administration.

The meager sociopolitical activity of employed women is often quoted as proof of the fact that the political involvement of women in our society has not improved, despite their great involvement in the economy. Moreover, sociological studies indicate that sociopolitical activity is an important factor in the social mobility of individuals in our society, that it is the element affecting many a "mechanism" of professional and social advancement.[17] Few women can be found in the channels of this type of mobility. Our research data show that only 9.2 percent of all employed women are members of the League of Communists compared to 15.9 percent of men; fewer women than men have a function in trade unions (36.7 percent of all have some function, which roughly corresponds to the proportion of women employed in the economic sector).

Frequent reproaches that women are not committed, expressed in formulations such as "they do not want to participate," "they avoid functions," etc., are not supported by our findings. As many as 49 percent of all the women surveyed expressed their willingness to assume some function in the trade unions. (We did not inquire about other sociopolitical organizations because they have smaller memberships.) The same question was answered in the affirmative by 53 percent of men.

We did not collect data on personal incomes, since such data are always unreliable when obtained by means of a questionnaire. Besides, we believe that gender-based discrimination related to personal incomes would be difficult to demonstrate, first, because women in our country actually get the same pay for the same work, and second, because the problem of discrimination through income is probably hidden elsewhere than in real or nominal personal net incomes. We agree with the economist who claims that the problem is not discrimination through income distribution but rather gender-based discrimination through differential accessibility to the conditions for equality in income distribution. Unequal accessibility to the conditions for income distribution exists when: (*a*) there is substantial segregation of jobs among different groups of the employed and (*b*) when certain jobs are predominantly performed by only certain groups defined in terms of gender, race, nationality, or in some other way.[18] Both of these conditions are confirmed by our data. It is obvious that the distribution of jobs among the employed varies very much between men and women; some jobs in our economy are occupied by more women than men. Some feminist sociologists claim that "on the average, women receive 84 percent of the average personal income, and in the economic sector as little as 81 percent. The decrease of personal incomes in a work organization is considered to be the indicator of some sort of economic crisis (of broader or narrower scope) and a potential political problem. Yet, the fact that women work constantly for 80 percent of personal income does not seem to jeopardize the constitutional stipulation of equal rights to work for men and women."[19] Similar facts were discovered ten years ago by a study of the development of Slovenia: "Irrespective of age, tenure, and activity, the personal incomes of men were considerably higher than the personal incomes of women. Employed women with higher education had 20 percent lower personal incomes than men of the same educational level, women with secondary education were paid 22 percent less, and women with grade school education 8 percent less than men. Highly skilled women workers were paid 20 percent less than highly skilled male workers, and the skilled, semiskilled, and unskilled women were paid 18 percent less than men of the same skill levels. These data indicate that it is more difficult for women to get higher valued jobs, despite their adequate qualifications."[20]

There is no reliable method, however, to prove gender-based discrimination in terms of income. Various studies assumed that in general two procedures are viable to find a solution. The first is the attempt to analyze the characteristics of the worker; the second is to analyze the characteristics of the work. In the former case, the possible differences between the incomes of men and women can be derived from factors that presumably determine differences in productivity, such as education and work experience. In the latter case, which we applied, the procedure is based on the assumption that there are differences of income among different branches and jobs and on the conclusion that there is a certain segregation in employment based on gender. In other words, there exists a positive feedback: the segregation in employment reproduces and expands itself, since it is difficult for a typically "female" branch or organization of associated labor to break the vicious circle of deprived activity because of its low accumulation. It is consequently in a position to attract only the labor which is cheap, or if not cheap because of large investments into its training, labor that does not have any aspirations for social mobility and higher status. In this way "female" branches expand and reproduce themselves, "female" factories, "female" occupations, "female" schools, and, some say, even "female" political factories.[21] This is how we come to the segmentation of the labor market. Thus, according to these findings, "discrimination" in incomes based on gender is in our conditions better called gender-based discrimination in the accessibility of the conditions for the acquisition and regulation of income.

13

Ivan Volgyes

Blue-Collar Working Women and Poverty in Hungary

In the past I have written extensively about the subject of the liberated females in the country of my birth.[1] This chapter concerns the dual problems of women at work and in poverty status in Hungary. It is not a complete treatment of all women in paid employment in Hungary. Nor is it a study of professional women. Rather, it focuses on those women who have not been the beneficiaries of high incomes, education, and social status: the working poor women of a socialist state.

The first section of the chapter presents statistical data concerning women at work in general. Section two deals with the relationship of income to other variables in the female work force. Section three deals with women in poverty status, living close to the minimal edge of existence in a society that is passing them by. Finally, the last section offers some explanations for the phenomena examined and suggests some reasons for the existence of structured discrimination against women and specifically against women in poverty.

Women at Work: Some General Trends

Efforts to change the status of women in communist Eastern Europe began on the basis of ideological imperatives. In Hungary, as elsewhere in the region, the equality of men and women was constitutionally affirmed and immediately made subordinate to the obligation to work. The percentage of women employed outside the home began to rise dramatically with the adoption of plans for rapid industrialization and modernization after 1948. The proportion of all women employed as active wage earners also grew rapidly, more than doubling between 1930 and 1980. While in 1930, only one out of every three women of working age was employed in a paid occupation, by 1980 three out of four women between the ages of fourteen

Table 13.1 Percentage of actively employed earners according to gender in Hungary (in percentages)

	1930	1949	1960	1970	1973	1975	1980	1983
Male	74	71	64	59	57	56	56	55
Female	26	29	36	41	43	44	44	45

Source: *A nök a statisztika tükrében* (Women in the mirror of statistics) (Budapest: Kossuth, 1974), p. 15; *Magyar Statisztikai Zsebkönyv, 1980* (Budapest: Statisztikai Kiado, 1980), p. 154; *Statisztikai Zsebkönyv, 1983* (Budapest: Statisztikai Kiado, 1983), p. 30.

and fifty-five were in paid employment. In addition, many women who have passed the official retirement age also continue to work.[2]

Hungarian women have made great progress in gaining access to every branch of commerce, industry, and agriculture since the 1950s. However, mobility crawled to a halt during the 1970s, and by the early 1980s the labor market was rather stagnant. Nonetheless, there are far more women in every branch of the economy now than in the 1950s. The increase has been especially great in the nonagricultural branches (see table 13.2). As in the rest of Eastern Europe and many other countries, women are overrepresented in commerce and services and underrepresented in other branches of the economy.[3] This pattern, while not unusual, is noteworthy because it contributes to differences in men's and women's earnings. The potential for high incomes exists in these fields, but for most women this potential is not realized.

The distribution of work is a more complex phenomenon than table 13.2 tends to indicate; employment of women is far from equal even within such fields as industry where women's representation most closely approximates the statistical average. If one breaks down the categories of industrial employment, men dominate in heavy industry and women in light industry (see table 13.3). In the latter branch of the economy, women's proportion of the labor force is below the proportion of the total labor force only in the paper and woodworking industries. In heavy industry, however, there is not a *single* branch where their representation is proportionate to their share of the total labor force.

Women have made gains in all other areas of the economy as well as in industry. Among medical and hospital personnel, for example, women account for 92 percent of the labor force, among draftspersons 85 percent, among clerical employees 71 percent; and among teachers 72 percent.[4] Having said this, however, we immediately have to qualify this success. As in the Soviet Union and in other parts of Eastern Europe, the occupations referred to above, as well as most other occupations in which women have

Table 13.2 Percentage of women employed in different economic sectors in Hungary

Economic sector	1950	1960	1973	1980
Industry	22.4	35.0	44.2	44.8
Construction	9.5	11.2	16.0	17.8
Agriculture	31.9	38.1	38.6	40.2
Transportation, telecommunication	11.3	17.0	23.1	24.7
Commerce	38.5	50.5	62.7	64.2
Service	41.4	45.2	58.7	61.3
Average	30.5	36.3	42.9	44.8

Source: *A nök a statisztika tükrében* (Women in the mirror of statistics) (Budapest: Kossuth, 1974), p. 16; *Statisztikai Évkönyv 1980,* p. 126.

made the greatest advances, are those that receive small financial rewards and carry rather minimal social prestige.[5]

Although women have entered the labor force in great numbers, they play a small role in economic decision-making. Women play a particularly small role in this respect in industry, although there has been some improvement in the last decade. Among all the managers of firms in the socialist sector in Hungary, for example, only 3.6 percent were women, and among chief engineers the ratio of women was only 1.4 percent in 1958. In 1965, of more than two thousand women employees of the Hungarian State Railroads, there was only a single woman station manager.[6] Even in commerce, the area clearly dominated by women in 1971, only 15 percent of store managers were women.[7] Not a single man was employed as a poorly paid cashier in that year. Nor is the picture any better in agriculture; while 6.3 percent of the men in agricultural occupations were employed in leadership or decision-making positions, only 1.5 percent of the women held similar posts.[8] Although later data from the 1980 census might seem to indicate a slight increase in upward mobility for women, especially at mid-level managerial posts, the improvements have been only marginal during the decade of the 1970s.

Even in the highest intellectual occupations, differences are evident in men's and women's work, training, and education. In spite of the fact that 6.5 percent of all men and 2.4 percent of women had obtained college diplomas by 1970, the proportion of women among the members of the Academy of Sciences was way below the expected figure.[9] Thus, among 181 academicians there were three women, of 523 doctors of sciences there were twenty-eight women, and of 3,627 of those holding the degree of candidate, there were only around 330 women.[10]

Table 13.3 Percentage of women employed in branches of industry in Hungary: 1972, 1979

Industry	1972	1979
Mining	14.4	15.7
Electricity	27.6	28.7
Steel	26.5	28.0
Engines and engine parts	25.4	25.7
Transport vehicles	30.8	29.0
Electric engines and parts	42.3	42.6
Telecommunications and vacuum technology	55.1	51.8
Tools	44.2	44.2
Consumer-oriented metallurgy	45.6	41.9
Construction materials	38.8	38.8
Chemicals	43.4	43.7
Heavy industry total	33.7	34.5
Woodworking	39.8	37.6
Paper	44.9	45.4
Printing	54.7	53.2
Textiles	67.5	66.8
Handicrafts	77.5	88.3
Leather, shoes, and furs	63.6	67.4
Synthetic textiles	81.9	84.4
Light industry total	64.3	69.1

Source: *A nök a statisztika tükrében*, p. 17; *Statisztikai Évkönyv 1979*, p. 182.

The question can rightfully be raised, whether it really matters where women are employed in a society where theoretically it matters little which branch of social production one works in. The answer, of course, lies in the area of remuneration. As the next section illustrates, these differences are important because they affect income distribution in Hungary.

Women's Qualifications and Wages

The factors that influence the inequality in men's and women's wages begin within, and hence are already determined by, the school system.[11] While it can be said that the socialization process begins very early with women's jobs in children's books tagged along the "traditional" lines (cook, doctor, wife, teacher, sales clerk, clerical employee), in the non-specialized levels of the primary schools (*általános iskola*), the role of women is relatively equal. Differentiation begins to creep in to a very great extent, however, as the children reach their seventh and eighth year of pri-

Table 13.4 Attendance in Hungarian secondary schools (1983)

School type	Number of students	Percentage of women among those students completing secondary education
Gymnasium	125,598	64.4
Specialized Technikum:	191,034	51.6
Industrial	92,812	16.5
Agricultural	13,147	20.0
Economic	37,797	89.8
Commercial	12,145	83.9
Restaurant	5,682	44.8
Transportation	3,101	30.4
Postal Service	3,918	87.6
Medical	15,557	98.8
Nursery-kindergarten	4,950	99.8
Artistic	1,925	63.4
Total	316,632	57.5

Source: *Statisztikai Évkönyv, 1983,* p. 300.

mary school and are being prepared to enter either the labor market or schools that will give further training. Here the bias against women getting certain types of education is visible among teachers and family alike: "this job is not for girls, you shouldn't try to study to be an engineer . . ."; these and similar stereotypes abound.[12] But more serious than the stereotypical responses received from parents at home is the deliberate channeling that takes place by teachers and principals in the schools. Their role in the "selection" process is enormous, and the counseling they give determines to a great extent what the child will do in the future. Without trying to investigate the intentions of the adults, let us at this stage simply examine the evidence: the resulting school structure between ages fourteen and eighteen broken down according to the ratio of men and women in the various institutions in Hungary (see table 13.4).

Clearly, women dominate in terms of numbers of students in gymnasia, economic and commercial high schools, and in the postal service, nursery/kindergarten, medical assistant, and artistic high schools, while men are overwhelmingly represented among the students of agricultural and industrial high schools and, although a little less heavily, in the food industry and transportation training centers. Two things should be kept in mind at this juncture: first, the gymnasia normally are the best road to a liberal arts college degree whose commercial value is the same as it is in the United States by itself, but the agricultural and technical high schools lead

Table 13.5 Average monthly wages according to occupation and gender in Hungary, 1979–81

	Percentage of men employed	Percentage of women employed	Average monthly wage (in forints)	Deviation from average
Heavy industry	91.6	8.4	5,860	+1,989
Light industry	44.8	55.2	3,771	- 100
Agriculture	58.0	42.0	5,210	+1,400
Clerical-economic commercial sector	11.0	89.0	3,200	- 571
Restaurant work	76.0	24.0	4,700	+ 829
Postal service	16.0	84.0	3,150	- 721
Nursery-kindergarten teachers	1.0	99.0	3,280	- 591
Medical assistants	2.0	98.0	2,800	-1,071
Average			3,871	

Source: Constructed from *Évkönyv, 1979, Zsebkönyv, 1980, 1981,* and *Cooperative Research Survey.*

to skilled worker/technician and—later on—supervisory positions in the economy; second, the preselection of the different kinds of schools, consequently, already sets the tone for income differentiation later on. As table 13.5, which shows the average monthly wage of skilled workers and those with a specialized high school qualification employed in Hungary, illustrates, there are important differences between the income of skilled labor in areas where men or women dominate.[13]

In those fields where men dominate as skilled workers, their wages are *above* the national average for skilled workers by 829 to 1,989 forints per month, while in sectors where women are the vast majority their wages are *below* that of the national average by 571 to 1,071 forints per month. Only in light industry—because of the wide dispersion of income and the relative evenness of the sexual distribution—do we find relative equality, but here, too, the vast number of women in lower-paying occupations tends to drag the average wage close to the national norm.

Income differentiation becomes even more visible if we look not only at the average income of trained and skilled laborers who have received the necessary education, but also at the income differentiation that exists between all employed women and men. In all areas of economic activity, approximately 78 to 91 percent of women earn less than four thousand forints per month, while the percentage of men who earn less than that amount ranges from approximately 41 to 58 percent. Put another way, women's income in Hungary is only slightly more than one half of the

Table 13.6 Monthly wages in the socialist sector according to gender in Hungary (1979)

	Forints/Monthly							
Sector	1,000 or less	1,001–2,000	2,001–3,000	3,001–4,000	4,001–5,000	5,001–6,000	6,001 and above	Percentage earning less than 4,000 forints
Industry								
Men	0.1	1.1	11.3	28.9	28.8	15.8	14.0	41.4
Women	0.3	7.2	44.7	34.2	10.1	2.4	1.1	86.4
Construction								
Men	0.0	0.9	10.3	29.6	29.7	15.4	14.1	40.8
Women	0.2	7.8	39.0	31.3	13.8	4.9	3.0	78.3
Agriculture								
Men	0.0	0.9	13.6	41.8	30.1	9.1	4.5	56.3
Women	0.3	11.1	51.2	28.6	6.7	1.6	0.5	91.2
Transportation & telecommunication								
Men	0.0	1.3	12.8	31.4	30.5	14.2	9.8	45.5
Women	0.7	7.1	42.0	34.3	11.5	2.8	1.6	84.1
Commerce								
Men	0.2	3.6	20.5	33.3	22.7	10.4	9.3	57.6
Women	0.8	10.4	43.8	28.7	10.4	3.7	2.2	83.7
Service								
Men	0.9	2.6	13.2	27.1	24.0	14.2	18.0	43.8
Women	2.5	13.8	37.2	24.0	13.9	5.4	3.2	77.5
Average								
Men	0.2	1.5	12.5	30.7	28.0	14.3	12.8	44.9
Women	1.2	10.1	41.8	29.5	11.5	3.7	2.2	82.6

Source: *Statisztikai Évkönyv, 1979,* p. 139.

income of men, a figure that is not that different from the wage differentials in many capitalist as well as other socialist countries.

Women in Poverty

Perhaps the worst aspect of the structural discrimination has been the unintended, though not unforeseeable, thrusting of a large number of women with low earnings into poverty. Their plight, exaggerated by the economic crisis of the early 1980s and Hungary's switch to a socialist-market economy, is by far the saddest plight, and the human face of the women at or below poverty levels is one that cannot be handled simply through the communist lens of "objective reality" or the Western lens of "objective social science phenomenon." As in many Western countries, the poor in Hungary are disproportionately female. Women in this status have many faces. In their tragic appearance they range from apparitions strongly resembling the "bag women" of New York to the desperately struggling working mother of a black family in any of the cities and towns of the United States, who tries to raise a large family with dignity and hard work but succumbs to the realities of minimal economic existence. They are women with many faces and many habits: some are habitual alcoholics bent on self-destruction, others are sad old women who live on measly pensions and fall further and further behind in their attempts to eke out a satisfactory existence.

The problem of poverty, of course, is not a new problem in Hungary: in the 1930s the land was rightly called that of 3 million paupers. The further pauperization of Hungarian society that occurred between 1945 and 1965 was only reversed as Hungary's demand for labor reached its peak between 1965 and 1975; during this period every segment of Hungarian society advanced, and it looked as though the problem of poverty could be solved in toto. But, as the world economic crisis of the late 1970s reached Hungary, as inflation took its toll, and as the market mechanism of the economy of Hungary drove consumer prices—especially food prices—sharply upward, the problem of poverty in Hungary became acute once again. Prompted by the alarming number of people tumbling into poverty status, the first coalescence of the relatively non-co-opted intellectuals and the working class took place in September 1979, culminating in the establishment of SZETA (Szegényeket Támogató Alap—Foundation to Assist the Poor), a private organization for the coordination of charities for supporting the poor. The purpose of the organization was to help "those individuals with low incomes and those who are unable to work [as well as those] families with many children [who are] unable to alter their circumstances through their own strength."[14] Through ups and downs of official disapproval and toleration the foundation has distributed clothes and financial aid (amounting to more than 250,000 forints) to a large number of people and assisted them generally in a manner similar to the antipoverty agencies that operated in the United States in the 1970s. The activities of SZETA, however, are inadequate when compared to the large number of people who really need their assistance.

Prior to discussing the relationship of women and poverty, it is important to emphasize the extent of the problem and the definition of poverty levels in Hungary. The official poverty level was defined by the Central Statistical Office of Hungary in 1969; based on their findings as of 1977, a per capita monthly income of 1,600 forints represented the poverty level.[15] According to the official sources in 1977, 20 percent of the population lived below this level with an average per capita monthly income of 1,965 and 1,862 forints for wages and pensions, respectively.[16] Due to the inflation and the rapid rise in the cost of necessities that occurred between 1977 and 1981, however, the poverty line in 1981 was at the level of 2,300 forints per capita.[17] Again, according to official figures of the Statistical Yearbook in 1980, 30 percent of the population had per capita earnings below the "official" poverty levels.[18]

Two social groups show up most frequently among the people below poverty lines: families with a large number of children and old people in retirement. In this study we will concentrate our attention on the families and especially the women with several children to care for. Out of 2,200,000 children under fifteen years of age, 720,000—32 percent of the total number—live in families where the per capita income does not reach the official poverty level.[19] Among the families below the poverty level, 30 percent have no wage earners at all; the ratio of adult women to men in this category is three to one. Seventy-three percent of those families where there are three children earn less than the minimum per capita monthly earning, and 94 percent of all those families where there are more than three children fall below the per capita poverty line.[20] In other words, fully 47 percent of *all* children today live below the official poverty line. To make it more explicit, since roughly 20 percent of *all* children are brought up in families headed by a woman (some two hundred thousand families), nearly *all* of those women in this category who have more than one child fall below the poverty line.[21]

The situation is especially critical for women who are employed in the socialist sector. Table 13.7 lists the percentage of women and men who earn less than three thousand forints, e.g., slightly *above* the poverty level of 2,300–2,400 forints monthly salary. Looking at women's salaries we find that those earning below three thousand forints range from a low of 47 percent (in construction) to a high of 62 percent (in agriculture), averaging 53.1 percent of all women employed in the socialist sector. In comparison to the men who earn less than that amount, a clear pattern of discrimination and pauperization can be established.

Some will argue, of course, that working women—by and large—"supplement" the income of the major breadwinner in the family. Such an argument may hold for some women, but it does not hold for the vast majority of working-class women, whose incomes often are essential for the maintenance of a minimal standard of living. Moreover, in one out of every five families for various reasons (divorce, death of the [male] spouse,

Table 13.7 Percentage of men and women earning less than 3,000 forints* per month in the various branches of the Hungarian economy in 1979

Branch	Men	Women
Industry	12.5	52.2
Construction	11.2	47.0
Agriculture	14.5	62.6
Transport and telecommunication	14.1	49.8
Commerce	24.3	55.0
Service	16.7	53.5
Average	14.2	53.1

Source: *Statisztikai Évkönyv, 1979,* p. 139.
*Poverty line income was estimated at 2,300–2,400 per capita monthly income in 1979.

desertion, alcoholism, etc.) the woman's income is the main or only income. Some would further argue that women who have low incomes supplement them from the second economy running rampant in socialist Hungary. But this argument ignores several basic points. First, the women examined in this study are those who possess few or none of the "convertible" skills so cherished in the second economy (e.g., such as those possessed by plumbers, electricians, translators, computer specialists). Suffering from a lack of higher qualifications and specialization in areas where the economy can use convertible labor, they benefit the least from the secondary economy. In addition, precisely because the women have both primary *and* secondary responsibilities (cooking, shopping, washing, ironing, childrearing), they are the ones who are left out of the secondary economy with its significant income supplement possibilities. Frequently, if there are large numbers of children (in the Hungarian context that means having more than two children), they are compelled to stay home on the "young mothers' leave," causing the family income to fall below the poverty line as their monthly income dwindles.[22]

Nor should one take seriously the family income supplement that people receive after each child. The amount of such a supplement in 1979 was less than five hundred forints per month per child,[23] an amount that barely covers 60 percent of the child's minimal needs.[24] Moreover, such an income supplement can only be paid to families where the "head" of the family worked at least twenty-one days a month, but precisely those in the lowest categories of income potential are forced to pick up the seasonal, better-paying jobs (such as harvesting, construction of special projects, dams, snow removal, etc.) and thus, in fact, frequently do not receive the family income supplements.

What conclusions can we draw from these data? First, it is clear that the structural differentiation discussed earlier has led to the pauperization of a large part of the population of working women. While it is true that the government has attempted to undertake some reforms to ameliorate their position (such as the reform of the family allowance system that began to be implemented in 1980), the vast majority of women analyzed in this chapter suffer not just from the "negritude" imposed upon them by the structure of the system, but also from the pauperization that resulted from the worsening Hungarian economic situation and their position within it. Ultimately, along with the old people existing on pittances, it is nonprofessional working women who have to pay the price of inequality of socialist Hungary.

Conclusions

Writers attempting to account for women's secondary status have looked at several factors. These include social roles as defined by tradition and social policies; lack of training and education; the selection process within the family, the schools, and the social ethos; differentiation in income in different sectors of the economy; and biological-physical roles that act as hindrances to the advancement of women.

One could examine each of these variables at great length and then might conclude that any policy the regime might follow as far as women are concerned is likely to be self-defeating. The leadership, for instance, can create more kindergartens—and there is a real need for that—but doing so will not help the crowded conditions caused by the lack of apartments that, in turn, acts as a limitation on the size of the family and *also* —indirectly—places the woman in a position of servitude toward in-laws, mothers, fathers, and other kinfolk, as *she* tries to be a major breadwinner, a servant, a wife, and a mother as well. Or, the regime can try to create the world's most liberal young mother's leave policy that allows the mother to stay home for three years with partial pay after giving birth.[25] This most humane policy has, indeed, been very successful in promoting the right of women to give birth and rear their children in relative peace at home; but it has also caused major disruptions in the careers of women who return to work after three or six years of the young mother's leave.

If we look specifically at women's economic situation, the primary reasons for the continued inequality between men and women in Hungary (as in other countries) are (1) the channeling of the children into "suitable" schooling; (2) the self-defeating and complacent attitudes still prevalent among women; and (3) the absolute lack of mobilized political power possessed by women.

Educational channeling is a phenomenon that is observable in most societies: the notion of what "women's jobs" should be is hardly restricted to the prejudices of communist dogma. But in communist Hungary a large part of the blame for the channeling is not restricted to society and societal attitudes only. Rather, it seems to be a conscious—or at best a subconscious—policy enforced and put into practice by the principals of grade schools (general schools), and more than 85 percent of these principals are men. In spite of all the policy directives to which Hungarian researchers refer, the fact is that no one can ever pinpoint a policy directive that encourages channeling women in high-income schooling directions (such as surgery, computer programming or electronic engineering on the higher levels, or transportation, telecommunication, or skilled heavy-industrial jobs on the lower levels).

Second, the attitude among women regarding their own role has not been altered significantly during the last three decades of communist rule as far as working women in nonelite jobs or in nonintellectual occupations are concerned. Physical or manual laboring women, blue-collar working women, and women clerical employees retain a view of themselves as second-rate earners of income and do not act in any significant way to change the conception of their role in society. Never mind that every tenth mother is a single head of a household,[26] never mind that more than twice as many women than men are below the poverty line: understandably tired after a hard day's work, after interminable crowded shopping battles, cooking, cleaning, tending to children, parents, and/or husbands, they simply have no energy to fight the battle for "female equality." And while in the United States and West European countries the battle for female equality has been waged largely by upper middle-class women in upper middle-class positions who desire an equal chance to get to the top, the women in Hungary who have made it into the elite and the upper stratum have neither the social consciousness nor the desire to fight for women at lower levels. Given the prevalence of attitudes such as, "well, if I made it, so can they!" or "we already have enough intellectuals," the female working stiffs can expect little real support from their upper-class *consoeurs*.

Finally, the very minimal leverage that women possess in the true positions of political power within the party and policymaking bodies and the political apparat in Hungary remains a significant limiting factor for the achievement of equality. Students of political science and theoreticians of public policy concerned with communist political systems should not pass by this phenomenon lightly. The party espouses egalitarianism but eschews any meaningful steps to bring women into equal participation. Influenced by the primitive sexist attitudes inherent in both the "movement" and the ideology and occupied with the practicalities of running a bureaucratic regime, the communist policymakers of Hungary have hardly begun to take the first steps toward making equality a meaningful concept for most Hungarian women.

14

Susan L. Woodward

The Rights of Women: Ideology, Policy, and Social Change in Yugoslavia

Commitment to equality among national groups and an explicit strategy to assure that equality transformed the Communist party of Yugoslavia from a victorious army of resistance into a governing party. Drawing support from all regions of the country, the party was thus able to construct a substantial majority against the sectional and protofascist appeals of its wartime opposition. It is less often noted, however, that the party's commitment to equality between women and men also distinguished it from its contenders for power over postwar Yugoslavia.[1]

The party's program of equality grew out of three traditions. The most obvious was ideological. To this Marxist party, the inferior position of women in the family, sanctioned by both cultural traditions and legal norms, was seen as clear evidence of the exploitation in Yugoslav society it was fighting to eliminate. Following Engels' analysis, the party's solution to both the emancipation of workers from the rule of capital and the liberation of women from their subjection to men would be found in the socialist state and its expropriation of bourgeois rights, especially to private property.[2] A second tradition was also ideological, but its origin can be traced to the tactics of local struggles in the Balkans. Since the late nineteenth century, advocates of social change, many of them important precursors of the communist movement, like Svetozar Marković, had emphasized the obstacles to progress that lay in women's status. Whether as mothers socializing their children or as public figures infecting the level of morality and civilization, women, in their ignorance, illiteracy, and "slavery,"[3] held back the general development of society. To these reformers, progress required not only increased wealth and its more egalitarian distribution, but also the education and enfranchisement of women. The third tradition might be called political. Although women were not always evident in leadership forums, they had been active members of the Communist party throughout the period of illegality and in the Partisans' struggle of the war.[4] However abnormal the demands of war, the party could hardly dismiss the contribution that women had made, any more than it could neglect their role once peace had been won. The old order was to be destroyed and so too the bases for the subordination of women in the traditional Yugoslav family.

As in its approach to the national question, the new leadership relied on constitutional guarantees of equal rights, both in society and in the family, to establish equality between women and men. To buttress these legal changes, the party also tried to diminish the influence of traditional authorities, in the belief that they were active opponents of equality and of the social changes required for equality to be realized. Thus the campaign against local clergy, for example, was based in large part on the assumption that the clergy promoted the view that women were inferior and suited only for the kitchen and nursery. These steps—erasing former legal permission to subordinate women and transferring authority to those who supported equality—completed the political stage. Directing its attention to economic development and the consolidation of political power, the new ruling group proceeded according to what Zsuzsa Ferge later called the "naive optimism" of the period, namely, the Marxist assumption that industrialization to lay the material base, acceptance of public responsibility for the provision of basic needs, and women's incorporation into productive labor to change consciousness would undermine traditional beliefs and allow relations between men and women to be restructured on the basis of equality.[5]

What have the consequences of this approach to changing social relations between men and women been in the period since the declaration of equal rights in 1945? Were the assumptions that social change would flow automatically from the political and economic changes instituted correct? What about the willingness to accept a relatively long time horizon for the goal of social equality? The discussion that follows is more an attempt to explore aspects of these questions than to provide definitive answers. It examines the process of change to identify some of the elements of any answer to these questions.

The Relation between Women and State Policy: The Pre-Socialist Period

The position of women in any society depends on how that society organizes basic human functions, such as reproduction, subsistence, and production. The ordering of social relations is constrained by ecological adaptation and, where populations live within states, by the demands and services of political authority. State policies to increase monetary revenues by taxing family income will influence the relations between men and women and hence their conceptions about women's roles in one way, policies to increase access to labor resources by taxing a child per year (the Ottoman *devshirme*) or by mobilizing all available adults, men and women, into voluntary work brigades, another. States that provide effective judicial and policing forces will place different demands on individuals and households than those that leave such tasks to private means. Where those states are alien impositions, as in the Yugoslav lands for the half millennium or so prior to 1918, the importance of the household in organizing social life is likely to be particularly great. This is because the services of the state are usually limited to the satisfaction of its extractive policies, and as subjects rather than citizens, the population can shape their social organization and satisfy their needs only within externally imposed and, therefore, largely arbitrary constraints that they can only attempt to adapt or evade.

The socialist program to create equality between women and men in Yugoslavia after 1945 did not take place in a vacuum but in a highly developed pattern of social relations shaped by the policies of earlier governments in the area. The policies of the new state, such as those designed to organize production, to obtain the resources necessary for its activities, to provide services such as securing social order, and to allocate the goods necessary to subsistence, were likely to require modification of the existing pattern of male-female relations at the same time as, and perhaps independently of, the adaptation required to the new rules promoting equality. To analyze the consequences of the socialist program, in other words, factors other than the explicit legislation creating equal rights must be examined. First, what social context do these new sets of state-defined rules encounter, and what is the nature of the adaptation that is being demanded? Second, what effect do other demands and services from authorities have on female-male relations in postwar Yugoslavia?

Although the two world wars and several regional wars during this century significantly reduced the number of available males, at midcentury adult identity for most women in Yugoslavia was inseparable from marriage and hence family. This was certainly the case for the 76 percent of the population still living in the countryside and probably true for a large proportion of the urban population. Certainly the 11 percent of the population engaged in industrial activities (by 1941) came from, and often still resided with, their rural families. Production, and hence labor, was organized by family-based units. The family, and more often than not home production that never entered a market, provided one's subsistence needs. Extensive alliances of mutual aid and obligation were created to expand the survival lifelines and the networks of cooperation for necessary tasks. Yet these, too, were all formed around a core of the marriage bond and lineage: alliances among generations within agnatic groups (*zadruge*) or with in-laws (*prijateljstva*); godparenthoods (*kumstva*); and, in the former military border, neighborhoods (also *zadruge*).

As a rule, the basic structure of human relations followed a pattern characteristic of most horticultural societies that anthropologists call "bridewealth societies" (in contrast to "brideservice" peoples).[6] Families were organized on patriarchal, patrilocal, and virifocal principles. Women married into their husband's families and were thus outsiders to the core social unit. Valued as sex objects, mothers, and workers, wives were acquired by the exchange of gifts, labor, and favors between men, which was seen as a payment for the *rights* to enjoy and to appropriate the products of women's labor, sexuality, and reproductive capacity. The indebtedness of the groom to those who made it possible for him to obtain a wife perpetuated the hierarchy and gerontocracy of the family. Tasks within the family were distributed according to a sharply differentiated division of labor along gender lines, and women's subordination both to all adult males in the family and to older women was essential to order, as can be seen by the conflicts that erupted when women acted otherwise. The basis of these hierarchical, unequal, rights-defined systems of obligations and reward was cemented in ritual separation of male and female spheres.[7]

Because each region in Yugoslavia had been subject to different feudal and imperial authorities, and thus to different policies, there were significant variations on this general theme.[8] In Slovenia, formerly a part of the Austrian crownlands, for example, primogeniture in land inheritance, extensive local services, crafts, roads, universal elementary education by the 1890s, and a well-developed local administration and police (all the product of Theresian policies of the eighteenth century to increase central revenues) had provided many more opportunities, as well as pressures, for both young women and men to find work, spouses, cooperative networks, and goods outside the family. Although the family was patriarchal, it was not patrilocal, and women were thus not always invaders of a close-knit, fortified bond among lineally related men. This was also the case in the urban administrative and professional families in most regions, although their numbers were small.

In the areas formerly under Ottoman control, on the other hand, for the Christian peasants at least (the majority of the population), the distance of the imperial administration and the extent of local autonomy under the millet system was such that households had to defend themselves and resolve their own conflicts. The solution was a pattern familiar in much of the Mediterranean:[9] the code of honor and the blood feud, along with stricter hierarchy, provided much of the required behavioral norms and unity. Alliances of the kind mentioned above were also more developed here because they had to provide protection and order in addition to labor as in the north. A woman's fertility was particularly important where large families were greater protection and even more necessary where families had annually to surrender one male child to the state (*devshirme*).

In addition to this great regional variation, political changes in the nineteenth century (such as the emancipation of the serfs in Austria-Hungary, the political autonomy of Serbia from Turkey, the annexation of Bosnia by Austria) and the creation of an independent state of the Kingdom of the Serbs, Croats, and Slovenes in 1918 had begun a process of change in the methods of gaining a livelihood and in the methods used by the state to extract resources from the population. Therefore, the social relations of production and control underwent a process of adaptation.

In Serbia and in the lands of Austria-Hungary, peasants were granted the right to own and inherit land. Reductions in the authority of feudal lords opened occupations such as commerce and governmental administration to former serfs. At the same time direct taxation increased substantially, and the growth of commerce and attempts by the states to encourage manufacturing activities by turning the terms of trade against the peasants or even forbidding the sale of manufactured goods in the villages (as in Serbia) increased both the need for cash as well as indebtedness of the majority. To cope, households had to develop strategies of accumulation. The increased competition over resources as well as the growing economic differentiation of the population as inequalities increased both intensified domestic tensions and led to changes in family relations. For example, men began to travel far in search of income, migrating for long periods to the Americas, Africa, and Asia. With rare exceptions (women recruited from Dalmatia as governesses in Cairo), women were left at home to tend the homestead. A few women went to work in textile and tobacco factories. The marriage dowry was introduced in Serbia and much of the Austro-Hungarian lands where it had no use before. Now women were sought for their wealth in land as well as their labor. Strategies of accumulation led to larger extended families (*zadruge*) than ever in much of the Austro-Hungarian territory. To counteract this tendency, and to increase its own revenues, the state permitted women to inherit property, which led to increased conflict within families. Coming from outside the still patriarchal family—an alliance of male relatives living with their externally recruited wives—these changes in women's rights created conflicts among brothers and between wives with their own property and other family members. Women became the focus of controversy and conflict. Conflicts that threatened to divide families, whatever their basis, were said to be caused by women who wanted to rule.[10]

The threat of disintegration in families, now far more significant because of the issue of property, led to a reassertion of patriarchal authority. Because marriage was still the moment where rights were distributed, especially where the state was still alien (everywhere but Serbia until 1918), it became the focus of family and even community conflict.

By the twentieth century, women began to attend school. In the 1931 census, illiteracy in women aged ten years or older had dropped to 6 percent in Slovenia, 24 percent in Vojvodina, 40 percent in Croatia, 77 percent in Montenegro, 78 percent in Serbia, 82 percent in Macedonia and 84 percent in Bosnia-Herzegovina. But the agrarian crises of the 1870s and 1880s and the 1920s and 1930s, the limits on industrial goods available in villages, the migration of men and war casualties, and the failure of the domestic economy to expand industrial employment all combined to keep women in the countryside and to increase their workload.[11] The scarcity of men only made them more valuable despite their unemployment because the family had not changed. New institutions to adapt, such as the purchase of sons-in-law (*kupovina zeta*) and a scale to measure male worth according to profession, status, wealth, and residence, developed after World War I.

Finally, with political independence (in Serbia in the nineteenth century and in the rest of the country after 1918), the domain of decision-making and power left the household, where women might at least have had informal influence, and sexual differentiation of political activities increased. By the interwar period, politically active women tended to be schoolteachers sent by the Ministry of Education to rural schools or organized university and professional women—educated women from urban families, who were frequently unmarried. The policies of the interwar governments to stimulate economic development by encouraging domestic industry, opening public schools, and reforming landholding patterns, appear to have furthered the processes of class differentiation begun in the previous century. The resulting changes in family structure and in women's roles were less dramatic than one might have expected, however, because of (1) the ability of various social forces to block implementation, for example, of the agrarian reform in the feudal south; (2) the privileged role of traditional authorities, especially church leaders, in the government's educational and family policies; and (3) the government's failure to adapt the legislation on family and inheritance from colonial days to the new circumstances. By 1941, and the outbreak of war again, each region was still governed according to its preindependence legal codes: the Austrian Civil Code in Slovenia, the Hungarian variant in Croatia-Slavonia and Vojvodina, the Serbian Civil Code of 1844 (based on the Austrian Code but prohibiting women's rights to property) in Serbia, the Montenegrin Code of 1855 in Montenegro, and in the south, the Ottoman Civil Code for Christians, with a layer of Austrian judicial interpretation in Bosnia since 1878, and Shar'ia law for Moslems.

As the socialist period approached, therefore, there were many more possibilities for women to have a social identity and to find subsistence outside of marriage and the patriarchal family. However, these opportunities reached only a very small number of women: the urban middle class, predominantly in the northern regions. But the family itself had not changed very much, apart from its increased tensions. The law still treated women by the patriarchal codes of the colonial period.

The Socialist policy

Into this social environment the new government introduced legislation granting equal rights to women. The 1946 constitution, for the first time, guaranteed Yugoslav women political, economic, and social equality with men. Women were given the right to vote, to hold public office, to be educated in any school, and to enter public employment without discrimination. The 1946 Basic Law on Marriage wrested control of marriage from the church and customary law and made it the jurisdiction of the state. Civil marriage became obligatory everywhere. Former customs discriminating against women, such as the dowry, bride price, *purda*, and the husband's right to total authority over domestic affairs and property, were forbidden. Husbands and wives were given equal rights over all family decisions, including the initiation of divorce, the care and treatment of children, determination of custody, and disposition of mutual property. Furthermore, for the first time in Yugoslav history, a single legal code for constitutional rights and family matters treated women the same regardless of region.

The government did not abolish the institution of the family itself, however. On the contrary, it viewed the family as a crucial source of social stability in a period of otherwise great upheaval from war, reconstruction, and establishment of a new order. As a result, it sought to strengthen the family as an institution that would be a "cradle of ties between personality and society."[12] Second, it viewed the family as the preferred institution to care for children and the elderly, at the very least to minimize the diversion of scarce public resources to such purposes. Third, it continued to view the family as the proper institution for the distribution of nonsocialized property. Thus the 1946 constitution also protected marriage and the family, on the argument that marriage was the most important basis for a family and that the family should be strengthened again. In a series of laws on old age, adoption, and relations between parents and children passed during 1947, the family was held responsible for the support of all *lineal* dependents.[13] In practice, furthermore, local officials regarded the many communal arrangements that grew out of wartime conditions and the resettlement migrations of the immediate postwar period as a "social evil." They reacted "energetically," as one scholar put it, to legalize these "wild marriages," as they were called by the colonists from Kordun and Dalmatia in the Vojvodina.[14]

These policies toward women and toward families, taken separately, seem quite reasonable given the goals of the new regime. Taken together, however, they clearly posit a model of the family that was foreign to much of the population, although closer perhaps to the small, urban, nuclear family of many of the policymakers or to the marriages of political and revolutionary comrades during the war or the radical days immediately preceding it.

In fact, the new policies papered over what was a compromise between the commitment to prohibit wholesale all those customs and laws that were seen to demean women, on the one hand, and the need for families to take responsibility for tasks the government was not ready to assume, on the other, with a vision of relations between men and women as equal, nurturing, voluntary, and free (that is, "private"). That this was a compromise, however, is apparent in the vagueness and ambiguity of the family law that was written, what one authority on the Yugoslav legal system referred to as the creation of "quasi-public law."[15] Marriage and divorce cases, for example, were placed under the jurisdiction of the civil courts, but family law was not integrated into the civil code. Instead, it was left as a separate "code" of only three laws plus "much that was left unregulated," with many legal contradictions as a result of hasty drafting and many other matters that were purposely left to provincial and local jurisdiction. The consequence of the last was that courts then filled in the gaps left by postwar legislation with prewar case law.[16]

The compromise is also apparent in the conflict between the declarations of party policy and the behavior of party members, on whom the implementation of policy depended in those early years. Local and district committees, according to complaints in the main party journal in 1950, rarely even discussed issues related to women. How to mobilize women for work in the economy; how to create conditions for them to take up public employment; how to eradicate illiteracy, the symbols of "slave relations" in the household (such as the veil), and prejudices and superstitions; and how to further the political and general education of women were neglected. Despite the party line of the Fifth Congress (1948) to enroll large numbers of the population into the party, less than 16 percent of adult women were being enrolled, even in factories with large numbers of women workers. Moreover, party members and demobilized Partisans were known to forbid their wives to become party members or members of the Anti-fascist Council of Women or to attend meetings of that council or party conferences. Party leaders frequently opposed giving governmental or economic leadership positions to women. The households of party members frequently included women still illiterate, still wearing the veil, and still forbidden from taking up jobs outside the home. Where new policies in agriculture, for example, clearly needed the mobilization and support of women for their effective implementation, party organizations ignored the task, paid no attention to creating political organizations for women or to the needed educational work, and showed no interest whatsoever in creating the institutions necessary to assist women workers, such as nurseries, extension services, and children's lunch programs.[17]

The consequences for women, as individuals and as members of families, cannot be assessed, however, without examining the effect of governmental economic policies on the actual pattern of social relations. In contrast to the policies of earlier governments, the socialist government aimed to maximize the resources available for social purposes and to gain access to those resources by direct control and organization of productive activities. In addition to nationalization and agrarian reform, to withdraw from private persons the right to withhold basic productive resources from social use, the new government proclaimed the equality of all citizens in order to eliminate social barriers to the full contribution of each to the country's development. It guaranteed the right to a free education and equal access to employment so as to utilize as fully as possible the country's abundant resources in labor. It directed a large proportion of societal surplus into industrial development, particularly infrastructure and capital equipment and plant, and it coordinated economic activity through planning so as to reduce the waste and misdirection of a market. Committed to improving the standard of living of the entire population, it also maintained relatively egalitarian wage rates by central control, set the prices of basic commodities such as food and housing, and provided a range of basic supports such as child allowances, pensions, and health care. In principle, at least, these governmental policies socialized the organization of labor and of productive activities and the responsibility for personal survival through physical safety and material security. Marriages were no longer necessary for survival: women could replace the marriage contract with a wage contract; men were no longer dependent on elders and kin for access to a wife. The workplace would replace the family (of birth for men, of marriage for women) as the source of social identity, community, duties, and taxation.

Very early on, the government found it difficult to maintain the flow of international resources it considered necessary to sustain this program. As a result of the economic blockade by the socialist states after the Cominform Resolution of 1948 and the sharp reductions in marketable agricultural produce at the time (due to drought and resistance to reorganization of productive activities in agriculture, among other reasons), the government had to find alternative resources for its program of socialist transformation. Public debate focused on the idea of a longer transition to socialism than the Soviet model posited as well as the need to adapt the path of change to the particular conditions of Yugoslavia. In practice this meant not only the use of the market and foreign trade, but also a scaling down of the scope of the socialist sector, to be favored as the core of a future socialist society within extensive private ownership of productive resources in the agricultural, handicrafts, and petty service sector (subject to regulation and limitation). It redirected its trading and financial relations to obtain Western aid, diversified trading links with the developing as well as the developed world, and began to use international trade and finance as a crucial source of additional accumulation for domestic growth. To adapt to these international links, to reinforce domestic support behind the party leadership under Tito, and to motivate workers and local administrators to higher productivity with the same resources the government decentralized control over much of the economy, introduced workers' self-management, and began to rely ever more on the market rather than planning to coordinate economic activity and allocate most resources and goods. Finally, it adopted economic criteria based on Western, developed standards that emphasized static allocational efficiency, comparative advantage, capital-intensive techniques of production, and human capital arguments. As more and more was allocated by the market, furthermore, the importance of individual and family incomes grew: governmental policy sought to improve living conditions by means of increased production of light consumer goods and then increased wages to create the demand necessary to sustain that production.

The Relation between Women and State Policy: The Socialist Period

Women's social identity

What have been the consequences for the status of women in Yugoslav society and the cultural conceptions of women and men of these sweeping legal changes and postwar economic policies? Above all, marriage is no longer essential to women as a means of subsistence or as the route to a culturally accepted place in society. Women have a place in Yugoslav society as individuals. Furthermore, the standards for measuring the worth of women and men are now the same: level of education, income, occupation, and maybe sexual attractiveness. Schooling has perhaps had the greatest impact on reducing differences. As Ruth Trouton observed by 1953 about changes in the early part of the century:

> Village schooling had a marked effect upon another of the main supports of the Yugoslav peasant family idea. The subordination of women to men was an unquestioned law of nature to most Yugoslav peasants. . . . Male peasants rationalized their authority over women by maintaining that women were stupid. Innumerable proverbs such as, 'Long hair, little wits,' 'Consult your horse or ox rather than your wife' were current. . . . But once schools were established and a few peasant girls . . . were allowed to go to school, it was found that they could hold their own in learning, so that the mass of the peasants had therefore to revise their opinion about the intelligence of women. When women teachers began to be appointed in the villages, the process went further, for peasant parents realized that there might be good sense in taking trouble over the education of their daughters now that a daughter as well as a son could be expected to reflect credit on the family and bring an income into it.[18]

Instead of providing for a daughter by marriage into as good a family as they could manage or by dividing family property among sons and daughters, with all its attendant conflicts, parents could now continue her schooling beyond the obligatory elementary school. This undercut the patrilocality and virifocality of families. Kinship could be reckoned bilaterally, marriages could potentially be a property exchange among equals, where bargaining over bride price and dowry disappears under the objective standards of schooling and income, and both men and women could be free to choose their mate since their livelihood did not depend on the choice. Families no longer extended their patrimony by children or profitable marriage settlements, so they began to have fewer children (an average of fewer than two by the 1960s) and focused instead on their children's education and employment. By the late 1960s, Denich found no difference in Serbian parents' aspirations for their daughters and sons, and Golubović and her students found that Serbian parents thought their daughters should actually receive more education than their sons because girls encounter greater obstacles to advancement in society.[19]

Women's incorporation into "productive" employment

This independence of women depends on the actual opportunities for employment outside the home, however, and here the goal of equality has been more elusive. One of the crucial initial conditions of postwar Yugoslavia, for example, was a labor surplus. The change in the early 1950s to a market economy, in principle, ended the commitment to full employment, gave preferences in employment and income to the highly skilled, and introduced the criteria of international competitiveness in investment and price policies. The pressures on women to enter the labor force that are familiar in the rest of Eastern Europe and the Soviet Union were never present in Yugoslavia. The share of women in the social sector labor force actually declined during the 1950s and has grown only gradually since 1957 to reach, by the late 1970s, those levels associated with Western European averages (about 33 percent) rather than those of the high participation countries of Scandinavia or Eastern Europe.[20] On the other hand, women have been disproportionately subject to unemployment since the government began gathering unemployment data in the early 1950s. Since the mid-1960s, women have been seeking work unsuccessfully in far higher numbers than men. As countrywide unemployment rates rose, furthermore, it was widely rumored that work associations did not like to employ women. Newspaper advertisements for jobs began to specify "military service completed," to signal that both women and youth need not apply. By the late 1960s, legislative commissions turned their attention to family policy, passing a law on contraception in 1969, excluding women from a wide range of activities to "protect" maternity in the Associated Labor Act of 1976, and, by 1978, creating extensive maternity benefits. Furthermore, because unemployment compensation is available only to people who have lost a job, not to those still seeking their first, and then only to those who cannot be supported by relatives, governmental policy tends to discourage women's independence of marriage and family for subsistence.

A major justification offered for women's higher rates of unemployment is their lower levels of skill, reducing the demand for their labor. Some of this is a consequence of generational change, but prejudices against women's schooling still can be found in rural areas and among Muslim families in the south. More important, perhaps, are the cultural conceptions of women's and men's work that seem to shape career choices. High school education is sharply segregated: women attend commercial schools, teacher training schools, and textile schools; men attend schools for engineering and construction trades. This segregation then extends to the workplace. Because wages and the many goods that are distributed through membership in a work association rather than on the market (winter food supplies, coupons for restaurant meals, apartments, vacation places, medical insurance, educational stipends, bank credit, and more) depend on an enterprise's profit, this segregation leads to fundamentally different rewards for women's and men's work. The main distinction appears to be that defined by the principles of international competitiveness and comparative advantage. Women work in those export sectors where the Yugoslav advantage is seen to be cheaper labor. In 1978, women were 78 percent of the labor force in the finished textile goods industry, 61 percent in linen and textiles, 68 percent in leather shoes and goods, 53 percent in variety goods, and 54 percent in foreign trade offices. This can also be seen in the growth of human services necessary to reduce the trade deficit. The tourist industry depends on female labor: more than half of the workers in hotels, restaurants, tourist agencies, and related services are women. In contrast, men work in those export sectors where the Yugoslav advantage is seen to be quality industrial equipment and wages are high. Even apart from the export sector, however, women are concentrated in occupations and enterprises that pay significantly less than the country average. Within firms, in addition, wage levels vary according to managerial responsibility and to seniority, to the advantage in both cases of men over women.[21]

Changes in the family and in gender-defined roles

Although women no longer require marriage for subsistence, neither the material conditions—inequalities in incomes and employment opportunities and housing shortages, for example—nor the social and legal norms concerning the importance of families encourage this independence. This does not mean, however, that the potential independence of women and the postwar policies discussed above have not changed the structure of families and male-female relations. The rise of a relatively effective state in maintaining internal order, the limitations on property ownership by individuals and families, the appropriation of resources for public use from work associations rather than families, and the expansion of opportunities to participate in community-based decision-making and politics have all reduced the functions families used to serve, above all those traditionally performed by men. Therefore, the institutions and customs that grew up to serve these functions, such as the blood feud, the code of honor, the hierarchical authority according to age and gender within the family, the displacement of blame for conflict onto women and the resolution of conflict onto brothers-in-law so as to maintain peace among lineally related males, and even the seclusion of women and male control over rules of sexual privilege, no longer had a base.

This was not the case for the traditional sphere of women's responsibilities. Although the government declared its intention to socialize the household tasks of women, investment policies long ignored the development of such services. Combined with the rising expectations of domestic comfort that improved standards of living bring, the result was an increased demand for women's unpaid household services.[22] The socialist commitment to the free or subsidized distribution of necessary goods and services succumbed by the mid-1950s to the changes in economic system and the decision to allow enterprises to allocate their earnings freely and individuals to purchase what goods and services they needed or desired. This means that women enter the labor market at times of economic recession or stagflation, when purchasing power declines, in order to supplement family income. That is, women enter the job market for reasons of their family's economic necessity, not self-liberation, and at a time when jobs are particularly scarce. Periodic stabilization policies designed to reduce the balance of payments deficits cut back increasingly on expenditures for services by local governments and by firms, transferring more and more of the responsibility for rents, food, childcare, and so forth, onto private incomes and domestic labor. The export orientation of the industrial growth strategy has led to periodic shortages in consumer goods and inadequate domestic links between the industrial and agricultural sectors. The resort to private, nonmarket means of obtaining necessary goods and services in response has been managed, as before the socialist period, by the family unit and usually women through extended networks among kin (between urban and rural relations and among generations). At the same time, the increasing use of the market for the allocation of most goods and services, unimpeded by governmental controls to influence distribution patterns, sets the stage for competition among families over standards of living and inequalities tied to the price system and personal incomes.

The former household sphere of women—the care of children, the provision of goods and clothing, housekeeping, perhaps a small vegetable garden to save costs—was not replaced, in other words, and the evidence is overwhelming that conceptions of women's and men's domestic tasks did not change either. For example, as the survey data from a national sample of employed women and their husbands in 1971 and a time budget study in Maribor, Slovenia, and Kragujevac, Serbia, during the middle 1960s both show (see tables 14.1 and 14.2), the strict differentiation of household tasks by gender remains. It does not respect regional differences of other kinds and is far more burdensome to women than to their husbands.

This traditional division of household labor is being perpetuated, furthermore, by agents of socialization. Children raised in this home atmosphere read school books that encourage boys to fight back, girls to withdraw. They teach girls to be neat, to cook, wash, iron, sew, and play with dolls and teach boys to climb trees and not to cry or play with dolls or cook.[23] Stories show mothers cooking dinner, ironing, washing, and caring for their appearance (makeup, dress) to be sexually attractive;

Table 14.1 Division of labor in the household in Yugoslavia

Task	Percentage who perform the task: Wife	Husband
Maintain and wash clothes	93	1
Clean house	91	13
Do major cleaning	90	31
Prepare food	88	14
Wash dishes	86	5
Make daily household purchases	75	37
Pay utility bills	61	47
Conduct business with educational and health institutions	54	59
Conduct business with post office or bank	44	68
Do minor repairs of shoes, household appliances, and other items	40	61
Conduct business with social services and government offices	40	68
Paint, whitewash, and lay rugs	30	56
Tend garden and feed livestock	20	19
Do apartment repairs	18	75
Conduct business with the courts	18	64

Source: Miro A. Mihovilović et al., *Žena Izmedju Rada i Porodice: Utjecaj zaposlenosti žene na strukturu i funkciju porodice* (Zagreb: Institut za Društvena Istraživanja Sveučilišta u Zagrebu, 1975), pp. 101–8.

fathers carry coal, do outside tasks, drive and repair automobiles, do home repairs, shave, and read the newspaper.[24] Even a study of secondary schools in Croatia, in 1970–71, found the school handbook of rules defining gender differences in dress: "Students, and especially the girls, must dress neatly and in keeping with their age."[25]

Men, on the other hand, find the locus of "their" activities shifted out of the home into the factory, the coffeehouse, and the political meeting. This does not appear to provide satisfactory substitutes for their reduced authority over women, however, as Simić's colorful essay on Yugoslav machismo suggests. Finding this behavior in Serbia and Bosnia in the mid-1960s, Simić posits a developmental relationship that would predict its presence in Montenegro and Herzegovina as well but its absence in Slovenia and parts of Croatia. The story he tells is of men, particularly the young, trying to live up to the former ideals of male excellence—heroic daring and aggressiveness, defense of honor, public demonstration of strength and initiative—in new circumstances. Public spaces (the café, the market, the street) are

Table 14.2 Time spent on household tasks in Yugoslavia (average hours per week, 1965)

	Employed men		Employed women		Housewives	
	Kragujevac[a]	Maribor[b]	Kragujevac	Maribor	Kragujevac	Maribor
Cooking	.7	1.3	9.4	10.7	19.2	20.2
Home chores	.5	1.1	7.4	8.4	12.2	14.7
Laundry	.3	.4	5.3	7.1	6.4	11.3
Marketing	1.5	.7	2.0	1.7	4.8	3.3
Garden, animal care	.7	4.2	.2	1.9	1.0	14.0
Errands, shopping	.7	.5	.6	.4	.4	.5
Other house tasks	3.3	4.6	1.8	1.4	3.7	3.7
Childcare	.3	.5	2.2	2.0	3.0	3.7
Other child	1.1	1.5	.9	1.3	.9	2.0

Source: Alexander Szalai, ed., *The Use of Time: Daily Activities of Urban Populations in Twelve Countries* (The Hague: Mouton, 1972), pp. 583–94.

a. Socialist Republic of Serbia.

b. Socialist Republic of Slovenia.

the new locale, while the substitute behaviors are the sexual double standard, male virility, heavy alcohol consumption, and exaggerated generosity.[26] The character of Yugoslav politics also suggests some of this transfer of male behavior from other spheres. Predominantly a male preserve still, men appear to seek positions less to change policy than to be able to create alliances (*veze i protekcija*, connections and pull, is the coinage of Yugoslav politics): to extend one's patrimony, so to speak. Within the family, furthermore, Olivera Burić reports from her study of the influence of wives' employment on family life in Serbia during the mid-1960s that men retain the old patriarchal concept of marital relationships but, forced by circumstances, actually behave like modern husbands. This loss of male dominance may be regretted by both partners, she finds, but among males there is tension between ideal and behavior: 80 percent reported being rude to their wives and solving disputes by aggression; 20 percent even admitted to beating their wives.[27] Finally, wage scales set by meetings of workers' councils reward seniority, formal education, and managerial responsibilities, although these provisions directly disadvantage women and youth and are unrelated to the idea of self-management or any social concern for the aged.

Changes in the nature of families and the relations between men and women in postwar Yugoslavia also vary by region, economic sector, and class. Because regional differences are really artifacts of historical legacies, one can suggest that change was negligible in most of Slovenia and among much of the old urban middle-class population. The change must have been enormous, in contrast, among families in southern Serbia, Bosnia-Herzegovina, Montenegro, and Macedonia (though the more isolated the village, the slower the pace). Yet there is evidence that the pattern of antagonism between the federal government and some minorities—in particular the Albanians of Kosovo—might have reinforced the traditional bases of family organization. Governmental policies of discrimination against them in education and employment until the mid-1960s and continued economic underdevelopment of the region may help to explain why the joint, extended family household (the *zadruga*) and its patriarchal culture have been preserved long past their decline elsewhere and, according to some, even have seen a resurgence in recent years. Some evidence can be seen in the divorce rate: against a country-wide average in 1968 of 1.0 per 1,000 inhabitants, Kosovo had 0.2 per 1,000 whereas Slovenia had 1.6 per 1,000. Also, the regional differences in the percentage of women seeking employment during the 1970s, where Kosovo contrasts sharply with the rest of the country (see table 14.3), cannot be explained by employment opportunities alone.

Sectoral differences in families, on the other hand, are a product of postwar policies. The decision to permit an individual, nonsocialized sector in agriculture and some services and handicrafts was of fundamental consequence for families and male-female relations because there the family remained the locus of production and organizer of labor. Again this is best illustrated by the complex, geographically mobile, economic networks of Albanian extended families, but it is most obvious in rural, agricultural families. The strategy of most rural families to maximize both income and security under these new circumstances was to resist incorporation into cooperatives, own their own land to assure subsistence, and then to send at least one family member to an industrial job for cash and the social welfare benefits for which individuals in the private sector otherwise have to pay. Because industrial location policies have not endeavored to link agricultural and industrial activities in Yugoslavia, this has meant substantial migration and commuting for the employed family member. Repeating an old pattern in most of the countryside, the men took on the commuting and left the women to care for the household and take over the agricultural labor (although the census tends to classify them as housewives).

The government's need to compensate for unfavorable terms of international trade in goods with revenue from factor services, in particular by sending workers temporarily abroad to northern Europe or on construc-

Table 14.3 Women seeking employment in Yugoslavia (percentage of total registered unemployed)

	SFRY	Bosnia-Herzegovina	Montenegro	Croatia	Macedonia	Slovenia	Serbia (inner)	Kosovo	Vojvodina
1970	49.0	38.2	51.3	61.1	43.6	66.8	56.8	9.2	54.5
1971	50.0	41.8	49.3	57.1	45.0	63.1	58.6	11.1	56.5
1972	50.0	45.5	48.2	55.3	46.5	60.7	58.7	11.3	55.4
1973	51.1	49.3	48.9	55.7	50.0	60.7	57.2	13.8	56.8
1974	51.9	48.4	56.2	56.8	50.1	62.0	58.1	13.7	59.2
1975	51.2	46.6	54.9	56.4	50.1	57.3	57.3	13.4	59.8
1976	50.7	46.7	57.7	55.3	50.7	55.8	55.7	14.8	57.3
1977	51.7	49.5	57.6	56.6	51.5	57.1	55.1	17.8	59.7
1978	53.7	53.0	59.0	62.7	52.3	57.3	55.6	19.0	65.8

Source: *Statistical Yearbook of the Socialist Federal Republic of Yugoslavia, 1979.*

tion crews in the Middle East, meant this migration would disrupt family life for long periods of time. Even when women joined their husbands or, after the mid-1970s, went in ever larger numbers themselves, they returned (usually alone) as soon as their children reached school age. Men thus joined the "modern" sector of industrial work, education, and politics,[28] leaving women in conditions that perpetuated cultural prejudices about their ignorance and traditionalism. Even the modernization of agriculture, meaning above all its mechanization, increased the burden of women's work on the farms because it enlarged the scale of production and thus the amount of nonmechanized hand labor done in preparation and finishing tasks, that is, women's work.[29] Evidence that this environment was not favorable to women can also be extrapolated from the behavior of young rural women. Although young males leave first for urban jobs, daughters have also sought a variety of strategies to escape: by selling their share in the family land to their brothers, by preferring to marry factory workers over farmers, and by avoiding agricultural high schools and colleges.

Managing the conflict between work and family

Even where family patterns from the presocialist period continue, the trend has been to break the bonds of earlier social obligation between husbands and wives, and parents and children, and to require adaptation to patterns of development within the economy. The difficulties for men have been mentioned above, in the loss of some roles and transfer of others to locales outside the home. For women, the adaptation has not only been difficult but has in other ways been impossible in the sense that the changes require women to accept, simultaneously, two not necessarily compatible roles. The compromises of the new government discussed throughout this chapter—between equal rights for women and restoration of the family; between socialist goals in socializing production and services and temporary concessions to private ownership; between developmental goals requiring independence and increasing dependence on international economic trends—present women with a particularly conflictual and ambiguous situation. Compromises are temporary solutions to incompatible goals and, as Davis reminds us, "people accept conflict in some relationships in the hope of avoiding it in others."[30]

The pattern of responses by women to this conflict brings an additional type of differentiation among families and women in Yugoslavia. One group of women continue to treat marriage as the only means of adult survival, usually because their parents are either too poor to forgo income during extended schooling or because they hold on to beliefs about women's inferiority. A second group of women treats marriage almost as incidental because it is unnecessary as a means of subsistence or status. This usually holds because their parents are able to provide the education, encouragement, and comforts necessary to a professional career or because they have risen to a position of independent status through political activity. The majority of the population still falls into a large middle group of women who find themselves torn "between work and family," as the title of a recent study argues, because they must combine both.[31] In other words, the autonomy given to domestic relations by the new government and an economy founded on market principles have tended to reinforce the importance of social origin—the economic and cultural inheritance from one's parents—in defining the set of opportunities and constraints within which most Yugoslav women operate.

The size of the first group of women is difficult to estimate because of the absence of research on the poor in Yugoslavia. Yet some sense that marriage is not a solution to subsistence that avoids the conflict between work and family can be gleaned from Silajdžić's study of testimony in divorce cases in Bosnia-Herzegovina between 1952 and 1972. Home life for these women appears to be one of bitter conflict, physical abuse, adultery, poverty, and neglect:

> My parents married me to the defendant and I had barely had a good look at him.
>
> I was persuaded to marry by others, because I am poor.
>
> The defendant became acquainted with my father, who told me one

day that I had to marry him or expect death. I tried to like him but it was no use.

I got married in the belief that I would find a solution to my material survival and to cease being a burden to my aunt since I am a war orphan. However, I have been completely disappointed by him. Ten days would pass and he wouldn't bring anything home; he would eat in town, and I survived only by the kindness of my neighbor.

I am in such an impoverished condition that it is impossible to live. I have an opportunity to marry another person, and the defendant has disappeared, so I'm asking for a divorce.

Ever since she found out that women had rights, she doesn't obey me.

He is particularly jealous since I got a job so he beats me constantly.

I am hungry, poorly clothed, and barefoot, and he spends his earnings on others.

Both the defendant and his mother beat me.[32]

At the other extreme are the women with political or professional careers. If they marry, they often hyphenate family names to affirm their identity with the status of their father and to reveal their independence. They marry men with the same level of education and, once working, try to arrange a relatively equal sharing of the household tasks. They socialize with friends from school and work, and because they frequently come from old urban families, their parents are nearby in case of need or to provide the important *baka-servis*.[33] If conflicts arise in their domestic relations, they often choose divorce. Many even choose to have a child alone, independent of marriage. At the same time, conflicts between domestic and work roles and between husband and wife are less likely for them, and they also have external resources with which to cope should they arise. The possibilities for conflict with men are more likely at their workplace instead.

Looking only at this group, many claim that equal rights have been achieved for women in Yugoslavia. As university students they tend to choose the same course of study. Faculties of law, economics, and medicine are fully coeducational, although women still prefer the faculty of philosophy more while men dominate in the faculties of electrical and mechanical engineering. Employment patterns suggest that careers are open regardless of gender. Yet since 1969 the rates of unemployment have been rising faster for women with secondary and higher education than for any other group of women or any group of men. The educational reform of the mid-1970s aimed to limit enrollments in the faculties where women congregate, and it did eliminate the *gimnazije* where women have long been in the majority. At the highest levels of skill and education, furthermore, men have higher rates of advancement than women, and women's salaries begin to decline faster with age than do those of men. The proportion of women in positions of political authority, finally, has dwindled since the 1950s.

For those caught in the real transition between traditional roles and new expectations—the vast majority of women—the level of potential conflict appears so great that they adapt by a sharp separation of male and female spheres and differentiation of sex roles. Thus, high school education for them is sharply segregated. For example, women attend commercial schools, teacher training schools, and textile workers' schools; men attend schools for engineering and construction trades. Data on marriages suggest that conflict may be avoided by maintaining the patriarchal and gerontocratic hierarchy of the traditional family: husbands are overwhelmingly five to ten years older than their wives, and women have lower skills and education than their husbands.[34] Women work at predominantly female workplaces, and the men will be found in managerial positions or in predominantly male workplaces. The conflict between family responsiblities and work, the double burden of women so common in Eastern Europe, is resolved for many in favor of the family: in an all-Yugoslav study of employed women, 38 percent chose to work in order to improve the family living standard and 48 percent would prefer not to work; 34 percent would quit work in order to take better care of their children, 11 percent more would quit in order to maintain good relations in their marriages and keep a good home, and only 3 percent more in order to have more time for themselves. Three-fourths of these women say that leisure time is for the purpose of excursions with their husband and child.[35] Yet, a Serbian study of the same period shows that husbands in the industrial working class spend almost every evening at the neighborhood café and that 55 percent rarely miss a soccer match.[36] A Macedonian study in 1976 asked people how they would pass the time if more leisure were available: 68 percent of the men would spend it in cafés and clubs whereas only 25 percent of the women would seek out these public spaces.[37] Finally, in this land of participation, women rarely become members of workers' councils or assembly delegations, giving as their reason (or legitimate excuse) that they are already overburdened with family responsibilities.

Conclusion

The state influences the position of women because its policies determine how society organizes the basic functions of production, reproduction, and subsistence. The system of property rights and the policies designed by those in political authority to obtain resources for the perpetuation of the state affect the basic structure of families. These policies are rarely part of an explicit program to define the status of women in society; rather, they are usually a consequence of decisions to accomplish other ends.

The Yugoslav socialist government, in contrast, attempted to intervene with an explicit, direct effort at social transformation. It set out in 1945 to create a "modern, egalitarian" society that included equal, nonexploitative relations between women and men. The result has been ambiguous. The party's comprehensive approach, first, has eroded historical, regional, and cultural differences and has made the legal rights of women in different parts of the country more uniform. Class differences among women are rapidly replacing the cultural divisions that formerly separated women of one region from another.

The set of acceptable roles for women in Yugoslav society has also expanded significantly. Women now can have a public identity independent of marriage where they are judged by the same criteria as are men. This new set of opportunities has not supplanted women's earlier role in the family, however, and in fact, the state's economic policies have increased the importance of these domestic tasks and of family units. Furthermore, a conflict exists between these two sets of roles; the burdens of time, psychological stress, and competing expectations are significant for those who attempt to combine the two identities, and in many instances the old roles interfere with the establishment of conditions necessary to women's enjoyment of their new rights.

Attitudes toward women appear to have changed the least. The characteristics of "bridewealth societies," in which women are valued as wife, mother, and sexual being, and where marriage grants men a "right" to these values, persist. Contemporary evidence of this abounds: (1) party leaders and governmental officials refuse to discuss publicly the problems of prostitution, rape, and wife beating; (2) men charged with rape have been acquitted because they come from "good families" and have families themselves; (3) women are portrayed as sex objects in journals, and photographs of nude women are published as a symbol of political freedom; and (4) abortion remains the main method of contraception because, as researchers point out, husbands and male physicians are unwilling to discuss contraception or sexual matters.[38]

Finally, the form of the current antifeminist backlash among young, middle-class males and party leaders alike reflects the pattern of patriarchal family governance and its attitudes toward women. By the late 1970s the cumulative impact of contradictions in state policies affected the means of family livelihood. The conflicts that developed focused on women because they are ultimately responsible for family survival. As in the past, kinship alliances and women's networks, whether through the *zadruga*, rural-urban family ties, and/or women's industrial employment, are extending the resources available for a family's survival. In the patriarchal, patrilocal family characteristic of most Yugoslav regions before the socialist period, women as outsiders, or the "foreign sex," were blamed when the unity necessary to social cooperation among the men of the agnatic core was threatened. Today the scapegoats for both family and political disunity are women who push for the realization of the regime's ideological commitment to equality.[39]

These developments demonstrate the difficulty of creating social change, despite ideological commitments to women's equality.[40] It is in the nature of states and systems of power to place priority on maintaining themselves and therefore on gaining access to the resources necessary for that power. To do so, the socialist government changed the system of property in Yugoslavia and determined the organization of production within the sphere of socialized ownership. This changed the functions of families working within the socialist sector, the functions of male authority in the family, and the social roles and property rights to which women had equal access. When women charged that these changes did not alter conditions sufficiently to create gender equality, party leaders insisted that the woman question can only be dealt with in terms of the class question. The government remained silent about the transformation of the domestic sphere.

Furthermore, the means by which subsistence is secured, that is, the allocation of goods and services, and of individuals among social roles, is organized according to market principles, reproducing rather than transforming thereby the pattern of change begun a century earlier. It appears that in this respect state policy in the current socialist period has made no difference.

What may be most significant for change in Yugoslavia is the way that women have chosen to adapt. Faced with a conflict between old and new roles, women have accepted the necessity of both work and family but have deemphasized their participation in the public sphere. Although time constraints are presented as a justification, this route is chosen because it lessens the most conflictual aspect of the change: the challenge to the system of authority itself and to women's jurisdiction in the home but not in society. However, this withdrawal from politics reduces the already limited bargaining power of women within Yugoslav society, thereby increasing the likelihood that the present structure of social relations will continue.

15

Bogdan Mieczkowski

Social Services for Women and Childcare Facilities in Eastern Europe

The role of women in Eastern Europe, emphasized in socialist planning more meaningfully than in its propaganda, is (1) that of providers of labor to be mobilized for the task of industrialization, provision of agricultural staples, and increase in the national product; and (2) that of the bearers of new generations of future workers, ensuring not only the simple biological continuation of the societies but, perhaps more importantly, reproducing and possibly enlarging the prospective future labor force.[1] The two roles of women tend to clash because the role of women as a source of population growth creates constraints on women's ability to supply their labor. Numerous analysts have found a negative correlation between the employment of women and the number of children they have.[2] There is an additional negative correlation between the social importance of the job held by a woman and the number of children she bears. The number of children is also related to educational background: the higher the education, the smaller the number of children.

The socialist state thus is forced to accept the second-best solution, which maximizes neither the economic mobilization of women for outside, out-of-home employment nor the net reproduction rate. The emphasis in that second-best solution may vary in time: during the early industrialization stage, the filling of jobs by women was stressed, while the resulting drop in the birthrates caused a later shift in the direction of a pronatalist policy. General societal conditions may also influence the relative emphasis of social policy as, for instance, in the East German need to make up for the earlier drain of manpower to West Germany; the Hungarian desire to increase the share of Hungarians in the total population; or the Romanian anxiety to provide a stronger demographic base for an independent policy vis-à-vis its neighbors. All of the above conditions tend to weaken the drive to employ women outside of their homes.

Shifts in the emphasis of public policy can, of course, be announced through propaganda outlets. But they can be most effectively brought to bear on the attitudes of women themselves through the creation of material incentives of one form or another or social services. In the pages to follow I discuss two kinds of social services: those in kind and those that augment money income. I also discuss some negative aspects of state activities concerning the economic and social roles of women and their impact on women's welfare. A section on the effects of the social service arrangements in Eastern Europe and conclusions wind up the chapter.

Social Services in Kind

The rendering of social services in kind in Eastern Europe is usually accompanied by some payment on the part of the beneficiaries, but such payments, if made, do not cover fully the cost of the services. For instance, parents' fees amount to only 7 to 12 percent of the full cost per child in nurseries in Poland.[3] In Czechoslovakia the parents' contribution to nursery schools covers only a minor part of the costs.[4] Consequently, budgetary subsidies have to cover the differential, in effect, constituting a net addition to the purchasing power of the beneficiaries but with a strict determination—by the state—of the consumption category on which that additional purchasing power can be "spent." The primary aim of the social services in kind that are considered in this chapter is to allow women to enter the labor force by freeing them from the necessity of staying at home. Other social goals also pursued by such social services will be indicated below.

There is one aspect of social services in kind that has not been mentioned in the relevant literature; namely, that they themselves provide jobs for women, create a demand for labor, and thus help mobilize women for work. The job category of social services has been feminized to a considerable extent in all of the East European countries. For instance, in Polish nurseries, with the possible exception of the physician, all the staff is usually female.[5]

Childcare

Childcare facilities are essential in both the West and in the socialist countries if women and men are to have an equal opportunity to participate in the labor force at least as long as it is still taken for granted that childcare is primarily the mother's responsibility. This is particularly true for mothers of small children. That is why quality childcare, subsidized by the state to lower its costs to individual families, is a necessity in Eastern Europe. While in the West, childcare is provided by a variety of sources

—private employers, community organizations, churches, labor unions, public and private schools, universities, and licensed-for-profit centers—in the socialist countries, such care, except for privately organized neighborly facilities, can be provided only by the state, although it is sometimes rendered by the state-owned enterprises that employ the mothers of small children.

Childcare services are divided in Eastern Europe into nurseries for children between the ages of five months and three years (in Poland and East Germany, a child can be left in some of these from Monday morning until Saturday noon) and the kindergarten program. At least in Poland and East Germany, there are also children's homes for orphans and children with only one parent who is unable to rear them, as well as for so-called "social orphans" or children with parents who are unable to provide adequate childrearing conditions for the development of their offspring. In addition, there are institutions for severely retarded children, whose separation from others may be a matter of social policy. The operation of childcare services is quite expensive and has to be highly subsidized.

Childcare is the most important single factor that binds a woman to her home. After the termination of the paid maternity leave, and in view of the general absence of a grandmother's services (Romania and Bulgaria by and large excepted) from the nuclear family in industrial-urban society, it becomes important to provide the mother with institutionalized care for her child, or children, until they reach school age. As table 15.1 indicates, there has been an increase in the capacity of both nurseries and kindergartens in Eastern Europe; this has occurred despite a tendency for birthrates to decline.[6] There has also been an increase in the number of children using these facilities and a rise in the proportion of children in the relevant age groups using these facilities.

More detailed information for Poland indicates that a substantially higher proportion of children in the relevant age groups are in kindergartens (97.8 per 100 in 1979) than in nurseries (32.2 per 100 in 1979), a relationship that continued into 1982.[7] In East Germany, the most advanced East European country in terms of institutions for childcare, 63.3 percent of children attended nurseries and 91.8 percent of children attended kindergartens in 1981.[8] Polish data indicate that a larger number of children use these facilities than there are places in them, a fact which testifies to overcrowding and to excess demand, even if it is granted that the exchange of one child for another in a nursery during the year may by itself raise statistical utilization to above 100 percent. There is no doubt that these trends also hold true for the other East European countries.

Despite the unquestioned achievements in providing institutionalized childcare facilities, the East European countries have experienced some

Table 15.1 Number of children in preschool establishments in Eastern Europe

	1960	1965	1970	1975	1977	1980
Number of children in nurseries (thousands)						
Poland	51.6	60.0	72.0	88.2	98.9	—
GDR*	105.0	142.0	183.0	243.0	268.0	285.0
Czechoslovakia	43.0	67.7	72.6	85.6	95.5	—
Hungary	32.0	40.9	41.8	55.4	67.4	—
Romania	12.8	11.8	30.1	73.1	88.4	—
Bulgaria	24.2	40.8	43.5	57.3	65.5	—
Number of children in kindergarten (thousands)						
Poland	450	547	636	892	1,007	1,223
GDR*	459	555	655	701	642	664
Czechoslovakia	286	330	378	475	580	695
Hungary	228	210	233	332	388	479
Romania	354	353	448	812	838	935
Bulgaria	279	316	325	385	390	416
Number of children in preschool establishments per 10,000 children of preschool age						
Poland	1,033	1,507	1,975	2,490	2,639	—
GDR*	3,200	3,801	5,045	7,088	7,806	—
Czechoslovakia	2,333	2,992	3,466	3,607	4,125	—
Hungary	2,913	3,615	3,710	4,750	5,103	—
Bulgaria	3,296	3,989	4,095	4,672	4,765	—

Sources: *Statistical Yearbook Comecon*, 1978, p. 436; *Rocznik Statystyczny 1983*, p. 555; *Statistiches Jahrbuch 1982*, p. 338.
*Number of places.

problems in that area. Even in Hungary, which—after the GDR—is at the forefront in providing childcare facilities, their inadequate provision, especially acute in view of the minor demographic wave that followed improvement in monetary and other encouragements to raise natality rates, has caused dissatisfaction. Both the number of the facilities and the number of teachers have been judged inadequate, particularly in rural areas.[9]

Even in 1972 it was estimated that in Hungary only about 10 percent of children five months to three years old (amounting to about 40 percent of children whose mothers were working) could be placed in nurseries, which obviously limited acceptances to children of sick or working mothers.[10] The provision of this service was therefore entirely inadequate, giving rise to preferential treatment of well-connected parents or parents who were able to pay bribes.

The kindergarten program is also insufficient, but to a lesser extent. For instance, in relatively well-endowed Hungary in 1971, only 58.9 percent of the entire three-to-five-year-old cohort were attending kindergarten, although the percentage tended to rise with age. Of the children entering regular school in 1971, 56.4 percent came from preschool. However, the geographical distribution of kindergarten attendance was quite uneven (the highest proportion of 82 percent occurred in Budapest), and some areas had attendance rates considerably below 50 percent.[11]

The insufficiency of childcare facilities is likely to indicate a social benefit/cost evaluation by the central planners in Eastern Europe who apparently decided that the addition to women's and possibly children's welfare and the expected increase in women's labor force participation rates created by new nurseries and kindergartens would be smaller than the incremental cost of such new institutions. It also reflects the decision made in many of these countries to attempt to increase the birthrate by increasing both paid and unpaid maternity leaves rather than expanding public childcare facilities. As Norton Dodge has noted in discussing the Soviet case,[12] the scarcity of childcare facilities is thus a result of specific social priorities accepted by the central planners.

Abortion

Abortion was made legal in the East European countries under consideration during the 1950s. Abortion is free and given in practice upon request, except in Romania where it is illegal because of an ambitious and rigid pronatalist policy.[13] Enacted in part to reduce the health risks to women posed by illegal abortions, laws allowing easy access to abortion also facilitate women's labor force participation. These laws obviously conflict with efforts to promote childbearing. Nonetheless, chances are small that they will be revoked. The GDR tried to proscribe abortion in 1968 but reinstated it in 1972, indicating existence of considerable social pressures in favor of abortion. A less drastic cycle of legal changes took place in Bulgaria at about the same time, and a still less radical change, involving the introduction of fees for abortion and restriction of the grounds for abortion, took place in Czechoslovakia. Hungary and Yugoslavia did some backtracking between 1969 and 1973, but the basic access to abortion was left there also. On the whole, one can conclude that a small modification of the completely permissive official stand on abortion did take place in Eastern Europe, but that, except in Romania, policymakers did not dare risk alienating the population and therefore continued their permissive policies in this regard. As a result, in several of these countries the number of abortions frequently has surpassed that of births in the 1960s and 1970s.[14]

A Polish student of the subject concluded that the fall in the birthrate constitutes a universal demographic law and that "abortions are not a cause of the decline in the birthrate but constitute a means whereby women implement their objectively determined desire to limit the number of their children. At a specific stage of demographic development, abortions may accelerate the process of transition to a lower birthrate, but they cannot initiate the process."[15] Except in Romania, East European leaders now seem to share his view that "all attempts at prohibiting abortion through administrative fiat are doomed to failure, as such attempts do not change the character and intensity of the socio-economic and socio-psychological factors that determine demographic processes, including above all the decline in the birthrate."[16]

Prenatal and postnatal care

Prenatal and postnatal care is a free social service and is unequivocally directed at promoting the role of women as procreators, although to the extent that it results in better health for both the mother and the child, it also makes a woman a more reliable member of the labor force and frees her to a greater extent from caring for sick children. It also maximizes the number of offspring who reach maturity per given number of pregnancies, thus maximizing the social cost-effectiveness of pregnancies.

The extension and expansion of pre- and postnatal medical care to women has been made possible by a significant expansion of medical staffs and of health facilities in Eastern Europe.[17] The distribution of these services is not even between towns and rural areas, but more rural clinics have been set up, in some cases run by midwives under the supervision of gynecologists from the towns. Considerable improvement has been achieved by the network of clinics, with a pronounced effect on general and infant mortality rates. The number of gynecologists and delivery personnel increased, for instance, in Poland from 1,576 in 1960 to 3,032 in 1970 and 4, 457 in 1980.[18] A similar increase took place in the number of hospital beds in obstetric wards. The proportion of doctor-assisted deliveries in hospitals rose from 41.6 percent in 1955 to 91.5 percent in 1975 and to 94.6 percent by 1978.[19]

Incentives also have been introduced to encourage pregnant women to use prenatal medical care in Eastern Europe. In Hungary, for instance, seeing the doctor three times before delivery has become a prerequisite to obtaining coupons for government-subsidized milk and a free layette.[20] In the GDR, two medical visits for prenatal care are a precondition for maternity grants.[21] In addition to medical checkups, there are visits from a district nurse designed to keep closer tabs on the health of the prospective mother and on the social condition of the family, presumably to provide relief in cases of dire need and to encourage the woman to follow approved medical and sanitary practices. The district pediatrician visits the child at home soon after birth, and a checkup for the mother with her gynecologist is also encouraged.[22]

The quality and accessibility of prenatal and postnatal care in Eastern Europe thus has to be evaluated quite positively. But, as the Polish case illustrates, there is still a good deal of disparity in the availability of those services between the towns and the villages. In 1977, pregnant women in villages received 9.8 percent of all consultations given to pregnant women. Yet, the proportion of women living in villages accounted for 37.4 percent of all women between the ages of fifteen and forty-nine in that year.[23]

The result of the expansion of medical care available to women has been a significant drop in the mortality rates connected with pregnancy and delivery, illustrated by a decline in Poland from .3 per 10,000 inhabitants in 1950 to .1 in 1960 and .0, or an insignificant proportion, in 1970 and 1979.[24] Mortality rates in Eastern Europe due to childbirth and complications of pregnancy are, except for Romania and Yugoslavia, quite low (see table 15.2). The high Romanian rates are likely to have been affected by the official ban on abortions (introduced in 1966) and the consequent resort to it under medically undesirable conditions. With the exception of Romania, these rates compare quite favorably with the death rates (per 100,000 population) connected with pregnancy and childbirth in West Germany (.6 in 1977 and .4 in 1981), France (.5 in 1976 and .3 in 1980), Austria (.4 in 1977 and 1981), Greece (.6 in 1976 and .4 in 1980), the United States (.4 in 1976 and .3 in 1979), and Japan (.7 in 1977 and .6 in 1981).[25]

A dramatic decline also took place in the infant mortality rates in Eastern Europe, undoubtedly contributing to the psychological welfare of the mothers. Infant mortality rates in 1981, expressed as the average number of children who died while under one year of age per 1,000 live births, were as follows: Poland—20.6, GDR—12.1 (1980), Czechoslovakia—16.8, Hungary—20.8, Romania—29.3 (1980), Bulgaria—18.9, Yugoslavia—30.6. For comparison, the USSR had a rate of 27.7 (1974), Austria 12.7, Belgium 11.7, Italy 14.1, West Germany 11.6, Switzerland 7.6, England and Wales 11.1, the United States 11.7, and Japan 7.1.[26] The East European rates, while higher than those in the Western countries above, were quite low in international comparison, especially when levels of per capita income are taken into account.

Other services

Gynecological and other medical care for women is included within the national health care systems, and women have free access to it—independently of cases connected with pregnancy. Undoubtedly, women are important beneficiaries of the free health care systems in Eastern Europe.

Table 15.2 Death rates per 100,000 women 15–56 years old resulting from complications of pregnancy, childbirth, etc.

	1970	1975	1977	1981
Poland	1.0	.5	.5[d]	.6[e]
GDR	.5[a]	.5	.7	.9[f]
Czechoslovakia	.6	.7	—	—
Hungary	1.1	1.0	.6	.5
Romania	4.7[b]	4.8[c]	5.6	4.7
Bulgaria	1.4	.9	1.1	.6
Yugoslavia	1.9	1.2[c]	.7	.3[f]

Sources: World Health Organization, *World Health Statistics Annual,* 1970, 1972, 1977, 1979, 1982, and 1983; *Statistiches Jahrbuch 1982,* pp. 345 and 375.
a. 1973.
b. Of which "other unspecified abortion" (other than "abortion induced for legal indications") was 3.0. In 1973 "other unspecified abortion" had a death rate of 3.5 out of the overall death rate connected with pregnancy of 4.7.
c. 1974.
d. 1976.
e. 1979.
f. 1980.

While mortality rates have declined in Eastern Europe for all age cohorts, those for females have kept well below those for males. The sex difference in life expectancy, which may indicate effective use of health care facilities by women, is also characteristic of the developed capitalist economies.

Unmarried mothers are encouraged to rear their children themselves and can utilize Homes for Mother and Child.[27] There are also programs to safeguard the welfare of children and youth in cases where parents are unable to provide satisfactory care due to hardship, incompetence, or carelessness. Where social intervention is deemed necessary, it is intended also to help the parents, as in cases of alcoholism of the father. Assistance is also given for adopted children, and a one-time payment is made for the purchase of clothing, school articles, and other necessities for such children.[28]

In addition to health care and services for children, some attention has been given to other services for women in Eastern Europe. The German Democratic Republic, in particular, stresses the effect of collective kitchens on the reduction of housework for women. Food for "collective consumption" is prepared in factories, nurseries, and kindergartens with apparently socially desirable results. Communal washing and dry-cleaning establishments also save women time and are also emphasized, particularly in the GDR.[29] Unfortunately, it is difficult to know how widely available these services are. In some countries, they are not widespread and do not result in much of a reduction of women's work.[30]

Women as well as men are the beneficiaries of the free educational services offered in Eastern Europe. Apart from making them more acceptable and adjustable as members of the labor force, education increases the upward mobility of women. Female/male literacy ratios have increased, especially in South-Eastern Europe, indicating a trend toward educational equality that is also evident in a comparison of men's and women's educational levels, particularly in younger age groups. The extension of free education to women also allows them to enter certain occupations that traditionally had been regarded as appropriate only for men, raises their lifetime incomes and social status, and provides greater satisfaction. As McIntyre and Heitlinger note in their chapters in this volume, education also affects adversely the number of children wanted and actually born, a phenomenon that is also familiar in the West.

As several of the authors in this volume note, some aspects of educational policy in Eastern Europe may serve to discriminate against women by pushing them into certain fields or occupations, offering sex-differentiated courses, applying different criteria during entrance exams, etc. Yet, with regard to removing some sex stereotypes, education in Eastern Europe has, indeed, achieved much. Women there have benefited from the extensive strategy of economic development with its stress on maximum utilization of the labor of both sexes and on upgrading the quality of labor.

Women also can use the services of state employment offices, but there is some indication that these offices benefit them less than men. The inadequate coverage of unemployment data indicates that, for instance, in Poland between 1960 and 1979, the number of women looking for work was about five times higher than the number of men; by 1982 the ratio changed to almost one-to-one. However, the number of men directed to work over the same period was about twice as high as that of women. Statistics on job vacancies divided by gender (indicating by that fact the existence of possible job discrimination) showed that vacancies for women ranged from one-sixth to one-half of those for men.[31]

Social Payments to Women

Women in Eastern Europe are the beneficiaries of several kinds of monetary payments. Maternity leaves with full pay are the rule in Eastern Europe. In Poland, they have been increased to sixteen weeks for the first delivery, eighteen weeks for each succeeding delivery, and twenty-six weeks for multiple births.[32] In the GDR, expectant mothers receive six weeks of prenatal leave with full-pay pregnancy allowance, followed by twenty weeks of maternity leave (twenty-two weeks in case of medical complications or multiple births) with a maternity allowance equal to their average net earnings before the leave.[33] A fairly high upper limit is in effect on these allowances. Shorter leaves are given to women who adopt an infant of less than four months. In Czechoslovakia the maternity leave covers a period of twenty-two weeks, and women taking it are entitled to 75–90 percent of their wage or salary for eighteen weeks and to 40–60 percent for four additional weeks.[34] In Hungary maternity leave with pay amounts to five months.[35] In addition, maternity grants are paid to women, amounting in Poland to three times the family assistance payments. Since 1978 a one-time flat sum is paid for any live delivery. A similar flat sum is paid in installments in the GDR.[36]

In several countries, including the GDR and Czechoslovakia, working mothers, after the end of their maternity leave, may apply for further leave from work for a full year after the birth of the second and any subsequent child. In the GDR, such a leave entitles mothers to a monthly allowance at a rate equal to the sickness benefit due after six weeks of unfitness for work, with a fairly generous lower limit for full-time workers. In Czechoslovakia the stipend depends on the number of children in the family.[37]

Family assistance payments are of two kinds: (1) for the children and (2) for the wife of an incapacitated husband. In Poland, for example, family assistance for children is given up to sixteen years of age, up to twenty-five if the child goes to school until that age, and without age limit if the child is handicapped. In 1980 this kind of assistance was extended to private peasants. Assistance is graduated according to the number of children and family income, and special consideration is given to orphans and handicapped children. Assistance given for adopted children is higher than for natural children, obviously to encourage their adoption. Assistance for the wife is given if she brings up at least one child to the age of eight years or if she or her child is handicapped.[38]

As Robert McIntyre notes in his chapter in this volume, East European leaders have enacted a number of other pronatalist measures designed to increase the birthrate. These include payments to women with young children to stay at home to care for them. A program introduced in Hungary in 1966, for example, allows a working mother to stay at home to care for her baby for as long as three years while receiving about one-half of the earnings of a beginning worker. About 65 percent of working mothers take advantage of this program, and the birthrate has risen perceptibly since its introduction.[39] The program has remained controversial within the Soviet bloc, although several other East European countries, including Czechoslovakia, have adopted similar policies. The social function of a mother formally has been recognized as deserving of a monetary remuneration.

Less radical variants of this idea include a reduction of the hours of work and a lowering of production norms for women with small children without loss of pay. These proposals are meant largely to be substitutes for institutional early childcare, but they run into conflict with the unavailability of part-time jobs.[40]

Women are also beneficiaries of the statutory sick leaves. In the case of a need to care for a sick child, Poland, for instance, grants leaves of up to sixty days with 100 percent pay.[41] Czechoslovakia has a similar paid leave system to allow for the care of sick children.[42] Women may also take leave without pay to take care of a sick child. Judging from the Polish case, many women use these unpaid leaves. Twenty-two thousand mothers used them in Poland in 1968; in 1970, fifty thousand mothers; in 1975, 219 thousand; and in 1977, 352 thousand. During such a leave, granted for up to three years to mothers with a child of up to four years of age, the mother can take up a course of study by correspondence or can accept half-time work at home for her own, or another, enterprise.[43]

Retirement pensions are given after at least fifteen years of activity, subject to compulsory insurance and upon reaching the retirement age, which varies for women in different East European countries from fifty-five to sixty years of age (five years less than for men). In the GDR the statutory minimum of fifteen years required to receive an old-age pension is reduced by one year for each child after the second for mothers of two or more children, as well as women who have brought up more than two children, provided they have been in insurable employment for at least five years. Mothers of five or more children are entitled since 1973 to old-age and disability pensions without any period of insurable employment in their own right. In general, however, the level of minimum old-age pensions established in Eastern Europe seems inadequate to meet the socially minimum requirements.[44]

Women also benefit from widows' and orphans' pensions. In East Germany, for example, these pensions are due if the deceased breadwinner would have been entitled to a pension in his own right or if death occurred as the result of a work-connected accident or illness. Surviving spouses below the retirement age receive a transitional bereavement benefit at the rate of the minimum pension for the duration of two years. A widow's pension amounts to 60 percent of that due to the deceased. Children who have lost one parent are entitled to 30 percent of the deceased's pension, with a low minimum; orphans who have lost both parents get 40 percent of that pension, with a higher minimum. Divorced spouses of insured, deceased breadwiners receive a maintenance pension at the rate of the alimony fixed by a court of law, up to a rather low maximum.[45] That these payments are sorely inadequate is shown by the fact that the Director of Warsaw University's Institute of Social Policies estimated in November 1980 that of 800,000 children of one-parent families (6.9 percent of those zero to nineteen years old in December, 1978, and 9.8 percent of those up to and including fourteen years old)—including divorced households—in Poland, 90 percent were living below the subsistence level.[46]

Unemployment assistance is granted in several East European countries. Countries that pay such assistance, either from the state social insurance or the enterprises that laid off the workers, are Poland and Yugoslavia.[47] To the extent that women have shown higher rates of unemployment than those of men, unemployment assistance tends to benefit them relatively more.[48]

Conclusion

A conscious effort has been made in Eastern Europe to solve the dilemma of the employment of women and of their demographic role. The effort has been moderately successful in mobilizing women for work outside of their homes. It has been less successful in counteracting the usual trend toward lowering of birthrates, attendant upon economic development. It also has been less successful in bringing about a true equality between the sexes—if such an equality had been, indeed, actually intended. Furthermore, the effort to change women's roles has been accompanied by several kinds of social disservices, which I have discussed elsewhere. The experience of rising labor force participation rates for women in Eastern Europe is not unique. A recent OECD study observed that in most of its member countries, there has been a rise in the proportion of working-age women participating in the paid labor market.[49]

The existence of social services in Eastern Europe does make the position of women somewhat easier. However, whether their situation is easier than that of Western women may be doubted, particularly since the general standard of living achieved by any society has a commanding influence on the economic welfare of its social groups, including that of women, and since that standard of living remains perceptibly lower in Eastern Europe than in industrialized Western Europe. Undoubtedly, partly because of the relatively low real income per person in Eastern Europe, the monetary assistance provided to women is quite low. Social services to women in Eastern Europe are not as comprehensive as might have been thought at first glance. For instance, Japan has provisions for a menstrual leave, unknown in Eastern Europe. Nor are the socialist achievements unique in other areas. For instance, in Japan the number of children attending nurseries almost tripled between 1960 and 1980, while the number of children attending kindergartens increased more than tenfold between 1950 and 1980.[50] Numerous West European countries also provide paid maternity leave.[51] (On the other hand, childcare arrangements and other services for working mothers are quite inadequate in many Western countries.) Appeals against sex discrimination also seem easier in the pluralistic industrial societies outside of the Communist bloc, as in Japan to the Central Equal Employment Commission[52] and to the courts, or in the United States to the National Labor Relations Board and to the courts. However, social services in kind are well-developed in Eastern Europe, and, although not abundant or in some cases not adequate, they are welcomed by the population.

The economic growth of socialist countries requires both women's labor and—to be sustained—their procreative powers. The provision of social services for women, therefore, can be viewed as part of the social costs of securing women's labor without discouraging their fecundity and, hence, retarding economic growth. It seems that a new consideration has been recently added in favor of an expansion of social services for women, and that is a recognition (rather slow) of women's special needs and rights. This reason for the provision of social services may be more enduring than the one that regards social services as a necessary, albeit perhaps unfortunate, cost of growth.

The subject of women and children and of their welfare has natural emotional connotations that can be subliminally exploited. The propaganda element in the socialist descriptions of their social services, therefore, cannot be disregarded. While this aspect of the problem does not, and should not, constitute a detraction from actual achievements, it should inject an element of caution into the final evaluation of the socialist social service systems. It also should prompt us to see social services for women against the background of the traditional socialist anticonsumption policy and its overall consequences in terms of the standard of living.

16

Robert J. McIntyre

Demographic Policy and Sexual Equality: Value Conflicts and Policy Appraisal in Hungary and Romania

The role, motive, and degree of success of public policy toward women in the various European socialist countries have been issues of continuing fascination for Western critics and social policy analysts. To some extent the attention has reflected a natural scientific interest in the playing out of familiar conflicts under structurally and to some extent culturally different circumstances. Beyond that there has been a current of concern that can only be described as ideologically motivated. The difficulties in achieving objectivity and perspective in the appraisal of very different social and cultural systems are compounded if the system under scrutiny also happens to be perceived as a threatening, or even rival, system to that of the observer.[1]

Culturally induced myopia in the Western approach to the study and evaluation of Soviet and Eastern European economies leads to a steady flow of research "findings" weighted more heavily with wishful thinking than clearheaded interpretation of fact. The particular psychological mechanism is simple and direct: once an undesirable pattern of behavior is discovered in Soviet or East European society, the questions of prevalence and intensity are bypassed and, by an unexamined logical transition, affairs are found to be "at least as bad" as in any Western society. This tendency is especially strong if the area in question has been one of the many in which the Soviets claim extraordinary achievement. It is impossible for Western specialists to pass up opportunities to poke holes in these pretensions. While we have gained valuable specific insights about how the Soviet system does function, this fact-finding dimension is regularly drowned in a tidal wave of popular and professional over- and misinterpretation of the initial findings. Quickly the "Eastern European" experience in question falls out of sight, by the polar dynamics suggested above: if clearly imperfect, then highly imperfect; and if so imperfect, not worthy of further attention or study. This pattern has appeared in a series of important areas, for example, income distribution, political participation, environmental quality, energy efficiency, and health care. I fear a similar cycle of selective perception and attention has already set in on the topic of women and socialism.[2]

Full economic and political participation for women was a fundamental tenet of nineteenth-century socialist thinking and standard programmatic element of the Marxian socialist and social democratic movements that transformed the European economic and social landscape in the twentieth century. By the force of events it was the Marxian socialists who confronted the task of constructing de novo social and economic relationships that include women as full and equal participants. This difficult undertaking, pursued singlemindedly at times, granted only lip service at others, was never abandoned as an explicit social goal.

Most modern societies are male-dominated, and many lack a strong commitment to full female social and economic equality. The question of whether, or to what extent, such a male-controlled society can transform itself in response to egalitarian norms is thus very important. The inherent tension between women's work life and fertility in modern industrial societies creates a set of countervailing social policy interests that are by no means unique to Eastern Europe. Numerous Western analysts have discussed the conflicts posed by women's dual responsibilities and analyzed the public policy implications of this conflict.[3] Attention to the directly relevant experience of women in Eastern Europe in this regard has lapsed for a variety of reasons, including the emergence of policy measures designed to equalize opportunities for women in some Western countries[4] and the sense that the achievements of the various Eastern European countries have fallen far short of their announced goals.

The purpose of this essay is to consider social policy developments in Hungary and Romania and use the comparison of these quite different countries to explore: (1) the extent to which egalitarian sex opportunity and achievement norms remain a vital force in public policy formulation; (2) to determine the extent to which a common political ideology and orientation have produced similar resolutions of the resulting policy dilemmas. Deducing the intentions of policymakers from observation of program accomplishments is often a difficult task, but the presence of a common ideological theme in Eastern Europe simplifies the situation so that analysis of differences in the policies developed in the face of common goal conflicts may be a useful exercise even though cultural and historical differences make clear assignment of weights to the various causal connections difficult.

Women's Work Life and Fertility

It seems plausible to argue that in a modern, urban, industrial society, a woman's work and maternal life are in fundamental contradiction—that attention to the one must detract from or damage the other significantly. The extent of this contradiction is strongly determined by structural features of work life, career development, and the household and social division of labor within a particular society, among other things. It is thus useful to inquire into the extent to which the social and economic structure of a particular society has been "designed" to eliminate the effects of gender on substantive life outcomes.

Fertility issues and fundamental economic planning choices often arise together in a society that stresses universal labor force participation. If women are encouraged to work and are provided assurances of equal treatment, *ceteris paribus*, and if performance of another socially valuable function, childbearing, systematically places women at a de facto career disadvantage, how far will society go to assure equality in (work) life outcomes? For a woman, fertility choices and work life choices (and outcomes) are so strongly intertwined that they can be viewed as dual aspects of a single policy issue—the extent and character of female participation in national life.

The scope of this discussion is limited to consideration of the question of the design and realization of "fertility policy" in the context of low fertility rates and current labor shortages. This combination of circumstances, which poses the worker-mother contradiction in its most painful form, prevailed in both Hungary and Romania during the late 1950s and early 1960s. But similar circumstances elicited nearly opposite policy responses in terms of the measures employed to attempt to reconcile "social" needs for higher fertility with the negative implication of realization of these goals for the work life and career outcomes of women. The Hungarian response to this dilemma was sophisticated, and while containing considerable "experimental" elements nonetheless managed to be both gradual and predictable. In addition, the measures selected for use in Hungary were almost exclusively facilitative, in the sense of being noncoercive and using what I have called elsewhere "positive incentives."[5] Romanian fertility policy was made famous by the extremity of its resolution of the same policy dilemma, which took the form of the nearly complete elimination of legal abortion (at that time the principal means of birth avoidance in Romania) and divorce, and decreased availability of modern contraceptives.

Historical Context

The experience of the Soviet Union, as the first avowedly socialist state, inevitably has a continuing influence in the Eastern European countries. The feminist theme evident in most prior socialist thought had a strong effect on the institutions constructed in the early years of the Soviet regime. Attempts to stimulate full female educational and labor force participation, which began almost immediately after the October Revolution, must be viewed largely as an ideological-philosophical manifestation, since they came long before the emergence of labor shortages as a policy concern. The full legalization and public provision of induced abortion in 1920 was a reflection of these broader trends, and the reversal of this step in the mid-1930s was a natural part of the Stalinist counterrevolution in most aspects of Soviet society that involved the family or sex roles. The 1935–36 restriction of abortion represents a foreshadowing of the tension between the fertility implications of readily available induced abortion and the strong pronatalist impulses of socialist planners and policymakers that became evident in a number of countries two decades later.

The restoration of the 1920 abortion provisions in mid-1955 was an early aspect of the de-Stalinization process, and similar legislation was shortly thereafter adopted by all the European socialist countries, except for the GDR and Albania. Fertility levels fell sharply in each country, and abortion availability was widely thought to have played a direct causal role.[6] That interpretation combined with strong reasons to prefer more rapid population and labor force growth soon suggested abortion restriction as a possible policy remedy. Mild restrictions occurred in Czechoslovakia in 1962–64, Bulgaria in 1967, Bulgaria and Czechoslovakia in 1972, and finally in Hungary in January 1974, and an abrupt and nearly absolute elimination of legal abortion occurred in Romania in 1966.

Pronatalist Predispositions

Population growth was viewed by socialist writers as a systems-differential phenomenon—the cause of misery in capitalist societies because of patterns of unequal entitlement to social resources but no threat to socialist society. A corollary is to view population growth as a sign of societal health. It is also obvious that sharp swings in the birthrate, as well as low population growth, have labor force implications that are of legitimate concern to economic planners. The former implies a delayed, but sudden, change in the size of the cohorts entering various levels of school, followed by the same effect on labor force growth. Slow population growth is especially important in light of the pattern of "extensive" growth commonly observed in "Soviet-type" economies, wherein output expands more from augmentation of the number of inputs used than from rising output per unit of input. If GNP growth has historically been based on this extensive model, and if the prestige and sense of legitimacy of the state are tied to continuing relatively rapid growth, it is reasonable to view lower fertility with considerable alarm.

The East European countries confronted the prospect of below-replacement fertility before similar developments in Western Europe and without large flows of immigrant workers to serve as a buffer against the adverse labor force consequences thereof. Even so, this pronatalist impulse is again finding expression in Western Europe as subreplacement fertility levels have become common in the years since 1970.[7]

Efforts to Reverse Abortion-Induced Fertility Decline

In the face of the rapid fertility decline of the late 1950s, the various Eastern European governments began to implement a series of explicitly pronatalist changes in both direct social support programs and the conditions of female employment.[8] These measures were diverse in nature and also in terms of the combinations and strength of the incentives adopted in specific countries.

The "positive" fertility inducements introduced in the early 1960s often worked through the payments mechanism of the established welfare system. Each socialist country had established a complicated structure of programs and policies directly or indirectly intended to ease the financial circumstances of large families, redistributing income as a matter of equity. As much as a quarter of total disposable income is distributed through social welfare funds whose payments vary with family size.[9] Additional assistance was provided by differentially subsidized housing and commodity prices, and childcare programs that directly underwrite some of the costs of childrearing. The labor shortages that emerged by the late 1950s mandated a high and steady level of female labor force participation. Pressure to maintain high participation rates was unfavorable to fertility and in some ultimate sense was a product of overall economic development policies. The explicitly pronatalist programs were thus added on top of the matrix of contradictory or at least countervailing programs and policies.

Hungarian pronatalist measures

Following the first postwar year of subreplacement fertility in 1958, the Hungarian government established a series of programs explicitly aimed at raising fertility. Over time these programs increased in strength and complexity and became more and more concentrated on stimulating second- and third-order births—a logical focus for a policy seeking to reverse the growing popularity of the one-child family. This carefully modulated pronatalism did not encourage reemergence of large families, which were believed to have negative implications for housing requirements and child "quality."

In 1959 the level of monthly payments through the Hungarian family allowance system was raised dramatically for third-order births. After six more years of low aggregate fertility, the strongest policy emphasis was shifted from third- to second-order births. The "marginal" monthly payment for second children (how much the total family allowance *increases* when a second child is born) was more than doubled, while the monthly payment for third births was cut in half. In 1966 family allowance payments were increased more or less proportionately for all birth orders and coverage was extended to agricultural workers, although at lower rates than for urban workers. In 1967 extensive reemployment guarantees and paid "postmaternity" leave of up to twenty-five months for female employees were introduced. The leave period began after the end of the normal five months of maternity leave at full salary and provided monthly payments of 600 forints in urban areas and 500 in agricultural areas. In 1969 the leave period was lengthened to thirty-one months, and in 1970 payments were equalized for rural areas.

At the beginning of 1972 renewed attention was directed toward encouragement of third- and higher-order births, monthly payments rising by 300 and 100 forints, respectively. Since a considerable increase in the number of first and second births had occurred since the low point in 1962, while the number of third- and higher-order births had continued to decline, this reorientation is easily understandable. When the prices of dairy products were raised as a part of a general price reform of 1973, both the family allowance and leave payments were raised in compensation with no change in the essential structure. Further changes in family allowance payments occurred in 1974, 1976, 1979, 1980, 1983, and 1985, in general aimed at offsetting the effects of rising real wages and inflation on the strength of the incentives. Table 16.1 shows the most significant shifts in the internal structure of the payments, involving the introduction of payments to families with a single child and a pattern of first decreasing and then reemphasizing incentives for third children.[10]

If the family allowance and paid postmaternity leave payments are evaluated in terms of the prevailing wage levels in the socialist sector of the Hungarian economy, we can see the rise in the relative significance of the payments over time. The even sharper increase in the buying power of the

Table 16.1 Marginal monthly family allowance payments and birth payments (Hungary and Romania)

		Birth order					
		1	2	3	4	5	6
Hungary							
1953	forints	—	75[d]	105	80	90	100
1959		—	75[d]	285	120	120	120
1965		—	200[d]	160	120	120	120
1966		—	300[d]	210	170	170	170
1972		150[a]	300[d]	510	270	270	270
1973		200[a]	400[d]	560	320	320	320
1974		200[a]	600[d]	560	320	320	320
1976		600[a]	720[d]	420	380	380	380
1979	130[b]	490[a]	850[d]	550	510	510	510
1980	130[b]	490[a]	850[d]	1,000	660	610	610
1983	130[c] 300[b]	600[a]	1,070[d]	780	660	630	630
1985	130[c] 410[b]	600[a]	710[d]	840	840	840	840
Birth payment[e]							
1972		1,100	1,000	1,000	1,000	1,000	2,000
1974		2,500	2,500	2,500	2,500	2,500	2,500
1985		4,000	4,000	4,000	4,000	4,000	4,000
Romania							
early 1960s	lei	100	100	100	100	100	100
late 1960s		130	130	130	130	130	130
1972[f]		150	160	180	180	180	200
1979		160	170	190	190	190	210
Birth payment—1967[g]		—	—	1,000	1,000	1,000	1,000

Source: Robert McIntyre, "Pronatalist Programmes In Eastern Europe." *Soviet Studies* 27, no. 3 (July 1975): 369; András Klinger, "The Impact of Policy Measures Other than Family Planning on Fertility," Research Report No. 18, Demographic Research Institute (Budapest, 1984), p. 24; Petre Muresan and Ioan Copil, "Romania," in Bernard Berelson, *Population Policy in Developed Countries* (New York: McGraw-Hill, 1974), p. 373; and Ioan Copil, personal communication, March 1980, and Buda Press, "Demographic Measures," no. 23 (1985): 1–3.

a. After January 1, 1972, payments were made to one-child families that had previously fallen into a higher parity class.

b. Single child younger than six years.

c. Single child six years of age and older.

d. Calculated with the assumption that all one-child families received the lowest possible payment.

e. Includes both maternity benefit and "layette" allowance.

f. Payments differ by family income and urban-rural residence. Figure cited is for lowest income group living in an urban area.

g. Prior to January 1, 1967, bonus payment applied to only tenth and higher births.

payments is partially concealed by the rising real wage level during these years.

The number of births rose in the late 1960s, especially among working women who were eligible for the new postmaternity leave. The increase involved mostly first and second births, while fourth- and higher-order births continued to decline at a somewhat reduced rate, suggesting at least the possibility that only timing and spacing were changing in response to the new incentives.

After many years of complete dependence on "positive" incentives to raise fertility, Hungary moved to make abortion somewhat more difficult to obtain as of January 1, 1974. The relatively mild restriction affected married women who were living with their husbands in adequate housing, were under forty years of age, and had fewer than two living children. During 1974 the family allowance payment was raised only for the second child, the birth payment was more than doubled for all first through fifth births, and the monthly postmaternity leave payment was raised and made progressive through the third child. After modest changes in family allowance payments in 1976, 1979, 1980, and 1983, a comprehensive package of incentives was introduced in 1985. The 1985 changes include higher payments for one-child families and higher payments for third and higher births, extended maternity leave arrangements, improved support for child-care expenses outside the home, and a considerable increase in the birth payment intended to cover "layette" and related one-time expenses. The 1985 changes appear to mark a return to more vigorous pursuit of an explicitly pronatalist policy in Hungary. There have been no major changes in the abortion legislation since 1974, although the age for automatic abortion request approval was raised to forty in 1979 and then moved back to thirty-five in 1982.[11]

After the restriction, abortion levels dropped and fertility rose substantially in 1974 and 1975, then declined again, falling to below replacement levels in 1978 until at least 1984. Even in 1976 and 1977 fertility levels were apparently viewed as insufficiently high. In November 1978 the Demographic Committee of the Hungarian Academy of Sciences, in an unusually direct statement, concluded that further measures were required to raise fertility levels:

> the aim of the population policy measures adopted at the beginning of the 1970s was to improve the age-structure of population, increase the birthrate over sixteen per thousand, and popularize a family type with three children. . . . the means applied in (that) period were not sufficient for the achievement of the aim set. If we don't want to change the aim, we have to change the means continuously. . . . we are not

Table 16.2 Cumulative family allowance and maternity leave payments as a percentage of the average annual wage in Hungary

	Birth order					
	1	2	3	4	5	6
Family allowance						
1966	—	16	27	37	46	55
1967	—	16	27	37	46	55
1972	—	13	35	47	59	70
1983	3	26	43	57	71	84
Maternity leave payment[a]						
1966	14	14	14	14	14	14
1967	41	41	41	41	41	41
1972	36	36	36	36	36	36
Total payment[a,b]						
1966	14	30	41	51	60	69
1967	41	57	68	78	87	96
1972	36	49	71	83	95	106

Sources: Calculated by the author; Hungary, *Statistical Pocketbook* (various years); *Demográfia* 11, no. 3–4 (1968): 480; and András Klinger, "Hungary," in Berelson, p. 248.

a. These calculations refer only to the time period in which the paid leave provision is in force, and not to the entire sixteen-year period of dependency as is the case for the family allowance payments. After the standard five-month maternity leave at full pay, a maximum of thirty-one months of postmaternity leave is possible, contingent on the number of children in the household.

b. A combined cash maternity payment and layette allowance does exist in Hungary. The development of these payments over time is not clear, but 1972 levels would amount to a 1–2 percent addition to the payments considered here.

> allowed to resign ourselves to the fact that for lack of financial means we should simply take notice of the decline in birthrates.[12]

Besides the direct pecuniary incentives and the measures designed to protect job and career interests of women, aspects of state policy on childcare, commodity price, credit, and housing allocation can be viewed as positive incentives to parenthood. Special assistance in renting or buying apartments is available for families with children under the 1971 housing reform, and rents are inversely tied to family size. Direct grants are available to defray up to 45 percent of the purchase price of an apartment. Young married couples can claim the latter subsidy in advance, subject to the requirement that one child be born within three years and two within six years. Efforts to expand preschools for children from three to six years of age continue, but the paid leave program appears to be preferred to state provision of day care for working women with children under the age of three. It is argued that Hungarian families prefer this arrangement, but it has clear negative career effects for women. The obvious question is why there have been no serious efforts to create a legal and attitudinal climate in which such "home leave" could be shared proportionally by the male.[13]

In Hungary there has been a long-term effort to devise a package of positive incentives sufficient to produce moderate population growth, and this shifting balance of policies had been moderately successful over the years 1959 to 1974.[14] The partial restriction of abortion availability in January 1974 is difficult to interpret under the Hungarian circumstances. According to the official description, "The aim was to reduce the risk of harmful effects on women and their later children." Terminations on request remain available for single, divorced, separated, and widowed women, and for married women in specific circumstances.[15] Health arguments are a convenient cover for demographically motivated behavior, and frequently have been used when abortion availability has been restricted in other countries, but the strong simultaneous effort by the Hungarian government to make modern contraceptives universally available and effectively used makes such an explanation more plausible in this case.[16]

Whatever the ultimate balance of motives, the 1974 restriction was not particularly traumatic for Hungarian women, since it was: announced in advance; written so as to leave considerable room for interpretation on the part of medical authorities and for appeal on the part of women denied abortion; interpreted flexibly in practice; and accompanied by a strong campaign to assure availability and use of modern contraceptive alternatives. In 1974, 98 percent of newly married couples were practicing contraception, mostly by means of modern, highly effective methods. Less than 3 percent of requests for abortion were denied in 1976, and it is likely that universally accepted contraindications accounted for most of the denials.[17]

Romanian pronatalist measures

While the Romanian abortion legislation was similar to the Hungarian in appearance, it was in practice even more accommodating. The practice of not requiring either application in advance through a medical commission or proof of identity resulted in a very high abortion level. In 1958 and 1959, 112,000 and 220,000 legal abortions were performed, and by 1965 the number reached 1,115,000—a ratio of four legal abortions for every live birth, far above the Hungarian peak of 1.4 (1964) and also higher than the unofficial Soviet figures.[18]

Romanian women had come to depend almost entirely upon abortion as a means of birth control. While other Eastern European countries which offered nearly equal access to legal abortion developed various monetary incentives to attempt to offset the resulting fertility decline, Romania delayed taking action until October 1966, when the legislation legalizing abortion was revoked without warning. The birthrate rose dramatically from the 13.7 level of the last three months of that year to 15.9, 22.8, and finally 39.3 in the succeeding three quarters of 1967. After more than fifteen years in which other means of birth control could presumably have been brought to bear, the Romanian birthrate remains at a level approximately four points above that which was obtained in the year of the counterreform.

Some pronatalist policy adjustments were finally made in 1966, including expansion of childcare facilities and part-time employment opportunities for women, modest increases in family allowances and maternity grants, and remarkably severe restrictions on divorce.[19] The experiences of Eastern European countries with much stronger and more comprehensive programs suggest that it is unlikely the modest Romanian incentive measures had much of an effect.

The decline in the birthrate after 1967 was aided by rising levels of both illegal and legal abortion. The decline in the number of legal abortions from more than 1 million in 1966 to 52,000 reported in 1967 is not the true net decline in the number of artificially terminated pregnancies as indicated in 1967 by the unusually large number of "spontaneous" abortions (153,000) and a sharp rise in both overall and abortion-related maternal mortality. By 1971 there were 330,000 "total registered abortions" ("spontaneous" and "legal-induced"), and the number reached 403,000 in 1979.[20]

Although the abortion policy actions of the government have been unusually drastic, and little has been done with indirect measures involving childcare and development of "market" substitutes for household services, Romania has gone further than other Eastern European countries in making part-time work available to mothers of young children. Recently Romania has returned to an emphasis on the direct productive role of women, stressing that promotions to policy-making positions are necessary to bring more women into the work force.[21] The decline in the Romanian birthrate in the early 1980s would appear to set the stage for the revival of strong and possibly coercive pronatalist measures.

Governmental Social Policy and Women's Lives

This discussion of the evolution of fertility policy in Hungary and Romania reflects the hope that light can be thrown on the closely related question of the motives and social values of those making policies that

Figure 16.1 Crude Birthrates for Romania, 1950–83, and by month, 1967–68

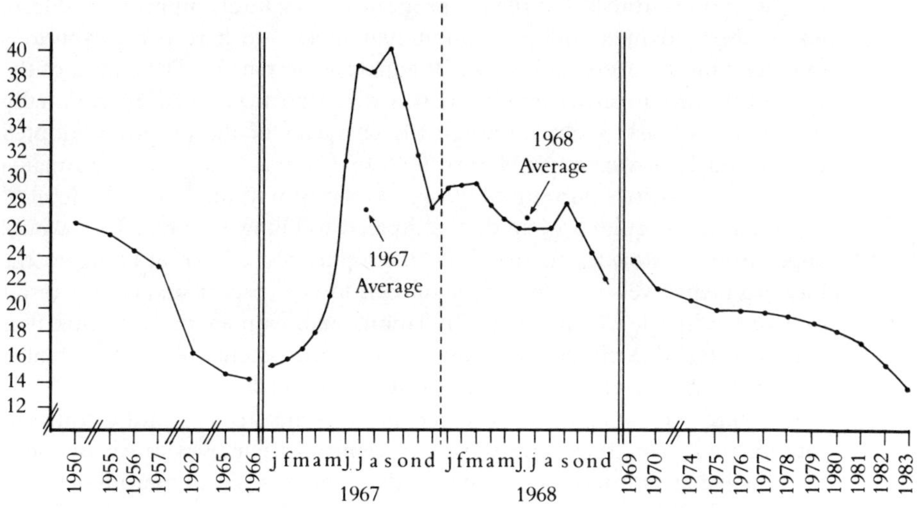

Sources: Romania, *Anuarul Demografic al Republicii Socialiste Romania, 1974* (1974), pp. 148–149, and *Anuarul Statistic al Republicii Socialiste Romania, 1984* (1984), p. 22.

affect the role and status of women in these two societies. To do this we must judge the extent to which the attitudes and values of the decision-making elite can be deduced from observation of the confusing real world manifestations of fertility policy.

If decision makers are assumed to pursue only immediate personal or group interest, then we have no problem. Since few women have occupied top party and state positions, we might assume that those high level bodies systematically protect existing male-predominance against the partly hostile and contradictory interests of women. The male party member or functionary operates under the offsetting pull of the explicit "feminist" theme that has been part of almost all systematic Marxist-Leninist thought.

Behavioral implications of "theoretical-level" feminism can be observed at both the attitudinal or consciousness level (considering the personality and value structure effects of the childrearing systems), and at the level of the extent to which the social and economic structure of society have been "designed" to eliminate the effects of gender per se on life outcomes. Have measures been taken to carry out the sexual-cultural revolution necessary to offset or at least begin to remedy the assumptions and attitudes accumulated within the partriarchal popular culture, and have exemplars of equal female achievement and competence been created ("allowed to arise"), so as to provide a tangible basis for shifts in the assumptions of both men and women about the implication of gender?

The various direct "fertility" programs—financial support, childcare leaves, reemployment and promotion guarantees—fit here as contributions to extending the observable range of female achievement. The efforts of the Eastern European governments in this direction have been exceptionally serious on a world scale, although the character of the program adopted differs widely, for example, between Romania and Hungary. In Romania the use of "positive" incentives has been relatively limited, and the level of the payments is quite low, so that compared to Hungary, pregnancy would appear to have strong negative financial implications. Even in Hungary the high payment levels have lost some of their force in recent years as the result of rising wage levels and some inflation, and women in large numbers appear to feel that either the income loss or professional retardation makes it necessary to return to work shortly after childbirth.

It is necessary to consider whether financial measures can fully compensate women, once they have started to think of their own career development as being as important as that of their spouses. As numerous scholars have noted in discussions of women's work and family roles in the United States and Western Europe, childbearing still entails many costs for working women.[22] Even programs that guarantee promotions while the woman is on childcare leave must surely refer to "automatic" movements, not promotion to new positions. After several years at home, a woman must have fallen considerably behind male cohorts, will appear to herself and others to have "lost qualification," and will at best have to struggle to catch up. Early retirement provisions introduced for women who bear children may reduce women's prospects for promotion in middle age and their likelihood of reaching leadership positions if the political and economic decision-making elites in question are to some extent gerontocratic. Still, strong reemployment guarantees such as have been adopted in Hungary are important on an absolute scale in minimizing the career damage and anxiety that go with pregnancy. Efforts to increase part-time positions in Romania are also positive steps.

Indirect "fertility" programs involving regulation of cost, availability, and quality of childcare, provision of "market" substitutes for household services, such as food preparation, cleaning, laundry, repairs, etc., and efforts to improve the internal supply situation to reduce the intense time pressure on working women may be more important than the direct programs in determining the potential for coexistence between full female economic participation and motherhood. It is sometimes suggested that the more highly developed "service" sector in advanced market capitalist economies permits the household (and women in particular) to sidestep the double burden by the purchase of various childcare, cleaning, food preparation, and other services. This advantage is largely illusory as a general solution to the problem raised, since it is only available to a narrow and relatively high income strata of society and probably presupposes even in that case that there is an available pool of service workers who must accept work at very low wages. In cases where such services are more broadly available, as in Sweden, Denmark, and the like, they are affordable only because they are funded as part of the public sector "social program" based on the taxing power of the central government. This is not to deny that expansion of the service sectors of all of the Eastern European countries would ease the existing pressure on women who work outside the home, but only to note that solution of the problem without a fundamental reallocation of roles and responsibilities within the household is a pipe-dream.[23]

If by historical and cultural impulse women are inclined to feel more responsible for the conduct of the household, they fall under what has come to be called a double burden. There is a cultural lag on the part of both men and women on the question of who is ultimately "responsible" for household duties in East European countries, and the person who has the quasi-managerial responsibility ends up doing far more of the actual work. (See Kulcsar's and Siemieńska's chapters in this volume.) As in other parts of the world, if women have been conditioned to assume that they are in charge in the home, and men have been conditioned to accept and expect to play a decidedly secondary role in the day-to-day running of the household and the raising of children, their resulting behavior will almost inevitably lead to negative career consequences for women (less education and training, inability to devote attention to the job while at home, inability to work overtime at times of crisis, etc.).[24] Given previous cultural expectations, it may prove difficult for many women to relinquish the sense of control and superior competence that they have found in the conduct of household affairs, despite the drudgery, and for men to assume an equal share of the drudgery.

Despite substantial achievement in creating a cultural milieu where economic involvement is assumed to be as central to the life and personal development of women as has traditionally been assumed for men, the East European governments have not moved very far in carrying out the structural or cultural transformation of society that would be required to permit achievement of equality of career *outcomes* for women who choose to bear children. The extension of eligibility for paid postmaternity leave to men in Hungary in 1982 is a promising but by itself insubstantial step in that direction. Both in terms of the socialization of conventional household tasks and in terms of the division of labor within the household, much remains to be done. Indirect fertility programs have emerged in most of these countries as openly acknowledged pronatalist measures—things that must be done in order to make maternity consistent with highly developed career expectations. But little has been done to apply cultural pressure on men to lift the double burden and absorb at least an even share of household obligations. In a perceptive analysis of the implications of this limited effect on the household division of labor, Heitlinger notes that "creation of equal opportunities in education and employment has led to a multiplication, rather than redefinition, of female roles."[25]

The problem of residual cultural assumptions about continued female responsibility for household tasks, even when women are employed full time outside the home, was directly acknowledged as a practical problem by Lenin, who observed:

> So few men—even among the proletariat—realize how much effort and trouble they could save women, even quite do away with, if they were to lend a hand in women's work. But no, that is contrary to the right and dignity of a man. They want their peace and comfort. The home life of a woman is a daily sacrifice to a thousand unimportant trivialities. The old master right of the man still lives in secret.[26]

The nature of the resolution of this problem and the locus of responsibility for its achievement was also clear: "The real *emancipation of women*, real communism, will begin only where and when an all-out struggle begins . . . against this petty housekeeping, or rather when its *wholesale transformation* into a large-scale socialist economy begins."[27]

It would appear that economic development level per se and its positive correlation with the size and complexity of the service sector is a significant part of the explanation of the current situation. The extent of the investment and labor force commitment that would be necessary to provide these services commercially is enormous and directly contradictory to planners' and party leaders' preferences for rapid expansion of heavy industry.[28]

Soviet efforts have by no means been trivial, but still they have been small in relation to the magnitude of the problem. The same may fairly be said for most of the East European countries, but there the more extensive family allowance and paid leave programs raise a further level of complexity in appraising the adequacy of the social policy response. In particular, to what extent is the improvement and enrichment of the "motherhood support" system directly subversive to the achievement of workplace equality?[29]

In the context of general acceptance of the double burden and the lack of very substantial efforts to change the uneven division of labor within the household, national programs that attempt to increase the number of pregnancies are inherently discriminatory, so that "the issue of pronatalism . . . raises the broader question . . . of the extent to which alternative social objectives may be legitimately pursued by a government committed to sexual equality."[30]

If women made the decisions about fertility policy, would pronatalism ever show its face, and if so, what forms of social support to offset the career effects of pregnancy would be observed? If the disproportionate role of the woman stopped at the moment of birth, and if all child and household duties beyond that point were equally divided, would the situation be very different? I think it would be, and that such changes would produce more female pronatalists. Still, as one observed the promotion patterns and career profiles of women and men under this new regime, it would be many years, and perhaps generations, before women occupied an equal share of the high economic and political elite positions because of the strong weight in the work force of older, but not old, workers raised under the earlier regime. And the "empirical" experiences of these senior decision-makers would make it difficult for them to be blind to gender in dealing with their younger subordinates, even if they were philosophically committed to the avoidance of gender-based discrimination. On both sides of the gender line, cultural values and assumptions change slowly and constrain the speed of possible progress toward real equality. The East European experience is very useful in suggesting the full extent of the social changes that would be or are necessary to reconcile maternity and full economic and political participation, as well as the inadequacy of measures that stop short of reorganization of the internal household economy. But unless absence of such a comprehensive household-cultural revolution is taken, by itself, as proof of lack of seriousness in pursuit of sexual equality, we are left with the barely begun process of explaining the link between political structure, ideology, and the policy measures actually taken.

This observation leads us back to the initial point. We know almost nothing about how the policies affecting women have been made. We do not know the goals or even (with complete certainty) the gender of the relevant decision-makers. Similar initial political systems appear in the case of Hungary and Romania to have resulted in nearly opposite policy approaches. The range of possible explanations is wide and the amount of real information about the policymaking process is close to zero. The appeal of a gender (male) conspiracy theory should not be allowed to divert researchers from the task of decoding the Eastern European social policy puzzles.

17

Alena Heitlinger

Passage to Motherhood: Personal and Social "Management" of Reproduction in Czechoslovakia in the 1980s

There has been considerable recent interest among Western feminist scholars in women's reproductive experiences, but this research has not been extended to the state socialist countries in Eastern Europe. This chapter attempts to remedy this situation by investigating the personal and social management of reproduction in one East European country—Czechoslovakia.

The process of reproduction examined in this essay is defined in terms of *transition to motherhood*. It refers to a reproductive sequence from coitus through birth control and conception to antepartum, intrapartum, and postpartum. The most recent works written from this perspective are those by Oakley,[1] but my use of this approach is significantly modified. While I agree with Oakley that structured eliciting of women's (and men's) accounts of reproduction and the integration of these accounts into interpretative feminist theories should constitute the chief goals of any current feminist research, it is not always possible to do this in practice, especially in Eastern Europe. Apart from short letters published in the press, first-hand accounts of "reproducers" themselves simply do not exist in Czechoslovakia. I could not conduct any formal interviews with a scientifically selected sample of women (and men) and was therefore unable to generate such data myself. Hence most of the data contained in this chapter are quite "conventional," supplied by "biased" Czechoslovak physicians, demographers, statisticians, psychologists, journalists, and sociologists in their official publications.

In spite of the limitation imposed by the paucity of data on Czechoslovakia, one can still make many meaningful comparisons. Reproduction is simultaneously individual and social in all societies. It is individuals and couples who make (or drift into) reproductive decisions, but such decisions are subject to considerable social manipulation and control and are influenced by structural, cultural, and individual elements. The major structural influences examined in this chapter include age, marital and economic status, and the medical management of reproduction. Culturally, the major influences are the pronatalist ideologies of motherhood and the specific norms prescribing and proscribing sexual behavior, methods of birth control, breast-feeding, and the "medicalization" of life. On the individual level, past and present experiences with sexual activities, contraception, abortion, pregnancy, and motherhood influence the various stages of reproductive decision-making.

How do we compare and evaluate these influences? I do not intend to draw a sharp dichotomy between "socialist" and "capitalist" transition to motherhood because such a rigid distinction would obscure variations among socialist and capitalist societies, as well as similarities between them. Furthermore, broad comparisons and evaluations of socialist and capitalist "management" of reproduction seem premature without more careful and informed case studies than are currently available.

The present chapter is intended as a contribution to this end. It reports on the following aspects of reproductive decision-making in Czechoslovakia: contraception, abortion, full-term pregnancy, childbirth, postpartum, and the repetition of the reproductive sequence.[2]

Contraception

In comparison with the United States and many other Western countries, modern contraceptive methods are of relatively recent origin and availability in Czechoslovakia. Postwar research and development in this sphere appear to have been slow. Domestically produced pills and intrauterine devices became available only in the mid-1960s, and they have been subject to periodic shortages, like all other consumer goods.

A 1977 article claims that while 41 percent of women were potential consumers of the pill in 1975, only 5 percent of Czech women and 2 percent of Slovak women were using oral contraceptives in that year. Compare this to the usage of 37 percent in Holland, 31 percent in New Zealand, 18 percent in West Germany and Australia, 21 percent in Austria and 19 percent in the United States in 1973.[3] If intrauterine devices and pills are statistically combined, the users increase to 19 percent in the Czech Lands and 9 percent in Slovakia,[4] both still well below Western levels.

Complaints of shortages and poor distribution of oral contraceptives often run concurrently with complaints about underdeveloped sex education. While certain analysts express general satisfaction with the current system of "education for parenthood," they are exceptions rather than the rule. Information advocating contraception is now incorporated into the eighth grade curriculum, but the subject is discussed only in three lessons.

Many health clinics have set up special contraceptive advice bureaus, but these institutions often suffer from shortages of printed materials to give their clients.[5]

All research findings confirm persisting general ignorance of modern contraception. Research conducted by the State Population Commission in the 1960s on the sexual life of young married couples showed that more than a quarter of the men and half of the women in the sample considered their sex education insufficient or nonexistent. Knowledge of contraception was generally absent; the majority of women depended on the responsibility and skill of their partners, both before and after marriage.[6] A more recent fertility survey, conducted in 1977, revealed only slightly improved knowledge. Thirty percent of women in the cities, for example, and 45 percent of those in rural areas had no knowledge of contraception at all, yet half of the women entering marriage had premarital "sexual experience" (presumably coitus).[7] It is estimated that every fourth woman in the city and every fifth woman in a rural area enters marriage pregnant.[8]

Contraceptive knowledge apparently improves with the length of marriage,[9] but theoretical knowledge is not always translated into practical use. While the women in the sample who were "informed" knew about all the major effective methods of birth control, coitus interruptus, one of the least effective techniques, was the one most frequently used. Two-fifths of Czech fertile women and half of Slovak women aged 18 to 44 use it. This is a smaller proportion than in 1956 when 68 percent of women relied on this birth control technique, but it is still very high. The findings of the survey also confirmed the continued general unpopularity of male contraception (e.g., condoms).

Surveys on sources of knowledge of birth control revealed that schools, youth organizations, mass media (television and radio), and fathers give little or no information on sexual matters. Books and friends seem to be the major sources of knowledge for both sexes, and mothers are significant for females. Lectures by specialists (usually medical doctors), who answer anonymous questions, constituted the most popular choice among respondents from the 1978 sample, but only 5 percent of males and females in an earlier sample claimed that they had actually learned anything significant from these sporadic lectures.[10]

Some doctors resent the fact that the inability of teachers and parents to talk freely about sexuality has shifted the major responsibility for sex education to them and argue that parents and teachers are more qualified than clinical physicians to discuss sexuality and parenthood systematically with young people.[11] Hence "jurisdictional" conflicts related to who is better qualified to perform a particular task also occur in Eastern Europe.

At present, researchers in Czechoslovakia seem to be resigned to the continued limited impact of contraception on fertility regulation, though they have spent little effort in trying to *explain* the persistence of birth control "conservatism." All we have are official medical pronouncements that it is unrealistic to expect contraception to become the major method of birth control and calls for research and development to focus on the improvement of techniques for both contraception and abortion.[12]

Abortion

Abortion was fully legalized in December 1957, following the lead of the Soviet Union in 1955. As things now stand, each woman seeking an abortion must first apply to a special abortion commission in her locality.[13] These commissions are composed of doctors, elected members of local national committees (municipal governments), representatives from the Population Commission, the trade unions, and the Council of Women. Their procedures have been criticized often for bureaucratic inflexibility, smug moralism, and hypocrisy. From the feminist standpoint, the greatest criticism concerns the almost total lack of men's responsibility for conception and its termination. The woman, not the couple, makes the application; she alone must go before the commission to receive a moralistic lecture about getting herself in "trouble" and be subjected to pressures to have the child and, if she is single, get married; she is the one who pays the fee, ranging from 200–800 crowns (approximately twenty to eighty dollars). The steepness of the fee is decided by the commission on the basis of an assessment of the "social acceptability" of the reasons for seeking an abortion. These bureaucratic practices are consistent with the general attitude toward contraception, which is also seen as a woman's responsibility. Male lack of accountability for reproductive decisions is in turn reinforced by the existing sexual division of labor, especially around childcare.[14]

On the whole, it is considered neither sinful nor disgraceful to terminate an unwanted pregnancy. Over the years, abortion commissions have turned down only 1 to 12 percent of requests, and a stricter attitude toward authorizing abortions has almost always been followed by a recorded increase in miscarriages.[15] Most pregnant women persisting in their applications have been able to obtain abortions; those who failed had recourse to a "spontaneous" miscarriage. Every third pregnancy is aborted in Czechoslovakia where the ratio of births to abortions is roughly two to one.

Less than 17 percent of women having an abortion in Czechoslovakia are childless, compared to 56 percent in the United States. In fact, "sufficient number" of children in a family (three and more) has consistently been the single most frequently cited reason for seeking an abortion and has accounted for 18 to 19 percent of all abortions. Thus two typical profiles of women seeking an abortion emerge from these data. On the one hand, we have a married woman in her twenties or thirties, who does not want any additional children; on the other side of the spectrum, we have a young, single woman, pregnant for the first time. It is the latter woman professional medicine is currently most worried about.

The documented health hazards of abortions have become the chief official concern, replacing an earlier worry about abortions contributing to declining birthrates. While Jerie et al. and Laně[16] claimed that 3 to 12 percent of all abortions led to "early" or "late" complications, the current quoted figure is 30 to 40 percent.[17]

Physicians in Czechoslovakia continue to rely chiefly on old-fashioned and more hazardous abortion techniques. The most widely used method in Czechoslovakia is that of dilation and curettage, which requires a greater dilation of the cervix (thus increasing the risk of incompetency of the cervix) than the more modern techniques of vacuum suction or menstrual regulation. In 1975 only one-third of all abortions in Czechoslovakia used the vacuum suction method, which is the most widely used technique in the United States and Canada. This was apparently due more to severe shortages of necessary medical technology (e.g., Czech- or Soviet-produced aspirators and vacurettes) than to doctors' unwillingness to use this method.[18]

Full Term Pregnancy

Pregnancies that are not terminated are also "managed" by the state and the medical profession. Maternity legislation in Czechoslovakia is, on the whole, superior to that existing in most Western countries, with the possible exception of Scandinavia. There is an extensive list of jobs forbidden to pregnant and nursing mothers, which is much longer than the list of jobs forbidden to women in general. These restrictions are not always followed in practice, but women have the right to request a transfer to easier work during pregnancy with no loss of pay. The difference between the wages earned in the permanent and the temporary job is made up from health insurance funds. If no suitable work can be found, the employing institution is required to lay the woman off and still pay her regular wage or salary.[19]

Dr. Michlíček, a plant gynecologist, claims that pregnant women often abuse this protective legislation. Many expectant mothers who are relocated to easier work, or to what Michlíček calls "pseudo-work," work, apparently deliberately, so poorly that the management prefers them not to be around. Many leading officials apparently put pressure on company physicians to declare "lazy" childbearing women as "disabled for work," thus forcing physicians into "conflict with the law, not to mention medical ethics."[20] On the other side of the spectrum, Baran found a high correlation between employment in sales and the risk of premature delivery, a risk minimal among housewives.[21] Childbearing women store assistants presumably would have been better off if they had "abused" the protective legislation and been sent home rather than continuing to work.

All childbearing women are guaranteed twenty-six weeks of maternity leave, eight of which can, and four of which must, be taken prior to the expected delivery date. Postpartum leave cannot exceed twenty-two weeks with the exception of premature births for which mothers are not penalized by the loss of four weeks of maternity leave.

Nearly every woman sees a medical specialist (an obstetrician and a woman's nurse) nine times during the course of her pregnancy and not later than sixteen weeks after conception.[22] But, while women in Czechoslovakia may well visit prenatal clinics more frequently than their counterparts in France or West Germany, if they do not or cannot follow medical advice, these visits become irrelevant and a waste of time, as we shall see below.

As in other developed countries, Czechoslovak medical prenatal care is supplemented by prenatal classes. Expectant mothers are also encouraged to read health-educational literature, which advises them on nutrition, physical exercises, and elimination of "bad" habits during pregnancy and postpartum. Most women seem to be well informed about what is "good" for them and their future babies, but the specialists' advice often is not or cannot be followed in practice. For example, Šabata and Fišerová and Trča[23] advocate lots of fresh fruit and vegetables in the pregnant woman's diet, but it is well known that these are not available in winter and early spring. Trča found that many women continue to smoke during pregnancy,[24] and few women exercise or participate in sports during pregnancy.[25]

Matters relating to "easy," "painless," or "prepared" birth are discussed under the term psychoprophylaxis in Czechoslovakia. As in other countries, psychoprophylaxis is portrayed "not as a radical alternative, but rather as a practical complement to medical practices during pregnancy and childbirth."[26] This medicalized ideology of "prepared childbirth" is echoed in all the popular and professional prenatal literature that I examined, and there is some indication that this is also how it works in practice. In a study of two small groups of women, only one of whom attended prenatal classes, the most significant difference between the two groups was not an easier and less painful childbirth but better cooperation with attending obstetricians by women who were appropriately socialized in prenatal classes.[27]

A course in psychoprophylaxis consists of six lessons in the anatomy and physiology of conception, pregnancy, labor, and delivery; it often also includes a visit to the maternity hospital. The six classes are attended twice a week during the last month of pregnancy, usually during the day, when the expectant mother is already on her maternity leave from work. They are not compulsory and attendance fluctuates across the country, ranging from 18 to 55 percent. The classes are led by women nurses at local health clinics, and they are designed exclusively for women.

There seems to be no general dissatisfaction among women in Czechoslovakia with their experiences of "medical management" of pregnancy, although relevant data are extremely limited (I was able to find only two references). The Institute for Research of Public Opinion (of the Federal Statistical Office) conducted a recent nationwide study on issues connected with children and the family and found that women are generally satisfied with the health care which they received during pregnancy and childbirth.[28]

Trča found that all respondents who attended prenatal classes liked them and preferred them to all other sources of knowledge. However, many women requested that some information be given to their husbands, either by the physicians or the nurse. Women in the sample were also critical of the home visit by a nurse, which they saw as useless and a waste of time.[29]

Childbirth

The rapid acceleration toward 100 percent hospital confinement in the 1950s marked the completion of the trend toward the "medical management of childbirth" in Czechoslovakia. While in 1950 more births took place at home than in the hospital, five years later only 20 percent of all deliveries remained at home. In 1960, 94 percent of all births were hospital confinements. The collection of statistics on births ceased in 1974 after hospital births exceeded 99 percent of the total.[30]

The process of "medicalization" of childbirth in Czechoslovakia has been intensified recently by the introduction of monitoring systems in intensive obstetrical care units. The large-scale use of fetal monitors, ultrasound machines, and incubators represents a serious drain on foreign currency reserves because this modern technology is imported predominantly from the West. The expenditure of precious hard currency for this purpose is justified by the assumed resulting decrease in perinatal mortality and morbidity.[31]

While the overall evaluation of mortality statistics is complex and controversial, Srp et al. and Petro[32] see a direct link between socialist obstetrical medicine and the visible postwar decline in maternal and perinatal mortality. Maternal mortality, while low to start off with, has declined consistently since the end of World War II, and the risk of dying while giving birth is now almost nonexistent. This reproductive "success" is attributed both to improved prenatal health care and to hospital births as well as to changes in maternal age and number of children.[33] The proportion of women having five and more children declined from 10.5 percent of all births to the current 2.9 percent, thus automatically lowering the overall number of high-risk pregnancies and potential perinatal deaths. Between 1948 and 1960, perinatal mortality decreased from 34.0 to 20.7 per thousand. It has remained stable since 1960, fluctuating between nineteen and twenty-three per thousand, and was 15.2 per thousand in 1982.

Czechoslovak analysts see the impact of the "scientific-technical" revolution on obstetrics as positive. Suk, for example, argues that interest in technical obstetrics ought to be encouraged among Czechoslovak physicians, though he warns doctors to maintain their "medical common sense and evaluation and not intervene unnecessarily."[34] However, most critics of current childbirth procedures in Czechoslovakia are much more concerned with the baby's than the mother's psyche. For the main part, the challenge to existing obstetrical hospital practices has come from psychologists, critical of the hospital environment for infant bonding, and pediatricians, who have been alarmed by the significant increase in early weaning.

Laboring women who enter the hospital are surrounded by complete strangers—hospital nurses and doctors as well as other laboring women, whose pain and cries are only too evident in the multi-bed laboring room. Neither husbands nor any other visitors are allowed in the hospital for the duration of the woman's stay (five to eight days).

In most hospitals today, the first contact between the mother and her baby is twelve hours after birth; further interaction is initially limited to two hours a day and gradually builds up during the strictly adhered to four-hour-long nursing intervals.[35] Dr. Švejcar, a prominent Czech pediatrician responsible for the postwar introduction of formula milk, has recently become an outspoken critic of these practices:

> Newborn wards, which were established in consideration of both the need for postpartum rest and the possibility of infections, took baby care in the wrong direction. A mother cannot have her peace after childbirth and simultaneously not disturb her relationship to the baby. Fear of infections did not take into account the enormous protection against them which the mother provides by her breast-feeding, which is much greater than the protection achieved by the separation from the mother.[36]

Dr. Švejcar is now a vocal advocate of introducing "rooming-in," a term for which the Institute for Czech Language has not yet found a Czech translation. The pediatric symposium in Olomouc in 1980 enthusiastically supported this system of care, which now exists in most hospitals in Western countries. Several hospitals in Bohemia and Moravia have transformed a number of multi-bed rooms (private rooms exist only in special party clinics) into wards for "rooming-in," but Prague is lagging behind, with "rooming-in" remaining in the experimental or planning stage.[37]

While Czech pediatricians are most concerned about the "optimal" environment for breast-feeding, psychologists are more worried about "optimal" infant and parental bonding. The author of an article on motherhood argues that babies born in the hospital find themselves in superb hygienic conditions and are cared for by professional nurses, but their environment is artificial and harsh, characterized by a hygienic but scourging shower, mass changing of diapers, and mass feeding at an hour specified by the hospital staff.[38]

Written before the emergence of the current debates about "rooming-in," the article recommends that mothers be allowed in the forbidden newborn ward. The author believes that nurses would both accept and benefit from mothers' help and that mothers themselves, especially new mothers, would learn more from direct observation and changing of babies than from one postpartum home visit by a nurse. The author is also critical of the exclusion of fathers from the birth event and of mothers who insist on exclusive childcare responsibility and control.[39]

Thus the evolution of a "medicalized" birthing system in Czechoslovakia has followed the Western pattern of interprofessional conflict, with the main challenge to modern obstetrics coming from pediatrics, psychology, and, most recently, also from the mass media. For the most part, critics are concerned with practices seen as harmful to the physical and mental health of babies; mothers' own feelings and satisfactions are a secondary concern. There has been no explicit recognition (as there has been in the West, thanks to the efforts of the feminist and women's health movements) that active, independent women may wish to "give birth" rather than "be delivered." In Czechoslovakia all matters relating to birth are decided and controlled by the medical and nursing professions.

Furthermore, there has been little awareness of the importance of the childbirth experience for the parents, as opposed to the baby, whose "birth trauma" has occupied several influential Czech psychologists, including the internationally known S. Groff, who currently lives in the United States. Czechoslovakia also lags behind the West in research and policy relating to men's role in the process of transition to motherhood. Trča's popular prenatal guidebook briefly mentions (in one sentence) that in France husbands are present during childbirth and adds (in another sentence) that, according to the results of one unspecified survey, male presence during childbirth is not desired by Czech women.

One could question this offhand conclusion. People generally do not respond to new "radical" suggestions with immediate enthusiasm because they need some time to consider the various pros and cons of the proposals. If the recorded positive experiences with "rooming-in" are anything to go by, allowing husbands into labor, delivery, and postpartum rooms will be welcomed by women in Czechoslovakia, though men's initial reaction is more difficult to predict, given the existing sexual division of labor in regard to birth control and childcare. Much would depend on the encouragement offered by the medical profession.

Postpartum

Dr. Švejcar recently said that babies are born twice, first in the hospital and for the second time when their mothers return home. He is, of course, referring to the sudden and dramatic transition to motherhood from being a helpless patient in the hospital, a transformation that is often accompanied by feelings of exhaustion, anxiety, depression, and insecurity. As a pediatrician, Švejcar is particularly concerned about the resulting decline in the supply of breast milk and the will to nurse. Ninety percent of mothers in Czechoslovakia nurse their babies while still in the hospital where breast-feeding is encouraged to the extent that it is the only opportunity a mother has to see her baby. However, within two weeks after childbirth, only 77 percent of babies are still nursed. After three months, the percentage drops to 30.[40]

Švejcar argues that "mothers' return home threatens most the nursing of babies," although he also blames nurses and doctors for advising too readily a recourse to bottle-feeding "if the baby does not seem to have enough." Švejcar advocates nursing without supplement for six months, unlike most other pediatricians in Czechoslovakia, who consider two months to be a sufficient period to begin solid foods.[41]

The majority of mothers wean their babies well before the expiration of paid maternity leave, despite the fact that maternity legislation enables them to nurse while working. A nursing mother is entitled to two half-hour breaks for breast-feeding a baby younger than six months and to one half-hour break for nursing a baby aged six to nine months. However, only mothers whose babies are cared for at nurseries in their place of work can take practical advantage of these provisions. Most infants and toddlers are cared for in nurseries run by the local authorities in the mother's place of residence, which means that in a big city nursing during work is not feasible. Furthermore, nursing in public is socially unacceptable, except for

Gypsy women. The latter can and generally do breast-feed in public, which, ironically, reinforces the prejudice against breast-feeding among the public given the general unpopularity of Gypsies.

Following the North American pattern, the decline in breast-feeding has coincided with an increasing reliance on formula milk, the consumption of which is now more than double the 1955 level.[42] Bottle-feeding entails more work and higher costs for the mother, and in Czechoslovakia there are additional problems with irregular supplies and less than adequate quality of formula products. These problems apply as well to ready-made solid baby food, which has only recently begun to appear in stores on a highly irregular basis. Disposable diapers are also not on sale. However, people seem to know that they are widely used in the West, and Matoušek even mentions them in his recent infant care guidebook.[43] On the other hand, there are sufficient supplies of cribs, carriages, and strollers, including collapsible strollers, an improvement on an earlier situation.

Most of the problems connected with the care of infants by married mothers pale in significance when we examine the desperate situation of single mothers. Single mothers are generally seen as "socially and mentally unprepared for motherhood."[44] The national statistics largely confirm this view, as the incidence of premature birth and stillbirth among single mothers is more than double that among married mothers.

Single mothers receive little or no help from the state but rely on their family of origin or the father of the child.[45] Single mothers are entitled to thirty-five weeks of paid maternity leave (as are mothers giving multiple births), which is nine weeks longer than the regular maternity leave, but this leave is meaningless if the mother has nowhere to live. A longitudinal study of mothers of all illegitimate children born in 1970 in Prague showed housing and low income to be the greatest specific difficulties they experienced.

A Home for the Unmarried Woman and Child, designed for eleven mothers and babies who can stay for up to a year, opened in Ostrava in 1965 and remains, to this date, *the only* such institution in the whole country. Women who passed through the Ostrava house apparently did not cope too well, and no additional institutions of this type are planned for the near future.[46] Mothers who are unable to stay with their family of origin have to rely on special nursing institutions, many of which accept the mothers for only two months or not at all; the baby can stay for up to a year before being moved to a children's home if the mother still has nowhere to live. I was told by one single mother that she was forced to agree to a research experiment on her baby son in order to get him accepted in the nursing institution and that this was only a temporary solution for her housing problem.

Existing data on the postpartum experience of single and married mothers allow only tentative comparisons. New mothers work under conditions of fatigue, inexperience, uncertainty, and often isolation in all socioeconomic systems. The situation of mothers in Czechoslovakia is made more difficult by shortages of consumer goods, smaller apartments (babies are generally kept in the same room with parents), and the persistent refusal of husbands to help with the less pleasant and more arduous household tasks. Many fathers are now willing to take the baby for a walk so that the mother can prepare dinner for the family (rather than simply rest), but domestic work (including diaper changing) is performed by women. There is no institutional postpartum support system (i.e., an ongoing, day-in, day-out access to a network of helpers rather than a limited short-term visit by a woman's nurse), but unlike their Western counterparts, most young mothers in Czechoslovakia get more help from their mothers and/or mothers-in-law, particularly in three-generation households. However, this situation creates a special paradox and leads to new kinds of tensions if mothers' and grandmothers' views on childcare differ.

Research on the psychic load of married women with at least one preschool child, carried out in Prague in 1975, showed that mothers tended to experience situational anxiety and decreased self-assurance much more frequently than women generally.[47] One can safely assume that situational exhaustion and insecurity are much greater among women who have just become mothers. It is therefore hardly surprising that women in Czechoslovakia do not want to experience motherhood too many times.

Becoming a Mother Again

According to the results of nationwide sample surveys among married women conducted in 1966–67, 1969–70, 1975, and 1977, an overwhelming majority of Czechoslovak women consider two children to be the "ideal" number of children in a family, both for themselves and in general. It should be noted, however, that one of the recent surveys indicates an increased proportion of women under age thirty desiring to be childless or to have only one child (see table 17.1).[48]

There are significant differences between Czech and Slovak women in their desired fertility. Virtually no Slovak woman desires to be childless and more than a third want to have at least three children, while the proportion of Czech women desiring only one child is almost double that of Slovak women. Schvarcová, a Slovak sociologist, sees the ideal family size as three children, which would be sufficient to solve the Czechoslovak "population problem." However, there is no longer official agreement that the population problem exists. According to Havelka, the Czech deputy minister of

Table 17.1 Number of planned children in a family in Czechoslovakia

	Ages of women			
	19–24	25–29	30–34	Total
Sample in total	335	569	132	1,036
Number of planned children				
None	108	287	88	483
One	143	195	30	368
Two	37	24	5	66
More than two	10	7	0	17
Do not know	20	31	5	56
Do not plan children	17	25	4	46
No further children wanted because of				
Health	30	82	18	130
Age	3	10	22	35
Employment status	7	19	4	30
Financial situation	36	51	10	97
Housing conditions	69	89	16	174
Domestic duties	8	10	1	19
Few children's facilities	20	28	3	51
Husband's attitude	13	14	0	27
Other reasons	96	170	23	184
Do not want to	53	96	35	289

Source: Antonín Šteker, "Průzkum populačních tendencí mladých rodin v ČSR," *Sociální politika* 5, no. 7 (July 1979): 150. A nationwide sample of 1,036 women who married after April 1, 1973, and who were then under age 30. One-third were aged 19–24, more than one-half 25–29, and the rest 30–34 at the time of the survey in 1977.

Labor and Social Affairs, the current crude birthrate of eighteen per thousand is sufficient to reproduce the Czechoslovak population at existing levels and ensure a stable proportion of productive population, set at 57 percent of the total.[49] There seems to be more concern now about the *quality* of the new population, including "the social burden posed by handicapped and retarded individuals,"[50] and the social and individual costs of unwanted children.[51]

The two-child family is the most common type in Czechoslovakia and the one-child family is the second most popular. There has been a slight decrease in the proportion of one-child families, but their popularity remains high in practice if not necessarily in theory. A substantial proportion of Czech women end up having fewer children than they consider to be "optimal," but the Slovak pattern, with more three-child than one-child families, is again different.[52]

A longitudinal analysis of fertility of women born in 1930–54 (who entered their reproductive period in 1945–69) showed that one-third of all women bear their first child before reaching the age of twenty-one and one-half before reaching age twenty-three. Only 10 percent of women remain childless. Ninety-five percent of mothers plan the timing of birth of subsequent children, and the preferred interval is three or more years, which is longer than the more common two-year interval in the West.[53]

Housing and financial difficulties are the most frequently cited reasons for not wanting more children (see table 17.1). Another survey revealed that 51 percent of women with two children would under "no circumstances" consider another child. The rest of the sample identified an increase in husband's income (32.9 percent), better housing (13.4 percent), and not having to work (13.2 percent) as required conditions for having a third child.[54] The substantial increases in the prices of many children's goods in 1979 (by almost 50 percent) and the official pronouncements on satisfactory population development indicate that no further family incentives are planned. In fact, the contrary may be the case. Hence most women will continue to "become mothers" only once or twice in their lives.

Conclusion

Examination of the passage to motherhood from conception to postpartum reveals many similarities and some differences between Czechoslovakia and North America. We noted the similarity in the material and social conditions under which reproductive choices on the timing and number of children are made. Contrasting experiences were seen in the reliance on abortion as the major method of birth control, the exclusion of fathers from prenatal classes and hospitals, and lesser reliance on bottle-feeding.

We have also seen the extent to which reproduction has become dominated by professional medicine. Medical control of reproduction is pervasive in both political systems, but it seems more monolithic in Czechoslovakia than in North America. The professional dominance of medicine in general and obstetrics in particular has come under considerable criticism in recent years from Western clinical psychology, sociology of medicine and the professions, the media, and the feminist and consumer health movements. No such broad critique is possible in Czechoslovakia, given the monopoly of power and doctrine by the Communist party, to which many top physicians belong. An independent feminist or woman's health movement of the current Western type cannot legally emerge in the communist countries to promote a discussion of reproduction as an issue detached from professional medical involvement. A truly radical reassessment of women's reproductive freedom seems to be possible only in Western democracies, which offer much wider scope to the efforts of organized social movements.

This, however, does not mean that no change in the social management of reproduction is possible or likely in Eastern Europe. There are many influential professionals in Czechoslovakia who have addressed reproductive issues with real concern and who have been critical of past and present policies in these areas. Czechoslovakia, like all the other East European countries (with the exception of Albania), is not a closed society. Public debates on controversial issues can and do occur, but they are generally initiated by experts rather than by lay people. Furthermore, changes tend to occur with considerable time lag behind the West.

On the other hand, proposals for change have often been inspired by Western developments. For example, the major theoretical rationales for advocating menstrual regulation as the major abortion technique or rooming in as a preferable system of newborn care reflect successful Western experiences in these spheres. Naturally, a successful experience in another socialist country, especially the Soviet Union (e.g., abolition or nonexistence of abortion commissions), provides an even better political rationale for change.

Thus some of the less radical changes in transition to motherhood currently occurring in the West may eventually filter through to Eastern Europe but in a modified way and co-opted by the medical profession. Czechoslovak doctors may not have high incomes in comparison with their Western colleagues (though obstetricians do not fare too badly considering the vast amounts of money they tend to receive in the black market as tips or bribes from their clients), but they are ideologically powerful because the socialist state has allowed them extensive control of the content of their work. In the absence of any active, articulate expression of women's (and men's) dissatisfaction with health care and the dominance of the "medical vision" in social life, reproduction will continue to be defined predominantly in medical terms. There are no Czech or Slovak equivalents to the Boston Women's Health Collective, the Canadian Serena, or the La Leche League that could challenge professional medical expertise as it has been challenged in the West.

V

Women's Voices

Alfred G. Meyer

Introduction

In Eastern Europe as elsewhere in the contemporary world, women's lives are changing as the society in which they live is changing. Indeed, the rapid transformation of society creates many pressures for women to change their lives, to join the urban labor force or to take over much of the rural labor while the men go off to work in the town; to participate in public life outside the place of work; to redefine their relationship toward their fathers, their husbands, and toward their traditional roles as child bearers. Pressures coming from outside, in their turn, may reinforce, or come into conflict with, changing attitudes on the part of women themselves.

In Eastern Europe as in other countries some attitudes and behaviors change only slowly or not at all. In particular, the image and self-image of women as predestined for motherhood and childcare often remains strong, despite significant changes in sex morals and the increased ability to prevent conception and birth. More generally, women's attitudes toward wage work, public life, and professional careers are likely to remain different from those held by men; or, if that be an overstatement, perhaps it should be argued that all people's opinions about the role of women in public life, in the world of work, in professional careers, and in the family are bound to remain highly controversial.

Modernization involves, among other things, cultural change—the substitution of urban for rural patterns of living, of the rhythm of the machine and the alarm clock for the rhythm of nature. A myriad of changes are involved in this replacement of one culture by another. In Western Europe and North America, this painful process occurred in unplanned, seemingly spontaneous, fashion. It began centuries ago and is still going on. In communist regimes, in contrast, it is instituted deliberately, on the basis of conscious planning, by people who are impatient to get it accomplished as quickly as possible. To be sure, in this attempt, communist parties often try to make use of elements from the very culture they seek to replace; or else, because they are themselves products of a particular national culture, their own behavior, attitudes, and language cause them to slip, however unwittingly, into the mold of that culture. As a result, the old and the new form a mix that is unstable, ever shifting, and unpredictable. At times one can observe interesting new syntheses emerging; at other times the clash between the old culture, seemingly rooted in the soil, symbolized by folkways and religious traditions, by language and myths, and anchored in the entire social fabric, and the new culture, which may appear to some traditionalists as the evil invention of alien usurpers, is particularly sharp.[1]

The sharpness is felt most painfully, perhaps, by women. In Eastern Europe as in many societies they have often been the principal agents for passing traditions and folkways down to the next generation. In their successive roles as maidens, wives, mothers, and mothers-in-law, they have often served as one of the most revered symbols of the entire nation. In their traditional roles women have been romanticized, and at times they have clung to the romanticized self-image even when they were painfully aware of the patriarchal reality concealed by it.

Communist regimes want to strip them of this halo. Marxism-Leninism is part of that urge toward a "rationalized" society, which Max Weber wryly described as "taking the magic out of the world." And yet communism also wishes to envelop its new society in a romantic veil of its own design. What the image of women will be once this fabric has been woven is still very unclear. The pattern is still very much in dispute. Some of the issues that are at stake here emerge from the essays in the final section of this volume.

18

Renata Siemieńska

Women, Work, and Gender Equality in Poland: Reality and Its Social Perception

As in the other socialist countries of Eastern Europe, the equality of the sexes has been invested in Poland's post–World War II social and economic system with both political and ideological significance. Basic documents, such as the 1952 Constitution, emphasize the equality of men and women as citizens. However, research shows that women's real status in society differs from that of men. What accounts for this is both the way official policy is put into practice and the persistence of traditional patterns of gender roles in social consciousness and practice.

The socioeconomic system developed in Poland after World War II offers, by virtue of its considerable centralization, greater opportunities for manipulating society than many other systems. The concentration of economic planning and decision-making at the center makes it possible to directly influence the extent of men's and women's participation in different spheres of life by creating employment opportunities for men and women; determining the pay structure in the predominant public sector; creating amenities and services for working women, including care and education for children; and providing educational opportunities for women. Appropriate images of women can also be created and spread through the mass media and politicians' speeches.

In Poland these and other means are used by the state in pursuing targets set in development plans[1] patterned on the Soviet model of five-year socioeconomic plans. Accordingly, the spheres of life listed above operate in a manner determined by the functions assigned to them by the plan. The question is whether their subordination to these functions is complete or whether some factors may modify their realization. The pages to follow examine the impact these plans have had on women's employment and popular attitudes toward women's roles in Poland.

The Structure of Women's Employment

In the post–World War II period there has been a clear interdependence between the goals of socioeconomic development and the employment structure in Poland. The proportion of women in the total labor force has grown steadily since World War I. In 1931 it stood at 33.5 percent, and women made up more than half the work force in the textile and garment industries. At that time, many women worked as domestic servants, but one white-collar worker in three was a woman.[2]

In the early 1950s industry and construction grew rapidly, creating job opportunities for both men and women, though the latter were mostly employed as unskilled laborers. Faced with a labor shortage, the government moved in 1952 to attract more women employees to the nationalized economy. Consequently, the growth rate of the number of employed women outstripped that of men, boosting the proportion of women in the total labor force from 31 percent in 1950 to 33 percent in 1954. An added aspect of this policy was that with real incomes stagnating, families could raise their living standards only if more of their members held a job. So the government's policy concerning the employment of women was formulated with an eye to the general economic situation in the country.[3] That was true also of the post-1954 policy; the investment drive had slackened and employment opportunities were reduced, and that reflected on the employment of women, so that between 1954 and 1960 their proportion in the total labor force remained constant at around 33 percent. Conversely, when investment picked up in the early seventies, women's proportion of the labor force began to grow rapidly and reached 43.2 percent in 1979.

In sum, although the number of working women has grown since World War II, that growth has not been linear. As described above, in some periods the proportion of women in the labor force leveled off; in others, new strategies of socioeconomic development propelled its renewed growth.

The government's development strategies and expectations concerning women's role in society have been mirrored by mass media content so that the images of women they created have changed with time.[4] In the early postwar period, the media strongly emphasized the need for women to participate actively in building the economic basis of Poland's new socioeconomic system. In the media image of women created then, the fact of their employment was taken for granted, and even their status in the family was shown to be determined by their occupational roles. In the seventies a different set of images prevailed. A content analysis of radio and television programs from that period shows that the exclusive stress on the occupational career of the fifties had now been broadened to combine work and family duties, with family duties in fact taking precedence over work.

The structure of women's employment has also changed. In the seventies the number of married women with children holding jobs increased significantly. In 1956 they constituted 30.3 percent of working women; in 1967, over 70 percent; and in 1970, 75 percent.[5]

The educational standards of working women have changed as well. The expansion of particular lines of education and the numbers of students attending particular types of vocational and secondary schools or institutions of higher learning were all planned by the central planners so as to meet the changing needs of the labor market. Thus, the level of education of both men and women grew between 1958 and 1973, but the number of women with secondary, basic vocational, and higher education showed particularly rapid growth. This fact and changes in the social division of labor, the organization of work, and modernization of technologies have led to changing proportions among blue- and, especially, white-collar workers. There are now many more women in white-collar jobs than ever before. The proportion of blue-collar workers among men, on the other hand, has grown slightly (see table 18.1).

Traditionally "female" occupations are becoming ever more so in Poland, although women are beginning to enter new occupations with relative ease. The number of women in traditionally "male" occupations, however, is increasing rather slowly. Women with higher education usually stay away from technical occupations and professions, and women in general tend to be concentrated in low-pay, low-prestige occupations that do not require prolonged studies. The concentration of women in particular areas of the national economy in turn reduces their chances of being highly paid.[6]

This employment structure results from, among other things, laws restricting the employment of women in jobs particularly hazardous to their health and quota systems specifying how many students of each sex are allowed to study certain subjects. However, the main reason is the traditional patterns of gender roles that exist in social consciousness. Women select their jobs and workplaces on their own but still prefer humanistic and medical studies, even though their number in technical, economic, mathematical, and natural sciences courses of study is growing steadily. Their number is lowest in agricultural, forestry, and veterinary studies, due in part to quotas restricting the number of women in these studies. Quotas also exist in medical studies. Differences also appear in secondary schools, where girls more often are found in comprehensive high schools and boys in vocational schools. Still, girls make up some 90 percent of the student body in vocational schools training employees for the health service, textile and garment industries, and the catering industry.

Table 18.1 Employees with university education in the Polish economy

	Occupational groups, by education					
	Engineers		Specialists in			
	Technical jobs	Agriculture, forestry, and veterinary doctors	Economists	Mathematics and natural sciences	Medicine	Humanities, history, and social sciences
Total						
1973	218,121	50,549	69,449	55,736	79,103	6,324
1977	273,031	61,531	81,349	75,050	87,129	9,925
1980	300,503	55,482	164,583	42,983	98,504	35,446
Women						
1973	34,964	16,145	31,184	32,751	42,687	4,268
1977	48,380	21,889	44,735	46,721	55,089	7,174
1980	59,724	20,368	82,875	24,954	62,597	22,275

Sources: *Rocznik Statystyczny 1980,* (Warsaw: GUS 1980), p. 58. *Rocznik Statystyczny 1984,* (Warsaw: GUS 1984), p. 62

In addition to these patterns of education, potential employers (usually men) prefer men to women workers. This is one of the reasons why women have more difficulties finding jobs than men. Enterprises and institutions usually report many more job openings for men than for women, although it always transpires later that if men are not available, women can be hired to fill at least some of those jobs. The proportion of job openings for men and for women reported by employers has changed over the years in favor of women. Jobs offered to women constituted 28.7 percent of declared vacancies in 1979, compared to 4.6 percent in the late 1960s.[7] While changing structures of employment certainly may account for this difference, another reason may be the overcoming of prejudices against women employees. However, the number of women looking for work remains several times higher than that of men. As elsewhere in Eastern Europe, women's wages are lower than men's, even if the women are better-educated and hold the same jobs. Women also hold a disproportionately low number of top economic positions.

Women's employment structure is also modified by processes arising spontaneously in response to government measures designed to utilize women as an additional source of labor. The female labor force does not admit of full and unrestricted manipulation. The media may shift from one preferred image to another, now presenting women as busily working and another time concentrating on women's role in bringing up children and

Table 18.2 Women in the labor force as a percentage of total employment in particular branches of the Polish national economy in 1955 and 1979

Branch of national economy	Percentages of the total number of employees in particular branches			Differences 1955–1979
	1955	1979		
Industry	30.2		39.0	+ 8.8
Construction	12.4		19.4	+ 7.0
Agriculture	20.5		27.0	+ 6.5
Forestry	6.4		19.6	+13.2
Transportation and communication	15.2		25.9	+10.7
Trade	51.4		71.6	+20.2
Municipal economy and services	31.1	29.3	32.8	+ 1.7
Housing	—	44.4		
Science and development	—	45.5	69.6	
Education	—	75.7		
Culture and art	56.6	59.7		+13.0
Health service and social welfare	76.7	80.3	78.5	+ 1.8
Sport, recreation	—	58.3		
Public administration and system of justice	38.8		60.7	+21.9
Finance and insurance institutions	57.0		83.4	+26.4

Sources: Calculated on the basis of *Rocznik Statystyczny 1975* (Warsaw: GUS, 1975), p. 53 for 1955; and *Rocznik Statystyczny 1980* (Warsaw: GUS, 1980), p. 59 for 1979.

looking after the home. In real life, however, women have shown a steadily growing interest in working, even though amenities and services to help them run the home and look after the children fall far short of what is necessary. Another uncontrolled factor is the unequal distribution of women graduates of universities and colleges. Women's particularly intense unwillingness to leave the large cities proves that human resources cannot be manipulated at will. Still, the centralized system makes it possible to bring considerable pressure to bear on members of society, and that is certainly one of its distinctive features.

Models of Women's Mobilization

In Poland we have a special model of women's mobilization that—to borrow a leaf from David Riesman—could be called "the other-directed model." In the pages to follow, I describe it in some detail, drawing on various research projects and direct observation of its functioning. The other basic model of women's mobilization is the "inner-directed model," where it is changes in the women's own ideas concerning their role in social life that prompt them to seek opportunities to be active outside family life. In the other-directed model, this role is played by external pressures.

The two models developed in different ways. In the inner-directed model, it is women's evolving consciousness, induced by changing living conditions, that produces changes in their behavior. The other-directed model emerges chiefly because of sudden and rapid changes in life circumstances that force women to go beyond accepted, traditional patterns of behavior and adjust to a new macrostructural situation that requires their participation in at least some new spheres of life. The end result of the operation of both models can be quite similar. Still, the ways of introducing the two models play an important role in determining relationships, as well as the degree of congruence between men's and women's attitudes toward women's active participation and behavioral patterns.

In the other-directed model, it is not so common for women to support —or claim—equal rights and equal participation with men in various spheres of life, including family life, even though countries where this model predominates have about the same percentage of women active in various spheres of social life as countries with the other model. Further, men are less likely than women to support equality of the sexes in all spheres of life, including the family. It is accepted mainly under the pressure of external circumstances, including material necessity.

These two models can be regarded as characteristic of the early stages of women's mobilization. This is especially true of the other-directed model, which is clearly of a temporary nature. It is followed by evolutionary changes that produce a more congruent pattern of relationships among various types of behavior on the one hand and among behavior and attitudes on the other. This congruence can be achieved in two ways that are not mutually exclusive. First, it can come about by a partial withdrawal of the model, a reduction of women's participation so that it becomes more selective and guided by personal preferences. Or, it can occur because of changes of attitudes and beliefs concerning women's activity.

Obviously the two models do not appear in pure form in practice and should be treated as ideal types. Various factors modify them by degrees, so different variations of them exist in real life. Macrostructural determinants also play a role in societies in which, it is assumed, the inner-directed model prevails (at least in some social groups). And the role of microstructural factors cannot be excluded from our considerations of women's participation in societies where the other-directed model prevails.

Models of mobilization prevailing in particular circumstances may be related to the social class of the women concerned. For example, the inner-directed model largely resembles the situation of middle-class women in highly developed Western European and North American societies in the 1960s. On the other hand, the other-directed model may characterize working-class women's mobilization in Eastern European countries. The other-directed model was typical of the socialist countries of Eastern Europe after World War II where it served to fill the gap between the size of the labor force needed to pursue plans of rapid development through industrialization and the number of male workers available.

The results of a study I conducted in Warsaw in 1978–79 as part of a larger cross-national project comprising research in Canada, Italy, Poland, Romania, and other countries show that the prevailing model of women's mobilization affects social perceptions of opportunities open to women. The questionnaire used in all the studies was jointly designed by an international team including T. Dobrin, M. Eichler, R. Siemieńska, and M. Vianello. In my study, some 1,000 inhabitants of Warsaw were interviewed, including 200 blue-collar and 200 white-collar workers, 200 teachers, 100 housewives, and 300 people in positions of economic and political leadership. The results of the study confirm some of the characteristics of the other-directed model as described below.

Work and Family Duties

The equality of the sexes in social and political life is often emphatically proclaimed in Poland, even though images of men and women disseminated by the media, their real roles in society, and traditional gender roles may not be fully in accord with such proclamations. I hypothesized that at a time of women's rapid educational advancement and influx into the labor force, they would be more likely than men to support the idea of equal family duties for men and women. Respondents were asked to accept or reject these two sentences:

> If to pursue her career a woman has to stay away from home for long periods of time, she should give up her career.
>
> If to pursue his career a man has to stay away from home for long periods of time, he should give up his career.

Respondents of both sexes from all socio-occupational groups replied in line with traditional models of gender roles[8] and agreed that women should give up work if it meant prolonged absence from home, i.e., neglect of family duties. In some socio-occupational groups more women than men adopted this view. On the other hand, women teachers and leaders were less likely to accept this point of view than men in the same categories. They were also more inclined than men to believe that the latter, too, should give up work if it were detrimental to family life.[9]

Attitude to Work

Empirical research has repeatedly shown that at the early stage of women's mobilization women generally accept conditions and circumstances of work that correlate strongly with their lack of skills. They also display little ambition with regard to work, a tendency that is reflected in, among other things, little interest in promotion if it means spending more time at work.[10]

It can be assumed that women's general educational advancement may affect these attitudes. If so, women's occupational roles should play a less marginal role than at the early stage of women's occupational mobilization. It also can be assumed that this attitudinal change does not happen uniformly in the entire society but is more pronounced among better-educated women holding managerial posts. Accordingly, I set out to test the following hypotheses:

(1) Women would be more likely than men to give up their jobs if they could afford to do so (reason: women go to work mostly for the money);
(2) The lower a person's education and social position, the more frequently he or she gives up work for shorter or longer periods of time (reason: statistically speaking, persons in this group, and particularly women, are less oriented to work as a set of specified activities);
(3) The higher a person's education, the lower his or her job satisfaction (reason: better-educated employees, particularly women, are more likely than those with lower education to perceive the inadequacy of their jobs and positions in the workplace compared to their real skills);
(4) The higher an employee's education, the more interested he or she is in promotion, as reflected in the acceptance of promotion actually offered and willingness to accept it if offered.

It has often been pointed out[11] that the primary reason why women, particularly less-educated women, work is to improve their financial situation and that many would gladly stay home. In my study, however, the clear majority (between 68 and 92 percent, depending on gender and socio-occupational category) would continue working, even if they were not under financial pressure to do so. Nor is it really true that men are much more strongly oriented to work as such than women. While male blue-collar workers and teachers did say more often (by about 10 percent) that they would want to continue working, for white-collar workers the proportions were reversed, and in the case of persons in managerial or leadership positions, they were identical for women and men (around 92 percent).

The reasons given for this willingness to continue working included the desire to be among people, to develop one's skills and interests, to do something useful for society, to be independent, and finally, to have more money. So the financial motive, once people have achieved the standard of living they wanted, seems to play a less important role compared to other values concerned with human relationships, place in society, and self-realization.

The view is widely current that women are less valuable workers than men, one of the reasons being that they give up their jobs more often than men when they cannot reconcile work with their duties as wives and mothers (particularly when they have small babies). My study confirmed this view to some extent. In each of the comparable socioeducational groups, women gave up work at least once in their careers 1.5 times more often than men, the exception being women in managerial and leadership positions who did so as rarely as men in the same category. The frequently observed rule was also confirmed that less-educated blue-collar workers give up their jobs more frequently. The higher the respondents' education and the more pronounced their work orientation (e.g., people in managerial posts), the smaller the number of people who have given up work even once. Among blue-collar workers, at least 27 percent of the men and 40 percent of the women have had breaks in their careers, while among the people in managerial positions the proportions were 7 and 11 percent, respectively. Men and women teachers discontinued work far more often than white-collar workers. Among the women, the decision to give up work was most often prompted by the need to look after children and the household. Among the men, it was attributed to family troubles and poor health.

As in similar research projects, respondents quite often gave an affirmative answer to a general question as to whether they were satisfied with their work. But while the proportion of those who are "quite satisfied" or "very satisfied" was generally relatively high, there were important differences in the evaluations of men and women, as well as of people in different socio-occupational groups.

More women than men claimed satisfaction with their current job, although differences between particular socioeconomic groups were quite similar in the case of men and women. Job satisfaction was lowest among blue-collar workers (65 percent of the women and 58 percent of the men). White-collar workers (79 percent of the women and 65 percent of the men), and teachers (women, 81 percent; men, 76 percent) were somewhat more satisfied, and job satisfaction was highest among persons in managerial and leadership positions (women, 92 percent; men, 85 percent).

Thus, my hypothesis concerning job satisfaction failed to find full confirmation in the study. Women are more likely than men to accept their working conditions, but the degree of satisfaction is the reverse of that assumed in the hypothesis and is strongly affected by the level of education and position held by the respondent. Dislike of manual work is probably the reason why persons performing it are less satisfied than persons with higher education in positions enjoying higher social prestige.

My study proved once again that women are less willing than men to accept promotion.[12] However, among both men and women, willingness to accept promotion was positively correlated with level of education (the exception being teachers of either sex who showed the strongest dislike of promotion).

The Woman as Boss

Very few women hold top positions, even in those branches of the economy where women form an overwhelming majority. Several causes can be distinguished: women's lack of requisite skills and experience; their unwillingness to accept promotion with its heavier time commitment; and the belief shared by both men and women that women lack the requisite leadership qualities and other traits needed in managerial positions.[13]

Since there are now many more women with high vocational skills in Poland than in the early postwar years and differences between men and women in their attitudes toward promotion are those of degree rather than complete opposition, I concentrated on the third group of causes for women's low level of representation in leading positions. It might be hypothesized that more men than women believe that women lack the leadership qualities and other traits needed to perform managerial roles. I also hypothesized that the lower the level of education (and consequently the social position) of respondents, the more likely all of them, regardless of gender, would be to believe that women lack traits needed in leadership roles. Finally, I hypothesized that there would be a positive relationship between having, or having had, a woman boss and the willingness to accept one in the future.

In a closed question intended to establish in what respects a respondent believed women are inferior, or equal to men, several components of leadership roles were distinguished: (1) solving conflicts among people; (2) getting people to understand something; (3) understanding people's needs; (4) knowing one's own mind; (5) persisting in one's own opinions even though others disagree; (6) the ability to reward or punish. Women scored highest on components three and four, as 90 percent of men and an even higher percentage of women answering the question said women were as good as men or even better (the split being roughly half and half). In the case of the other traits, fewer respondents, especially men, said women were as good as men or better.

The hypothesis that better-educated respondents would more readily accept women in nontraditional roles and therefore would be willing to revise the traditional image of women and their abilities was not confirmed. Male leaders were most likely to believe women lacked the ability or gift listed in the question, but female leaders also shared this attitude. On the other hand, blue-collar workers (both men and women) were least likely to adopt this attitude.

Only in rare cases did respondents (men or women) declare a preference for a woman boss. Otherwise, they clearly prefer men, or they say the boss's sex makes no difference to them. These two groups can be identified in equal numbers in all socio-occupational groups covered by the study. Slightly more women than men prefer male bosses or say the boss's sex is of no importance. Female leaders and male teachers relatively more often than other respondents prefer a woman boss or say the boss's sex is of no importance.

There is no statistically significant relation between having a woman boss and a clear preference as to the boss's sex. In other words, the experience of working with a woman boss does not affect preference in this respect either positively or negatively. The preferences are either traditional (for a male boss) or—and this is a certain novelty—respondents say it makes no difference to them whether they have a man or a woman boss.

The Equality of Women and Men in Social Perceptions

Respondents were also asked to evaluate the actual opportunities that men and women have to obtain vocational training, get a job, achieve a position of leadership, and the likelihood that women would be the first to be fired in a job squeeze. The following scale was used: (1) "Women are strongly favored"; (2) "Women tend to be favored"; (3) "There is equality between the sexes"; (4) "Men tend to be favored"; and (5) "Men are strongly favored." The results were that all the social groups covered by the study agree that men and women stand an equal chance of getting vocational training. In the area of getting a job, respondents stated that there is less equality because men tend to be favored. The tendency to favor men is much stronger when it comes to filling positions of leadership.

Different groups of respondents, distinguished according to the criteria of gender and membership in different social groups, hold quite similar

Table 18.3 Indices of satisfaction with women's participation

	Men							
	Blue-collars		White-collars		Teachers		Leaders	
Indices of satisfaction	Mean	SD	Mean	SD	Mean	SD	Mean	SD
Chances for vocational training	.102	.65	−.079	.78	.101	.75	.143	.50
Chances for a job	.375	.87	.188	.92	.333	.88	.611	.68
Chances for positions of leadership	.458	.85	.396	.86	.414	.79	.835	.82
General satisfaction (based on training, job, and leadership)	.313	.58	.168	.74	.283	.66	.529	.50
Chances to be fired first	.361	.96	.316	.87	.177	.88	.284	.94

Note: SD = standard deviation.

views concerning men's and women's opportunities, but there are still differences between them concerning the perception of the actual opportunities men and women have in real life. Less-educated respondents were more likely than better-educated ones to give both genders relatively equal chances, and men were more likely to do so than women. Various circumstances may account for those differences. A higher level of education, for example, usually gives a person a better awareness of the situation and a better ability to judge one's own chances and those of others.

Another important question is the relation between the actual levels of women's participation in different spheres of life and men's and women's views as to what that participation should be like. As has been suggested earlier, the introduction of the other-directed model of women's mobilization can result in a divergence between the more traditional norms accepted by people and their actual behavior (or at least its perception). Constructed indices allow us to judge the relationship between norms and perceptions of real opportunities concerning men's and women's chances to obtain vocational training, job opportunities, chances to hold a position of leadership, and chances of being fired first. We have called this index the "index of satisfaction."

Table 18.3 shows the distribution of the means for the index of satisfaction. The situation is satisfactory, in the definition adopted here, when attitudes concerning women's participation are congruent with their perceived real chances and the mean index is close to zero. Positive numbers signify that men are favored more than they should be. The sign "−" signifies that women are favored more than they should be.

Women									
Blue-collars		White-collars		Teachers		Housewives		Leaders	
Mean	SD	Mean	SD	Mean	SD	Mean	SD	Mean	SD
.102	.62	.462	.89	.290	.79	.170	.60	.231	.61
.333	.79	.962	.82	.650	.86	.490	.86	.865	.82
.521	.93	1.087	.99	1.070	.89	.720	.91	1.385	.77
.319	.56	.837	.75	.670	.65	.460	.65	.827	.61
−.134	.76	−.379	.96	−.103	.88	−.040	1.00	−.638	.85

As table 18.3 illustrates, men and women believe that women should have more opportunities than they really enjoy. However, women are more dissatisfied with their real opportunities than men. Men and women differ least in their perception of women's opportunities for vocational training and chances of being fired before men. Differences in men's and women's attitudes are more pronounced on the question of job and leadership opportunities for women.

Responses are also differentiated by membership in particular social groups. The disparity between reality and beliefs is much more marked among better-educated people, especially among educated women. On the other hand, there are considerable similarities among male and female blue-collar workers. Generally speaking, women's attitudes to their role in society change more rapidly when new opportunities open before them not only to get a job but also to pursue higher education. Among blue-collar workers of both genders, on the other hand, attitudes change much more slowly.

Women's Expectations Concerning Their Future Opportunities

Respondents also were asked about their expectations concerning the near future (the next five years). We found that women are more inclined than men to believe that men will continue to be more favored than women. Blue-collar workers of either gender are more likely than other members of society to believe that men and women will get equal treat-

Table 18.4 Indices of optimism I (for more equality for women in future) (based on comparison of expectations for the future and perception of the current situation)

	Men							
	Blue-collars		White-collars		Teachers		Leaders	
Indices of optimism I concerning	Mean	SD	Mean	SD	Mean	SD	Mean	SD
Chances for vocational training	–.133	.57	–.010	.52	–.061	.45	–.022	.30
Chances for a job	–.271	.70	–.079	.54	–.121	.67	–.156	.49
Chances for positions of leadership	–.242	.60	–.178	.54	–.222	.53	–.264	.44
General satisfaction (based on training, job, and leadership)	–.218	.46	–.083	.42	–.135	.41	–.148	.28
Women's chances to be fired first	–.216	.82	–.184	.72	–.021	.48	–.244	.69

Note: SD = standard deviation. The minus sign means that respondents assume more equality of the sexes in the future; the plus sign signifies the reverse tendency.

ment in the future. Better-educated respondents tend to assume that men will be favored in all the above-mentioned areas of life, except access to positions of leadership. People in such positions believe that men and women have equal opportunities to achieve them. There is a clear correspondence between the respondents' perception of the current situation and expectations for the future. Those who believe there is equality today assume that equality will be even more perfect tomorrow.

Two indices of optimism were used to describe expectations for the future. Indices of "optimism I" show the differences between expectations for the future and perception of the current situation. They are presented in table 18.4. Indices of "optimism II," presented in table 18.5, show differences between attitudes concerning equality between men and women and expectations for the future.

Table 18.4 shows that, generally speaking, both male and female respondents assume that there will be greater equality in the future. They expect the greatest changes to occur in the field of job and leadership opportunities. As for opportunities to obtain vocational training, they perceive equality in this sphere already. There is less optimism concerning equality of firing practices. Respondents expect that women will be fired first less often than now, but there is a wider distribution of replies here than in other cases. For example, female blue- and white-collar workers believe

Women									
Blue-collars		White-collars		Teachers		Housewives		Leaders	
Mean	SD	Mean	SD	Mean	SD	Mean	SD	Mean	SD
−.040	.67	−.115	.66	−.030	.76	−.070	.43	.000	.34
−.177	.82	−.183	.60	−.110	.65	−.250	.74	−.115	.38
−.333	.81	−.165	.61	−.170	.62	−.320	.57	−.192	.51
−.191	.60	−.152	.46	−.103	.50	−.213	.44	−.103	.29
.010	.70	.029	.68	−.227	.73	−.050	.69	.000	.41

that the tendency to fire women first will be even stronger in the future than today. Female leaders are of more or less the same opinion.

Women tend to be less optimistic than men, although the difference is not great. Better-educated respondents (especially women) are not very hopeful concerning equal chances for opportunities for men and women in the future.

A comparison of tables 18.4 and 18.5 shows that respondents' expectations fall roughly halfway between the current situation as they see it and the ideal of equality they think should prevail. In other words, they expect some, but not too much, improvement. The pattern of differences is similar to that in "optimism I." Women are more pessimistic than men, and women's opinions vary according to occupational grouping. There is little difference in the scores of female and male blue-collar workers on the "optimism II" scale. Educated women, on the other hand, do not have high expectations for the future, although women leaders are somewhat more optimistic than other educated women. Some groups of respondents believe women will be excessively favored in some spheres of life. Blue- and white-collar workers, for example, are convinced that women's access to education will be too easy and that too few women will be among the first to be fired.

Additional analysis of the differences in scores of both indices "general

Table 18.5 Indices of optimism II (for more equality for women in the future) (based on comparison of attitudes toward equality of both sexes and expectations for the future)

Indices of optimism II concerning	Men							
	Blue-collars		White-collars		Teachers		Leaders	
	Mean	SD	Mean	SD	Mean	SD	Mean	SD
Chances for vocational training	.031	.53	.069	.71	−.040	.57	−.121	.42
Chances for a job	−.102	.74	−.109	.87	−.212	.79	−.462	.65
Chances for positions of leadership	−.216	.86	−.218	.84	−.192	.78	−.571	.76
General satisfaction (based on training, job, and leadership)	−.289	.53	−.086	.71	−.148	.58	−.385	.47
Chances to be fired first	−.143	.64	−.152	.59	−.155	.80	.086	.65

Note: SD = standard deviation. The minus sign signifies that women will enjoy less equality in the future than they should; the plus sign signifies the opposite tendency.

optimism I" and "general optimism II" (t-test, level of significance less than .05 with reference to all groups covered by the study) shows that differences in scores of general optimism I are statistically significant only between male blue-collars and male teachers, and between male white-collar workers and housewives. Differences in scores of "general optimism II" are more often statistically significant. Male leaders differ from all other men, who have fairly similar scores. All women respondents differ from all male respondents (with the exception of female blue-collar workers who score similarly to male blue-collar workers and male teachers).

Conclusion

To sum up, the results of the Warsaw study, which can be considered relevant for the Polish urban population generally,[14] show that the introduction of the other-directed model of women's mobilization more than thirty years ago has undoubtedly been instrumental in changing men's and women's attitudes toward women's work and their role in social life in Poland. Due to the lack of comparative data, we cannot determine the magnitude of the change, although differences in attitudes between members of particular socio-occupational groups clearly show that a process of change is sweeping the whole society, even though the pace of change differs from group to group.

Women									
Blue-collars		White-collars		Teachers		Housewives		Leaders	
Mean	SD	Mean	SD	Mean	SD	Mean	SD	Mean	SD
−.041	.72	−.346	.81	−.260	.88	−.100	.54	−.231	.70
−.155	.73	−.779	.84	−.540	.76	−.240	.68	−.750	.84
−.188	.90	−.932	.91	−.900	.93	−.400	.80	−.192	.84
−.128	.60	−.689	.73	−.567	.70	−.247	.57	−.724	.67
.112	.67	.350	.74	.320	.75	.090	.85	.580	.84

Research has shown that some attitudes are linked with level of education and social group, which is significant in that educational standards have increased very markedly in postwar Poland. Still, there is no simple cause-and-effect relationship (namely that the higher a person's education, the less traditional his or her views on women's role in society and the greater the similarity of views on women's employment and the sharing of home duties). Nor is it always true that women are less traditional in their attitudes than men. These tendencies are observable, but deviations from them are common. Simply put, attitudes do not form cohesive entities that can be placed in a specified spot on the traditional-nontraditional continuum. In some cases women perceive their role in a more traditional way than men. In other cases, better-educated respondents in higher social positions (in leadership roles) are more traditional in their views on men's and women's possibilities than people with less education.

These deviations from general rules are found more often when we analyze ideological indices concerning men's and women's roles in society than those concerning actual behavior and attitudes involved in work. By ideological indices we mean general statements regarding the relations between work and family, comparisons between men's and women's leadership qualities, and normative beliefs as to the equality of the sexes in various spheres of social life.

The views of leaders of both genders are important in promoting egalitarian processes. Leaders in our sample view contemporary reality in a more optimistic light than other socio-occupational groups and believe that women are less predisposed to perform leadership roles than men. So we can assume that leaders, including women, will not actively promote women's more active participation in various spheres of life. On the contrary, they may find the current situation quite satisfactory in various respects.

In sum, social perceptions of the situation of both men and women appear to reflect the real circumstances of life more than the more egalitarian views promoted by politicians. The attitudes of men and women toward work egalitarianism and the lack of cohesion of these attitudes are not characteristic of Poland alone, however. Some processes and phenomena recur in many countries,[15] leading to the conclusion that processes of modernization and of breaking through traditional patterns tie in with identical transformations in countries with differing political systems and initially widely different processes of women's mobilization.

19

Gail Kligman

The Rites of Women: Oral Poetry, Ideology, and the Socialization of Peasant Women in Contemporary Romania

The transformation of all customs and practices . . . is a work of decades. (Lenin)

As you can see, we have had an easy time constructing factories. But it is incumbent on us to transform man at the same rate, so that he will be capable of mastering new techniques . . . and new ways of thinking. (Ceauşescu, President of Romania)

Romania is a communist country ideologically dedicated to equality between the sexes. While women do comprise an increasingly significant factor in the wage labor force (45 percent of the total labor population), women's labor force participation has not really altered their status in the family in cities or in rural areas where slightly more than half the population lives. If anything, there has been an accentuation of the double burden situation for women.[1] This chapter is a preliminary treatment of aspects of the socialization of women in Romanian peasant society, a peasant society that is changing due to the socioeconomic demands imposed by the goals of communist state planning. These goals reflect the "production mentalities" of state planners whose priorities have been focused upon effecting rapid transformation in the economic, political, and social realms. In this process, cultural transformation has been considered an essentially derivative phenomenon. However, recent studies stress the need to devote serious attention to this residual realm as a means to gain insight especially into the persistence of "traditional" patriarchal values and behavioral norms in the face of otherwise dramatic change.[2] With regard to family relations, the "traditional" hierarchical structuring of relations between and among the sexes continues to be reproduced. Thus, it is to the "traditional" that we turn.

Traditional peasant society in Romania as well as elsewhere is structured upon generalized sex-bound delineations of public/private domains of activity that reflect separately organized spheres of productive relations.[3] Men tend to deal with the public sector; women, the private. Men are the formal representatives of households, the public arbiters of interfamilial relations. Women are the informal managers of domestic affairs, the private mediators of intrafamilial relations. Viewing the overall social organization, it may be stated that social relations are hierarchically structured: men dominate women; women do not readily have access to the male domain.[4] But women are not without power. In the private domestic world, they dominate. Because in the extended family household women interact mostly with each other, they dominate each other. It is this—the socialization and domination of women by women—that I explore in this chapter. To do so, I focus upon the wedding ritual as a "metaform" of social organization. Weddings are rites that confirm the norms governing women's behavior. Weddings address the private domain of familial life but in a public context. Moreover, as effective symbolic action, the wedding is a rite of passage that manages the incorporative shaping of the social persona. Hence, it constitutes a meaningful focus within which to explore aspects of the socialization and domination of women by women.

Socioeconomic Transformation in a Maramureş Village

Data were collected during fieldwork in 1978–79 in Ieud, Maramureş, an isolated region in northern Transylvania. Maramureş is surrounded by mountains to the west, south, and east. The Tiza River forms the northern border along the Russian Ukraine. Ieud is one of the oldest and largest villages in Maramureş, with a population of approximately 5,500. Historically, it is a village of nobles, *nemeşi*.[5] Religion has had profound influence in Maramureş and in Ieud particularly: Ieudeni (people from Ieud) attribute high natality and no divorce to the tenacity of tradition, religious and secular.[6] Ieud used to be one of the wealthiest villages in Maramureş. Forced cooperativization in 1950 and 1962, as well as nationalization of the forests, has radically altered this status; Ieud is now one of the poorest villages.[7] The primary motivation for cooperativization in Ieud was not based on economic rationality; rather, it was aimed at undermining the authority of the Church and destroying the wealthy, landed peasant class of *chiaburs* descended from titled nobility. This process was met by violent resistance. However, in 1962, the *chiaburi* were successfully inscribed in the cooperative farm; Ieud was left semicooperativized.

As everywhere, these imposed changes transformed the economic organization of the village. They also led to the diversification of the family with one or more persons entering the wage labor force to supplement the family's income. In Romania rapid industrialization has occurred simultaneously with planned urbanization. Industrial centers are dispersed throughout the country rather than concentrated in a few target areas. One consequence of this strategy is the increase of commuters to and from factories and mines. Rural-urban contact is daily, as approximately 20 percent of the labor force commutes on an everyday basis. However, these commuters are disproportionately male. Agriculture has been steadily feminized, and women now account for approximately 70 percent of the agricultural work force.[8] Interestingly, the feminization of agriculture has unintentionally reinforced traditional roles and norms. Men used to commute to the forest; now they go to the city. Women have become the nurturers of the state as well as the family.[9]

As is generally true throughout the world, the results of socioeconomic transformation have been fraught with contradictions.[10] Most strikingly, in Ieud, it is the ritual system—religious and secular—that has emerged as the stable organizational factor in a much altered village life. The church calendar broadly dictates the rhythm of activity. Seasonal laborers leave the village at the beginning of Lent to return for Easter. This cycle is repeated for Pentecost, St. Mary's in August, and Christmas. The villagers remain in residence through the cold winters during which time most weddings take place. Death of a family member supersedes all other obligations at any time. Again, socioeconomic change has unexpectedly emphasized the ritual system. (The tendency to highlight the ritual system with respect to local social organization seems to occur in areas where there is a high proportion of *transhumant*, or migrant laborers, who comprise the local population. Otherwise, the general trend in both urban and rural areas, collectivized and noncollectivized, is for rituals to become ceremonially less complex but materially more extravagant. This reflects the changing conditions of socioeconomic welfare as well as of modes of production. Nonetheless, ritual continues to redistribute wealth and structure a system of reciprocal relations.)

The Dynamics of Ritual

Ritual, seen as effective symbolic action, is a dramatic form that articulates the relationship between a symbolically constructed order of meanings, which some writers term "culture," and a system of interpersonal and institutional relationships, often referred to as "society." Because of the intrinsic characteristics of symbols and symbolic systems, ritual is able to mobilize perceptions and values that are often not consciously recognized but, rather, remain in the background of experience. Life-cycle rituals, in particular, may be viewed as synthetic expressions of the nature and dimensions of social relations and exchange. Weddings, like funerals, are of special import because (1) they socially effect realignments of social relations and, hence, affect central economic institutions and (2) are ego-focused rites that require collective participation and, hence, "state" the ritual transformation of the individual as a transformation of the whole. The power of ritual lies in this ability to articulate the nature of social consciousness while incorporating the individual's experience into it.[11]

In this chapter, I explore the dynamics of ritual by focusing on selected aspects of the wedding rite, namely, symbolic bargaining. Weddings in Maramureş are complex cultural dramas[12] that involve elaborate ritual action and ritual language. Nuptial *strigături* (shouted verses) in the form of rhymed couplets either traditional or improvised include literal and metaphorical commentary upon general matters such as morality, drinking, kinship, and aging, as well as upon more precise problems of socialization, dispute, change, and personal trauma. *Strigături* constitute the primary mode of communication during weddings. The ritual context in which they occur invites the crystallization of existing norms and values in every symbolic mode. How the wedding ritual proceeds from the directly personal and/or interpersonal to the sociocentric thereby effecting transformation of the individual, all the while reifying the social as the context for this transformation, can be demonstrated. For objectifying experience, ritual language and ritual action comprise a powerful symbolic medium through which to understand the lived-in world of the participants. As we shall see, weddings provide public forums for introductory as well as advanced discourses on womanhood and marriage.

The Bridal Veil of Tears

"Don't worry, if she doesn't cry, I've got onions," the young bride's mother assured me as she watched her daughter with embarrassment.[13] Her daughter had just offered me a welcoming smile. But it was her wedding day; she was about to be dressed, and she smiled? Unthinkable, or rather, unacceptable. She *must* cry—a ritual imperative that at the same time is symbolic of women's raison d'être.

Becoming a woman begins at the moment of birth. Like all babies, the newborn girl cries. But so do her mother and female kin because "she" is not a "he."[14] Later in life at another's wedding, the young girl may publicly acknowledge her mother's suffering with a *strigătură*:[15]

When you bore me mother
How happy you were
You thought you had a son
But you had only sorrow and longing

When you saw I was a girl
Your whole body ached.

What's so bad about having a girl? As one mother stated, "A girl is a worry; after all, she may become pregnant out of wedlock, God forbid. Boys drink and all, but that's different. Anyway, when my son marries, it'll be his wife's worry, not mine." A daughter is yours always, and her mother knows what being a daughter-in-law means. There is an implicit acceptance of women's subordination to men and, through them, to mothers-in-law. It must be noted that the daughter's compassionate mother does not recognize that she is simultaneously the tyrannical mother-in-law of her son's wife. Since the birthrate in this village is high, most women usually experience having at least one pitiable daughter and one scapegoat daughter-in-law. A mother-in-law toasted her new daughter-in-law:

Poor mothers with daughters
For a long time they are dearly kept
Then she gives them away and doesn't see them
I assure you I have kept them
I gave them and didn't have them
I was left with five sons
And with each I will take a daughter-in-law
Dear Lord, take care of what I've taken
So I won't be the laugh of the village.

In "taking a daughter-in-law" the mother-in-law exercises her rights of dominance vis-à-vis the new bride; however, the mother-in-law also realizes that her own position is hierarchically relative. The community at large acknowledges a mother-in-law's "rights," but if the daughter-in-law is not well-behaved, then it reflects badly upon the elder woman's authority. A daughter-in-law is expected to obey her mother-in-law, to work arduously, and to be sexually honorable. Otherwise, the mother-in-law will be publicly ridiculed.

When a daughter marries, she cries, and so do all of the women present. Yet the major concern of girls between the ages of sixteen and twenty is getting married. Twenty-one already signifies "old maiden" (*fată mare*). Later, when a woman dies, other women cry and lament for her; when others die, she cries and laments. From beginning to end, a deluge of tears obscures women's clear vision of their circumstance. Why? What is the process that fosters this traditional malady? Any woman can tell you the basic reason. Women suffer and rightfully so. Eve sinned. Humanity's depravity is her fault, a deed for which women should atone.[16] Religious training and commensurate practice teach a girl inherent shame.

And with this shame she becomes a woman. The moment that publicly marks a girl's formal entry into the hierarchically ordered world of women is her wedding. As mentioned above, the wedding emphasizes normative behavior; it is hardly ordered by concern for the individual bride's own personal feelings. The wedding has everything to do with the collective identity of women. Thus, the wedding provides an occasion to reflect publicly upon being a woman as the bride is introduced to her new status and role. The bride's individuality is tamed. The vocalized commiserative support of other married women cajoles her into passively accepting her lot. The individual is lost to the generalized group of married women. The wedding is a subtle act of incorporation into a subordinate position.

The first incidence of domination occurs when the wedding agreement is finalized. That a wedding will take place is never certain until the bride and her future mother-in-law shake hands through their woolen aprons worn over their chemises. Fathers, the economic heads of households, can agree, but there is no binding symbolic conviction in that. Traditionally, men conclude business transactions with a handshake and toast.[17] However, a bride's dealings will be primarily with her mother-in-law rather than with her husband and father-in-law. Hence, the seemingly innocent gesture overtly symbolizes cooperation between these two women; nonetheless, it simultaneously signifies submission on the part of the bride to the will of her future mother-in-law. The handshake must be done through woolen aprons. Wool symbolizes prosperity.[18] It is important to note that sheep are tended by men; women utilize the products of sheep—milk, meat, wool—secondarily. In like fashion, the link between the mother-in-law and daughter-in-law is secondary; women are not directly connected but, rather, are related through men. Hence women must shake hands through their aprons. Hope springs eternal, silencing the words heard so many times at weddings:

Poor girls
If only they would die
And let their mothers bury them
Let them bury them among the flowers
Rather than become daughters-in-law
Let them bury them among the lilacs
Rather than live among strangers.[19]

Given preferential patrilocal residence, when a girl marries, it is most often she that leaves home to live "among strangers." As rite of passage, the wedding ritual publicly dramatizes this separation of the bride from her natal family and her incorporation into a new family. Thus, the three-day proceedings both facilitate as well as demarcate changes within corporate households. The wedding offers an occasion for the bride to acknowledge her fulfillment of obligations to her natal family and, likewise, they to her. When the wedding is over, the bride leaves home to become a member of another family. She will contribute her share to the groom's family by working and bearing children. For a corporate household to function smoothly, it is crucial to secure the allegiance of women and children to it. As noted similarly in Macedonia, incorporation of a bride—an outsider—into established family routine poses a threat to household organization; however, at the same time, the continuity and growth of the household is dependent upon the successful incorporation of outside women into it.[20]

While certain economic benefits may ensue as a result of marriage, economic considerations are not of primary import in the wedding itself. In Romania, as in neighboring countries, what is transferred through the weddings are mainly the rights to the bride's reproductive powers; the transfer does not necessarily involve alienation of other forms of productive power, i.e., land, animals.[21] The implicit concern throughout the wedding is sexuality and, more specifically, the bride's virginity—for it is this that symbolizes the potential to create sacred life, thereby guaranteeing the continuation over time of the family and its honor. The emphasis on virginity, in part, reflects the dominant values of Greek Catholicism that still permeate the worldview of Ieud.

The Wedding

Again, the wedding is an elaborate three-day event that enacts the transference of the bride from her natal family to that of her husband.[22] The ritual dramatizes the complex status and role changes that occur among the participants, thereby exemplifying effectively "the iconic relationship between the structure of rituals and that of the social transitions they mediate."[23] Hence, the unfolding of the ritual sequences represents in condensed but parallel form the social transformations that occur due to and through the process of marriage.

On the evening preceding the religious ceremony, the groom's flag is made and danced by bachelor friends. Afterward, the young men accompany the groom to the bride's house where her bridal crown will be danced by unmarried friends. The flag and crown are obvious sexual symbols. Then everyone leaves, except the members of the bride's immediate family, her bride's maid, the groom, and his flagbearer. Following a brief meal, the first of three symbolic bride bargainings commences. This is the only ceremonial interaction that occurs directly between the principals, the bride and groom themselves. The bargaining results in the groom giving the bride white ribbons that he has purchased to link her braids together, and the bride offering the groom woolen wrist bands that she has woven for him to wear under his billowing shirtsleeves. That concludes the evening's activities.

The next day following the morning church service, all of the bride's girlfriends as well as close female relatives and neighbors, young and old, gather at the bride's home. The bride is to be dressed. This requires a minimum of two hours, most of which is spent braiding the bride's hair and sewing fresh greenery into her long braids which will be tied together with the groom's gift of white ribbon. Older women do the honors, just as they later will wind the new bride's braids around her head, indicating her status as a married woman.[24] During the bride's dressing, musicians (always male and preferably gypsy) play songs specific to the occasion. The girlfriends and unmarried female relatives accompany the musicians with songs of separation or with *strigături*. These deal with the bride's leaving home to live among strangers, her not being a maiden anymore, and so on. The dressing of the bride is the formal mark of her separation from the cadre of girls (*fete*). It is appropriate that only girls sing at this time. The married women remain silent. It is an emotional time; there is poignant crying. The bride must cry; ritual crying is prescribed. And the older women will not let her get away with merely a glum look—there must be tears, even if induced by onions. (However, it should be pointed out that such measures are rarely required.) It is submission and domination. The texts speak for themselves.

Mother, strangers are coming for me
Please ready my things
God help you

Let me kiss you both
Because I am leaving you
The flowered paths remain
Full of girls and boys
I am setting out on a path with thorns
To live among strangers
Thank you for raising me
And for all that you did for me

Your green crown
How it takes you from us
And puts you among married women
It's nice being a girl with sweethearts
It's rough with young babies
It's nice being a girl
It's awful bathing babies.

The bride is embarking on a "path with thorns"; her crown, like that of Christ, is symbolic of her martyred existence. When the bride is dressed, a young boy places her crown upon her head. It is believed that this will insure a male first-born. Formal leave-taking from her immediate family follows. (This sequence also occurs at the groom's house.) There is continuous toasting and tears until all family members have clinked glasses with the bride. Then everyone proceeds to the church where the groom is waiting. Tradition allows the bride to walk as slowly as she desires; it is said this is the last time in her younger years that she will command when things are done. It is a last gesture of independence from her soon-to-be husband and mother-in-law. However, tradition also cautions the bride not to walk too slowly thereby aggravating her waiting groom and mother-in-law. In part, the slow, dirgelike pace underscores the symbolic equation of marriage with death.

During the church service, unmarried friends dance outside. When it is over, the groom and his party go to his house; the bride, to hers. After a meal, ritual exchanges of bread and brandy occur between the two households. Representatives from the groom's entourage go to the bride's home bearing their symbolic gifts of food and drink; upon their return, members of the bride's party reciprocate. The order in which these presentations occur is unequivocal, reflecting power relations between the wife-takers and the wife-givers.[25] The reciprocal, and equivalent, offerings establish ties of exchange between the two families.[26] Having constituted a basis for interaction, it is appropriate to go after the bride, to bargain symbolically for her.

Once again, it must be mentioned that marriage entails an exchange resulting in the acquisition of something specific: the bride's reproductive power. In an idealized situation such as the wedding, that which is normative is presumed to exist. The bride's virginity is an expected reality. At this juncture in the wedding, two ritual "plays" or scenarios highlight this preoccupation with sexuality and virginity by means of a symbolic lexicon articulated primarily through verbal dueling. The metaphors employed in these plays borrow from the cultural vocabulary associated with bargaining. A propos, one is cautioned that "a marriage is a type of negotiated exchange like that in the market; if you bargain with closed eyes, you'll pay dearly." The word for "negotiated exchange," *tîrg*, connotes both the market place and the bargaining that characterizes activity within it.

The first of these ritual plays is known as "asking for the bride." The groom's party consisting of his relatives and close neighbors arrives at the bride's house around 1 A.M. In former times, a ritual fight, reminiscent of bride capture, occurred between male members of the bride's and groom's respective groups; more recently, however, elaborate verbal dueling is found in its stead. The bride's father and groom's godfather, his ritual sponsor, are the principal actors. This is as it should be, for in public dealings men represent the corporate households. They officiate over interfamilial matters. The initial pretext for the verbal exchange is that the groom's party is lost in the night. They were enroute either to the market or the forest, the referential categories being determined by the location of the bride's house in the village. If enroute to the forest, signaling that the bride lives in the upper part of the village,[27] then the weary travelers are searching for the first flowers of spring. (Most weddings occur in the winter.) If off to the market, then they hope to acquire a fine white lamb. Both are symbols of purity and vitality.

Nonetheless, there is an implicit ambivalence associated with these symbols. Lambs and sheep are sacred animals; women, because of their natural condition of pollution, are not permitted to milk them for fear of causing the milk to curdle. Regarding flowers, the euphemism for having one's menses is "having flowers on one's skirt." Virginal girls wear brightly colored, floral-patterned skirts. Married women customarily do not. Also, water from a baby girl's first bath is showered over patches of flowers in the garden so that she will have many suitors; that of boys is thrown only over one flower patch so that he will acquire first off that which he seeks. In the wedding the groom's party attributes the lateness of their intrusion to their eagerness to be the first to find the flower or the lamb as the case may be. This points to competition over eligible women as well as to matters of honor. For the sake of argument, I will continue the account in reference to the flower.

The tone of these opening exchanges is polite. The host offers customary respite: bread, drink, and shelter. However, he repeatedly inquires about the true nature of their intentions; strangers in the night are highly suspect, particularly since the neighboring village is reputed to be one of thieves. This notwithstanding, the travelers are invited in. The bride's guests must accommodate them, which, owing to the small rooms, usually means they must exit from the room and crowd around the door and windows.

Once inside the house, the groom's godfather implores the host to search for a flower in his home. He points to the white scarf on the groom's flag, thereby indicating the flower's purity of color. The host obliges and returns with a young girl of four or five years. She is dressed in white bridal attire with the exception of a floral-patterned skirt. The integrity of the symbolic system is evident as is the ambivalence. The girl is displayed before the groom and his party. She recites the following verse, the only fixed-phrase text in this ritual play:

If I please you, I please you
If not, then I won't force you to take me
I'll put my bridal crown in the hope chest
And remain a maiden yet another summer.

The text is fixed, traditional, just as the ideal unfolding of any girl's life. This episode presages her own hoped-for eventual status as a bride. The godfather looks her over but politely refuses: "She's lovely—to her health; may she too be a bride someday."

He then asks again that the bride's father search for something whiter. Skillful bargaining requires subtle manipulation, give-and-take. The intensity of the verbal exchange heightens with the host accusing his guests of unwarranted pretentions. He's given them food and lodging, and yet they are unsatisfied: "Once a gypsy, always a gypsy," he challenges. "Ah, but effort never meets death," the godfather responds to his host's retort, meaning that if his intentions were dishonest, then he would not bother to ask; he would simply steal, a reminder that conjures up memories of bride theft and again comments on the unfortunate reputation of the neighboring villagers as well as of gypsies. It should be noted that conflict, if and when it arises during ritual bargaining, is resolved through the use of proverbs which therein function so as to impose constraint upon that which threatens the transformative progression within the ritual structure itself and the "goal" of the ritual.[28]

Having calmed the host's temper, he is again persuaded to look for a "whiter" flower and returns with the bridesmaid. She also wears a floral-patterned skirt. Hence, she is not quite what they want either, but she is designated the future property of the groom's flag-bearer. In this manner, a symbolic betrothal takes place, insuring continual reproduction of the social order.

The scene repeats, and on the third try, the father enters with his daughter, the bride. The white flower has blossomed forth. In fact, she is dressed entirely in white. It should be noted that the variegated flowers of youthful skirts give way to pure white; the bride is purest and is thus sacralized for "sacrifice." (Once again, it is interesting to recall the relationship between marriage and death.) All is well that ends well. The father's social graces are vocally applauded. Having reached an agreement, the two men shake hands whereupon the godfather proposes a toast to the flower that has been picked by the groom. The flower is now theirs.

In this manner a deal (between households) is concluded. To reiterate, bargaining is dependent upon successful manipulation. This accounts for the unformalized "text" thereby allowing each to exercise his skill and wit.

The progression of events is developed via metaphoric discourse. While the verbal duel continues on the level of metaphor, metonymic acts refine the ambiguity of the symbolic content. Of course, in the end, the object of transfer or, rather, acquisition is substantive not symbolic.

The conclusion of the first ritual play satisfies the wedding guests' curiosity. Their stated purpose in attending the wedding is "to see what the groom bought," "to see how he bargained." In point of fact, the groom's ritual sponsor bargained for the bride in this public scenario. The groom interacted directly with the bride only on the evening preceding the church ceremony; that symbolic bargaining occurred in the privacy of the bride's immediate family. Clearly, as the ritual unfolds, it becomes increasingly more symbolic; emphasis is displaced from actuality. The discussion moves from one about *the* marriage to one about marriage.

Hence, in the ritual play, "asking for the bride," the groom (as represented by his godfather) seeks to acquire purity, a virgin bride. After considerable negotiation, the host produces his daughter. As in any bargaining situation, the buyer looks for the best; the burden lies upon the seller to convince his prospective customer that what he has to offer *is* the best. However, bargaining is an age-old verbal art, and the best often has little to do with real quality but rather more to do with verbal agility. It is no different when seeking a bride. All brides are virgins, even if it takes a chicken's blood to prove it. Be this as it may, honor demands that the bride's quality be publicly certified.

This is accomplished in the second ritual play, the "selling of the hen." Briefly, the bride's symbolic mother, in reality the woman who prepares the wedding meals (and, in this case, gives the wife-takers what to eat literally and metaphorically), attests to her "daughter's" virginity through a versified dialogue with the symbolic mother-in-law, the groom's godmother. As in the preceding ritual play, the bargaining has shifted from the interpersonal level between bride and groom to the socially interpersonal. The cook, in the symbolic role of the bride's mother, carries through the room crowded with the groom's party a cooked hen bedecked in greenery and necklaces of bread. (Just as the bride's braids are adorned with fresh greenery, so the hen is similarly fashioned into an icon of the bride.) As the cook progresses through the jammed room, she bargains in *strigături* with the "mother-in-law" to sell her the hen. After extended banter, the "mother-in-law" buys the hen which is then eaten. In part, this play dramatizes the process of appropriation: the cooking of food may be seen as a metaphor for reproduction. The cook, just like an unmarried girl's mother, transforms raw meat into cooked meat.[29] The hen is cooked in the kitchen and then carried to the point of consumption. When appropriated, it is consumed.

In the first play the principal actors were the bride's father and groom's godfather who, in the public realm, are the heads of households. It is through them that approval of the exchange is granted publicly. But in the private realm, that is, the home, women rule. As with the handshake through woolen aprons, the bride's subjugation to her mother-in-law is stressed repeatedly. Once the bride takes leave of her mother, her interaction will be primarily with her mother-in-law. This mother-in-law/daughter-in-law relationship is exceedingly troublesome.[30] Again, while assuring the continuation of the family, the presence of a bride simultaneously threatens the solidarity of the corporate household and the authority of the mother-in-law. Because marriage signals the termination of the mother/daughter bond and the commencement of the mother-in-law/daughter-in-law relationship, it is again appropriate that the bargaining over the "hen" occur between these two women. And thus it begins:

Hey, Auntie, what are you thinking?[31]
Come and bargain with me
I'll give a little, you add a little
For bargaining has no anger.

The hen as a ritual icon for the bride is not arbitrarily determined; there is a metonymic connection in the economic realm. Poultry—their care, preparation, and sale—are the responsibility of women. Hens are particularly valuable to a household because they provide eggs for both nourishment and additional income. So it is with the bride. The symbolic similarity is readily stated: "a bride is like a hen." In extolling the virtues of this "hen" during the play, the "mother" incorporates into her sales pitch those virtues most desired in a bride:

My hen is a good one
I fed her well,

meaning that she is from a good family, well-raised, and healthy:

My hen is really plump
With fat on her backbone
She's well prepared
Fit for a wedding.

This alludes to the preference in Maramureş for women who are *grase şi frumoase*, fat and beautiful. Bigger is better, healthier and more capable of childbearing and hard work. A girl's constitution is carefully scrutinized.

Even more so her virginity: it is crucial to the upholding of social norms and the well-being of the community.[32] This refers to the maintenance of peaceful relations between women who, after all, are the crux of the matter. Despite the fact that men are known to be more promiscuous, women believe that they themselves are the perpetrators of sexual corruption, which can only foster social disharmony.

Everyone, in fact, awaits the end of the wedding when the virgin bride will lose her innocent status. Anticipation of this event brings to the surface heretofore unmentioned sexual tensions. Therefore, in this play, the "selling of the hen," codes governing sex and sexuality are explored. But social norms do not permit forthright discussion of sexual matters in public; this must be carried out on the level of metaphor, safeguarded within the frame of ritual. To this end, the *strigături* exchanged between the two women become increasingly suggestive. These verses are necessarily joking verses, the joke being a convenient vehicle to voice that which is normally suppressed if not repressed. Woman, the temptress, here in the person of the cook, teases:

Enroute to the wedding
I injured my thigh
If you don't believe me
Well, godfather, lift my skirt
And see for yourself!

But propriety prevails as she continues:

Hey, behave yourself
Don't lift it from the front!

Verses addressing the form of payment provide the mechanism by which to manipulate more explicitly a discussion on sexual behavior. It should be noted that the payment transferred at the end of this play goes to the cook; there is no bridewealth in Maramureş. The godmother may offer:

I'll give you ten lei to buy earrings[33]
I'll give you ten zlotys to buy underpants.

(Underpants are meant to discourage temptation by covering the genitals.) To which the cook may reply:

My husband bought me some
It's not the responsibility of the village.

A less reserved cook may begin an exchange tauntingly:

I won't ask a high price for my hen,
Godmother dear
Just once with the godfather.

But the godmother will have none of that:

My husband is a big scoundrel
He doesn't desire just anyone
He wants only me
I'll give you money, land
But, I won't sell you my husband.

Depending on the dynamics of the situation, the cook may persist:

The godmother is pretty
But my mouth is sweeter
The godfather has many lovers
But the godmother doesn't know.

And so on. The primacy of sexuality and sex is evident. The content of these *strigături* often becomes blatantly pornographic, ribald, much to the temporary enjoyment of all. The cook might begin:[34]

My, the poor godfather.
Because I've brought him a hen.
And given the godfather a hard-on.
The godfather is a well-behaved man
And puts his shirttail down in front!

The hen has nine eggs
The godfather has only two
Whoever knows, you've guessed well
I think you've squeezed (tickled) them!

In keeping with the idealized superior/inferior status relations between the households of the bride and groom, it should be noticed that it is the bride's "mother" who acts as ribald temptress; the groom's godmother makes order prevail. True to tradition, the woman's side is unvirtuous; the man's virtuous. Marriage is necessary to continue the moral order. And so it does. In the end, the traditional norms and values are hailed. Much to the relief of everyone, religious and moral tenets are reaffirmed; the sociocultural order is celebrated.

Eventually, the "mother," or cook, succeeds in selling the hen for which she is paid. Inflation has raised the payment from twenty-five to a hundred lei—about nine dollars. Inclinations toward conspicuous consumption encourage innovation. While waving the bill for all to see, she proclaims:

Conditions are easier in the world today
I want to buy a television.

The intent is partially satirical. In the traditional verses, the woman brags that she will buy new boots to wear to the Sunday dance, the traditional form of entertainment. Now, no longer having land to be worked due to cooperativization means that many people have a little more leisure time to be in their homes—to watch television.[35] The "buying of a television" also points to the ongoing reconstruction of value represented in a system of objects.

The conclusion of this transaction publicly finalizes the bride's change of status and household allegiance. The "sale" of the bride to her mother-in-law presages her own attainment to this status and position. Womanhood entails sex, a topic also discussed in *strigături* to introduce the bride to it and incorporate the couple into the existing realm of relations among married couples. Processual changes within the structure of the households are symbolically indicated and demarcated.

Upon completion of this play, nonstop toasting of the bride begins. It is her day. Men usually toast the bride or the couple with nonspecific *strigături* about enjoying the guests, wishing the couple, godparents, or whomever, good luck and good fortune. The concern of men is the general well-being of the community. In terms of interhousehold relations, men represent individual families as undifferentiated discrete units. But, within the individual households, relations *are* differentiated, and women use the occasion of a wedding to vocalize the nature of this differentiation. Because a wedding effects the transference of a woman from one household to another, the liminality experienced during the rite of passage temporarily breaches the boundaries between discrete household units. Accordingly, so the constraints on internal privacy are also breached.

Hence, during the wedding, the primary toasts are those of married women to the bride. Women elevate intrahousehold matters to the level of communal concern. In this way, the toasts constitute a form of collective cathartic expression that at one and the same time legitimates the position of women and protests it. Thus, unlike the toasts offered by men, women's toasts are specific: they tell the bride about the professed conditions of married life. For all the celebrating, the bride dissolves into tears as she listens to her fate. This type of toasting by any one woman may continue for ten to fifteen minutes uninterrupted.

When you were at your mother's house
You were never troubled
You slept only with a woven blanket
She let you sleep later
But now you'll sleep in your husband's arms
And get up at dawn
And your mother-in-law isn't your mother
Don't think that she won't beat you

My dear little bride
Listen to me if you'd like
What I'll tell you isn't a lie
You'll see that it shall be
Sweet bride, your crown
Finely braided
And worn but little
Your green crown
How it takes you from maidenhood
And puts you among us
It is fine to be called wife
But it is never like being a maiden
Because you won't go where you please
Your husband will order you
He isn't your brother
Don't think he won't beat you
He won't hit you with a stick
But he will sting you with harsh words
That will break your heart . . .

Little bride, take heed
You will give your crown for the married woman's scarf
And this scarf is very heavy
Trouble and worry are under it
But don't fret my dear
Because we all wear it . . .

At this point, the bride was crying intensely, so the woman toasting her, after having produced this hysterical state, tried to soothe her:

Your husband is from my family
So I think it won't be bad
I think it will be fine
Little bride, your husband
If he is like mine
Since we've been married
He's never hit me
We've lived happily together.

If lengthy toasts are directed to the groom, then they call his attention to the "flower" beside him and to the fact that in his home she will have no one but him. They also beg him to take good care of her.

The wedding ends at the bride's house with her ritual undressing. This refers to the ritual taking off of the bride's crown to be replaced by the married woman's scarf. The crown, which had been positioned by a young boy, is removed by the bride's godmother who then places the crown on the head of a young girl. It is hoped that she too will wear the crown one day. This event, as opposed to the dressing of the bride discussed earlier, is accompanied by songs sung by married women linked together in a unified circle around the bride:

Take off your crown, bride
And give it to the circle of women
In your mother's garden
Where your crown will be left
Will grow basil
For you won't be a girl at the dance
You won't come and go
Your husband will make love to you
And your mother-in-law isn't your mother
Don't think she won't urge him on!
From now on
The paths are forbidden to you
Only three are permitted:
To the garden for onions
To the well after water
And occasionally to your mother's.

While songs often blame the husband for limited freedom, in reality, the mother-in-law is to blame. She dictates where the bride may go and when. With the exception of infrequent visits to her mother, those places where the bride must go are associated with tears and submission and not with flowers and vitality. Hence, when the bride's godmother places the married woman's scarf on her head, the bride refuses it by throwing it off. She does this three times. And then it is all over. The married women sing:

Outside it is snowing and raining
We have a new married one
Be quiet, stop crying
Let the others cry
Who remain unmarried.

With the end of the wedding another bride is successfully incorporated into the fold of married women, the latter thereby assuring themselves of their normative appropriateness. The wedding succeeds in making her, the bride, like all married women. This one is no different:

Sweet little bride
You were a rose in your mother's garden
But when you blossomed forth
Your mother sold you
That's how it is with girls
Not just for one, but for all. . . .

Her position and status will improve as she herself bears children and progresses through the stages of the life cycle. Eventually she too will be not only a mother but also a mother-in-law, reproducing the social order.

Conclusion

In summary, Romania is ideologically dedicated to the "equal involvement of men and women in productive activity,"[36] that is, to the incorporation of women into the economic sphere of production as the means to dissolve sexual inequality. If this alone would liberate women from their tears, then important inroads have been made. But the tears keep flowing. Women do comprise an increasingly significant factor in the labor force, but if there has been a shift in public externalized relations between men and women, it has not significantly influenced the structure of interaction between them within the household. Furthermore, the relations between women have not changed.

Ideological loyalty to sexual equality reflects support of an abstract formulation. In Romania, as in other communist countries, the ideological cadres have paid little attention to the family per se. As a consequence, the implementation of five-year plans for socioeconomic transformation has inadvertently reproduced the traditional structure of social relations, particularly at the local level. The commuter strategy alleviated the problems that would have been engendered by lack of infrastructural resources in the burgeoning urban areas. To that end, the plan was generally successful. However, it resulted in a predominantly male commuter population, as women continued to be constrained by traditional household and childcare obligations. A female core remained at home; agriculture was feminized. By unintentionally keeping women in the village, this mode of their integration into the national economy has actually accentuated many of the traditional patterns of relations and intensified the tensions inherent in them: i.e., women are economically subordinate to men, even if women hold industrial jobs. Men hold higher status positions within the local political economy. Women usually do not, although they do shoulder the responsibility for many of the tasks formerly performed by fathers, husbands, and sons. These, however, are added to the already established routines of women. Hence, in view of the female core in the village, not only do the traditional norms and values persist, but they may be perceived to be exacerbated.[37]

As I have tried to demonstrate in this chapter, at the local level, the nuances of daily interaction are effectively articulated in weddings which constitute a symbolic microcosm of the sociocultural order. Throughout the wedding, the hierarchical structuring of social relations according to age and sex within both public and private domains is dramatically presented. The wedding enacts social process normatively in terms the society constitutes and "understands": a woman is alienated from her natal family and incorporated into the family of her husband. The central focus of the ritual, therefore, is upon women. By addressing the private domain of familial life in a public context, weddings serve to explicate the nature of power relationships in the public domain. (Given the patriarchal character of the regime in Romania,[38] this analysis may be extended to include relations of dominance between the Communist party and population—but this is a subject for another essay.)

Thus, the ritual moves from the directly interpersonal in a private context (the initial bargaining between the bride and groom) to the socially interpersonal in a public context (the "asking for the bride" and the "selling of the hen"). As the wedding progresses, ritual discourse and action become more remotely symbolic, transforming the "discussion" into one about marriage in general. In the end, society generates marriage through the godparents, removing interpersonal relations to the communal sphere. The ritual succeeds in objectifying and categorizing subjective experience.[39] Nonetheless, the wedding rite is not primarily concerned with specific individuals' actual experience of personal history but rather with their experience of the sociocultural order within particular historic contexts. Society dictates that marriage represents the finest expression of individual and social humanity, hence, marriage is culturally elaborated and celebrated via the wedding ritual.[40] This rite symbolically encodes a normative system (constituted within the terms of patrilineality and patriarchy) of hierarchical social relations between and among the sexes (irrespective of the state's ideology of equality for women). At the ideational level, marriage signifies subordination and hardship for women. However, at the experiential level, marriage entails ongoing negotiations of relationships between individuals. Hence, relations with the ubiquitous mother-in-law may or may not be deeply troublesome. Place of residence and the cyclical nature of life serve to temper structural ambivalence: aging mothers-in-law often express concern that their daughters-in-law may take revenge during the former's old age, especially should the husband's death precede hers or should she be infirm. Marriage may or may not mean that women suffer verbal humiliation and physical abuse; raising children is burdensome, notably for women, but this burden is one wrought of pleasure. The wedding rite underlines the social transformations that marriage engenders, emphasizing the position of the bride because she is the pivotal person in this system of alienation and incorporation. The ritual dramatizes the norms and values of the sociocultural order; however, the dramatization of social rules and meanings is not necessarily translated verbatim into actual belief and behavior. Norms and values are meant to be exemplary and constraining, but they are not totally determinant. Ritual may be perceived to be "cultural work," but it is also "cultural play." Hence, its meanings and messages are open to interpretation.

This is in contrast to the primary concerns of state ideology, which is normative in scope at the formal institutional level only. State ideology lacks a transformative quality, especially at the level of action. It is programmatic and progressive but does not *effectively* articulate the relationship between the individual and the sociocultural order as experienced in everyday terms.[41] As long as the existing nature of social interaction between and among the sexes hierarchically structures relations in terms of dominance, women will continue to cry when a girl is born and when she marries. This does not, however, preclude the possibility of change over time in respect of the life cycle. Reinforcing the discrepancy between formal state ideology and praxis, girls and women upon the occasion of each wedding will again shout the traditional words of wisdom:

If only girls realized
What happened to brides
No matter what payment given
They wouldn't marry

Oh, bride, your crown
How it takes you from your mother
And gives you to your mother-in-law

Eat, little bride, eat dinner
In your mother's house
Because from now on
You'll eat the white meat of hens
With a mother who is a stranger.

20

Dorothy Rosenberg

The Emancipation of Women in Fact and Fiction: Changing Roles in GDR Society and Literature

Women's status in a given society is determined by the interaction of political, economic, and cultural forces. Germany provides the unique example of an industrialized, highly sophisticated Western European country that has been divided into two distinct societies. Contemporary East and West Germany are the products of thirty-five years' application of contrasting political and economic systems to a single cultural and historical foundation. By examining legal status and employment statistics, we can establish the obvious structural changes in women's position in East Germany. Their representation in literature provides us with a more subtle picture of changing roles in private as well as public life, giving us a clearer insight into the status of East German women.

It is a precept of Marxist theory that relationship to the means of production is the primary factor in the analysis of any social question. Accordingly, orthodox Marxists have treated the oppression of women as a contradiction arising from the class struggle rather than as a separate problem. Thus, the oppression of women can only be alleviated in the course of achieving socialism. The mechanical application of this conclusion resulted in both theoretical and strategic limitations in the orthodox Marxist approach to the emancipation of women.[1]

In the Weimar Republic the strategy of the German Communist party (KPD) for the emancipation of women rested on a program of demanding formal legal equality, political activation, and the full integration of women into economic life. After the interregnum of the Nazi period, which had systematically excluded women from the public sphere, the KPD program from the 1920s was reestablished as the party's goal for women in the "anti-fascist-democratic" phase of the GDR (1945–50).

With the assumption of state power by the Socialist Unity party (SED), which was the amalgamation of the prewar KPD and SPD, in 1946, the first demand for formal legal equality was promptly and easily fulfilled. The legal equality of women was declared in the 1946 party program and the first Constitution and was included in several laws between 1950 and 1960. The demands for political activation and integration into economic life were rather more complex. While both tasks were promptly undertaken, it was for quite different reasons and with unsurprisingly different results.

Political Activation

The political activation of women in East Germany began as early as May of 1945 with the formation of local antifascist women's commissions,[2] whose primary concerns were women's and children's issues. In October 1945, in an open letter to the City Council of Berlin, the Central Women's Commission demanded not only legal equality but: "Active participation of women in public life, education, science, and the professions . . . occupational retraining programs open to all women, new health and safety laws, equal pay for equal work, and health care for women and children, especially orphans."[3] Equal pay for equal work had already been declared law by the Soviet Military Administration in their sector in August 1945.[4] After intense debate, the demand for special training programs for women was included in the paragraph of the SED program guaranteeing women equal rights in 1946.[5]

In March 1947 the women's commissions were consolidated into the German Democratic Women's Organization (DFD) with committees for social, educational, cultural, constitutional, and legal issues. The primary function of the DFD was to organize the unorganized. In the 1950s and 1960s, with the massive shift of women into factory work where the majority joined unions, the DFD's sphere of influence gradually contracted to preparatory and political education courses for housewives. Although it exists today with a membership of over 1.4 million, approximately 30 percent of whom are housewives, and has a block of thirty-five seats in the Volkskammer (Parliament), it has little direct political power. Instead, the responsibility for the representation of women was assumed directly by the SED.

The report of the Second Party Congress on September 24, 1947, included the following resolution: "The active participation of women is of decisive importance for the safeguarding of democracy. Therefore, it is an urgent task of the party to increasingly entrust women with political assignments and to support women's promotion to responsible work in the whole of public life. The SED will do everything to promote this development and to prepare women for their responsibilities."[6]

According to Gabriele Gast in *The Political Role of Women in the* GDR, this resolution was the result of three political considerations. In part, it rested on Lenin's thesis that the construction of socialism required the complete emancipation of women and the equally conscious and active participation of men and women. In addition, leaders of the party realized that both their own power and the internal consolidation of the state depended on women's active support. This required ideologically reliable women who could participate in party political work. The SED expected the integration of women into public life to result in their involvement in general political struggles and a maturing of their ideological consciousness. Finally, the resolution also reflected women's own ambitions and demands to have an influence on social, economic, and political relations in the new state.[7]

Legal Guarantees

One result of the formal party resolution was the inclusion in the Constitution of a guarantee of women's equality and a series of laws expanding its implications. The wording gives a clear picture of the double role of worker and mother expected of women. In the October 7, 1949, Constitution, article 18 declared that women's employment merited special legislation and that special arrangements were to be made to guarantee that women's responsibilities as citizens and workers were made compatible with their duties as women and mothers; article 32 declared that motherhood deserved special protection.

Following a directive from the party political bureau of April 18, 1950,[8] the Volkskammer passed the Mother and Child Protection Act, which included a number of measures to protect women's health and productive capacity, with special concern for pregnant women. It included sections on the promotion of working women, women's position in the family and the professions, and the creation of childcare facilities. The work code passed on April 12, 1961, declared that "in order to make possible an equal and complete participation in the work process for women, measures will be taken for the promotion and further qualification of women, the relieving of women's housework duties, and the social care of mother and child."[9]

Finally, the family code of December 20, 1965, reiterated that men and women were equal within the family. It stated that both partners were required to support the full development of the other's abilities and emphasized the fact that the education of children was the responsibility of the entire society. It also stated that large families and single parents would receive special aid and that relations between the partners were to be arranged to make women's professional and social responsibilities compatible with motherhood.[10]

Political Power

The integration of women into party political work falls into three phases. The first, from 1946 to 1950, was characterized by an intensive effort to recruit women. At the same time, women party members were systematically assigned to deal with women's issues and, to a certain extent, formed their own faction within the party. The first party statutes guaranteed women a minimum representation in all party organs including leadership roles.

This guarantee was dropped in the second phase, which began in 1950. At the 1949 Party Congress, Elli Schmidt declared: "The development of the SED as a party of the new type requires that a whole series of bad habits in the area of women's work be completely overcome. In the Social Democratic party special women's groups existed which stood near the party. Such a division between men and women can (not) and may not exist in a Marxist-Leninist party."[11]

The reorganization of the SED from a mass party to a cadre party between 1948 and 1950 negatively affected women in particular, and the ensuing reduction of the party bureaucracy resulted primarily in women losing their posts. At the same time, the principle of "rising through the ranks" was applied, with the result that most women were relegated permanently to the grass roots. The slogans "Let the women really work" and "More women comrades in leadership" that had been heavily propagandized in the party press of the 1940s quietly disappeared. As happened in other East European states, from 1950 onward the SED line insisted that in the GDR the "woman question" had been solved.

The year 1967 marked the beginning of the third phase. In that year the underrepresentation of women at leadership levels of the party again came under discussion, and a new campaign was launched to increase the number of women in Parliament and in mid-level positions such as mayors. But the number of women in top positions remained virtually unaffected. With Erich Honecker's assumption of power in May 1971, the issue was again dropped, and there has been no significant change in women's status in the party since that time. Although women comprise about a quarter of the SED membership, they are concentrated in primarily advisory or representative party posts in which they can vote but have no influence on political decision-making. As in other communist, as well as noncommunist, countries, at higher levels of power the percentage of women drops rapidly.[12]

Gast is pessimistic about any change in the near future because of the number of factors weighing against women. These include prejudice against career women and distrust, particularly of young women, by state and party functionaries; the lack of women in lower- and middle-level administrative party posts and organizations; the close personal connections between the party-state and economic apparatus that exclude women; and the concentration of women in specific subareas of politics. Women's double burden of public employment and domestic labor also hinders their participation, as does the time-wasting style of work in leadership bodies. Finally, there is no suitable organization to represent women's demands.[13] Despite women's greater involvement in political work in the GDR and their extensive legal rights and equality, they are still effectively shut out of social and political decision-making processes.

Economic Integration

In contrast, the integration of women into the economic life of the GDR has been highly successful. As of 1982, 88.5 percent of women between the ages of twenty and sixty were employed, compared to 42.7 percent in the United States and 38.4 percent in West Germany.[14] While bringing women into the work force was one of the central demands of the old women's movement as well as of the SED after 1945, the political significance of women's productive labor was completely overshadowed by simple economic necessity.

Ever since its foundation, the GDR has suffered from an acute and chronic labor shortage. Following World War I, Germany suffered from what was referred to as an "excess of women," a ratio of 32.2 million to 30.2 million men in 1925.[15] A result of the war, the imbalance was concentrated in the twenty-to-forty age group, which in turn negatively affected the birthrate. As the ratio approached a balance in the next generation, World War II began. This again resulted in a disproportionate loss of male population, prolonged by the slow release of prisoners of war by the Soviet Union. The labor shortage was exacerbated by the exodus to the West of predominantly working-age males, especially skilled workers, technicians, and professionals, from 1954 until the borders were closed in 1961. The situation was complicated by the small size of the industrial base in the primarily agricultural eastern part of Germany, the absence of a postwar source of capital investment, and the Soviet Union's reverse Marshall Plan of dismantling and removing factory installations and goods. These factors contributed to the development of a highly labor-intensive system of production.

Postwar economic conditions were sufficient to draw a comparatively high percentage of women into the work force. Single, widowed, and abandoned women took jobs to survive. Their numbers, however, were not adequate to satisfy the need for labor. More workers and especially more dedicated and reliable workers were needed. The SED began a series of campaigns to get women into the labor force.

After the first big push to get women into the factories, the SED supported subsequent campaigns on ideological rather than economic grounds. The party emphasized not only the emancipatory effect that an independent income and a public role outside the home had on women, but also the political and educational effect of participation in socialized labor in the workplace.[16]

While the primary goal for women during the early or "construction" (*Aufbau*) phase of the GDR was simply to get them into employment, the declaration in 1963 that the GDR was a "developed socialist society" led to a new emphasis on integrating women into previously "male" jobs and professions.[17] Party Secretary Ulbricht stated in 1963: "I know that there is an old attitude that women should work only in the so-called light jobs. But, dear comrades, we cannot build socialism with hairdressers alone. I, too, am in favor of attractive hair styles, but the technical professions are actually the most interesting and important."[18]

On July 7, 1966, a new regulation on Training and Advanced Training of Women in the Technical Professions was issued. It emphasized that as technical qualification and social and professional work experience were the preconditions for assuming a leadership position, factories and organizations would be required to develop special programs to recruit, develop, and promote women into middle- and upper-level management posts.[19]

A series of factors reflecting both economic pragmatism and political theory lay behind the new emphasis on technical qualifications for women. As noted earlier, the GDR had experienced a steady loss of skilled workers, technicians, and professionals to the West. Despite the border closure in 1961, this drain continued, although at a slower rate. With the introduction of the New Economic Policy (NOS) and the declaration that the GDR had become a "developed socialist society" in 1963, the need for trained workers in these areas was urgent. Women constituted a still relatively untapped potentially skilled labor pool; and women had, for a variety of reasons, shown themselves less likely than men to abandon the GDR for an uncertain future in the West. Second, continuing income differentials between men and women, resulting from women's relegation to low- or unskilled jobs and the lack of training programs or promotion opportunities for women, tended to reduce their commitment to work outside the home, undermining both the economic and political education goals that had been set by the party. Finally, the recognition in the mid-1960s of the lack of women in social and political leadership posts and the broad negative implications of this failure to integrate women into the power structure underlined the need for a change of tactics.

By 1970, 76 percent of women between the ages of twenty and sixty were regularly employed.[20] As a result, by the late 1960s the "woman question" in the GDR began to move beyond the mechanical goal of integrating women into political and economic life to address the quality of their participation. Other aspects of the emancipation of women came increasingly to the forefront.

With the steadily rising percentage of women working in the public sphere and expected to remain in it throughout their working lives, women's labor in the private sphere became an increasingly pressing question. This leads us back to Engels' third condition for the emancipation of women—the socialization of domestic work and childcare—and the one aspect of his strategy that was not included in the original party program. The GDR's record on this question is uneven.

In the area of childbirth and childcare, the record is very positive. Currently, women are legally guaranteed a pregnancy leave of six weeks prior to and twenty weeks following childbirth at full pay plus a grant of a thousand marks per child. Women have the option of up to a full year's leave at reduced pay with the right to return to the same or an equivalent job. A full year's leave is guaranteed at the birth of a second or higher-order child. Women also receive paid sick leave during the illness of a child. Despite the legally established obligation of the husband to share equally in childcare and housework, men do not receive sick leave for a child's illness unless they are single parents or can offer other supporting circumstances. Adequate state-supported infant and childcare facilities are available, although in some areas space has begun to lag behind demand.[21] In addition, unrestricted abortion was legalized in 1972, and contraceptives are freely available.

This favorable situation can be explained perhaps more convincingly by economic pragmatism than by political commitment to women's emancipation alone. Given the GDR's reliance on the female labor force and its equally pressing need to encourage a high birthrate to increase its population and work force (the birthrate did not equal the death rate until 1977),[22] adequate childcare and economic support of childbirth are necessities. The gradual liberalization of abortion and contraception policy also appears to be primarily a pragmatic response to social and political pressures.

Progress in the area of domestic work is less advanced. According to a 1971 study, the average time spent on household tasks in the GDR IS 47.1 hours per week. Despite their legal equality in the home, women perform 78 percent of this work,[23] thus putting in nearly another full work day after the completion of their daily paid duties. The official approach to solving this problem is through the limited socialization of domestic labor.[24]

Despite the nod to the principle of equality in the home, the party's approach in the GDR, as in other East European countries, assumes that domestic work is a woman's responsibility rather than a social problem. The question of "double burden" or women's full-time participation in the paid labor force followed by a "second shift" of unpaid reproductive labor in the home became a focus of concern among Western feminists and scholars in the early 1970s.[25] The GDR leadership defined this as a pragmatic rather than a theoretical problem and accordingly instituted palliative measures without reopening the question of the male-female division of reproductive labor, thus avoiding a series of theoretical complications that have faced Western Marxists. "Double burden" has been extensively discussed in the GDR, but the discussion has taken place in literature rather than in political theory.[26]

Although the issue of domestic work has not been totally ignored, the degree to which public resources have been committed to its solution indicates that it is not a high priority. It is also questionable to portray any increase in consumer goods and services as a step toward the emancipation of women. While childcare is accepted as an economic necessity and pregnancy leave is vital to maintaining the population, transforming unpaid private housework into socialized domestic labor is seen as an expensive political goal lacking in urgency. Measured against Engels' third criterion, this party practice reflects the continuing prejudice against women and resistance to full emancipation, especially in the private sphere.

To what extent is this a result of the cultural component in the interplay of forces on the social status of women? A study of East German works written for or about women can provide some insight into this question.

East German Women in Literature

Literature plays an active as well as a passive role in socialist societies. "Agitation and propaganda," later "cultural work," were regarded as weapons in the class struggle from the earliest days of the socialist movement. The power of art and particularly literature to reflect or affect ways of thinking has been taken very seriously in subsequent socialist societies as shown by their continuing preoccupation with censorship and political control over both the form and content of creative works.

Hence, it is legitimate to ask what literature can show us about women in socialist societies, both through its conscious application as a tool for change and in its capacity as an unconscious mirror of the culture which produces it. In giving us deliberately constructed role models for women, literature illustrates changes deemed necessary but not yet accomplished. Failure to emphasize certain roles and the portrayal of situations as normal and not of special interest indicate that change has taken place and has been accepted. And as numerous American and West European writers have demonstrated,[27] sexist stereotypes and negative images of women without didactic motivation betray continuing unexamined discriminatory attitudes.

In the hands of socialist writers, literature has proved to be a weapon applied not only in the interest of the state but also in opposition to it. East German literature provides surprisingly frequent examples of thinly veiled social and political criticism conveyed by the realistic narration of contemporary conditions. Thus literature, in providing a reflection of society from the inside, can give us a sharper and perhaps more accurate picture of the social status of women in the GDR, augmenting the analysis provided by purely historical or sociological approaches.

The cultural foundation

The German cultural attitude toward women at the end of World War II was similar to that generally in force in other Western societies. Women were regarded as passive, weak, irrational, and dependent. These views were exacerbated by twelve years of fascist rule that had disenfranchised women, barred them from the professions, and banned them from the public sphere, giving force of law to the slogan, "Politics is men's business" (*Politik ist Männersache*). While women were being drafted to work in war industries, Nazi propaganda continually declared that women's role was to serve as wives and mothers of the race, and that their place was in the home.[28] The first task of the new GDR government was the dismantling of this image.

The writers available to carry out this task and considered reliable enough to print were almost exclusively Communist party (KPD) members from the 1930s, who had recently returned from Soviet exile. KPD writers had had a very uneven record in the construction of literary role models for women during the late 1920s and early 1930s.[29] Nonetheless, given the straightforward task of recruiting women as workers and supporters of the new order, they produced a creditable collection of working-class mothers and heroines of the resistance, rubble clearers, and factory workers.

The worker heroines

The literature of the 1950s reduced the question of women's emancipation solely to their function as workers, with entry into formerly male skills considered to be particularly emancipatory. The primary reason for this trend was the economic situation that forced the GDR to mobilize all available reserves of potential workers. This campaign manifested itself in a literature set in the arena of material production and the creation of "factory novels" with worker heroines. Women factory workers and female construction workers especially were shown as positive role models. Bredel's character, Petra Harms,[30] stubbornly overcomes female resentment of her vanity and ambition and male resistance and ridicule, as well as pain and physical suffering, in order to become a bricklayer rather than a simple hod carrier.

Regine Haberkorn[31] is a somewhat more typical factory novel, giving us a better idea of the role models and attitudes toward women prevalent in the 1950s. Elfriede Brüning, born in 1910, joined the KPD and its writers' group, the Organization of Proletarian-Revolutionary Writers (BPRS) in 1930 and was arrested for antifascist work in 1935. After a prison term, she spent the fascist period writing trivial literature and rejoined the party in 1945. Brüning is a very popular writer in the GDR, writing light fiction for women from a fairly conservative socialist perspective. Her best-known novel, *Regine Haberkorn*, was first published in 1955 and by 1974 had gone through sixteen printings with a total of 123,000 copies.

The plot is simple and fairly standard for novels of the time. After fifteen years as a housewife, Regine gets a job in order to earn enough money to buy a new bedroom set. Although her only previous work experience was as a laundress before her marriage, she is hired as an assembler at the local factory where her husband also works. He reluctantly agrees to her working, provided that it is temporary and does not interfere with her housework.

Most workers in the factory, especially the women, are portrayed as indifferent toward their jobs. The women are almost entirely young and single or older and widowed and hold jobs out of necessity. There is no childcare provided, and children are left unsupervised while their mothers are at work. Good workers are recognized by management from the top and resented by their coworkers. The plant leadership, including the factory director, a female engineer, a party representative, and the shop foreman, are all very positive characters. Interestingly, the factory director and foreman are portrayed as having bad marriages with petit bourgeois wives who do not understand their revolutionary dedication to labor.

Regine, of course, quickly becomes a model worker, is praised by the leadership, improves the morale of her whole line with technical innovations and personal concern for her fellow workers, and loves her work. Conflict is provided by the husband who, incensed at having to reheat the supper she had left for him, demands that she quit after the first week. He moves out and starts an affair with a widow from the factory canteen but returns home when he realizes that she is a bad worker who only wants to marry him so that she can quit work and be a housewife. Regine takes him back but keeps her job.

The book emphasizes the effect that economic independence and social recognition of her labor have on a woman's self-respect and self-confidence. The comparison between the steadfast Regine and her timid housewife neighbor underscores the improvement in Regine's status and bargaining position in her home. However, Brüning in no other way contradicts the traditional womanly role. Regine's nurturing qualities of empathy, patience, and caring for others are simply extended to the workplace. Her job merely broadens her field of operation without reducing the amount of unpaid labor expected of her.

From today's perspective, this little socialist-realist soap opera delivers a number of oddly ambiguous messages. While transmitting the ideologically expected views on work and production, *Regine* hints broadly that there are flaws in the system. Along with the recruitment slogans about the emancipatory effects of socialized production, it shows that the complete lack of childcare facilities makes it impossible for women with young children to participate. It also contains a number of illustrations of the double burden of industrial and domestic work. The novel depicts authority in a positive light, approving the top-down system of management, yet portrays the leaders as having unsatisfactory personal lives. The open contradictions are portrayed as elements of the class struggle, either petit bourgeois class background or lack of a sufficiently developed working-class consciousness, but the attitudes of most of the workers are shown as rather realistically unenthusiastic about socialist labor.

Aside from a few exceptional role models, women appear as backward and conservative. They must be taught and led, generally by middle-aged men who are experienced workers and party members. The depiction of the female population as a huge conservative mass to be prodded and lured into the workplace where the process of socialized labor will turn them into emancipated women is the key characteristic of the literature of the 1950s. As economic reconstruction moved ahead, these politically backward housewives and naive young students would be transformed into enthusiastic model workers; all that was required was the heady taste of economic independence and self-confidence gained on the production line, supervised, of course, by a fatherly or brotherly male party secretary.

The rise of the professionals

The second phase in GDR literature, beginning in the early 1960s, was ushered in by the writers' conference held in late 1959 in the industrial town of Bitterfeld. The conference declared the founding of a new cultural revolutionary movement to bridge the gap between workers and intellectuals. In practice this meant sending writers into the factories to gather experience of the working class through direct participation in labor. It also encompassed the organization of worker-writer groups to recruit new writers from the working class. As a cultural revolution, Bitterfeld was a failure, and after initial fanfare the worker-writer programs were allowed to die quietly. It was, however, not without influence on further literary developments.

Brigitte Reimann, a former schoolteacher, became active in the Bitterfeld movement and through it, became closely involved with a construction brigade in Hoyerswerda.[32] Her 1961 novel, *Ankunft im Alltag* (Arrival in Daily Life),[33] describes the conflicts and experiences of a class of high school seniors assigned to work on a heavy construction site. Its title eventually became the slogan (*Ankunftsliteratur*) for a new literature that looked beyond the factory production line to other types of work and increasingly into the private sphere. This development was encouraged and supported by the 1961 change in party line discussed above that led to a new policy emphasizing the education and training of women as skilled workers and encouraging women's entry into the professions.

By the mid-1960s and early 1970s, heroines had become jurists, architects, librarians, teachers, and journalists, instead of machinists and bricklayers. The move from the sphere of production to that of the technically qualified professions allowed authors to focus on a host of new problems and conflicts. Instead of worrying about how to overproduce the quota or streamline the production line, women in literature began to struggle with the contradictions between career and motherhood, professionalism and interpersonal relationships.

Another of the Bitterfeld novels, Christa Wolf's *Der Geteilte Himmel* (Divided Heaven, 1963),[34] illustrates another new trend in the novels of the 1960s, the increasingly positive portrayal of female characters. With the success of the campaign to integrate women into the work force (69.8 percent were employed in 1960 and 76.2 percent in 1965),[35] a gradual change of literary emphasis occurred. As women characters became increasingly positive heroines and role models, they began to be shown not only as morally superior to men but also as more creative and flexible. Men, on the other hand, began to be portrayed as cynics and opportunists who hinder the ethically more developed women.

Wolf's novel was a forerunner of this trend. Set during the period leading up to the closing of the border in 1961, the central conflict is not production but commitment to socialism and the GDR. The main character, Rita, is a student who works in a railroad car manufacturing plant in the summers. Her fiancé is a medical student about to receive his degree. Driven by his mother's petit bourgeois influence and his own weakness, he decides to flee to West Berlin and asks Rita to join him there. She meets him once in the

West but returns to the East. There, unable to resolve the conflict between his demands and her own convictions, she attempts suicide. Rita typifies another literary innovation of the 1960s, the positive mixed character. She is a step away from the socialist-realist cartoon heroes and toward believable character development.

The increasingly honest portrayal of women and the trend toward a more subjective presentation were also by-products of contemporary politics. At the Seventh Party Congress in 1967, Ulbricht declared that antagonistic class contradictions had been resolved and that the GDR had achieved a socialist community.[36] Ulbricht's announcement provided the theoretical justification for a policy of suppressing class differences that had been in effect for some time. The official statement, however, created a literary opportunity that was promptly seized by GDR authors. It constituted an unexpected victory in a long-term cultural-political struggle over the place of conflict in socialist literature.

In the 1950s the SED had taken the position that every conflict had a societal dimension and that the depiction of conflict in literature reflected class conflict. The party also maintained that class differences were disappearing in the GDR and with them the basis for societal conflict. Thus, the party required literature, which must reveal the laws of historical inevitability, at least to show that conflict tends toward resolution. On these grounds, the portrayal of unresolved conflicts or insoluble contradictions was criticized as modernist and formalist. Such literature (e.g., existentialism) could be published only with great difficulty or not at all.

The policy of harmonization advocated by the SED in the 1960s denied the existence of antagonistic class differences in the GDR. Consequently, as conflict could no longer be regarded as an expression of class differences, the opportunity arose for literature to portray unsolved or insoluble conflicts as individual rather than class problems. Where the literature of the 1950s had argued that the solution of individual problems lay in social change, since the 1960s society no longer has all the answers, and in a few cases, individual problems are admitted to be social in nature.

This apparently minor political point had tremendous implications for literature and for women. It made possible the presentation of conflicts that were more than minor obstacles in the broad path of historical inevitability. Since it was no longer necessary to treat questions principally from their class aspect, it became possible to write about subjective perceptions and personal problems. New aspects of the woman question could now be discussed in literature. Finally, as it was no longer necessary to resolve every conflict raised within the work, complex problems could be touched on and unanswered questions asked.

The rise of the Superwomen

The third phase of GDR literature began in the late 1960s and developed in the 1970s under these new conditions. Thc 1970s are marked by women becoming the center of literary attention and by a fairly consistent split between the works of male and female writers in the portrayal of women characters. By this point the integration of women into the working world is taken for granted. While female role models for women characters remain scarce (the standard fatherly party secretary remains male), women's involvement in and dedication to their work is believable and presented as normal. Active participation in party work after finishing school, however, is portrayed as being rather unusual. Female characters tend to be older, as the idealistic young students of the Bitterfeld period have matured into women in their mid-twenties to mid-thirties with one or two children. Marital problems are common; childless women over twenty-five are very rare.

While both the men and women writers of this period tend to agree on these general characteristics of their female figures, they disagree sharply over their true status in GDR society. Contemporary male authors such as Gunter deBruyn, Eric Neutsch, Dieter Noll, and Benito Wogatzki ascribe a great measure of superiority to their female characters.[37] Mature women appear as givers of guidance and wise mothers, as tolerant and patient wives; young women appear as rekindlers of the lost idealism and waning sexuality of mature men. Ostensibly main characters, the women in these works continue to play their traditional literary role as objects in the lives of men.

The Superwomen not only manage to compete successfully with men in the workplace but simultaneously carry the entire burden of housework and childcare, attend night school to qualify themselves for a profession, and retain their health, looks, and faith in socialist humanism. In contrast, the same works show men as not merely authoritarian and patriarchal but frequently opportunistic and morally unreliable. While idealization of women into Superwomen is a clumsy attempt to grasp and reflect the changes in women's status that have taken place in the last ten years, the simultaneous clinging to worn sexist stereotypes reveals a continuing fear and rejection of those changes.

In her 1977 novella, *Partnerinnen*, Elfriede Brüning presents the Superwoman image in a very different light. "Later I could only laugh when I read about women who managed everything effortlessly: they shone in their work, and took correspondence courses as well, they cared for their husbands, and always knew how to fascinate them . . . and on the side, as if it were child's play, raised their sons and daughters to be perfect socialists.

I was never one of these Superwomen . . . and I don't believe in them." Later in the novella a thirty-year old says, "we will age prematurely under our multiple duties, if we don't just physically collapse."[38] These comments could be taken for Brüning's apology for her complicity in the creation of the Superwoman image. It is at least a clear repudiation of Regine Haberkorn, who did quite a lot of effortless coping.

On the positive side, the question of whether married women should work is almost a dead issue and socialized day care almost equally widely accepted. Women do not appear as victims; they are shown as more flexible, more resilient than men. This less blatant idealization of women still leaves them a heavier responsibility in interpersonal relationships and in the family. Male writers seem to be very ambivalent toward their female characters, alternating between admiration, envy, and insecurity on the one hand, and male egotism and dominance on the other. This inconstancy may well be an accurate reflection of male attitudes in GDR society.

The Revolt Against the Superwomen

The current situation is presented from a different perspective in the works of women writers, which can be divided roughly into two generations. The older group is represented by four important novels which appeared between 1974 and 1976: Brigitte Reimann's *Franziska Linkerhand* (1974);[39] Gerti Tetzner's *Karin W.* (1975);[40] Christa Wolf's *Nachdenken über Christa T.* (1975, Thinking about Christa T.);[41] and Irmtraud Morgner's *Leben und Abenteuer der Trobadora Beatriz* (1976, The Life and Adventures of Troubadora Beatrice).[42]

Morgner's book is unusual in that it is both openly feminist and an allegorical fantasy that spoofs the Superwomen legend. It had a major impact on both East and West German audiences. The other three novels are realistic studies of contemporary women. The main characters are all qualified professionals who are or have been married, are in their late twenties or early thirties, and are attempting to come to terms with their careers, their relationships with men, and their families. They have rejected the Superwoman model and are trying to reexamine not just how they fit into the system but the system itself.

The second group is actually composed of several age cohorts who have been born since 1940 and thus have grown up within GDR socialism. These writers began appearing in 1976 with volumes of short stories that constituted an explicit revolt against the Superwomen image. They include Helga Königsdorf's *Meine ungehöriger Träume* (1978, My Illicit Dreams); [43] Brigitte Martin's *Der rote Ballon* (1978, The Red Balloon);[44] Helga Schubert's *Lauter Leben* (1975, Unvarnished Life);[45] and Christine Wolter's *Wie ich meine Unschuld verlor* (1976, How I Lost My Innocence) and *Die Hintergrunds-*

person oder Versuche zu lieben (1979, The Background Person, or Attempts to Love).[46] These authors are the daughters of the single mothers of the forties and fifties and have grown up in GDR society expecting to work for a living, have children, and be able to support them. None of them is a professional writer, and several are divorced with small children. They write extremely unromantic, critical, and straightforward descriptions of women's lives in contemporary GDR society. Surveying the wreckage of the nuclear family (the GDR has one of the highest divorce rates in the world, with the majority of actions being brought by women), they discuss women who are seeking companionship but are wary of men, struggling to support and nurture their children. While they do not regret their independence, they suffer no illusions about its price.

The above authors have continued to publish. They have been joined by Renate Apitz, *Evastöchter* (1982, Eve's Daughters) and *Hexenzeit* (1984, The Witching Hour);[47] Beate Morgenstern, *Jenseits der Allee* (1979, On the Other Side of the Avenue);[48] Maria Seidemann, *Der Tag an dem Sir Henry starb* (1980, The Day Sir Henry Died) and *Nasenflöte* (1983, Noseflute);[49] and Angela Kraus, *Das Vergnügen* (1984, The Amusement)[50] among others, who have expanded the categories of women, career, and family to include middle-aged and elderly women, the emotionally isolated, or developmentally disabled.[51]

This literature is unique in the forthrightness with which it addresses problems and remarkable for its abandonment of the requirement to provide solutions. Its central issues are the problems of single motherhood, divorce, the contradiction between work and family, and the failure of men to support or adapt to women as equals. Other problems are described almost casually but with startling clarity and openness, such as the continuing discrimination against women in the party and their second-class status in the power structure, the apartment shortage and the destructive effects of the lack of living space on relationships, shortages of consumer goods and services, and the failure to accept or integrate individuals outside the mainstream of GDR society.

These works offer a unique insight into both the situation of women and the function of literature in the GDR. In them we can see the positive role that literature can play in supporting social change by showing women as active, effective people. We also see it serving as a forum for critical reflection and discussion of problems and speculation on possible solutions. Women writers in the GDR seem to be very conscious of both the power they have and the responsibility they bear in a society in which literature is accepted as a political force.

The consensus from Brüning to Morgner to Wolter is that while legal and economic equality are necessary preconditions to emancipation, until women are equal in the home and in their private lives, they will continue to suffer discrimination and exploitation in both the public and the private sphere. In literature in the GDR, then, private relations have become a political question. Even more surprising for a socialist society, writers like Wolf and Morgner have used literature as a public forum to go beyond criticism of existing conditions and question whether women should struggle to integrate themselves into the institutions of male hierarchy and power. They reject the concept of women as male-defined and argue for the recognition of the differentness and value of women's perception and experience of life.

The GDR discussion of these questions has taken a very different shape than the politicization of the personal in the West. The Western European feminist movement has been much more polemicized and isolated than the relatively broad-based American feminist movement. In contrast to both, women writers in the GDR have until recently not described themselves as "feminists" in the hope of avoiding the polarization which has occurred in the West. GDR women writers have taken great pains not to attack anyone; instead they have concentrated on describing and often satirizing the problematic conditions under which women live and work. Consistent with a Marxist analysis, they accept a necessary connection between socialism and the emancipation of women and locate the causes of contemporary conditions in inherited systems of social and economic organization that have not yet been adequately converted to socialism. Even the most outspoken self-defined feminist critic, Irmtraud Morgner, criticizes the pace of change, not its direction.

This consensus among GDR women writers places their discussion of the emancipation of women on a different theoretical as well as experiential foundation than much of the Western debate. The GDR response to the Western "new conservative feminism" and especially to its use of female differentness to define women out of the public sphere would probably be to classify it as openly reactionary and suspiciously reminiscent of theoretical arguments used to support the Nazi ideology of women's social role.[52]

In the GDR both women and literature seem to be finding their own directions and are beginning to slip away from state control. Women are aware of the concrete advantages they have in a socialist society but are not content with the status quo. They are still exluded from the centers of political and economic power, still carry a double burden of full employment and unpaid domestic labor, still face discrimination, lower status, and other familiar results of sexism.

A generation of independent, self-reliant women has developed in the GDR today. The general feeling among the women I interviewed in a series of visits to the GDR in 1980, 1982, and 1984 was critical but fairly optimistic that they will continue to improve their status. Given the degree of change in the past thirty years and the difference between their position and that of women in West Germany, their optimism is not unjustified. In an interview in May 1980, Irmtraud Morgner said that when women step outside the nuclear family at the age of thirty or thirty-five, it begins to dawn on them that something is missing, and they start to ask questions.[53] They may find some very interesting answers.

Notes

Introduction

1 The relationship between the public and private spheres has been discussed extensively by numerous analysts. See Michelle Zimbalist Rosaldo, "Women, Culture, and Society: A Theoretical Overview," in Michelle Zimbalist Rosaldo and Louise Lamphere, eds., *Woman, Culture, and Society* (Stanford, Calif.: Stanford University Press, 1974), pp. 17–42; several of the essays in Rachel Kahn-Hut, Arlene Kaplan Daniels, and Richard Colvard, eds., *Women and Work: Problems and Perspectives* (New York: Oxford University Press, 1982); Eva Gamarnikow, David Morgan, June Purvis, and Daphne Taylorson, eds., *The Public and the Private* (London: Heinemann, 1983); Barrie Thorne and Marilyn Yalom, eds., *Rethinking the Family: Some Feminist Questions* (New York: Longman, 1982); and Virginia Sapiro, *The Political Integration of Women* (Urbana-Champaign: University of Illinois Press, 1982), for examples of these discussions.

2 See Ester Boserup, *Woman's Role in Economic Development* (London: Allen & Unwin, 1970), for one of the earliest discussions of the impact of development on women. See Wellesley Editorial Committee, *Women and National Development: The Complexities of Change* (Chicago and London: The University of Chicago Press, 1977), and the essays in *Signs* 6, no. 2 (Winter 1981), for more recent discussion of the impact of development on women in various settings. See Jane S. Jaquette, "Women and Modernization Theory: A Decade of Feminist Criticism," *World Politics* 34, no. 2 (January 1982): 268–84, for a recent review of the literature on women and development.

3 We are indebted to several scholars who have studied women's roles in other regions of the world, and particularly to Phyllis Palmer, for pointing out these commonalities.

4 See Kenneth Jowitt, "An Organizational Approach to the Study of Political Culture in Marxist-Leninist Systems," *American Political Science Review* 68, no. 3 (September 1974): 1171–91.

5 See Sharon L. Wolchik, "Ideology and Equality: The Status of Women in East-

ern and Western Europe," *Comparative Political Studies* 13, no. 4 (January 1981): 445–76, for a summary of some of these differences.

I Conditioning Factors

1 Feminism, Socialism and Nationalism in Eastern Europe

1 For a trenchant critique of Marxist economic theory from a feminist point of view, see Batya Weinbaum, *The Curious Courtship of Women's Liberation and Socialism* (Boston: South End Press, 1978).

2 The fragmentary essay on money in Marx's *Economic-Philosophic Manuscripts of 1844* expresses this in forceful tones of moral indignation. See Karl Marx and Friedrich Engels, *Werke*, Ergänzungsband, vol. 1 (Berlin: Dietz-Verlag, 1968–71), pp. 565–67.

3 Marx and Engels, *Die heilige Familie*, Ergänzungsband, vol. 2 (Berlin: Dietz-Verlag, 1968–71), pp. 205–8. For other pertinent citations of works by Engels and Marx, see Alfred G. Meyer, "Marxism and the Women's Movement," in Dorothy Atkinson, Alexander Dallin, and Gail Warshofsky Lapidus, eds., *Women in Russia* (Stanford, Calif.: Stanford University Press, 1977), pp. 85–112.

4 I will come back to this point toward the end of this essay when I will make some judgments about the place of women in East European societies today.

5 Zetkin expressed these views in numerous articles and editorials in the journal she edited for many years, *Die Gleichheit*. She summarized them in *Die Arbeiterinnen- und Frauenfrage der Gegenwart* (Berlin: Vorwärts-Verlag, 1889).

6 For a typical complaint of this kind, see her letter to Wilhelm Liebknecht, May 26, 1872, in Marx and Engels, *Werke*, vol. 33, p. 702.

7 Luxemburg's letters have been translated and edited by Elżbieta Ettinger, *Comrade and Lover: Rosa Luxemburg's Letters to Leon Jogiches* (Cambridge, Mass.: MIT Press, 1979).

8 The term is used by Werner Thönnesen, *The Emancipation of Women: The Rise and Decline of the Women's Movement in German Social Democracy, 1863–1953* (London: Pluto Press, 1973).

9 On Zetkin, see Jean H. Quataert, *Reluctant Feminists in German Social Democracy, 1885–1917* (Princeton, N.J.: Princeton University Press, 1979). On Krupskaia, see Robert Hatch McNeal, *Bride of the Revolution: Nadezhda Konstantinovna Krupskaia* (Ann Arbor: University of Michigan Press, 1972). On Kollontai, see Barbara Evans Clements, *Bolshevik Feminist: The Life of Aleksandra Kollontai* (Bloomington: Indiana University Press, 1979), and Beatrice Farnsworth, *Aleksandra Kollontai and the Russian Revolution* (Stanford, Calif.: Stanford University Press, 1980).

10 Bernstein's Revisionist ideas have been published in English translation under the title *Evolutionary Socialism*.

11 An important contributor to this kind of Revisionism was Lily Braun (1865–1916), whose biography I have written; it has been published by

Indiana University Press (1985).

12 These terms occur quite frequently in the documents discussed in Dietrich Geyer, *Kautskys Russisches Dossier: Deutsche Sozialdemokraten als Treuhänder des Russischen Parteivermögens*(Frankfurt, New York: Campus Verlag, 1981).

13 The term is used by Quataert in her *Reluctant Feminists*.

14 For a glimpse at radical women in Ireland, see the following works: Elizabeth Coxhead, *Daughters of Erin: Five Women of the Irish Renaissance* (London: Secker & Warburg, 1965); Anne Marreco, *The Rebel Countess: The Life and Times of Countess Markievicz* (London: Weidenfeld & Nicholson, 1967); and Jacqueline Van Voris, *Constance De Markievicz: In the Cause of Ireland* (Amherst: University of Massachusetts Press, 1967).

15 For interesting accounts of the role of women in communist revolutionary movements see Richard Stites, *The Women's Liberation Movement in Russia* (Princeton, N.J.: Princeton University Press, 1978); Sheila Rowbotham, *Women, Resistance, and Revolution* (New York: Pantheon, 1972); Barbara W. Jancar, "Women in the Yugoslav National Liberation Movement: An Overview," in *Studies in Comparative Communism* 14, nos. 2–3 (Summer/Autumn 1981): 143–64; also by the same author, *Women under Communism* (Baltimore: Johns Hopkins University Press, 1979).

16 For an historical analysis of the double burden, from feudal society to socialism, see Eli Zaretsky, *Capitalism, the Family, and Personal Life* (New York: Harper Colophon Books, 1976).

17 As suggested in this essay, this generalization may not be true for the German Democratic Republic and for Albania. In Cuba, too, the pattern may be quite different, and even more so under the Sandinista regime of Nicaragua. See Sharon L. Wolchik, "Eastern Europe," in Joni Lovenduski and Jill Hills, eds., *The Politics of the Second Electorate* (London: Routledge & Kegan Paul, 1981), pp. 252–73, for an overview of women's political roles in the region. See Section III for studies of women's roles in politics in Romania, Albania, Poland, and Czechoslovakia.

18 The classic statements of this position can be found in August Bebel, *Die Frau und der Sozialismus* (Women and Socialism), first published in 1879, and the later work by Friedrich Engels, *The Origins of the Family, Private Property, and the State*.

19 See Margaret Benston, *The Political Economy of Women's Liberation* (Toronto: New Hogtown Press, 1973); Wally Secombe, "The Housewife and Her Labor under Capitalism," *New Left Review*, no. 83 (January–February 1974): 3–24; several articles in Richard C. Edwards et al., *The Capitalist System* (Englewood Cliffs, N.J.: Prentice-Hall, 1972); Marilyn Power Goldberg, "The Economic Exploitations of Women," in David M. Gordon, ed., *Problems in Political Economy: An Urban Perspective* (Lexington, Mass.: D. C. Heath, 1971).

20 Gail Kligman, one of the contributors to this volume, has called my attention to the striking analogy between this position—in society but not of society—that liberal ideology attributes to the propertylessness and the situation of women within patriarchal kinship structures: they are, typically, in the family but not of the family.

21 For a contemporary scholar who also recognizes women as the reserve army of socialist countries, see Gail Warshofsky Lapidus, *Women in Soviet Society: Equality, Development, and Social Change* (Berkeley: University of California Press, 1978), especially chapter 3.

22 A number of writers have criticized Marxism for paying insufficient attention to the persistence of patriarchal culture and to the possibility that there might well be such a thing as socialist or state-socialist patriarchy. See Isaac D. Balbus, *Marxism and Domination: A Neo-Hegelian, Feminist, Psychoanalytic Theory of Sexual, Political, and Technological Liberation* (Princeton, N.J.: Princeton University Press, 1982), p. 62; Zillah Eisenstein, ed., *Capitalist Patriarchy and the Case for Socialist Feminism* (New York: Monthly Review Press, 1979); and Nancy Hartsock, *Money, Sex, and Power: Toward a Feminist Historical Materialism* (New York: Longman, 1983).

2 The Precommunist Legacy, Economic Development, Social Transformation, and Women's Roles in Eastern Europe

1 See A. J. P. Taylor, *The Habsburg Monarchy, 1809–1918: A History of the Austrian Empire and Austria-Hungary* (New York and Evanston: Harper and Row, 1965); Robert A. Kann, *A History of the Habsburg Empire* (Berkeley and Los Angeles: University of California Press, 1977); Alan Palmer, *The Lands Between: A History of East-Central Europe since the Congress of Vienna* (New York: Macmillan, 1970); Hugh Seton-Watson, *The Decline of Imperial Russia, 1855–1914* (New York: Frederick A. Praeger, 1952); Robin Okey, *Eastern Europe, 1740–1980: Federalism to Communism* (Minneapolis: University of Minnesota Press, 1982); Peter F. Sugar, *Southeastern Europe under Ottoman Rule, 1354–1804* (Seattle and London: University of Washington Press, 1977); Charles Jelavich and Barbara Jelavich, *The Establishment of the Balkan National States, 1804–1920* (Seattle: University of Washington Press, 1977); Hugh Seton-Watson, *Eastern Europe between the Wars, 1918–1941* (New York: Harper and Row, 1967); C. J. Macartney and A. W. Palmer, *Independent Eastern Europe* (London: Macmillan; New York: St. Martin's Press, 1966); and Joseph Rothschild, *East Central Europe between the Two World Wars* (Seattle: University of Washington Press, 1974), for standard sources on Eastern Europe under the empires and during the interwar period.

2 Andrew Janos, "The One-Party State and Social Mobilization: East Europe between the Wars," in Samuel P. Huntington and Clement H. Moore, eds., *Authoritarian Politics in Modern Society: The Dynamics of Established One-Party Systems* (New York and London: Basic Books, 1970), p. 208.

3 Ibid. Approximately 77 percent of the population in Yugoslavia, including 80.2 percent in Serbia and 75.2 percent in Croatia, was dependent on agriculture in 1930.

4 Ibid. There were also important regional differences in this respect in Czechoslovakia, where 29.7 percent of the population was agricultural in the Czech Lands, but 60.6 percent in Slovakia. See Nicholas Spulber, *The Economics of*

Communist Eastern Europe (New York: Massachusetts Institute of Technology and John Wiley and Sons, 1957), pp. 9–20, for a brief overview of relative levels of industrial development in the region during this period. Spulber notes that Czechoslovakia alone accounted for over 37 percent of the total labor force employed in large-scale industries (defined here as industry with five or more workers) in the region; the industrial labor force was also considerably larger in Hungary and Poland than in the rest of the region. See Legislative Reference Service of the Library of Congress, *Trends in Economic Growth: A Comparison of the Western Powers and the Soviet Bloc* (Washington, D.C.: U.S. Government Printing Office, 1955), pp. 230–32, for a discussion of the important contribution the lands that later became East Germany made to total German industrial production and agriculture during the precommunist period.

5 See Vera St. Erlich, *Family in Transition, A Study of 300 Yugoslav Villages* (Princeton, N.J.: Princeton University Press, 1966), for a discussion of family forms in Yugoslavia; see Bette S. Denich, "Sex and Power in the Balkans," in Michelle Zimbalist Rosaldo and Louise Lamphere, eds., *Woman, Culture, and Society* (Stanford, Calif.: Stanford University Press, 1974), pp. 243–62, for a brief discussion of research on the family in the Balkans.

6 See Peter R. Prifti, *Socialist Albania since 1944, Domestic and Foreign Developments* (Cambridge, Mass., and London: MIT Press, 1978), pp. 90–94; and Stavro Skendi, ed., *Albania* (New York: Frederick A. Praeger, 1956), pp. 148–51, for brief discussions of family forms in precommunist Albania.

7 Brian R. Mitchell, *European Historical Statistics, 1750–1975* (New York: Facts on File, 1981, 2nd rev. ed.), pp. 86, 124–30.

8 Illiteracy rates were much higher in Slovakia and Ruthenia than in the Czech Lands in 1921 and remained higher throughout the interwar period. Despite progress in all areas, in 1930 8.1 percent of all inhabitants ten years of age and older in Slovakia and 30.8 percent of all inhabitants of Ruthenia, compared to 1.2 of all persons in Bohemia and 1.5 percent of all inhabitants in Moravia and Silesia, were illiterate. Státní úřad statistický, *Statistická ročenka republiky Československé 1937* (Prague: Orbis, 1937), p. 12. By 1930, however, only 4.1 percent of the total population (3.3 percent males and 4.8 percent females) was illiterate in Czechoslovakia as a whole. UNESCO, *Literary Statistics from Available Census Figures* (Paris: Education Clearing House, 1950), p. 19. Approximately 10 percent of the population six years of age and older was illiterate in Hungary by 1930 and 23 percent of the population ten years of age and older in Poland in 1931. UNESCO, *Progress of Literacy* (Paris: UNESCO, 1963), pp. 162–63; UNESCO, *Literary Statistics*, p. 21.

9 Approximately 32 percent of the population ten years of age and older was illiterate in Bulgaria in 1934; in Romania, 43 percent of the population seven and over was illiterate in 1930, while in Yugoslavia, 44.6 percent of the population eleven years of age and older was illiterate in 1931. In Albania, where information is not available for the pre-World War II period, 54 percent of the population nine years of age and older was illiterate as late as 1950. UNESCO, *Progress of Literacy*, pp. 162–63; Directia Centrală de Statistică, *Anuarul Statistic Romanii, 1937* (Bucharest: Directia Centrală de Statistică, 1937), pp. 76–77.

10 Approximately 43 percent of women seven and older in Bulgaria in 1934, 54.2 percent of women seven and older in Romania in 1930, and 56.2 percent of women eleven and older in Yugoslavia in 1931 were illiterate. UNESCO, *Progress of Literacy*, pp. 162–63.

11 Approximately 41 percent of men nine years of age and over were illiterate in Albania in that year. UNESCO, *Statistical Yearbook, 1963* (Paris: UNESCO, 1963), p. 27.

12 *Statisticheski godišnjak Bol'garii*, pp. 697–98; Státní úřad statistický, *Statistická příručka Československa, 1938* (Prague: Orbis, 1938), p. 34; Central Statistical Office, *Statistical Yearbook of Hungary, 1957* (Budapest: Central Statistical Office, 1957), pp. 317, 494–95; Savezni zavod za statistiku, *Statistički godišnjak Jugoslavije, 1969* (Belgrade: Savezni zavod za statistiku, 1969), p. 291.

13 Skendi, p. 274.

14 See Janos, pp. 212–34; Seton-Watson, *Eastern Europe between the Wars*; Macartney and Palmer, *Independent Eastern Europe*; and Rothschild, *East Central Europe between the Two World Wars*, for area-wide discussions of political developments in the region during this period.

15 Women were only enfranchised in 1945 in Hungary, 1946 in Romania and Bulgaria, and 1947 in Yugoslavia. Elsie Boulding, Shirley A. Nuss, Dorothy Lee Carson, and Michael A. Greenstein, *Handbook of International Data on Women* (New York: John Wiley and Sons, 1976), pp. 250–51. In Albania women formally received the vote in 1946, when a new constitution was adopted, but women's equality and equal rights to participate in politics had been proclaimed by Communist party leaders in November 1944, just prior to the establishment of a communist government in Albania. Skendi, pp. 62–64; Prifti, pp. 97–98.

16 See Victor S. Mamatey and Radomír Luža, eds., *A History of the Czechoslovak Republic, 1918–1948* (Princeton, N.J.: Princeton University Press, 1973), for more information.

17 See David W. Paul, *The Cultural Limits of Revolutionary Politics* (Boulder, Colo.: East European Quarterly, 1979), chapter 2, and Hans Brisch and Ivan Volgyes, eds., *The Heritage of Ages Past: Essays in Memory of Josef Korbel* (Boulder, Colo.: East European Quarterly, 1979), for discussions of this tradition.

18 See Leila J. Rupp, "I Don't Call that *Volksgemeinschaft*": Women, Class, and War in Nazi Germany," in Carol R. Berkin and Clara M. Lovett, eds., *Women, War & Revolution* (New York: Holmes & Meier, 1980), pp. 37–54, and Gisela Bock, "Racism and Sexism in Nazi Germany: Motherhood, Compulsory Sterilization, and the State," in *Signs* (Spring 1983): 400–421, for discussions of the impact of Nazism on different groups of women.

19 See Sharon L. Wolchik, "Ideology and Equality: The Status of Women in Eastern and Western Europe," *Comparative Political Studies* 13, no. 4 (January 1981): 445–76, for a brief area-wide review of women's status on several indicators of equality; Barbara W. Jancar, *Women under Communism* (Baltimore: Johns Hopkins University Press, 1978), also includes the East European countries.

20 See Gail Warshofsky Lapidus, *Women in Soviet Society: Equality, Development, and Social Change* (Berkeley: University of California Press, 1978) and "Sexual Equality in Soviet Policy: A Developmental Perspective," in Dorothy

Atkinson, Alexander Dallin, and Gail Warshofsky Lapidus, eds., *Women in Russia* (Stanford, Calif.: Stanford University Press, 1977), pp. 115–38, for this argument in regard to the Soviet Union.

21 See H. Gordon Skilling, *The Governments of Communist East Europe* (New York: Thomas Y. Crowell, 1966), especially pp. 48–68; and Zbigniew Brzezinski, *The Soviet Bloc* (Cambridge, Mass.: Harvard University Press, 1967), especially pp. 67–155, for more information concerning the East European adaptation of the Soviet model. Both authors note that diversity once again increased in the region after the death of Stalin, but the political systems remain organized according to common principles.

22 See Fred Singleton, *Twentieth Century Yugoslavia* (New York: Columbia University Press, 1976), and Dennison Rusinow, *The Yugoslav Experiment* (Berkeley: University of California Press, 1977, published for the Royal Institute of International Affairs, London), for discussions of Yugoslavia's evolution since 1948.

23 See Hilda Scott, *Does Socialism Liberate Women*? (Boston: Beacon Press, 1973); Alena Heitlinger, *Women and State Socialism* (Montreal: McGill-Queens University Press, 1979); and Sharon L. Wolchik, "Women's Status in a Socialist Order: The Case of Czechoslovakia, 1948–1978," *Slavic Review* 38, no. 4 (December 1979): 583–602, for discussion of the impact of this factor on women in socialist states.

24 This tendency became particularly pronounced once the Stalinist system was consolidated, as the mass women's organizations were disbanded in several of these countries, and political elites proclaimed that the institution of socialism had fundamentally solved women's problems. See Scott, pp. 96–103, and Sharon L. Wolchik, "Elite Strategy toward Women in Czechoslovakia: Liberation or Mobilization?" *Studies in Comparative Communism* 14, nos. 2 and 3 (Summer/Autumn 1981): 123–42.

25 See Brzezinski, pp. 97–104, and Alex Nove, *The Soviet Economy* (New York: Frederick A. Praeger, 1961), for brief discussions of the main elements of the strategy for economic development adopted at this time.

26 See Lapidus, *Women in Soviet Society*, for the Soviet case; see Scott, pp. 72–99, and Wolchik, "Elite Strategy toward Women," for discussions of this approach to women's issues in Eastern Europe.

27 Gregor Lazarcik, "Comparative Growth, Structure, and Levels of Agricultural Outputs, Inputs, and Productivity in Eastern Europe, 1965–79," in Joint Economic Committee, *East European Economic Assessment, Part 2, Regional Assessments* (Washington, D.C.: U.S. Government Printing Office, 1981), p. 592.

28 Prifti, p. 61.

29 Ibid.

30 Approximately 30 percent of the population remained dependent on agriculture in Poland and 25 percent in Bulgaria in 1979; approximately 19 percent of the total population in Hungary, 13 percent in Czechoslovakia, and 10 percent in East Germany continued to work in agriculture in that year (Lazarcik, p. 592).

31 Approximately 24 percent of the total population fifteen years of age and older

(12 percent men and 34 percent women) was illiterate in Yugoslavia in 1971. United Nations, *Demographic Yearbook 1973* (New York: United Nations, 1973), p. 493.

32 Approximately 28 percent of the population nine years of age and older, including 20 percent of men and 37 percent of women, was illiterate in Albania in 1955, the last year for which such information is available.

33 Paul Marer, "Economic Performance and Prospects in Eastern Europe: Analytical Summary and Interpretation of Findings," in Joint Economic Committee, *East European Economic Assessment, Part 2, Regional Assessments* (Washington, D.C.: U.S. Government Printing Office, 1981), p. 25.

34 Regional disparities in living standards are still particularly noticeable in Yugoslavia, where national income per capita in the most developed republic was 4.4 times greater than in the least developed region (Kosovo) in 1956. Differences between the more and less developed regions persisted throughout the 1970s; in 1977, for example, per capita income in Slovenia was 6.5 times that in Kosovo. Laura d'Andrea Tyson and Gabriel Eichler, "Continuity and Change in the Yugoslav Economy in the 1970's and 1980's," in Joint Economic Committee, *East European Economic Assessment, Part 1, Country Studies, 1980* (Washington, D.C.: U.S. Government Printing Office, 1981), p. 165.

35 Vera Pilić, *Karakteristika i problemi ženske radne snage u Jugoslaviji* (Belgrade: Institut za Ekonomiska Istrazivanje, 1969).

36 See David Lane, *The End of Inequality?* (Middlesex, England: Penguin Books, 1971) and *The Socialist Industrial State: Towards a Political Sociology of State Socialism* (Boulder, Colo.: Westview Press, 1976); Walter D. Connor, *Socialism, Politics, and Equality: Hierarchy and Change in Eastern Europe and the USSR* (New York: Columbia University Press, 1979), and Archie Brown and Jack Gray, eds., *Political Culture and Political Change in Communist States* (New York: Holmes & Meier, 1979).

37 As Kenneth Jowitt, in "An Organizational Approach to the Study of Political Culture in Marxist-Leninist Systems," *American Political Science Review*, 68, no. 3 (September 1974): 1171–91, notes, communist elites have not tried to change all elements of the traditional value systems; rather, they have selectively incorporated certain traditional elements into the new value systems they have tried to promote.

38 See Chalmers Johnson, "Comparing Communist Nations," in Johnson, ed., *Change in Communist Systems* (Stanford, Calif.: Stanford University Press, 1970), pp. 1–32, and Richard Lowenthal, "Development vs. Utopia in Communist Policy," in ibid., pp. 33–116, for discussions of some of these unanticipated consequences.

39 See Henry P. David and Robert J. McIntyre, *Reproductive Behavior: Central and Eastern European Experience* (New York: Springer, 1981); Alena Heitlinger, "Pronatalist population policies in Czechoslovakia," *Population Studies* 30, no. 1 (March 1976): 123–35; and John F. Besemeres, *Socialist Population Politics: The Political Implications of Demographic Trends in the USSR and Eastern Europe* (White Plains, N.Y.: M. E. Sharpe, 1980), for discussions of the causes of the fall in the birthrate in these countries.

40 See David and McIntyre, pp. 3–19, and individual country chapters.

41 Live births per 1,000 population decreased from 44.5 in 1955 to 27.4 in 1978 in Albania. Dudley Kirk, "Albania," in David and McIntyre, pp. 301–2. Yugoslavia also has avoided adopting an explicitly pronatalist approach at the federal level; pronatalist incentives exist but are regulated and enacted by the republics. See David and McIntyre, pp. 146–75.

42 See Lapidus, "Sexual Equality in Soviet Policy," pp. 135–37, for indications that discussion concerning women's issues also has increased in the Soviet Union in the last decade and a half. However, debate and research on women's issues currently appear to be more open and to touch a broader variety of topics in many East European countries than in the Soviet Union.

43 See Morris Bornstein, Zvi Gitelman, and William Zimmerman, *East-West Relations and the Future of East European Politics and Economics* (London and Boston: Allen and Unwin, 1981), for discussions of the impact of these factors in Eastern Europe.

44 See Zvi Gitelman, "The World Economy and Elite Political Strategies in Czechoslovakia, Hungary, and Poland," in Bornstein, Gitelman, and Zimmerman, pp. 127–61, for an elaboration of this argument.

II Women in the Precommunist Period

Introduction

1 East European women were also active in a variety of more partisan political organizations at the time, including socialist parties and movements.

2 See Jo Freeman, *The Politics of Women's Liberation: A Case Study of an Emerging Social Movement and Its Relation to the Policy Process* (New York and London: Longman, 1975); William H. Chafe, *Women and Equality: Changing Patterns in American Culture* (New York: Oxford University Press, 1977), and Philip S. Foner, *Women and the American Labor Movement: From Colonial Times to the Eve of World War I* (New York: Free Press, 1979), for discussions of this tendency in the American case. See Marilyn Boxer and Jean Quataert, eds., *Socialist Women: European Socialist Feminism in the Nineteenth and Twentieth Centuries* (New York: Elsevier New Holland, 1978); Carol Berkin and Clara Lovett, eds., *Women, War and Revolution* (New York: Holmes & Meier, 1978); Jean Quataert, *Reluctant Feminists in German Social Democracy, 1885–1917* (Princeton, N.J.: Princeton University Press, 1979); Richard Stites, *The Women's Liberation Movement in Russia: Feminism, Nihilism, and Bolshevism, 1860–1930* (Princeton, N.J.: Princeton University Press, 1978); Elizabeth Croll, *Feminism and Socialism in China* (Boston: Routledge & Kegan Paul, 1978); and Jane Slaughter and Robert Kern, eds., *European Women on the Left: Socialism, Feminism, and the Problems Faced by Political Women, 1880 to the Present* (Westport, Conn.: Greenwood Press, 1981), for discussions of attitudes toward women's issues in socialist and other reform movements in Western Europe, China, and Russia.

3 See Gregory J. Massell, *The Surrogate Proletariat: Moslem Women and Revolutionary Strategies in Soviet Central Asia: 1919–1929* (Princeton, N.J.: Princeton

University Press, 1974), for a discussion of this phenomenon in Central Asia in the Soviet Union; see Gail Warshofsky Lapidus, *Women in Soviet Society: Equality, Development, and Social Change* (Berkeley: University of California Press, 1978), for a discussion of the impact of modernization in the Soviet Union more generally.

3 Medical Education for Women in Austria: A Study in the Politics of the Czech Women's Movement in the 1890s

1 For a modern survey of the First Czechoslovak Republic, see Victor S. Mamatey and Radomír Luža, eds., *A History of the Czechoslovak Republic* (Princeton, N.J.: Princeton University Press, 1973); for data on women in twentieth-century Czechoslovakia, see Bruce Garver's chapter in this volume; Alena Heitlinger, *Women Under State Socialism: Sex Inequality in the Soviet Union and Czechoslovakia* (New York and London: McGill-Queens University Press and Macmillan, 1979); Hilda Scott, *Does Socialism Liberate Women?* (Boston: Beacon Press, 1974); and Sharon L. Wolchik, "The Status of Women in a Socialist Order: Czechoslovakia, 1948–1978," *Slavic Review* 38, no. 4 (December 1979): 583–602.

2 There is no general history of the Czech women's movement. For a detailed discussion to 1908, see "Ženská emancipace," in *Ottův slovník naučný*, 27: 803–11. See also Bruce Garver, "Women in Czech Society, 1848–1914," unpublished paper delivered at the Midwest Slavic Conference, May 1977.

3 See the detailed and fascinating book by Priscilla Robertson, *An Experience of Women: Pattern and Change in Nineteenth-Century Europe* (Philadelphia: Temple University Press, 1982), especially chapters 19, 20, 23, 24, 30, and 31 on early feminists in France, Germany, and England.

4 Unless otherwise noted, "Austria" in this paper refers to the Austrian half of the Dual Monarchy, the "kingdoms and countries represented in the Reichsrat"—or Cisleithania, as it is sometimes called. After 1867 "Austria" and Hungary shared only the ministers of the army, foreign affairs, and finance; education and other social institutions developed quite differently in each half of the realm. Although Bohemia and the other constituent parts of Austria had autonomy in certain areas, most decisions concerning education had to come from Vienna—the Reichsrat, the Ministry of Education (Ministerium für Cultus und Unterricht), or the Emperor. Unless otherwise stated, "Austrian women" refers to all women in Austria, not just Germans. German Bohemians, one-third of the population of Bohemia in 1890, are not treated here; in Prague, their intellectual center too, they numbered less than 10 percent of the population and their university was half the size of the Czech. No independent Bohemian German women's movement seems to have existed before 1900.

5 On women in 1848, see Stanley Z. Pech, *The Czech Revolution of 1848* (Chapel Hill: University of North Carolina Press, 1969). The first, short-lived women's organization, the Society of Slavonic Women, emerged during the Revolution.

6 On women's education in Europe, see Phyllis Stock, *Better than Rubies: A History of Women's Education* (New York: Putnam, 1978), and an English translation of the arguments of a late nineteenth-century German feminist, Helene Lange, *Higher Education for Women in Europe*, trans. L. R. Klemm (New York: D. Appleton, 1897). By the 1870s women could attend universities (though not in all cases with the same rights as men) in France, Russia, England, and most West European countries. See Kaethe Schirmacher, *The Modern Woman's Rights Movement—A Historical Survey* (New York: Macmillan, 1912 [translation of German original, 1909]).

7 During the Counter-Reformation, Charles University merged with the Jesuit College of St. Clement into a single institution to which Emperor Ferdinand III (1637–57) lent his name. In 1882, after a long campaign by Czech nationalists, the Charles-Ferdinand University of Prague (1654–1918) was divided into two parallel universities known in common parlance as the German University and the Czech University. Comenius elucidated these principles of universal education in his *Didactica magna* (1628–32; trans. M. W. Keatinge, 1896); *The Great Didactica of John Amos Comenius* (London, 1896, reproduced 1967).

8 Czech primary schools had been increasing in numbers since the 1830s, but the Law on the Rights of Citizens of December 1867 delcared the right to education at all levels in one's native tongue, and the school law of 1869 guaranteed state support of these schools. In 1869 as well, the requirement for instruction in German in Czech secondary schools was abolished.

9 *Městská vyšší dívčí škola.*

10 *Ústav ke vzdělání učitelek—Dívčí pedagogium.*

11 The courses of the *Ženský výrobní spolek* had served several thousand women by 1900.

12 Eliška Krásnohorská, "Pro ženské studium v Čechach," *Kalendář paní a dívek českých* 4 (1891): 50.

13 "Před prahem České university," *Ženské listy* 10 (1882): 18–19.

14 They could be auditors beginning in 1895 at the discretion of each individual professor.

15 See some of the recent literature on women in the Third World for comparison. For example: Torill Stokland, Mallica Vajrathon, and Davidson Nicol, eds., *Creative Women in Changing Societies: A Quest for Alternatives* (Dobbs Ferry, N.Y.: Transnational Publishers, 1982) (copyright by the UN Institute for Training and Research—UNITAR); and Roslyn Danber and Melinda L. Cain, eds., *Women and Technological Change in Developing Countries,* AAAS Selected Symposium, no. 53 (Boulder, Colo.: Westview Press, 1981), especially part 1.

16 Some Czech charitable organizations had been permitted to function as early as the 1850s. One, the Society of St. Ludmila, began as an organization for providing aid to widows; in 1865 it reorganized into a sponsor of a school that would teach those widows to support themselves. For women who first joined the national effort as daughters, wives, and mothers, see Garver, "Women in Czech Society, 1848–1918."

17 Other women literati of this period were Karolina Světla (1830–99); the

founder of the Women's Industrial and Commercial Training Association; Tereza Nováková (1854–1912); Sofie Podlípská (1833–97); and Eliška Krásnohorská (1847–1926). Světla and Krásnohorská were primarily poets, the others prose writers. All were active in the national and women's movements. Arne Novak, *Czech Literature* (Ann Arbor: Michigan Slavic Publication, 1976).

18 The best single introduction to late nineteenth-century Czech politics is Bruce Garver, *The Young Czech Party, 1874–1901, and the Emergence of a Multi-Party System* (New Haven: Yale University Press, 1978).

19 On the students, who included the "woman question" as an integral part of their program in the early 1890s, see Karen J. Freeze, "The Young Progressives: The Czech Student Movement, 1887–1897" (unpublished Ph.D. dissertation, Columbia University, 1974).

20 After 1900 many of these groups and parties sponsored women's activities and publications.

21 See Stock, chap. 8 and bibliography; Mary Walsh, *Doctors Wanted: No Women Need Apply—Sexual Barriers in the Medical Profession, 1835–1975* (New Haven: Yale University Press, 1977); and two unpublished papers from the 1978 Berkshire Conference on the history of women: Regina M. Morantz, "Women Physicians, Coeducation, and the Struggle for Professional Standards in Nineteenth-Century Medical Education"; and Christine Johanson, "Bureaucratic Politics, Public Opinion, and Women's Medical Education during the Reign of Alexander II, 1855–1881."

22 Russia and Britain were under particular pressure to recognize women doctors for religious reasons—and did so.

23 See Stock, chap. 8, and Walsh.

24 Elizabeth Blackwell, who received her degree from Geneva in 1849, was the first.

25 See *Ženské listy* 18 (1890): 105–6; Kamil Harmach, "Otázka vyššího vzdělání žen a rakouský parlament" in Albína Honzáková, ed., *Československé studentky let 1890–1930: Almanach na oslavu ctyřicatého výročí založení ženského studia Eliškou Krásnohorskou* (Prague, 1930), pp. 20–24.

26 On Krásnohorská, see Pavla Antošová, ed., *Chudým dětem Eliška Krásnohorská* (Brno, 1947); Honzáková, *Československé studentky*; Ferdinand Strejček, ed., *Eliška Krásnohorská: Literární konfese* (Blatna: Jihočeské nakladatelství Bratří Řimsové, 1947); and Krásnohorská's memoires: *Z mého mládí* (Prague-Smíchov: Vaněk a Votava, 1920) and *Co přinesla léta*, 2 vols. (Prague-Smíchov: Vaněk a Votava, 1928).

27 On the German women's education movement, see Hildegard Ries, *Geschichte des Gedankens der Frauenhochschulbildung in Deutschland* (Westphalia, 1927); Hans Sveistrup and Agnes v. Zahn-Harnack, comps., *Die Frauenfrage in Deutschland: Strömungen und Gegenströmungen, 1790–1930. Quellenkunde* (Burg bei Magdeburg: Hopfer, 1934), an annotated bibliography; and Albína Honzáková, "Ze světového studia ženského," in Honzáková, pp. 303–30.

28 On Bayerová and Kecková, see *Ženské listy* 11 (1883): 58 and 10 (1882): 7; E. Krásnohorská, "V pamět druhé lékařky české," and "Slovo k prvním abiturientkám naším," in Honzáková, pp. 45–50 and 9–15.

29 *Ženské listy* 17 (1889): 109–17; Bayerová's reply urging the women to campaign for the legal recognition of women doctors in ibid., pp. 229–31.

30 *Ženské listy* 18 (1890): 65–68.

31 For a list of professors and other prominent Czechs who signed the petition, see *Ženské listy* 18 (1890): 81. Even before the petition had been presented to the Reichsrat, its favorable reception by the Czech press inspired optimism. See ibid., pp. 64–68.

32 An economic depression had plagued Central Europe since 1873; it would not abate until the mid-1890s.

33 All other countries but Germany, according to the petition, admitted women to universities; all but the Balkan states recognized women doctors and professors; and everywhere but Austria secondary schools were open to women (ibid., pp. 65–66).

34 "Regular" study (*řadné, ordentlich*) was full-time, leading to a degree, and normally required the completion of an eight-year gymnasium course as a prerequisite. Women students were not even allowed to be "irregular" or "extraordinary" (*mimořadní, außerordentlich*) students nor, the least desirable status, auditors (*hospitantky, Hospitanten*).

35 *Stenographische Protokolle über die Sitzungen des Hauses der Abgeordneten des österreichischen Reichsrathes*, Session X, 11 March 1890, pp. 13709, 13750–51.

36 *Ženské listy* 18 (1890): 106, 127. The petition from Pilsen represented both men and women, many of them prominent in the town. "Jungmann" was a society of students from the Prague region.

37 Ibid., p. 128. *Ženské listy* expressed pleasure at the recognition the German Viennese women were giving the Czechs as initiators of the cause.

38 Honzáková, "Za Eliškou Krásnohorskou," p. 25; Anna Kellnerová, "Eliška Krásnohorská a její místo v českém ženském hnutí," in Antošová, pp. 57–58. Krásnohorská was elated at the response of the city council but still had to convince Bohemian governor Thun, whose wife opposed the idea of academic education for women.

39 "Provolání: Vzdělanstvu Českému!" A four-page brochure.

40 The first year was to be a preparatory for the four upper grades of the gymnasium course that would follow. It was a strenuous program embracing all four lower gymnasium years of classical languages and other subjects hitherto not found in girls' schools.

41 Honzáková, "K zápasu o lékařské studium," in Honzáková, pp. 66–74.

42 *Ženské listy* 18 (1890): 195–98, 213–19; and 19 (1891): 168–70; Krásnohorská, "Pro ženské studium," *Kalendář paní a dívek, pp.* 54–57 and *Co přinesla léta*, vol. 2, pp. 123–44; Honzáková, pp. 16–19.

43 *Ženské listy* 19 (1891): 136, 139.

44 See Krásnohorská, "V pamět druhé lékařky české," and Anna Honzáková, "Působení A. Bayerové v Bosně," in Honzáková, pp. 51–53; *Ženské listy* 19 (1891): 257. This explicit recognition of women doctors by the government led Czech women to believe they could expect to have their own women doctors in the near future. Krásnohorská's persistent optimism is reflected in the reaction of *Ženské listy* to the government's every move. Over a year before, in the

announcement about Minerva, the journal praised the School Board (*Zemská školní rada*) for approving the curriculum and expressed the view that university entrance would be granted "today or tomorrow." (*Ženské listy* 18 [1890], insert).

45 See Freeze, pp. 132–37.

46 Harmach; *Ženské listy* 19 (1891): 245–50; *Neue Freie Presse*, 31 October 1891.

47 *Ženské listy* 19 (1891): 245; Harmach, pp. 22–23; *Stenographische Protokolle*, October 30, 1891, p. 2834. Masaryk and others also suggested that girls should not have to attend "our imperfect schools"—another reason for prompt reform.

48 *Ženské listy* 19 (1891): 246–47; *Neue Freie Presse*, November 4, 1891, p. 2; *Stenographische Protokolle*, November 3, 1891, p. 2861. *Neue Freie Presse* reported applause at Gautsch's definition of the main task of women's education; the *Protokolle* noted the affirmation "Sehr richtig!"

49 *Ženské listy* 19 (1891): 247.

50 This comprehensive exam was the climax of the eight-year academic gymnasium and its successful completion the prerequisite for university admission.

51 The text of Minerva's petition is in *Ženské listy* 19 (1891): 234–36 and *Stenographische Protokolle*, November 6, 1891, p. 2989. For a report on the discussion following see *Ženské listy* 19 (1891): 248–49.

52 Honzáková, "K zápasu," p. 67, mentions Krásnohorská's eagerness for women to go into medicine—perhaps because women met more opposition here than in most other fields (see Kellnerová, p. 61).

53 Honzáková, "K zápasu," p. 68; Vlasta Rostočilová, "První promoce absolventek dívčího gymnasia 'Minerva' na české universitě v Praze," *Acta Universitatis Carolinae—Historia Universitatis Carolinae Pragensis* 12 (1972): 241. Not until 1907 could Minerva examine its own students for a valid *maturita*.

54 Krásnohorská, "Slovo k prvním abiturientkám naším," in Honzáková, pp. 9–15. She also appealed to the graduates' patriotism in urging them to use and continue their education.

55 But then they had not been a real threat earlier. See *Ženské listy*, 25 (1897): 52, 100; also *Čas*, December 12, 1896, p. 796.

56 Hamza, *K dějinám českých medíků* (Prague, 1895), p. 104. German students were more demonstrative in their protest; see the report on extremists in "Hallští studenti proti vyšším studium, *Ženské listy* 27 (1899): 135–37.

57 Honzáková, "K zápasu," p. 71; Rostočilová, p. 244; "Ženské studium universitní," *Almanach Slavie*, 1899–1900.

58 See review and discussion by E. Vlasák, "Ženská otázka v lékařství," in *Rozhledy* (1896), pp. 145–49, 226–31, 300–303.

59 See ibid.; M. Kronfeld, *Die Frauen und die Medicin* (Vienna: Professor Albert zur Antwort, 1895); E. Hannak, *Professor Alberts Essay: "Die Frauen und das Studium Medicin"* (Vienna, 1895).

60 Honzáková, "K zápasu," pp. 69–72. Rostočilová, pp. 241–42 (from an interview with Eliška Vozabová, one of Honzáková's fellow medical students). Honzáková tells of their precarious existence at the German university due to radical German students who wanted them expelled. There were no German women students in the faculty. See *Ženské listy* 25 (1897): 235.

61 The Badeni language ordinances of April 1897 precipitated an explosion of passions on both sides, among politicians as well as students. See Garver, *Young Czech Party*, chapter 9, and Arthur J. May, *The Hapsburg Monarchy 1867–1914* (Cambridge, Mass.: Harvard University Press, 1968), pp. 325–28.

62 The decree of March 19, 1896, on "Nostrification der von Frauen im Ausland erworbenen medizinischen Doctordiplome" is in Leo Beck-Mannagetta and Paul Kelle, *Die österreichische Universitätsgesetze* (Vienna, 1906), p. 566. All legislation pertaining to *Frauenstudium* up to 1906 is assembled on pp. 562–83 of this volume. See also Berta List-Ganser, "Das Akademische Frauenstudium," in *Frauenbewegung, Frauenbildung und Frauenarbeit in Österreich* (Vienna: Bund Österreichicher Frauenvereine, 1930), pp. 192–99.

63 *Frauenbewegung*, p. 193.

64 *Ženské listy* 25 (January 1897): 16.

65 "Ženské studium vitězí," *Ženské listy* 25 (1897): 91–95. See Beck-Kelle, p. 566, for the text of the law.

66 Honzáková, "K zápasu," p. 71, reminisced how the petitions were returned, stamped "Not possible at this time because of existing ordinances."

67 Ibid., pp. 71–72. Another ministry representative expressed surprise to these young women that the desire to study medicine should emerge among Czech women in Prague. He advised them to go abroad to study.

68 Ibid., p. 72. That fall a new prorector at the University of Vienna spoke highly of the women philosophy students and expressed hope that other faculties might be opened to women. See *Die feierliche Inauguration des Rektors der Wiener Universität, 1899–1900*, pp. 12–13.

69 Beck-Kelle, p. 570. The decree was made public on September 15. *Neue Freie Presse* (September 16, 1900) published a favorable report.

70 Honzáková, "K zápasu," pp. 73–74. Honzáková recalls how one sympathetic professor told the crowd of men students who came to hear her exam that he was glad they had come because they finally heard how one should perform at a *rigorosum* exam. Some hospital administrators did not think people would have confidence in women doctors and therefore refused to employ them. Honzáková, like many who followed, chose obstetrics-gynecology as a specialty because she felt it was where she was most needed and because of the "possibility of educational and moral influence" among women, especially the young.

71 Rostočilová, p. 244.

72 See description in ibid.

73 See Ries, pp. 94–95, and Honzáková, "Ze světového studia ženského," for dates and history. Women were not admitted to the law faculties until 1918.

74 Both outside observers and the Czechs stressed the role of the national movement in the development of the women's movement. See the translation of a report by Russian educator A. L. Petrov in *Ženské listy* 19 (1891); Schirmacher, pp. 230–32; Kellnerová, especially pp. 54–61. Krásnohorská frequently contrasted the productive work of the Czech movement—especially its major achievement, Minerva—with the "passive" activity of the Austrian women proper. See, for example, her comments on the forthcoming Austrian women's

congress in *Ženské listy*, 19 (1891): 192–95; in "Pro ženské studium," p. 51; and in a report on Minerva, *Ženské listy* 19 (1891): 168–70. Yet Czech women in the 1890s did not become internationalists; they refused to participate in the first Austrian women's congress in 1892 because the Austrian women would not recognize the demands of the Czechs in Vienna for their own schools, an issue seemingly unrelated to the major issues of women's rights. See *Ženské listy* 19 (1891): 192–95.

75 The women's political movement began in earnest around 1904, though the demand for voting rights had been expressed in the late 1890s. The socialist women broke off from the larger women's movement after 1900.

4 Women in the First Czechoslovak Republic

1 Few works treat the status, aspirations, and political activity of Czech and Slovak women in the Czechoslovak Republic (1918–38). Relatively more is published on Czech and Slovak women during the years of National Revival (1781–1866), Dual Monarchy (1867–1918), and Communist rule (1948–1985). Little is said about women in the better surveys of the Czechoslovak Republic, all of which emphasize domestic politics, the economy, and foreign policy. These include Victor S. Mamatey and Radomír Luža, eds., *A History of the Czechoslovak Republic, 1918–1948* (Princeton, N.J.: Princeton University Press, 1973); Vera Olivova, *The Doomed Democracy: Czechoslovakia in a Disrupted Europe, 1914–1938* (Montreal: McGill-Queens University Press, 1972); Alice Teichova, *An Economic Background to Munich* (Cambridge: Cambridge University Press, 1974); and Jan Kapras, Bohumil Němec, and František Soukup, eds., *Idea československého státu* (Prague: Národní Rada československé, 1935). On late nineteenth-century developments affecting women, see Karen Johnson Freeze, "The Young Progressives: The Czech Student Movement, 1887–1897," (unpublished Ph.D. dissertation, Columbia University, 1974); and Bruce M. Garver, *The Young Czech Party, 1874–1901, and the Emergence of a Multi-Party System* (New Haven: Yale University Press, 1978). Earlier developments are surveyed by Joseph Kočí, *Naše národní obrození* (Prague: Státní nakladatelství politické literatury, 1960), and Stanley Z. Pech, *The Czech Revolution of 1848* (Chapel Hill: University of North Carolina Press, 1969).

2 See Robert Bezucha, ed., *Modern European Social History* (Lexington, Mass.: D. C. Heath, 1972); Renate Bridenthal and Claudia Koonz, eds., *Becoming Visible: Women in European History* (Boston: Houghton Mifflin, 1977); Berenice A. Carroll, ed., *Liberating Women's History: Theoretical and Critical Essays* (Urbana-Champaign: University of Illinois Press, 1976); Mari Jo Buhle, *Women and American Socialism, 1870–1920* (Urbana-Champaign: University of Illinois Press, 1981); Sheila Rowbotham, *Hidden from History* (New York: Pantheon, 1974); and Linda Frey and Marsha Frey, eds., *Women in Western European History: A Select Chronological, Geographical and Topical Bibliography: The Nineteenth and Twentieth Centuries* (Westport, Conn.: Greenwood Press, 1984).

3 Edvard Vondruška, "Československá pozemková reforma," pp. 74–88, in Josef Gruber et al., *Sociální politika v Československé Republice* (Prague:

Sociální ústav ČSR, 1924).

4 Surveys include Karel Pichlík, *Zahraniční odboj 1914–1918 bez legend* (Prague: Svoboda, 1968), and Vojta Beneš, *Československá Amerika v odboji* (Prague: Pokrok, 1931) and *Vojáci zapomenuté fronty* (Prague: Památník Odboje, 1923).

5 Statistical Office of the Czechoslovak Republic, ed., *Manuel statistique de la République Tchécoslovaque*, vol. 4 (Prague: State Statistical Office, 1932), pp. 13–16. The Czechoslovak National Socialist party, established in 1898 and appealing to lower middle-class Czechs, civil servants, and skilled workers, was patriotic, social reform-minded, non-Marxist, civil libertarian, and not anti-Semitic.

6 Alois Hajn, *Ženská otázka v letech 1900–1920: Retrospektiva a kulturně historický dokument* (Prague: Pokrok, 1939); Teréza Nováková, *Ze ženského hnutí* (Prague: Jos. R. Vilímek, 1909).

7 Garver, *Young Czech Party*, pp. 283–88, and Josef Beran, *Gabriel Schneider: Zakladatel kongregace chudých Sester de Notre Dame v Čechách* (Horažd'ovice: Sestry de Notre Dame, 1931).

8 Statistics in this chapter on birthrates and death rates come from *Masarykův slovník naučný* 1: 1056 and *Atlas obyvatelstva* ČSSR (Prague: Ústřední správa geodézie a Kartografie, 1962), pp. 38–47.

9 Tomáš Čapek, *Naše Amerika* (Prague: Orbis, 1925), and Bruce M. Garver, "Czech-American Freethinkers on the Great Plains," pp. 147–69, in Frederick Luebke, ed., *Ethnicity on the Great Plains* (Lincoln: University of Nebraska Press, 1980).

10 *Manuel statistique de la République Tchécoslovaque* 4: 14, 333.

11 Statistical Office of the Czechoslovak Republic, ed., *Aperçu statistique de la République Tchécoslovaque* (Prague: State Statistical Office, 1930), pp. 11–12, 233–34.

12 Leonard Bianchi et al., *Dejiny štátu a práva na uzemí v období kapitalizmu 1848–1945*, vol. 2 (Bratislava: Slovenská Akadémia Vied, 1973), pp. 129–30, and Francis H. Stuerm, *Training in Democracy: The New Schools of Czechoslovakia* (New York: Inor Publishing, 1938).

13 Albína Honzáková, ed., *Kniha života: práce a osobnost F. F. Plamínkové* (Prague: Melantrich, 1935), pp. 531–45, 556–59, 571–73.

14 *Aperçu statistique* (1930), pp. 233–35, on all above school enrollments for the period 1921–22 through 1927–28.

15 Chapters on women in arts, letters, and history appear in Jan Kapras, ed., *Česká žena v dějinách národa* (Prague: Novina, 1940), and Arne Novák, *Dějiny českého písemnictví* (Prague: Sfinx, 1946). Biographical sketches of prominent Czech and Slovak women may be found in Jaroslav Kunc, *Kdy zemřeli . . . ? 1937–1962* (Prague: Státní Knihovna ČSSR, 1962); Ján Tibenský et al., *Slovenský literárny album* (Bratislava: Obzor, 1968); Zděnka Pešata, ed., *Čeští spisovatele z přelomu 19. a 20. století* (Prague: Československý spisovatel, 1972); and Stephen Taylor, ed., *Who's Who in Central and East Europe*, 2nd ed. (Zurich: Central European Times, 1937).

16 For example, Czech racing car driver Eliška Junková won twice at Sicily's Targa Florio and in 1927 in the Nürburgring. Jaroslav Hausman and Miloš

Kovářík, *Vteřiny za volantem* (Prague: Nakl. Dopravy a spojů, 1968), pp. 5–39, discuss her career.

17 On women in religion, see Beran, *Gabriel Schneider*; Miloslav Kaňák, ed., *Padesát let Československé církve* (Prague: Husová československá bohoslovecká fakulta, 1970); and Egon Hostovsky et al., *The Jews of Czechoslovakia* (Philadelphia: Jewish Publication Society of America, 1968).

18 Honzáková, *Kniha života*, pp. 137–49, 482–84.

19 *Sbírka zákonů a nařízení státu československého* (Prague: Státní tiskarna, 1918–38). Law 91 (1918), pp. 81–83; Law 29 (1920), pp. 38–43; and Law 420 (1919), pp. 563–66.

20 Evžen Štern, "O osmihodinové pracovní době," pp. 13–18, in Gruber. *Sociální politika*.

21 *Sbírka zákonů* (1920–22): Laws 15/1920 and 241/1922. Vladimír Procházka, "Volná chvíle dělnictva v Československu," pp. 19–33, in Gruber.

22 *Sbírka zákonů* (1918–22): Laws 63/1918, 157/1919, 89/1920, 47/1921, 267/1921, 482/1921, 489/1921, and 400/1922, and Bianchi, *Dejiny štátu* 2: 119–21 ff.

23 Statistical Office of the Czechoslovak Republic, *Volby do Národního shromáždění v dubnu 1920 a všeobecné volby . . .* (Prague: State Statistical Office, 1920), p. 33; table I, "Poslanecká sněmovna," pp. 3–13; and table I, "Senát," pp. 73–81. Statistical Office of the Czechoslovak Republic, "Volby do Poslanecké sněmovny v květnu 1935" (Prague: State Statistical Office, 1935), pp. 3–13.

24 *Protokol XII. sjezdu čs. sociálně demokratické strany dělnické konaného ve dnech 27.–30. prosince 1918* (Prague: Ústřední dělnické knihkupectví, 1919), and *Protokol XIII. řadného sjezdu čsl. soc. demokratické strany dělnické jenž se konal 25.–28. IX. 1920* (Prague: Ústřední dělnické knihkupectví, 1920).

25 O. Frankenberger and J. Kubícěk, *Antonín Švehla v dějinách čs. strany agrární* (Prague: Novina, 1931), discuss the Agrarian party's growth through 1929.

26 Among the best books on Masaryk and women are T. G. Masaryk, *O ženě. Se statí F. F. Plamíkové*, 2nd ed. (Prague: Čin, 1929); T. G. Masaryk, *Mnohoženství a jednoženství*, 2nd ed. (Prague: B. Kočí, 1925); and F. F. Plamínková, *Masaryk a ženy*, 3rd ed. (Prague: Ženská Národní Rada, 1930), vol. 1.

27 Alice G. Masaryková, *Dětství a mládí: Vzpomínky a myšlenky* (Pittsburgh: Masaryk Publications Trust, 1960); Charlotta G. Masaryková, *Listy do vežení* (Prague: Vladimír Žikeš, 1948); and Ruth Crawford Mitchell, ed., *Alice Garrigue Masaryk, 1879–1966* (Pittsburgh: University of Pittsburgh, 1980).

28 Honzáková, *Kniha života*, pp. 239–47. Three of these international organizations were founded in London: the International Congress of Women (1898); the International Alliance of Women (1902); and the International Federation of University Women (1919).

29 František Soukup, *Revoluce práce*, vol. 2 (Prague: Ústřední dělnické knihupectví, 1938), pp. 1344–47, 1619.

30 First in circulation and political influence was the *Časopis učitelek*, "the organ of the Women's Central Teachers Union in Bohemia," whose thirty-third year began in 1918.

31 Unless otherwise indicated, information below on newspapers and periodicals comes from František Roubík, *Bibliografie časopisectva v Čechach z let 1863–1895*

(Prague: Česká Akademia Věd a Umění, 1936), and the Czechoslovak Bibliographical Institute, ed., *Bibliografický katalog časopisectva Republiky Československé za rok 1920* (Prague: Josef Springer, 1921).

32 Information on Communist party periodicals and newspapers appears in Ústav dějin KSČ, ed., *Časopisy a noviny vydávané KSČ v krajích v letech 1921–1938* (Prague: Ústav dějin KSČ, 1958), and *Časopisy a noviny dělnické a sociálně demokratické, vycházející v krajích v letech 1867–1920 a pokrokové mimo KSČ z let 1921–1938* (Prague: Ústav dějin KSČ, 1958).

33 František Taborský, ed., *Paní Renáta Tyršová: Památník na počest jejích sedmdesátých narozenin* (Prague: Národní Rada Československá, 1926), is the most detailed account.

34 Data on membership are from V. Procházka, "Volná chvíle dělnictva v Československu," in Gruber, p. 25.

35 Archiv Národního Shromáždění, ed., *Ročenka Národního Shromáždění Republiky Československé 1923–24* (Prague: Archiv Národního Shromáždění, 1924); *Poslanecká sněmovna ve III. volebním období* (Prague: Archiv Národního Shromáždění, 1930); and *Senát ve IV. volebním období* (Prague: Archiv Národního Shromáždění, 1935), provide electoral data.

36 Rud. Tayerle et al., eds., *Hospodářské poměry, sociální politika a odborové hnutí v letech 1926–1929: Zpráva k. IX. sjezdu O.S.Č.* (Prague: Archiv Národního Shromáždění, 1930), pp. 112–15.

37 Outstanding Czechoslovak Social Democratic women were Karla Máchová (1853–1920), a journalist; Božena Eksteinová (1871–1930), an editor of *Právo lidu*; Betty Karpíšková, representative in Parliament from 1923 to 1938 and editor of *Ženské listy*; and Emma Koutková, a postal official and, after 1935, a state senator.

38 *Zpráva ku XV. řádnému sjezdu čsl. soc. dem. strany děl.* (Prague: Lidová knihtiskarná A. Němec a spol., 1927), p. 156.

39 *Program a zásady čsl. strany nár. soc.* (Prague: Melantrich, 1933), pp. 169–70.

40. Ibid., pp. 254, 264.

41 The best work on Plamínková is Honzáková, *Kniha života*.

42 Josef Doležal, *Politická cesta českého katolicism 1918–28* (Prague: Ústřední Křesťansko-Sociální Dělnické Organizaci v Čechach, 1928), p. 44.

43 In 1928 the party continued to support this legislation that had "benefited ordinary men and women from the poorer strata of society." Doležal, *Politická cesta*, p. 37.

44 The Slovak People's party, the most vocal interwar advocate of autonomy for Slovakia, supported the establishment of a Slovak Republic in March 1939 and became the leading party in that state. Before 1939 it won 25 to 30 percent of the Slovak vote.

45 The outstanding National Democratic woman was Anna Vetterová-Becvářová, an educator and wife of a professor, who was elected once to the lower house and twice to the upper house of Parliament. *Senát ve IV. vol. období*, p. 99.

46 Václav Havel expressed this view at a public lecture at Yale in April 1968.

5 Ukrainian Feminism in Interwar Poland

1 Considerations of space prevent a discussion of feminism; for the purposes of this article I have dealt with women activists in general. Only materials directly relevant to this chapter are cited, although the information for it is culled from a book I am currently writing on Ukrainian women. I would like to thank the American Association of University Women for granting me the Founder's Fellowship that enabled a year for research; the International Research and Exchanges Board for funding a research trip to the USSR; Fulbright Fellowship for research in Poland; the Ukrainian National Women's League of America and the World Federation of Ukrainian Women for initiating and supporting the project. My special thanks go to Jaryna Turko Bodrock of Widener Library, Liubov Abramiuk Volynec and Svitliana Lutska Andrushkiv of the New York Public Library, and Basil Nadraga of the Library of Congress for help in locating elusive publications; and to Professor Ivan L. Rudnytsky, of the University of Alberta, for making the papers of Milena Rudnyts'ka available to me. According to M. Felinski, *Ukraincy w Polsce odrodzonej* (Warsaw, 1931), *Provista* in 1928 had eighty-four branches and 2,916 reading rooms. Among the other major Ukrainian organizations in which women were active were the *Sil's'ky Hospodar* (Village Farmer), the Association of Day Care Centers, the Temperance Union, Marian Sodalities, women's sections in political parties, and some philanthropic societies. The Union was the most numerous and the most effective, hence it serves best as the focal point for this essay. Most women accepted it as their representative in the international arena. The Polish authorities prevented the establishment of a united Ukrainian women's organization for all Ukrainians in the Polish territories; letter of Milena Rudnyts'ka to Hanna Chykalenko-Keller, 15 July 1923, in the Ukrainian Academy of Arts and Sciences, New York, UVAN, Chykalenko-Keller Archive, uncatalogued.

2 Demographic data for this period may be found in Marian Marek Drozdowski, *Społeczeństwo, Państwo, Politycy II Rzeczypospolitej* (Cracow: Wydawnictwo Literackie, 1972). On the political background, see Miroslawa Papierzyńska-Turek, *Sprawa Ukrainska w Drugeij Rzeczypospolitej, 1922–1926* (Cracow: Wydawnictwo Literackie, 1979); Antony Polonsky, *Politics in Independent Poland 1921–1939: The Crisis of Constitutional Government* (Oxford: Clarendon Press, 1972); Stephan Horak, *Poland and Her National Minorities* (New York: Vantage Press, 1961); Ivan Kedryn, *Zhyttia, Podii, Liudy: Spomyny i Komentari* (New York: Chervona Kalyna Publishing Cooperative, 1976).

3 The discussion generated on women and development by the UN-sponsored decade of women, particularly as it refers to the nonindustrialized countries, illustrates these similarities. See, for example, the articles in "United Nations Decade for Women World Conference," *Women and Politics* 4, no. 1 (Spring 1984).

4 Firm statistics on the Union are not available and the information we have is not consistent. According to *Sprawozdanie z zycia mnieszosci narodowei*, 1936, no. 1, p. 35, as of March 29, 1936, the membership of the organization was

50,000, an increase of 11,000 from the previous year. The report of the Union on the work of 1936 mentioned that the organization had sixty-seven branches, 1,101 circles and 45,000 members. In a letter from the Ukrainian Women's Union to the Ukrainian Women's League of America in April 1937 (no exact date given; letter in the uncatalogued archives of the Ukrainian Women's League in New York), seventy-five branches are mentioned, and 1,150 peasant circles, with a total of 50,000 members. That is also the number given by Konstantyna Malyts'ka, "Pislia rozviazannia soiuzu Ukraiinok," *Zhinochy svit*, June 1938. C. Mikulowska [Lucja Charewiczowa], *"Ukrainski" ruch kobiecy* (L'viv, 1937), p. 11, quoted the number 39,199 as having been officially announced by the Union itself in 1936. Milena Rudnyts'ka, "Ideolohichni pozytsii i zavdannia matirnoho soiuzu Ukraiinok," *Informatsyiny lystok Matirnoho Soiuzu Ukraiinok*, May–June 1951, p. 4, insisted that on the eve of World War II, the Union in Galicia alone numbered 100,000. *Entsyklopediia Ukraiinoznavstva* 8: 2986 noted that 25 percent of the villages with a Ukrainian population had circles of the Union.

5 See especially Natalia Kobrynska, "Pro pervistnu tsil' Tovarystva rus'kykh zhinok v Stanislavovi," in N. Kobrynska and Olena Pchilka, eds., *Pershy Vinok* (L'viv: Drukarnia im. T. Shevchenka, 1887), pp. 457–63; a facsimile edition was published by the Ukrainian Women's League of America in New York in 1984. The monthly journal *Zhinocha dolia* (Woman's Fate), published and edited by Olena Kysilevs'ka in Kolomya between 1924 and 1939, offers the best concrete examples of the approach. The Ukrainian women, however, failed to produce a theoretical analysis of their work. Among the women in imperial Russia, the psychological motivation resulted in dedication to idealistic terrorist politics; see Barbara Alpern Engel, *Mothers and Daughters: Women of the Intelligentsia in Nineteenth-Century Russia* (Cambridge: Cambridge University Press, 1983).

6 The writing of the women socialists that contradicts this statement was mostly from before 1914 and is part of a different story.

7 Polonsky, p. 22, estimated that 20 percent of the coal mines, 99 percent of the basalt mines, 60 percent of the chemical industry, 20 percent of oil refineries, and 30 percent of the metal industry were in government hands. Railways, merchant marine, posts, telegraphs, and telephones were about 95 percent government-owned. All commercial aviation and all armaments were in the hands of the government.

8 Ivan Martiuk, *Tsentrosoiuz* (n.p., 1973), p. 30. Martiuk errs somewhat, as the Peasant Cooperative moved toward organizing women en masse only in 1936.

9 But Levchanivs'ka's failure to attend the Eleventh Congress of the Suffrage Rights of Women, held in Rome in 1923, was particularly painful; see letter of Olena Zalizniak to Chykalenko-Keller, in Keller, UVAN archives, uncatalogued, dated June 15, 1923.

10 Parliamentary experience weakened the already tenuous international cooperation among feminists in Eastern Europe. The little cooperation there had been among Polish and Ukrainian women became open antagonism during the liberation struggle, which was never buried again. Some Polish deputies at times

defended the Ukrainians in the legislature; of the women only Wanda Pelczynska of Vilnius (then the Polish Wilno, but claimed as the capital by Lithuanians)spoke against discrimination against Ukrainians and other minorities, especially at the session of Feburary 10, 1937. Even a projected law that would drop married women from jobs if their husbands were employed was not enough to warrant closer cooperation among women; *Sprawozdanie stenograficzne Senatu Rzeczypospolitej* session of the Senate, March 9, 1936.

11 *Zhinka*, March 1, 1937; a later editorial in the paper commented: "Organized [Ukrainian] women must forcefully oppose the blind aping of foreign models of fascist dictatorial systems which would reduce the role of women and circumscribe their activities, as we see happening in Italy and Germany," ibid., September 15, 1937.

12 Editorial in *Hromandianka*, December 15, 1938, defending the journals published by Olena Kysilevs'ka; Maria Strutysn'ka, "Materyn'stvo u feministychnomu svitohliadi," *Zhinocha Dolia Almanach*, 1930, pp. 22–27. By far the most interesting Ukrainian feminist was Natalia O. Kobrynska (1855–1920). See my two articles, "Kobrynska: The Feminism Movement," in Andrei Markovits and Frank Sysyn, *Modernization and Conflicts of National Identity* (Cambridge, Mass.: Harvard University Press, 1982), and "Socialism and Feminism," in Tova Yedlin, ed., *Women in Eastern Europe and the Soviet Union* (New York: Praeger, 1980), pp. 44–64.

13 *Zhinocha dolia*, September 1925, pp. 5–6.

14 *Zhinochy svit*, August–September 1933, p. 18.

15 Full text of the resolutions in *Zhinocha dolia*, no. 15/16, 1934, and no. 17, 1934, as well as in *Zhinochy svit*, July–September 1934, pp. 4–6, and the following issue. They were also published in L'viv as a separate booklet.

16 The Catholic Action was an ideological organization formed by the Catholic Church in the 1920s to organize the laity into groups that would offer a positive social and economic goal as an alternative to the politics of the extreme left and extreme right. It gave the group authority from the church in pursuing its political and social actions.

17 "Vybory bez zhinok," communiqué and article that were censored from *Zhinka*, no. 15/16, 1935; text in Rudnyts'ka's personal files.

18 Letter from Lidia Burachyns'ka, former editor of *Nova Khata*, to author, July 16, 1981.

19 "Dopovid' na zahal'nomu z'iizdi Soiuzu Ukraiinok," *Zhinka*, no. 21/22, November 1937, gives a résumé of Rudnyts'ka's speech, with some parts quoted. The above is a direct quotation.

6 Peasant Women of Croatia in the Interwar Years

1 This has been documented in numerous studies, particularly for Chinese and Soviet women. For examples see, Sheila Rowbotham, ed., *Women, Resistance, and Revolution: A History of Women and Revolution in the Modern World* (New York: Vintage Books, 1972), and Marilyn B. Young, ed., *Women in China* (Ann Arbor: University of Michigan Press, 1973).

2 For information on Croatian women during the Yugoslav resistance, see Mary E. Reed, "Croatian Women in the Yugoslav Partisan Resistance, 1941–1945" (unpublished Ph.D. dissertation, University of California, Berkeley, 1980). Also see Reed, "The Anti-Fascist Front of Women and the Communist Party in Croatia," in Tova Yedlin, ed., *Women in Eastern Europe and the Soviet Union* (New York: Praeger, 1980), pp. 128–40. For an overview of the activities of Yugoslav women during this period, see Barbara W. Jancar, "Women in the Yugoslav National Liberation Movement: An Overview," *Studies in Comparative Communism* 15, nos. 2 and 3 (Summer–Fall 1981): 143–64.

3 See Wayne S. Vucinich, "Interwar Yugoslavia," in Vucinich, ed., *Contemporary Yugoslavia: Twenty Years of Socialist Experiment* (Berkeley: University of California Press, 1969), pp. 12–15. The most valuable source on Yugoslav peasants during the interwar period is Jozo Tomasevich, *Peasants, Politics, and Economic Change in Yugoslavia* (Stanford, Calif.: Stanford University Press, 1955). For information on the Croatian Peasant party, see Robert G. Livingston, "Stjepan Radic and the Croatian Peasant Party, 1904–1929 (unpublished Ph.D. dissertation, Harvard University, 1959).

4 The most complete investigations of the position of the Communist party toward feminism and women's movements are those for the Soviet Union. Two recent works on this subject are Gail Warshofsky Lapidus, *Women in Soviet Society* (Berkeley: University of California Press, 1978), and Richard Stites, *The Women's Liberation Movement in Russia* (Princeton, N.J.: Princeton University Press, 1977). The larger issue of the Communist party's political strategy concerning rural women is explored in Gregory J. Massell's study of Moslem women, *The Surrogate Proletariat* (Princeton, N.J.: Princeton University Press, 1974). For a comparative study of women in the Soviet Union, Eastern Europe, Cuba, and China, see Barbara W. Jancar, *Women Under Communism* (Baltimore: Johns Hopkins University Press, 1978).

5 The newspapers of the Croatian Peasant party and women's publications such as *Ženski svijet* and *Žena danas* describe in detail these gatherings and the acclaim with which the peasant speakers were received.

6 Unfortunately our sources on Croatian peasant women are quite meager. This is due to the preoccupation of Yugoslav historians with the political aspects of the workers' movement and the Communist revolution and the virtual disappearance of the Croatian Peasant party soon after the war. An indispensable source on peasant women in the interwar period is the anthropological work, Vera Stein-Erlich, *Family in Transition* (Princeton, N.J.: Princeton University Press, 1966). The three-volume series published by the Konferencija za Drustvenu Aktivnost Žena Hrvatske (successor to the Anti-Fascist Front of Women in Croatia) contains valuable documents on women in the workers' movement and the National Liberation War. See *Žena Hrvatske u Radničkom Pokretu* (Zagreb: Konferencija za Drustvenu Aktivnost Žena Hrvatske, 1967) and *Žena Hrvatske u Narodnooslobodilačkoj Borbi* (Zagreb: Konferencija za Drustvenu Aktivnost Žena Hrvatske, 1955), vols. 1 and 2. Other information can be gleaned from the pages of women's magazines, particularly *Žena danas*, published in Belgrade, and *Ženski svijet*, in Zagreb, and from the newspapers

of the Croatian Peasant party. Nada Sremec's monograph *Mi Nismo Krive* (We Are Not to Blame), published in Zagreb in 1940, describes the condition of women in Slavonia, the fertile agricultural area of Croatia.

7 Accounts of the treatment of women in various parts of Yugoslavia can be found in several autobiographical sources. See, for example, Louis Adamic, *The Native's Return* (New York: Harper, 1934), Louisa Rayner, *Women in a Village* (London: Heinemann, 1957), and Milovan Djilas, *Land Without Justice* (New York: Harcourt, Brace, 1958).

8 Erlich's study divides Yugoslavia into regions corresponding to stages of development from patriarchal family structures in the Albanian parts of Macedonia to modern regions along the Dalmatian Coast and in Slovenia where women were relatively independent. In the transitional areas, including Croatia, Serbia, and parts of Christian Bosnia-Herzegovina, family life was characterized by discord along with a new sense of independence among family members.

9 Examples of this can be found in Adamic, pp. 211–12; Rayner, pp. 41–42 and Djilas, p. 6.

10 Erlich's study shows that life expectancy for women was less than for men due to the greater dangers posed by pregnancy, childbirth, and abortion. In addition, the ratio of female to male deaths in the prime childbearing years, twenty to forty, was greater in Macedonia (13.7 to 9.1 percent) than in more progressive Croatia (13.0 to 11.1 percent).

11 Erlich attempts to prove this statistically by analyzing over three hundred questionnaires she received from villages throughout Yugoslavia. The responses were grouped according to geographical-ethnic region and then described as either patriarchal, transitional, or modern.

12 The anthropologist Joel Halpern in his assessment of life in a Serbian village agrees with Erlich's observation that the disappearance of the large family unit, the *zadruga*, increased the work load considerably more for women than for men. He notes that the responsibilities of a wife of a peasant were extremely burdensome and that although the position of women in the traditional *zadruga* was subservient in many ways, in some of these large households women enjoyed a significant degree of power and independence through their economic roles. See Joel Halpern, "Yugoslavia: Modernization in an Ethnically Diverse State," in Vucinich, p. 332.

13 *Ženski svijet*, May 1939, p. 14.

14 Erlich notes that attitudes among peasants were not entirely hopeless. She felt that these women were beginning to perceive an end to their subjugation. However, protests were still generally confined to the household. See, for example, pp. 64–65.

15 Interview with Milka Kufrin, Zagreb, May 1976.

16 Anica Roje provides one example of the connection between the two movements. Her name appears as one of the speakers at a large meeting of women in Split who were demonstrating their support of women's suffrage. Roje, then forty-seven years old, identified herself as representing women agricultural laborers and the Women's Branch of the Peasant party. After the

occupation she joined the Anti-Fascist Front of Women in Split and spoke at other regional meetings of that organization. See *Žena Hrvatske u Radničkom Pokretu* (hereinafter ŽHRP), pp. 274–75; *Žena Hrvatske u Narodnooslobodilačkoj Borbi* (hereinafter ŽHNOB) 1: 151 and 411 and 2: 32.

17 Stojan Pribičević, *World Without End* (New York: Reynal and Hitchcock, 1939), p. 280. Mara Matočec is also described as heading the Women's Branch of the Peasant party and as one of the foremost peasant poets in Andrija Stampar, "Croat Peasant Literature," *The Slavonic Yearbook*, vol. 19 of the *Slavonic and East European Review* (1939–40), p. 294.

18 Tomasevich, *Peasants, Politics and Economic Change in Yugoslavia*, p. 257.

19 *Seljački dom*, September 1938, pp. 3–4; Erlich, p. 30; and Sremec, pp. 48–49.

20 These experiences were recounted by Marija Zmirič in *Seljačka sloga*, October–November 1940, pp. 285–89.

21 In an issue of *Ženski svijet*, Matočec declared that throughout Croatia she heard the same complaint, "There is no justice," and everywhere there was one desire, "Teach us so that we can better take care of our lives." *Ženski svijet*, February 1939.

22 *Ženski svijet*, May 1939.

23 *Seljačka misao*, April 1937.

24 Ibid.

25 *Žena danas*, December 1938, p. 4.

26 *Seljačka sloga*, March 1939.

27 *Seljački dom*, December 1929, pp. 8–9.

28 *Seljački misao*, December 14, 1939.

29 *Seljačka sloga*, February 1939.

30 Kata Pejnović, the heroine of the Anti-Fascist Front of Women, was a notable exception. She lived and worked exclusively in the rural areas of Lika. A short biography of Pejnović appears in ŽHNOB 1: 184–85. A monograph on Pejnović is now also available. See Marija Šoljan Bakarić, *Kata Pejnović* (Zagreb: Savjet za Pitanja Društvenog Položaja Žene, 1977).

31 *Borba*, August 23, 1923, in ŽHRP, p. 111. The organizational plan of the Central Secretariat of Women appears in the same volume, pp. 178–79.

32 *Proleter*, February–March 1935, in ŽHRP, p. 239.

33 References to infiltration of these groups can be found in ŽHRP, p. 308; ŽHNOB 1: iv–v; and in Vida Tomsic's address to the Fifth Congress in 1940, in ŽHNOB 1: 6.

34 *Ženski svijet*, November 1939, p. 20.

35 The independent newspaper *Glas mira* made this point in its first issue by stating that peasant women had difficulty in realizing their own position of subjugation in society and were only rarely interested in their equality with men or in their own rights. *Glas mira*, January 1937, in ŽHRP, p. 316.

36 Both Matočec and Balenovic affirmed that peasant women had an advantage over city women because they lived on their own land, had bread to eat, and were with their children during the day. They urged peasant women to be thankful for this and proud of their peasant heritage. See Matočec in *Seljačka sloga*, October 1939, and Balenovic, *Seljački dom*, September 8, 1938.

37 Tomšič's address to the Fifth Conference of the Yugoslav Communist party, November 1940, Zagreb. The portions pertaining to work with women are quoted in ŽHNOB I: 2–8.

III Women and Politics

Introduction

1 See Gail Warshofsky Lapidus, "Political Mobilization, Participation, and Leadership: Women in Soviet Politics," *Comparative Politics* 8, no. 1 (October 1975): 90–118, and *Women in Soviet Society*, pp. 198–231; Jancar, *Women under Communism*, pp. 88–121; Heitlinger, *Women and State Socialism*, pp. 104–7, 159–60; and Wolchik, "Eastern Europe," in Lovenduski and Hills, pp. 252–77, for other discussions of women's political roles in the Soviet Union and Eastern Europe. See Lovenduski and Hills for brief overviews of recent research on women in politics in the United States and other Western countries.

2 See Robert D. Putnam, *The Comparative Study of Political Elites* (Englewood Cliffs, N.J.: Prentice-Hall, 1976); and the essays in Lovenduski and Hills, and Cynthia P. Epstein and R. L. Coser, eds., *Access to Power: Cross National Studies of Women and Elites* (London: Allen and Unwin, 1981), for discussions of these tendencies. See the sources in note 1 for more detail on the characteristics of leaders in the Soviet Union and Eastern Europe.

3 See Margherita Rendel, ed., *Women, Power, and Political Systems* (London: Croom Helm, 1981), pp. 15–21, for a discussion of the family as a source of political power for women in Western Europe and the United States.

4 See the sources listed in note 1 and also Joel C. Moses, "Indoctrination as a Female Political Role in the Soviet Union," *Comparative Politics* 8, no. 4 (July 1976): 525–48; Nelson, however, found that women in his sample of local leaders did not differ markedly from men in education or age.

5 Partial exceptions include Yugoslavia, where small groups of young professional women have identified themselves as feminists in the last decade, and East Germany, where certain women writers write from a feminist perspective. In neither case are the numbers involved very large. See Tatyana Mamonova, ed., *Women in Russia* (Boston: Beacon Press, 1984), for writings of recent Soviet feminists.

6 See Sandra Baxter and Marjorie Lansing, *Women and Politics, The Invisible Majority* (Ann Arbor: University of Michigan Press, 1981), and Lovenduski and Hills for illustrations of these tendencies.

7 It is also possible that women in Eastern Europe, as has been argued in the case of West European and American women, have little interest in politics as it is currently conceptualized because this conceptualization leaves out many of the communal activities women engage in or because the content as well as the forms of what is generally considered the political have been defined by men and based on the male understanding of power and male, rather than female, experience in other areas. While it is difficult to determine the reasons for women's lack of political interest in Eastern Europe, the

monopoly of political life by the Communist party and its officially approved mass organizations does mean that East European women have less opportunity to take part in the less structured, voluntary, ad hoc forms of communal activity thought to be important aspects of women's political activism (although, until recently not often included in definitions of political participation) in the West. See Jane S. Jaquette, "Introduction," in Jaquette, ed., *Women in Politics* (New York: John Wiley and Sons, 1974); Kay Boals, "Review Essay: Political Science," *Signs* 1, no. 1 (Autumn 1975): 161–74; Jane S. Jaquette, "Review Essay: Political Science," *Signs* 2, no. 1 (Autumn 1976): 147–64; and Berenice A. Carroll, "Review Essay: Political Science, Part I: American Politics and Political Behavior," *Signs* 5, no. 2 (Winter 1979): 289–305, for reviews highlighting problems in how political activity is conceptualized. See Virginia Sapiro, *The Political Integration of Women* (Urbana-Champaign: University of Illinois Press, 1981), for a recent study that defines women's political activity more broadly. See Nancy C. M. Hartsock, *Money, Sex, and Power: Toward a Feminist Historical Materialism* (New York and London: Longman, 1983), especially chapters 9 and 10, for an interpretation of how differences in men's and women's experiences in other areas of life are reflected in their conceptualizations of power and politics.

8 The head of the women's organization is currently a member of the secretariat, politburo, or comparable party body in Czechoslovakia, East Germany, and Romania.

9 See Rosabeth Moss Kanter, *Men and Women of the Corporation* (New York: Basic Books, 1977), for a discussion of how small numbers hinder independent action and encourage conformity to group norms and values on the part of women in the American business world.

10 See, for example, the accounts of women activists in the United States in Irene Tinker, ed., *Women in Washington: Advocates for Public Policy*, Sage Yearbooks in Women's Policy Studies, vol. 7 (Beverly Hills, Calif.: Sage Publications, 1983).

7 Women in Romanian Politics: Elena Ceauşescu, Pronatalism, and the Promotion of Women

1 For a detailed treatment of the Ceauşescu cult, see my "Idol or Leader? The Origins and Future of the Ceauşescu Cult," in Daniel N. Nelson, ed., *Romania in the 1980's* (Boulder, Colo.: Westview Press, 1981), pp. 117–41. On current issues, see Walter M. Bacon, Jr., "Romania: Neo-Stalinism in Search of Legitimacy," *Current History* 80, no. 465 (April 1981): 168–72, 184–85.

2 Public opinion surveys in Romania on this topic are not possible, and so my assertions about "Romanian" attitudes toward Elena Ceauşescu and her husband can only be impressionistic, based on six research trips from 1973 to 1982.

3 See, for example, the discussion in J. M. Taylor, *Eva Peron: The Myths of a Woman* (Chicago: University of Chicago Press, 1979), especially chapter 1; Elena Ceauşescu might be a puritanical version of the "Woman of the Black

Myth" described there. A closer political parallel, which would not bode well for Elena Ceauşescu's future, is the case of Chiang Ch'ing in China.

4 According to recent historiography, Nicolae Ceauşescu and Elena Ceauşescu met in the late 1930s when both were involved in communist activities. They were married after the war. See Donald Catchlove, *Romania's Ceauşescu* (London: Abacus Press, 1972), pp. 67 and 83, or *Omagiu Tovarăşului Nicolae Ceauşescu* (Bucharest: Editura politică, 1973), p. 24.

5 On June 16, 1970, for example, *Scînteia* reported on a visit to France by "the President of the Council of State, Nicolae Ceauşescu, and his wife, Elena Ceauşescu." That same formulation was used on May 18, 1971, when President Heinemann of the Federal Republic of Germany visited Romania with his wife. On that occasion, even the wife of the president of the Romanian Council of Ministers, Elena Maurer, was included by name along with her husband.

6 *Scînteia*, July 9 and 24, 1971. The August visits were to the seaside, to Tulcea, to a market in Bucharest, and to Harghita; *Scînteia*, August 5, 6, 13, and 16, 1971.

7 *Scînteia*, October 4, 1971.

8 The quotations are from *Scînteia*, January 6, 1979, p. 1; January 7, 1981, p. 1; and March 9, 1982, p. 3.

9 The best summary of Romanian demographic policies in English is Henry R. David and Robert J. McIntyre, *Reproductive Behavior: Central and East European Experience* (New York: Springer, 1981), especially pp. 176–97. For the Romanian view, see Ion Blaga, *Populaţia activă a României* (Bucharest: Editura politică, 1979). Demographic data are from *Anuarul demografic al* RSR, *1974* (Bucharest: Direcţia centrală de statistică, 1974), pp. 132–33. On the labor shortage, see Marvin R. Jackson, "Industrialization, Trade, and Mobilization in Romania's Drive for Economic Independence," in U.S. Congress, Joint Economic Committee, *East European Economies Post-Helsinki* (Washington, D.C.: U.S. Government Printing Office, 1977), pp. 886–940, especially 932–38.

10 See, for example, *Scînteia*, October 1, 1966, p. 5; October 2, 1966, p. 1; February 18, 1967, p. 2.

11 David and McIntyre, pp. 183, 193. See also William Moskoff, "Child Care in Romania: A Comparative Analysis," *East European Quarterly* 15, no. 3 (September 1981): 391–97. Since Moskoff's comparison is with the United States, his conclusions regarding Romania are quite positive.

12 On this last point, see Jackson, p. 932, and Sharon L. Wolchik, "Ideology and Equality: The Status of Women in Eastern and Western Europe," *Comparative Political Studies* 13, no. 4 (January 1981): 445–76, especially table 3 and pp. 452 and 465.

13 The CC plenum was reported in *Scînteia*, June 19–20, 1973. Ceauşescu's speech was printed June 20, pp. 1, 3, and translated in his collected speeches, Nicolae Ceauşescu, *Romania on the Way of Building Up the Multilaterally Developed Socialist Society* (Bucharest: Meridiane, 1973) 8: 601–8. Jackson also notes the failure to raise the birthrate and the potential role of women in alleviating the labor shortage, pp. 932, 936–38. On economic patterns of sex discrimination and the conflict between female recruitment and population growth, see Wil-

liam Moskoff, "Sex Discrimination, Commuting, and the Role of Women in Rumanian Development," *Slavic Review* 37, no. 3 (September 1978): 440–56.

14 Ceauşescu, *Romania on the Way* (Bucharest: Meridiane, 1969), 1: 64.

15 As he stressed to a CC plenum, *Scînteia*, 16 April 1966, p. 1.

16 Ceauşescu, *Romania on the Way* 1: 476–77.

17 Ibid., pp. 478, 477.

18 In 1960 only 17 percent of RCP members were women; by 1974 the share was 25 percent; from November 1979 to December 1980 it remained at 28 percent. By 1982 the figure was still "below 30," although 46 percent of new members in 1981 were women. The data were given at each party congress by the party leader; for 1980 to 1982, see Ceauşescu's speeches in *Scînteia*, March 26, 1981, and April 2, 1982. On the Central Committee, see table 7.1.

19 Ceauşescu, *Romania on the Way* (Bucharest: Meridiane, 1970), 4: 299.

20 See Gail Warshofsky Lapidus, *Women in Soviet Society: Equality, Development, and Social Change* (Berkeley: University of California Press, 1978), p. 179.

21 Ceauşescu, *Romania on the Way* (Bucharest: Meridiane, 1969) 3: 192.

22 Ceauşescu, *Romania on the Way* (Bucharest: Meridiane, 1973) 8: 601–8.

23 See Radio Free Europe Research, *Rumanian Situation Report*/38 (September 27, 1973), pp. 8–9.

24 The 1973 plenum did stimulate a number of books on the issue of women's economic participation. See, for example, Georgheta Dan-Spînoiu, *Factori obiectivi şi subiectivi în integrarea profesională a femeii* (Bucharest: Editura Academiei RSR, 1974); Ana Glubacov, *Afirmarea femeii în viaţa societăţii: Dimensiuni şi semnificaţii în România* (Bucharest: Editura politică, 1975); Aneta Spornic, *Utilizarea eficientă a resurselor de muncă feminine în România* (Bucharest: Editura Academiei RSR, 1975); Ecaterina Deliman, *Femeia personalitate politică în societatea noastră socialistă* (Bucharest: Editura politică, 1977); and Stana Buzatu, *Condiţia femeii, dimensiune a progresului contemporan* (Bucharest: Editura politică, 1979).

25 The comparative literature on women in politics is growing steadily. For analyses focusing on the USSR and Eastern Europe, see Lapidus; Wolchik, "Ideology and Equality"; Wolchik's dissertation, "Politics, Ideology, and Equality: The Status of Women in Eastern Europe" (University of Michigan, Ann Arbor, 1978), and the sources cited. On China, see Elizabeth Croll, *Feminism and Socialism in China* (Boston: Routledge & Kegan Paul, 1978); Margery Wolf and Roxane Witke, eds., *Women in Chinese Society* (Stanford, Calif.: Stanford University Press, 1975); Marilyn B. Young, ed., *Women in China*, Michigan Papers in Chinese Studies, no. 15 (Ann Arbor: Center for Chinese Studies, University of Michigan, 1973). On American women in a comparative context, see Jane S. Jaquette, ed., *Women in Politics* (New York: John Wiley and Sons, 1974). Among the comparative works on women and revolution, see Sheila Rowbotham, *Women, Resistance and Revolution* (New York: Pantheon, 1972); and Carol R. Berkin and Clara M. Lovett, eds., *Women, War, and Revolution* (New York: Holmes & Meier, 1980).

26 The usual method by which a woman exercised political power in Romania had been through a male; see Walter M. Bacon, Jr., "Queens, Concubines, and

Wives: Women in Romanian Politics," a paper presented at the meetings of the American Association for Southeast European Studies, Columbus, Ohio, April 1981.

27 The Executive Committee was renamed the Political Executive Committee in 1974 at the Eleventh Party Congress when the Bureau was created.

28 Lina Ciobanu had been involved in party work in Bucharest in the 1960s, and from 1974 to 1978 she was president of the National Women's Council; this post was added to the Council of Ministers in March 1975, making her the first woman on that body in almost twenty years. From 1975 to 1984 she was Minister of Light Industry and in 1984 served briefly as the first woman since Ana Pauker on the Central Committee Secretariat.

29 The total size of the PEC was twenty-seven full and eighteen candidate members, making the female proportion 19 percent and 22 percent, or exactly 20 percent overall. By mid-1984 there were only twenty-two full and nineteen candidate members and three women in each category: 14 and 16 percent, or just under 15 percent overall.

30 In most political systems, the participation of women is concentrated in symbolic rather than decision-making bodies; see the literature cited in note 25 above.

31 Soviet figures range from a high of 9.7 percent in 1917 (the next highest was 8.3 in 1912 and then 4.5 by 1918) to a low of 2.2 percent in 1934 and 1939. In 1976 the proportion was 3.3 percent. See Lapidus, table 28, p. 219.

32 See the chapter on Czechoslovakia, for example, in Wolchik, "Politics, Ideology, and Equality."

33 Ionaş is evidently Hungarian, so she fills two quotas among the ranks of the county first secretaries: nationality and sex.

34 Wolchik, "Politics, Ideology, and Equality," p. 418.

35 There may actually be a larger number of male local party officials among the full CC members than table 3 reveals. The "unknown" category would be mostly local party officials plus individuals directly involved in production, some of whom would not have appeared in the press as yet. A few of the male "unknowns" could be local party workers.

36 For a discussion of low retention elsewhere in Eastern Europe, see Wolchik, "Politics, Ideology, and Equality," especially pp. 207, 418.

37 Wolchik makes a similar point in "Ideology and Equality," p. 462.

38 See my discussion of the Romanian Central Committee in "The Romanian Communist Party and Its Central Committee," *Southeastern Europe* 6, pt. 1 (1979): 1–28, especially 17–20.

39 Women make up 60.6 percent of the labor force in education, science, and culture; see *Recensămîntul populaţiei şi al locuinţelor din 5 ianuarie 1977*, vol. 2, *Populaţie: structura social-economică* (Bucharest: Directia centrală de statistică, 1980), p. 370.

40 For example, 25.59 percent of the delegates to regional, city, district, and communal People's Councils in 1956 were women (*Scînteia*, March 14, 1956, p. 4), and in 1957 16.9 percent of the deputies to the Grand National Assembly were women.

41 For example, forty-one of forty-five deputies in heavy industry are male; eighteen of twenty-two in light industry are female; fifty-eight of the seventy-seven directors are male; eighteen of nineteen women directors are in light industry or agriculture.

42 For a detailed discussion of the 1975 elections, see my "Participatory Reforms and Political Development in Romania," in Jan F. Triska and Paul M. Cocks, eds., *Political Development in Eastern Europe* (New York: Praeger, 1977), pp. 217–37.

43 The only 1975 race in which a male and female ran against each other involved two directors of collective farms. The woman won.

44 In 1980 nineteen races involved both sexes: nine two-candidate contests of which the males won seven, and ten three-candidate contests in which five victors were male and five female.

45 Ana Pauker had been Minister of Foreign Affairs, and Stela Enescu had served briefly as Minister of Social Services in 1953–54. The only other RCP woman minister had been Constanţa Crăciun, a party member since the 1930s who had spent the war years in Romanian prisons. She became a CC member and president of the Union of Democratic Woman in 1948 and served as Minister of Culture from 1953 to 1957.

46 Suzana Gâdea had been professor of physics and engineering at the Bucharest Polytechnic Institute, and from 1963 to 1974 she was president of the National Women's Council. In August 1979 Gâdea was appointed president of the Council on Socialist Culture and Education and candidate member of the PEC.

47 Aneta Spornic had taught at the Academy of Economic Studies and chaired the Bucharest Women's Committee until 1977. From November 1975 until August 1979 she was Deputy Minister of Labor, and from 1979 to 1982 she served as Minister of Education and Instruction. She held ministerial status on the State Planning Committee from 1982 to 1984 and then became president of the State Committee on Prices.

48 Cornelia Filipaş was a high official of the party youth organization in the early 1950s, then worked in the Ministry of Education, at the State Committee for Culture and Art, and more recently at the Central Council of Trade Unions where she has been secretary since 1976. In 1982 she was suddenly dropped from both the Council of Ministers and the PEC. Gâdea, Spornic, and Filipaş all fit the pattern of female specialization found by Joel C. Moses in the Soviet Union; see his "Indoctrination as a Female Political Role in the Soviet Union," *Comparative Politics* 8, no. 4 (July 1976): 525–47.

49 Ana Mureşan worked in the Ministry of Internal Trade during the 1960s before moving to the trade union council and then to the National Union of Agricultural Production Cooperatives. Since 1978 she has been president of the National Women's Council. From 1978 to 1980 she was vice-president of the Council on Socialist Culture and Education, and since 1980 she has been Minister of Internal Trade.

50 This heightened consciousness was illustrated by the appearance of a selection of statements by Ceauşescu himself on the issue in 1980. Nicolae Ceauşescu, *Creşterea rolului femeii în viaţa economică şi social-politică a României*

socialiste (Bucharest: Editura politică, 1980).

51 See Lapidus, pp. 50–55. For more on the Bolsheviks and the Russian background, see Richard Stites, *The Women's Liberation Movement in Russia: Feminism, Nihilism, and Bolshevism, 1860–1930* (Princeton, N.J.: Princeton University Press, 1978), and Dorothy Atkinson, Alexander Dallin, and Gail Warshofsky Lapidus, eds., *Women in Russia* (Stanford, Calif.: Stanford University Press, 1977).

52 Stites, p. 339.

53 Romania is far behind its socialist neighbors in producing key consumer items like refrigerators or washing machines; see Radio Free Europe, *Romanian Situation Report/8* (April 7, 1978), p. 14.

54 Wolchik, "Politics, Ideology, and Equality," p. 427.

55 In fact, a new pronatalist campaign began in March 1984 when the 1983 birthrate was reported to be 14.3 live births per thousand, as low as 1966 when abortions were still legal. A variety of party and state organs, including the Ministry of Health, were given special responsibilities in "fulfilling the demographic policies and ensuring appropriate population growth." See *Scînteia*, March 3, 6, and 8, 1984.

8 From Courtyard to Cabinet: The Political Emergence of Albanian Women

1 See Gregory J. Massell's study of Moslem women under communism in Central Asia, *The Surrogate Proletariat: Moslem Women and Revolutionary Strategies in Soviet Central Asia, 1918–1929* (Princeton, N.J.: Princeton University Press, 1974).

2 Stavro Skendi, "Crypto-Christianity among the Balkan Peoples under the Ottomans," *Slavic Review* 26, no. 2 (June 1967): 2.

3 Ismail Kadare, *The Wedding* (Tiranë: Naim Frashëri Publishing House, 1968), p. 72.

4 *Problems of the Struggle for the Complete Emancipation of Women* (New York: Gamma Publishing, 1973), p. 14.

5 Ramadan Marmullaku, *Albania and the Albanians* (London: C. Hurst, 1975), pp. 89–91.

6 Peter Prifti, *Socialist Albania since 1944* (Cambridge, Mass., and London: MIT Press, 1978), pp. 93–94.

7 See Z. Xholi's remarks in *Problems of the Struggle*, p. 46.

8 E.g., the idea of "imbecillitas sexus" that passed from Roman law (*Problems of the Struggle*).

9 See F. Gjinali's article in *Problems of the Struggle*, pp. 254–66.

10 An excellent example of this hero-type is found in the epic, "The Song of Bagdad," in Albert B. Lord, ed., *Serbo-Croatian Heroic Epic Songs* (Cambridge, Mass., and Belgrade: Harvard University Press and the Serbian Academy of Sciences, 1954). The singer is Albanian.

11 Prifti, p. 90. See also M. Shutëriqi's comments in *Problems of the Struggle*, pp. 122 ff.

12 The remark is made by one of three sisters whose experiences are treated by

Sulejman Krasniqi in his short novel, *Tri Motra Tri Histori* (Tiranë: Naim Frashëri Publishing House, 1972), p. 76.

13 See remarks made in an interview by Liri Belishova in Dymphna Duxack, *Illyria Reborn* (London: Heinemann, 1966), p. 109.

14 Anton Logoreci, *Europe's Forgotten Survivors* (Boulder, Colo.: Westview Press, 1978), p. 192.

15 In Zog's Albania the illiteracy rate was about 80 percent. In the more remote areas and among women it reached 90 to 95 percent. See *Answers to Questions About Albania* (Tiranë: Naim Frashëri Publishing House, 1969), p. 250. Also, Logoreci, pp. 157 ff.

16 The "traditional patriotism" of the Albanians (which is also taken to mean their antireligious tradition) is even seen as a "moral motive force." Nexhmije Hoxha, *Some Fundamental Questions of the Revolutionary Policy of the* PLA *About the Development of the Class Struggle*, (New York: Gamma Publishing, 1978), p. 35.

17 Logoreci. Reference is made to Professor Arshi Pipa's article, "Panorama of Contemporary Albanian Literature," in *Zeitschrift für Balkanologie* (Munich: Dr. Rudolf Trofenich, 1969/70), vol. 7, nos. 1–2.

18 Kadare, p. 57. For more information on Ismail Kadare and his place in modern Albanian literature, see Arshi Pipa's article mentioned above. See also references to Kadare in Anton Logoreci's study mentioned above, in which he also examines writers and poets, including Arshi Pipa, who have seen the inside of Albania's labor camps, perhaps the darkest side of the country's Stalinist legacy.

19 *The Albanian Woman: A Great Force of the Revolution*, (Tiranë: The "8 Nentori" Publishing House, 1978), p. 18.

20 The phrase appears in the writings of the Rev. Alexander Thomson, the agent of the British and Foreign Bible Society in Constantinople who struggled for thirty years (1865–95) to produce and distribute reading material for the Albanians in their own language.

21 It is difficult even to guess how far efforts of the government have gone to relieve Albanian women of the double burden of working and managing their households, particularly in areas outside the major industrial and agricultural centers.

22 A term ridiculed in the Albanian press in its harsh criticism of the Yugoslav leadership and its handling of the spring 1981 demonstrations in Kosovo.

23 Ibid., p. 46.

24 Ibid.

25 Ibid.

26 *The Eighth Congress of the Women's Union of Albania* (Tiranë: the "8 Nentori" Publishing House, 1978), pp. 51–52.

27 English-language publications, e.g., *New Albania*, occasionally refer by name to women serving, like Thomai, in top administrative posts.

28 Prifti, p. 108.

29 See Radio Free Europe Research reports prepared by Louis Zanga, who periodically provides valuable profiles not only of the "losers" in Albania's politi-

cal upheaval, but also the "winners" who are relatively unknown. The rise and fall of political figures may also be traced to a degree in National Foreign Assignment Center publications, *Directory of Officials of the People's Socialist Republic of Albania* (Washington, D.C.: Library of Congress, 1974, 1977, 1979, 1980). It is apparent, however, that even the few primary sources in Albanian (e.g., *Zëri i Popullit*, to say nothing of statistical yearbooks or journals available to the general public) do not allow for penetrating looks at the system that, on the surface, has indeed moved women into the twentieth century.

30 In Dibër she came into contact with Hekuran Isai, who had been elected to the Central Committee in 1971. In 1975 he was elevated to the party's secretariat and politburo.

31 I do not have information on these women that would enable me to make any useful comparisons with their male counterparts.

9 Women in Local Communist Politics in Romania and Poland

1 Sidney Verba, Norman Nie, Jae-on Kim, *Participation and Political Equality: A Seven Nation Comparison* (New York: Cambridge University Press, 1979), p. 256.

2 Ibid., p. 265.

3 George Cioranescu, "The New Romanian Communist Party Central Committee," Radio Free Europe Research, *Background Report/24* (5 February 1980), p. 10. (See also Fischer in this volume.)

4 Barbara W. Jancar, "Elite Analysis in Applied Research on Women in Communist Society," *Women and Politics* 1, no. 2 (Summer 1980): 51; Sharon L. Wolchik, "Eastern Europe," in Joni Lovenduski and Jill Hills, eds., *The Politics of the Second Electorate: Women and Public Participation* (London: Routledge & Kegan Paul, 1981), pp. 261–62. See Gail W. Lapidus, *Women in Soviet Society* (Berkeley, Calif.: University of California Press, 1978), for a discussion of the Soviet case, and the essays in Lovenduski and Hills for discussions of similar trends in the United States and Western Europe. See Wolchik, and Barbara W. Jancar, *Women under Communism* (Baltimore: Johns Hopkins University Press, 1978), for overviews of women's political roles at the national and local levels in Eastern Europe.

5 The latter, of course, refers to citizen political activity that is autonomous. Mobilization concerns externally organized involvement in which "elements of spontaneity, volition, and autonomy are largely absent." Manipulation is distinguished from mobilization because of the "deception of those politically involved." See Vernon V. Aspaturian, "Political Participation in Eastern Europe: A Conceptual Critique," paper prepared for the Second World Congress of Soviet and East European Studies, September 30–October 4, 1980, Garmisch, FRG.

6 Because most literature in political science tends to use "involvement" with reference to psychological concern for political life, I prefer to substitute the term "activity" for "involvement" in Aspaturian's typology, while retaining his

three-fold distinction. Activity connotes specific behaviors in politics, while involvement suggests one's attitude while performing such activity.

7 See, for example, "Subnational Political Elites in a Communist System," *East European Quarterly* 10, no. 4, (December 1976): 459–94; "Issues in Local Communist Politics," *Western Political Quarterly* 30, no. 3, (September 1977): 348–96; "Background Characteristics of Local Communist Elites," *Polity* 3, (Spring 1978): 398–415; and "Subnational Policy in Poland: The Dilemma of Vertical vs. Horizontal Integration," in Roger Kanet and Maurice Simon, eds., *Background to Crisis: Policy and Politics in Gierek's Poland* (Boulder, Colo.: Westview Press, 1980), pp. 65–93.

8 The sample was biased toward urban-based deputies, which, in turn, raised the educational level and skewed the occupational distribution of the sample. These are discussed with weighting procedures to "correct" for sampling biases in Daniel N. Nelson, *Democratic Centralism in Romania* (Boulder, Colo.: East European Monographs, 1980), appendix C.

9 These data and other statistics cited in this paragraph are from Jacek Tarkowski and Krzysztof Zagorski, *Radni i Członkowie Prezydiow Rad Narodowych 1958–1969* (Warsaw: Głowny Urzad Statystyczny, 1972), p. 23.

10 Oral communication, January 1977, in Rataje Osiedle.

11 From data provided to the author by Judeţul Timiş authorities, July 1978.

12 Data provided to the author by Judeţul Cluj authorities, 1973 and 1978.

13 The Romanian samples are used here since the *N* is larger and more internationally comparative.

14 Marcia M. Lee, "Toward Understanding Why Women Hold Public Office: Factors Affecting Participation of Women in Local Politics," in Marianne Githens and Jewel L. Prestage, eds., *A Portrait of Marginality* (New York: Mackay, 1977), p. 126.

15 Krzystof Jasiewicz, *Rołe Społeczne Radnych Wojewodzkich Rad Narodowych* (Wrocław: Zadład Narodowy im. Ossolinskich, 1979), p. 63.

16 Ibid., pp. 63–64.

17 Ibid., p. 67, indicates male/female distribution within the sample. Research was conducted in cities with *powiat* status, which after the 1969 elections had from 20.9 to 25.5 percent female membership in people's councils, as compared to the sample's 26 percent.

18 Nelson, *Democratic Centralism*, p. 98.

19 Ibid., p. 99.

20 Regarding such an expectation and women's political roles in other systems, see the essays in Lovenduski and Hills.

21 Githens notes that in the U.S. case, women's "prior occupations limit them in their activities in the legislature once they get there and force them into somewhat dysfunctional role orientations and styles." See her "Spectators, Agitators, or Lawmakers," in Githens and Prestage, p. 208. See Wolchik in Lovenduski and Hills, pp. 252–77, and Fischer in this volume for similar trends in Eastern Europe at the national level.

22 Comparative evidence of such limitations can be found in Lovenduski and Hills.

23 The forty-two elite interviews are examined in Nelson, "Background Characteristics."

24 This is a mean based upon data provided to the author in 1978 interviews in Timiş, Cluj, Brasov, Iaşi, Constanţa, and Bucharest.

25 This is a common pattern in many political systems. See the studies in Lovenduski and Hills. See Sandra Baxter and Marjorie Lansing, *Women and Politics: The Invisible Majority* (Ann Arbor: University of Michigan Press, 1981), for the West European and U.S. cases.

26 Deputies to people's councils were asked "What function do you fulfill in the people's council system?" Several alternatives were suggested: (*a*) president, vice-president, or secretary of a standing commission, (*b*) member of the executive committee, (*c*) president, vice-president, or secretary of the executive committee, (*d*) functionary in the apparatus of the people's council, (*e*) employee in one of the units subordinate to the people's council, (*f*) other. The same question was used in 1973 and 1978 in Romania. See Nelson, *Democratic Centralism*, appendix B, p. 153. Once they responded by indicating a role, I would then follow up by seeking specific arenas of responsibility (e.g., what kind of functions? what specialization does the committee have?). This question was less systematically applied in the Polish sample during my 1977 research, although I determined with reasonable certainty their formal role as well as arena of responsibility.

27 I am extrapolating from data provided to the author by Judeţul Timiş authorities, 1973, and interviews conducted in both 1973 and 1978.

28 These socioeconomic conditions are discussed in a comparative perspective in Daniel N. Nelson, "Inequality of Regional Development in Romania," paper presented at the Eastern Economic Association Annual Meeting, Montreal, May 1980.

29 Oral communication, August 1978.

30 These characterizations are based on data reported in Gheorgheta Dan-Spinoi *Factori Objiectivi şi Subjectivi în integrarea Profesionala a Femeii* (Bucharest: Editura Academiei, 1974). Another study, which suggests limitations on female participation in Yugoslavia, is Milan Mesić, "Političko kultura samoupravijanja zagregackih radnica," *Žena* 2 (1978): 47–61.

31 The conflict of values between those ascribed to women and those of political activism has been researched in depth in the American context. See, for example, Judith M. Bardwick and Elizabeth Douvan, "Ambivalence: The Socialization of Women," in Vivian Gornick and Barbara Moran, eds., *Women in Sexist Society* (New York: Basic Books, 1971), and Ralph H. Turner, "Some Aspects of Women's Ambitions," *American Journal of Sociology* 70, no. 3, (November 1964): 270–85. The limitations imposed on women's political activity because of children are considered, for the U.S. case, by Cornelia B. Flora and Naomi B. Lynn, "Women and Political Socialization: Considerations of the Impact of Motherhood," in Jane S. Jacquette, ed., *Women in Politics* (New York: John Wiley and Sons, 1974), pp. 37–53. One must add that men, too, regard the familial roles of women as primary, thereby adding an expectation and socialization "pressure" toward deference to them in political life.

32 See, for example, Jerry Hough's summaries of conversations with women in the scholarly community in *The Soviet Union and Social Science Theory* (Cambridge, Mass.: Harvard University Press, 1977), pp. 150–51, indicating rather (in my judgment) traditional views of women's roles.

33 Lee, p. 132.

34 These results for Romania, without distinguishing responses by gender, are found in Nelson, "Issues in Local Communist Politics." These findings parallel those discussed by Hough, pp. 143–46, in which Soviet women deputies spoke most at sessions on topics concerning health, culture, education, and public services.

35 Alex Inkeles and H. K. Geiger, "Critical Letters to the Soviet Press," in Inkeles, ed., *Social Change in Soviet Russia* (Cambridge: Cambridge University Press, 1968), p. 309. Their findings were based on research undertaken in the early 1950s.

36 Jan Adams, "Critical Letters to the Soviet Press: An Increasingly Important Public Forum," in Donald E. Schulz and Jan S. Adams, eds., *Political Participation in Communist Systems* (Elmsford, N.Y.: Pergamon Press, 1981), p. 124. See also Hough, p. 151.

37 Numerous studies in Eastern Europe indicate that women have much less leisure time than men. See Heitlinger, *Women and State Socialism*, pp. 86–96 and 144–46; Jancar, *Women Under Communism*; and Wolchik, "Status of Women," pp. 596–97, for summaries of several of these studies and discussions of their implications for women's political roles. See Lapidus, *Women in Soviet Society*, pp. 280–84, for the Soviet case.

38 A few of these studies include Marjorie Lansing, "The American Woman: Voter and Activist," in Jacquette, pp. 5–24; Naomi B. Lynn and Cornelia Butler Flora, "Motherhood and Political Participation," *Journal of Political and Military Sociology* 1, no. 1, (March 1973); Veronica Heiskanan, "Sex Roles, Social Class, and Political Consciousness," *Acta Sociologica* 14, nos. 1–2, (1971): 83–95; Bardwick and Douvan; Anthony Orum, Roberta Cohen, Sherri Grasmuck, and Amy W. Orum, "Sex, Socialization, and Politics," *American Sociological Review* 39, no. 2 (April 1974): 197–209; and Lee, pp. 118–38.

10 Women in the Opposition in Poland and Czechoslovakia in the 1970s

1 The literature on opposition movements in Eastern Europe has expanded rapidly in recent years. Among those works that should be mentioned are Jiří Pelikán, *Socialist Opposition in Eastern Europe* (New York: St. Martin's Press, 1976); Vladimir Kusin, *From Dubcek to Charter 77* (New York: St. Martin's Press, 1978); Rudolf Tökés's well-edited book, *Opposition in Eastern Europe* (Baltimore: Johns Hopkins University Press, 1979); H. Gordon Skilling, *Charter 77 and Human Rights in Czechoslovakia* (London and Boston: Allen and Unwin, 1981); and A. Ostoja-Ostaszewski et al., eds., *Dissent in Poland: Reports and Documents, December 1975–July 1977* (London: Association of Polish Students and Graduates in Exile, 1977).

2 See the above sources for discussions of dissent elsewhere in the region.
3 Radio Free Europe Research, *Background Report/221 Poland* (August 3, 1981), p. 207; and telephone interview with Tadeus Walendowski, United States–Polish Helsinki Watch Representative, Washington, D.C.
4 Radio Free Europe Research, *Background Report/284* (October 6, 1981), mimeographed, pp. 7–10.
5 See author's discussion of job formalization in Barbara W. Jancar, *Women under Communism* (Baltimore: Johns Hopkins University Press, 1978), pp. 17–18 and 33.
6 *Poland: A Chronology of Events, July–November 1980*, Radio Free Europe Research, RAD *Background Report/91 Poland* (March 31, 1981), p. 37.
7 Charter 77, Document No. 5.
8 Radio Free Europe Research, *Czechoslovak Situation Report/35* (October 5, 1977), p. 4, and *Czechoslovak Situation Report/37* (November 17, 1978), p. 6.
9 Radio Free Europe Research, *Czechoslovak Situation Report/11* (May 7, 1980), p. 2.
10 *Newsletter in the Defense of Human Rights in the Soviet Union and Eastern Europe* 5, no. 21 (March 1981), p. 34; Radio Free Europe Research, *Czechoslovak Situation Report* (August 19, 1984).
11 See letter to Zuzana Dienstbierová, March 18, 1977, from Dr. Beihilf, cadres and personnel manager, Prague Building Enterprise, as translated in *White Paper on Czechoslovakia* (Paris: International Committee for the Support of Charter 77 in Czechoslovakia, 1977), p. 102.
12 Charter 77, Document No. 6, and letter of Peter Uhl to Judr Jaromír Prokop, Senior Prosecutor, February 8, 1977, *White Paper*, pp. 65 and 234–35.
13 *Newsletter in Defense of Human Rights* 5, no. 21 (March 1982): J1 and 4, nos. 18–19 (September 1981): A5.
14 As reported by Reuters (Vienna), March 8, 1982. See also the report in Radio Free Europe Research, 7, no. 14 (April 9, 1982): 10–11, mimeographed.
15 Discussion and interpretation derived from Radio Free Europe Research, RAD *Background Report/251* (September 3, 1981).
16 For a short account in English of the strike, see Rupnik, "Dissent in Poland," p. 73, and Jancar, p. 170.
17 *The New York Times*, October 26, 1981.
18 *Poland: A Chronology of Events, July–November 1980*, p. 20.
19 See the open letter of Josefa Slánská to Dr. G. Husák, Prague, January 17, 1977, photocopy of typewritten version, for an example of these.
20 Hana Ponická, speech to the Third Congress of the Slovak Writers' Union, March 2, 1977, as published in *Le Monde*, May 14, 1977. Ms. Ponická was not allowed to attend the congress, having been expelled from the Writers' Union. As a result, her speech was never delivered but made its way to the West. "500 proti realité," *Svědectví* (Testimony) 14, no. 53: 4.
21 Vlasta Chramostová, Letter to Western Intellectuals, March 1, 1977, as translated in *White Paper*, p. 170.
22 Marta Kubišová, letter to Young Pop Singers, *White Paper*, p. 180.
23 See the *White Paper* and Ostoja-Ostaszewski et al. for documents and state-

ments written by male spokespersons.

24 Charter 77, Document No. 7, *White Paper*, pp. 88–89.

25 *Poland: A Chronology of Events July–November 1980*, appendix I, p. 11.

26 Ibid., appendix II, p. v.

27 See Siemieńska's essay in this volume for Polish male attitudes toward women's roles.

28 *Poland: A Chronology of Events, July–November 1980*, pp. 53 and 55.

29 *Poland: A Chronology of Events, November 1980–February 1981*, Radio Free Europe Research, RAD *Background Report/263 (Poland*, September 11, 1981), p. 75.

30 *The New York Times*, October 26, 1981.

31 Helena Klímová, "Právo na osud druhého" (The Right over Another's Fate), *Svědectví* 15, no. 58 (1979): 271–73.

32 Eva Kantůrková, *Douze femmes à Prague* (Twelve Women in Prague), trans. from the Czech by Catherine Fournier (Paris: François Maspero, 1981). It is worth noting the publication in 1984 of a book on women in dissent in the Soviet Union edited by Tatyana Mamonova. *Women and Russia* follows the same interview format of Kantůrková's study, and indeed the style is so similar that it begs some prior knowledge by Mamonova of the Czech work. However, the content of *Women and Russia* is much more oriented toward Western feminist concerns, treating directly of Soviet women's perceptions of women's status in the USSR. Mamonova now resides in the West. Tatyana Mamonova, ed., *Women and Russia: Feminist Writings from the Soviet Union*, trans. by Rebecca Park and Catherine A. Fitzpatrick (Boston: Beacon Press, 1984).

33 Kantůrková, p. 227.

34 Ibid.

35 Ibid., p. 188.

36 Ibid., pp. 208–9.

37 See Hilda Scott, *Does Socialism Liberate Women?* (Boston: Beacon Press, 1974); Jancar, *Women under Communism*, chapter 5; Sharon L. Wolchik, "Elite Strategies toward Women in Czechoslovakia: Liberation or Mobilization?" *Studies in Comparative Communism* 19, nos. 2 and 3 (Summer/Autumn 1981): 123–42, for discussions of the activities of the official women's organizations in Czechoslovakia and elsewhere in Eastern Europe.

38 Many Western feminists also argue that women's liberation is only possible in the context of changes in the larger society that would liberate men as well. The difference lies in the fact that for East European women in opposition, fundamental change in the larger system appears to be seen as an end in itself, rather than as a necessary step toward eventual improvement in women's situation.

39 *Newsletter*, p. A5.

40 For Charter 77 positions on events in Poland since 1980, see Martin Hybler and Jiří Němec, "In Search of an Answer" (n.d., 1980), in Skilling, *Charter* 77, pp. 324–27; and "The Position of Charter 77 in the Polish Crisis," signed by the three spokesperson signatories in Prague on January 7, 1982, as published in *Listy* 12, no. 1 (February 1982): 10.

41 Ružena Vintrová, Jan Klacek, Václav Kupka, "Ekonomický růst v ČSSR, jeho bariery a efektivnost" (Economic Growth in the CSSR, Its Barriers and Efficiency), *Politická ekonomie*, no. 1, (1980) p. 38. The leadership has taken cognizance of the problem in its recent cautious decision to stop subsidizing production units that operate at a loss except under exceptional conditions and to give more autonomy and responsibility to the enterprises. (Radio Hvezda, October 22, 1984 and Radio Budapest, October 29, 1984.)

42 Charter 77, Document No. 4, *White Book*, pp. 129–35, and letter of Helena Trojánová to UNESCO, *White Book*, pp. 135–40.

43 Letter of Vera Chytilová to Dr. Husák, October 8, 1975, *White Book*, pp. 177, 179.

44 For a discussion of the relation of Charter 77 to the national issue in Czechoslovakia, see Skilling, pp. 191–93. The national issue in Poland is well validated by the restoration of former national holidays during 1981. For discussion of the mobilization of women to the national cause, see Barbara W. Jancar, "Women in the National Liberation Movement in Yugoslavia," *Studies in Comparative Communism* 14, nos. 2 and 3 (Summer/Autumn 1981): 143–64.

45 See my discussion of female self-image in Jancar, *Women under Communism*, pp. 179–205.

46 Václav Havel, "Letter to Gustav Husák, General Secretary of the Czechoslovak Communist Party," *Survey* (London) 21, no. 3 (Summer 1975): 173.

47 See my discussion of these aspects of women's situation in Jancar, *Women under Communism*, chapter 2.

IV Women and Work: Production and Reproduction

Introduction

1 See the essays in Rachel Kahn-Hut, Arlene Kaplan Daniels, and Richard Colvard, eds., *Women and Work: Problems and Perspectives* (New York: Oxford University Press, 1982); Martha Blaxall and Barbara Reagan, eds., *Women and the Workplace: The Implications of Occupational Segregation* (Chicago: University of Chicago Press, 1976); Donald Treiman and Heidi Hartmann, eds., *Women, Work, and Wages* (Washington, D.C.: National Academy Press, 1981); and United Nations, *The Economic Roles of Women in the ECE Region* (New York: United Nations, 1980), for recent discussions of these issues in the United States and Western Europe.

2 Women's work roles have received a good deal of attention from scholars in Eastern Europe since the 1960s; they also have been examined by several Western scholars, including Jancar, *Women under Communism*, especially chapter 4; Heitlinger, *Women and State Socialism*, chapters 10 and 15; Scott, *Does Socialism Liberate Women?* chapter 6; and Wolchik, "Politics, Ideology, and Equality," chapter 3. See Lapidus, *Women in Soviet Society*, chapter 5; Atkinson, Dallin, and Lapidus, eds., *Women in Russia*, part 2; Gail Warshofsky Lapidus, ed., *Women, Work, and Family in the Soviet Union* (Armonk, N.Y., and London: M. E. Sharpe, 1982); Alistair McAuley, *Women's Work and Wages in the Soviet Union* (London: Allen and Unwin, 1981); and Michael Paul Sacks, *Women's*

Work in Soviet Russia (New York: Praeger, 1976), for discussions of women's economic roles in the Soviet Union.

3 The relationship between women's work and family roles, the impact of the "double burden," and the importance and ramifications of the sexual division of labor within the home have remained central themes in analyses of women's roles in the United States and Western Europe. See Joseph H. Pleck, "The Work-Family Role System," pp. 101–22; Janet G. Hunt and Larry L. Hunt, "Dilemmas and Contradictions of Status: The Case of the Dual-Career Family," pp. 181–91; and other essays in Kahn-Hut, Daniels, and Colvard; Karen Wolk Feinstein, ed., *Working Women and Families*, vol. 4, Sage Yearbooks in Women's Policy Studies (Beverly Hills, Calif.: Sage Publications, 1979); Michael Geerken and Walter R. Gove, *At Home and at Work: The Family's Allocation of Labor* (Beverly Hills, Calif.: Sage Publications, 1983); and Heidi Hartmann, "The Family as the Locus of Gender, Class, and Political Struggle: The Example of Housework," *Signs* 8 (Spring 1981): 366–94, for discussions of these issues. See Feinstein, *Working Women and Families*; Irene Diamond, ed., *Families, Politics, and Public Policy: A Feminist Dialogue on Women and the State* (New York: Longman, 1983); and Carolyn Teich Adams and Kathryn Teich Winston, *Mothers at Work: Public Policies in the United States, Sweden, and China* (New York: Longman, 1980), for examples of the literature on public policies in regard to women in the West. The contradictions that exist between the demands of the work and home worlds are posed particularly sharply in Eastern Europe, given the high employment levels of women. See Lapidus, *Women in Soviet Society*, and H. Kent Geiger, *The Family in Soviet Society* (Cambridge, Mass.: Harvard University Press, 1968), for discussions of men's and women's roles in the family in the Soviet Union.

4 See Lapidus, *Women in Soviet Society*, chapters 3, 4, and 8, for a discussion of this tendency in the Soviet Union; see Heitlinger, *Women and State Socialism*, chapter 17; Jancar, *Women under Communism*, chapter 6; and Wolchik, "Politics, Ideology, and Equality," chapters 6 and 7, for earlier discussions of the East European case.

5 Gail Warshofsky Lapidus, "Sexual Equality in Soviet Policy: A Developmental Approach," in Dorothy Atkinson, Alexander Dallin, and Gail Warshofsky Lapidus, eds., *Women in Russia* (Stanford, Calif.: Stanford University Press, 1974), pp. 115–38.

6 See Lapidus, *Women in Soviet Society*; Geiger; and Gregory Massell, *The Surrogate Proletariat: Moslem Women and Revolutionary Strategies in Soviet Central Asia, 1918–1929* (Princeton, N.J.: Princeton University Press, 1974), for Soviet experiments in this regard.

7 As in, for example, the essays in Barrie Thorne and Marilyn Yalom, eds., *Rethinking the Family: Some Feminist Questions* (New York: Longman, 1982); Betty Friedan, *The Second Stage* (New York: Summit Books, 1981); and the contributions to Jean Bethke Elshtain, ed., *The Family in Political Thought* (Amherst: University of Massachusetts Press, 1982).

11 The Socioeconomic Conditions of Women in Hungary

1 Zsuzsa Kovács-Orolin, *A falusi nök helyzete* (The Conditions of Women in the Country) (Budapest: Kossuth Kiadó, 1970).

12 Theory and Reality: The Status of Employed Women in Yugoslavia

1 Vida Tomšič, *Women in the Development of Socialist Self-Managing Yugoslavia* (Belgrade: Jugoslavenski pregled, 1980), p. 63.
2 Ibid.
3 *Mesecni statisticni pregled* SR *Slovenije* (Ljubljana: Zavod SRS za statistiko), vol. 30, no. 2 (1981), p. 54.
4 Ibid., p. 49.
5 *Statisticni letopis* SRS (Ljubljana: Zavod SRS za statistiko, 1979), p. 114.
6 *Statisticni letopis* SRS (Ljubljana: Zavod SRS za statistiko, 1981), p. 59.
7 *Mesecni statisticni pregled* SR *Slovenije*, (Ljubljana: Zavod SRS za statistiko), vol. 30, no. 1 (1981), p. 61.
8 Stipe Suvar, "Promjene u strukturi rada—osnove promjena u obrazovanju žena," *Žena* 36, no. 1 (1978): 50–52.
9 Vida Tomšič, *Ženska, delo, družina, družba* (Ljubljana: Komunist, 1976), p. 148.
10 Stipe Suvar, "Društveni položaj i uloga žene u razvoju socijalističkog samoupravljanja," *Žena* 38, nos. 4–5 (1980): 13–23.
11 Slaven Letica, "Prioriteti u strategiji razvoja—ekonomsko, socijalno i politicko pitanje," *Žena* 36, no. 1 (1978): 18–23.
12 Katarina Prpić, "Negativna selekcija u zapošljavanju žena u SR Hrvatskoj," *Žena* 35, no. 2 (1977): 19–28.
13 "Zakljucci Predsjedništva Centralnog komiteta Saveza komunista Jugoslavije o zadacima Saveza komunista na daljnjem poboljšavanju društvenog položaja i uloge žene danas," *Žena* 38, nos. 4–5 (1980): 30.
14 Tomšič, *Ženska, delo, družina, družba*, p. 148.
15 Letica, p. 20.
16 Prpić, p. 19.
17 Silva Mežnarić, "Social Changes and Intergenerational Mobility of Women in Yugoslavia," in English in Institut za sociologijo Univerze v Ljubljani, *Some Yugoslav Papers Presented to the* 8th ISA *Congress, Toronto* (Univerza Ljubljana, August 1974), pp. 276–325.
18 Donald Treiman and Heidi Hartmann, eds., *Women, Work, and Wages: Equal Pay for Jobs of Equal Value* (Washington, D.C.: National Academy Press, 1981), p. 16.
19 Vesna Pusić, "Žena i zaposlenost," *Sociologija* 23, nos. 3–4 (1981): 338.
20 Zavod SRS za planiranje and Zavod SRS za statistiko, *Družbeni razvoj* SR *Slovenije* (Ljubljana: Komunist, 1974), p. 158.
21 Letica, p. 18.

13 Blue-Collar Working Women and Poverty in Hungary

1 Ivan Volgyes and Nancy Volgyes, *The Liberated Female* (Boulder, Colo.: Westview Press, 1977). The data in this chapter are taken from statistical sources published in Hungary, interviews conducted in Hungary during the period 1974–81, and a major research project of the Cooperative Research Institute undertaken in 1977–78. Support for my research has been given by the International Research and Exchanges Board and the Fulbright-Hays Grant program; the Cooperative Research Institute's findings have been made available to me by Dr. Antal Gyenes, the Director of the Institute, and Dr. Pal Juhasz, the principal investigator of the project.

2 *Statisztikai Évkönyv, 1979* (Budapest: Statisztikai kiado, 1979), pp. 6, 126 (hereinafter *Évkönyv*).

3 See Donald Treiman and Heidi Hartmann, eds., *Women, Work, and Wages* (Washington, D.C.: National Academy Press, 1981), for a recent discussion of these trends in the United States. See Michael P. Sacks, *Women's Work in Soviet Russia* (New York: Praeger, 1976); Alistair McAuley, *Women's Work and Wages in the Soviet Union* (London: Allen and Unwin, 1981); Gail W. Lapidus, *Women in Soviet Society* (Berkeley: University of California Press, 1978); Barbara W. Jancar, *Women under Communism* (Baltimore: Johns Hopkins University Press, 1978); Alena Heitlinger, *Women and State Socialism* (London and Toronto: Macmillan and McGill-Queen's University Press, 1979) and Volgyes and Volgyes for earlier discussions of Soviet and East European trends in this regard.

4 *Népszabadság*, August 10, 1979.

5 *Müszaki Élet*, April 14, 1960. The tendency for occupations in which women predominate to have lower salaries and less social prestige is found in the United States and many West European countries as well, even though the particular occupations in which women predominate differ.

6 *Népszabadság*, March 13, 1965.

7 *Népszabadság*, April 6, 1971.

8 Ibid.

9 István Monigl and János Timár, "A nök iskolázása, szakképzése és pályaválasztása," *Tanulmányok a nök helyzetéröl* (Budapest: Kossuth, 1972), p. 57.

10 Márta Tömöry, "As egyenlöség ára," *Élet és Irodalom*, May 13, 1972, p. 57.

11 József Rózsa, *Szociálpolitika Magyarországon* (Budapest: Kossuth, 1978).

12 Volgyes and Volgyes, pp. 46–48, discuss this problem in considerable detail.

13 Because of the limited scope of this chapter, I have ignored the income earned from the second economy, which, while very important in Hungary, should be dealt with separately.

14 "A Szegényeket Támogató Alap," *Irodalmi Ujság*, January–February 1981, p. 1.

15 István Kemény, "Miért vált idöszerüvé a szegénység problémája Magyarországon?" *Irodalmi Ujság*, March–April 1981, p. 4.

16 *Statisztikai Évkönyv, 1977* (Budapest: Központi Statisztikai Hivatal, 1977), pp. 341, 369.

17 Hungarian sources, as late as 1980, however, still regard the 1,600 forints per capita figure as acceptable for defining the poverty line, in spite of an officially admitted 21.3 percent inflation between 1977 and 1980. It is the 1,600 forints figure that is used in the seminal study of Zsuzsa Ferge, "A gyermekes családok jövedelmi helyzete," *Valóság* 8 (1980): 57–67.

18 *Statisztikai Évkönyv, 1980*, pp. 341, 386.

19 "A Szegényeket Támogató Alap," p. 1.

20 Kemény, p. 4.

21 Ferge, p. 59.

22 The "young mothers' leave," or *gyes* as it is popularly referred to, is described in detail in Volgyes and Volgyes, pp. 153–60.

23 *Statisztikai Évkönyv, 1979*, p. 386.

24 Ferge, p. 66.

25 Katalin Sulyok, *Egy ország gyesen* (Budapest: Kozmosz, 1979).

26 Julia Turgonyi and Zsuzsa Ferge, *Az ipari munkásnök munka és életkörülményei* (Budapest: Kossuth, 1969), p. 31. See Judit H. Sas, *Életmód és család* (Budapest: Akadémia Kiadó, 1976) and *Azópari munkások munka és életkörülményei* (Budapest: Közgazdasági és Jogi Könyvkiado, 1967).

14 The Rights of Women: Ideology, Policy, and Social Change in Yugoslavia

This chapter is taken from a larger manuscript, "Family and the State: A Perspective on Changing Sex Role Conceptions in Yugoslavia," that benefited greatly from the careful attention of Drude Dahlerup, David Powell, Jean Quataert, and Hilda Scott. I would like to thank them here and especially to thank Gail Kligman for midnight assistance and for sharing a title, my father-in-law for illumination on the finer details of sex and gender, and Steven J. Rosenstone for cheerful editorial labor.

1 On the Chetnik bias against women, in contrast to the Partisans, see Jozo Tomasevich, *War and Revolution in Yugoslavia, 1941–1945: The Chetniks* (Stanford, Calif.: Stanford University Press, 1975), pp. 188–89.

2 Friedrich Engels, *The Origin of the Family, Private Property, and the State* (1884) (New York: International, 1942). For a Yugoslav version of Engels's argument, see Vida Tomšič, *Women in the Development of Socialist Self-Managing Yugoslavia* (Belgrade: Jugoslovenska Stvarnost, 1980).

3 This argument can be found in Svetozar Marković's version in Jovan Djordjević, ed., *Žensko Pitanje: Antologija Marksističkih Tekstova* (Belgrade: Radnička Štampa, 1975), pp. 186–88.

4 According to Tomasevich, "the Partisan fighting ranks numbered between 15 and 20 percent women." Tomasevich, p. 188. One of those women, a member of the party from the interwar years, later wrote of their contribution thus: "More than two million working women, peasants, housewives, students, and intellectuals took part in the great struggle to achieve the independence of the people and a new social order in which they would also enjoy equality. They

bore arms in military units, helped carry out subversive activities [and] acts of sabotage in the cities, performed clandestine political activities in the occupied territories, served as couriers and gathered intelligence, and collected and concealed weapons and medical supplies. Their homes became meeting places, hospitals and workshops; women also served in military units or partisan hospitals as nurses, ministering to the wounded, cared for the children of fighting men or of victims of the fascist terror, and provided clothing and food for the liberation army. Under the most adverse conditions, women cultivated the fields and kept the harvest from the hands of the enemy" (Tomšič, p. 25).

5 Zsuzsa Ferge, *A Society in the Making: Hungarian Social and Societal Policy 1945–75* (White Plains, N.Y.: M. E. Sharpe, 1980), pp. 61–64.

6 See Jane F. Collier and Michelle Z. Rosaldo, "Politics and Gender in Simple Societies," in Sherry B. Ortner and Harriet Whitehead, eds., *Sexual Meanings: the Cultural Construction of Gender and Sexuality* (Cambridge: Cambridge University Press, 1981), pp. 276–81. This article was unusually helpful in clarifying my own thinking on these matters.

7 In contrast to brideservice societies, Collier and Rosaldo (p. 279) write, "Bridewealth peoples . . . tend in their rituals and cosmology to display a preoccupation with female reproductive capacities; women are valued as mothers, but feared for their polluting blood. Characteristically, men in their rituals stress the rejection of feminine qualities; femininity is threatening to maleness, and male adulthood requires rejection of childhood ties to a feminine world." The research by Olga Supek on Carnival in Croatia, where the main theme is always sex role reversal, provides a Yugoslav example. See, for example, Olga Supek, "The Meaning of Carnival in Croatia," *Anthropological Quarterly* 56, no. 2 (April 1983): 90–94.

8 This variation is best demonstrated by Vera St. Erlich, *Family in Transition: A Study of 300 Yugoslav Villages* (Princeton, N.J.: Princeton University Press, 1966). Sources of information on changes in the Yugoslav family include: Jozo Tomasevich, *Peasants, Politics, and Economic Change in Yugoslavia* (Stanford, Calif.: Stanford University Press, 1955); L. S. Stavrianos, *The Balkans Since 1453* (New York: Holt, Rinehart, and Winston, 1958); Perry Anderson, *Passages from Antiquity to Feudalism* (London: Verso, 1974); Perry Anderson, *Lineages of the Absolutist State* (London: Verso, 1974); Wayne Vucinich, "The Nature of Balkan Society under Ottoman Rule," *Slavic Review* 21, no. 4 (December 1962): 597–616; Traian Stoianovich, "Factors in the Decline of Ottoman Society in the Balkans," *Slavic Review* 21, no. 4 (December 1962): 623–32; Robert F. Byrnes, ed., *Communal Families in the Balkans: The Zadruga, Essays by Philip E. Mosely and Essays in His Honor* (Notre Dame, Ind.: University of Notre Dame Press, 1976); Eugene A. Hammel, *Alternative Social Structures and Ritual Relations in the Balkans* (Engelwood Cliffs, N.J.: Prentice-Hall, 1968); Lorraine Barić, "Levels of Change in Yugoslav Kinship," in Maurice Freedman, ed., *Social Organizations: Essays Presented to Raymond Firth* (London: Cass, 1967), pp. 1–24; Lorraine Barić, "Traditional Groups and New Economic Opportunities in Rural Yugoslavia," in Raymond Firth, ed., *Themes in Economic Anthropology* (London: Tavistock, 1967), pp. 253–78; Robert Donia,

"East European Moslems: Community Organization and Mobilization in Bosnia, 1878–1914," (unpublished manuscript, 1977), and E. A. Hammel, "Economic Change, Social Mobility, and Kinship in Serbia," *Southwestern Journal of Anthropology* 25, no. 2 (Summer 1969): 188–197.

9 Several examples from the extensive literature on honor and shame in the culture of the Mediterranean are J. Davis, *People of the Mediterranean: An Essay in Comparative Social Anthropology* (London: Routledge & Kegan Paul, 1977); Julian Pitt-Rivers, *The Fate of Shechem, or the Politics of Sex: Essays in the Anthropology of the Mediterranean* (Cambridge: Cambridge University Press, 1977); Jane Schneider, "Of Vigilance and Virgins," *Ethnology* 10 (January 1971): 1–24; J. G. Peristiany, *Honour and Shame: the Values of Mediterranean Society* (London: Widenfeld and Nicolson, 1965); and J. G. Peristiany, ed., *Mediterranean Family Structures* (Cambridge: Cambridge University Press, 1976).

10 The word used, *gospodariti*, means to govern on the basis of land ownership, but it often took on the meaning "to boss" because of the sense that rightful authority was being usurped. On this common consequence of the patriarchal paradox, see also the chapter by Gail Kligman in this volume. This is one of several similarities with the Romanian case and why my title intentionally draws the parallel between these two chapters. On the extension of this conflict to communities, also when legal changes stimulate strategies to increase membership and internal cohesion as preconditions of increased power, see Donia's discussion of the ethnic conflict in Bosnia-Herzegovina after its annexation by Austria in 1878.

11 On the agricultural labor of "housewives" in the interwar period, see Tomasevich, *Peasants, Politics, and Economic Change in Yugoslavia*, pp. 453–54.

12 Darinka Kostić-Marojević, *Promena društvene sredine i promene u porodici* [Change in Social Environment and Changes in the Family] (Belgrade: Institut Društvenih Nauka, 1968).

13 Law on Relations Between Parents and Children, Article 32; see A. G. Chloros, *Yugoslav Civil Law: History, Family, Property* (Oxford: Clarendon Press, 1970), p. 237.

14 Kostić-Marojević.

15 Chloros, p. 50.

16 Divorce cases, according to judicial decisions rendered in the Vojvodina in the first decade, continued to be governed by prewar legislation, ignoring the new rights of women. Ibid.

17 Mara Naljeva, "Neka Pitanja Partiskog Rada Medju Ženama," [Some Questions about Party Work among Women] *Partiska Izgradnja* 2, no. 1 (January 1950).

18 Ruth Trouton, *Peasant Renaissance in Yugoslavia* (London: Routledge & Kegan Paul, 1952), pp. 110–11.

19 Bette Denich, "Sex and Power in the Balkans," in Michelle Zimbalist Rosaldo and Louise Lamphere, eds., *Woman, Culture, and Society* (Stanford, Calif.: Stanford University Press, 1974), pp. 243–62; Bette Denich, "Women, Work, and Power in Modern Yugoslavia," in Alice Schlegel, ed., *Sexual Stratification: A*

Cross-Cultural View (New York: Columbia University Press, 1977), p. 225; Zagorka Golubović, personal communication; see also Zagorka Golubović, *Porodica Kao Ljudska Zajednica: Alternativa Autoritarnom Shvatanju Porodice Kao Sistema Prilagodjenog Ponašanja* [The Family as Human Community: An Alternative to the Authoritarian Conception of the Family as a System of Adaptive Behavior] (Zagreb: Naprijed, 1981).

20 Tea Petrin and Jane Humphries, "Women in the Self-Managed Economy of Yugoslavia," *Economic Analysis* 14, no. 1 (1980): 69–90.

21 *Žena u Društvu i Privredi Jugoslavije* [Women in Society and Economy in Yugoslavia], Statistički Bilten No. 788 (Belgrade: Savezni Zavod za Statistiku, 1973); Thomas Hendrik, "Personal Income Distribution in Yugoslavia: A Human Capital Approach to the Analysis of Personal Income Differences in the Industry of a Labor-Managed Economy" (unpublished Ph.D. dissertation, Cornell University, 1973), p. 41.

22 In the wealthiest area, Slovenia, for example, a study in 1977 found that women's traditional role in the home was being revived in a majority of the families surveyed in response to the family's demand for higher quality food, cleaning, and service than commercial services provide; as a result, women were leaving paid employment to resume domestic tasks. See Anuška Ferligoj, Silva Mežnarić, and Mirjana Ule, "Raspodjela Svakodnevnih Uloga u Porodice Izmedju Želja (Društva) i Stvarnosti (Porodice)," [The Division of Daily Tasks in the Family between Wish (Society) and Reality (Family)], *Sociologija* 21, no. 4 (1979): 419–39.

23 Dr. Vera Čolanović, "Uticaj Porodice na Socijalizaciju Uloge Pola Kojem Dete Pripada," [Family Influence on Childhood Socialization to Sex Roles] in *Porodica i Socijalizacija Mladih: Prilozi sa Simpozijuma* [The Family and the Socialization of Youth: Excerpts from a Symposium] (Belgrade: Radnička Štampa, 1970), pp. 76–87.

24 Additional evidence can be found in Mirjana Morokvasić, "Changing Role of Women in Yugoslav Society" (unpublished manuscript, September 1978).

25 Susan L. Woodward, "Training for Self-Management: Patterns of Authority and Participation in Yugoslav Secondary Schools" (unpublished Ph.D. dissertation, Princeton University, 1974), appendix B.

26 Andrei Simić, "Management of the Male Image in Yugoslavia," *Anthropological Quarterly* 42, no. 2 (April 1969): 89–101.

27 Olivera Burić, *Promene u Porodičnom Životu Nastale pod Uticajem Ženine Zaposlenosti* [Changes in Family Life Originating under the Influence of Women's Employment] (Belgrade: Institut Društvenih Odnosa, 1968).

28 Local community councils in rural areas are overwhelmingly male and the proportion of women in parliamentary delegations from agricultural communities has, since the system was introduced in the mid-1970s, been less than 2 percent.

29 See *The Yugoslav Village* (Zagreb: Institute for Rural Sociology, 1972), particularly the articles by Ruža First-Dilić, Cvetko Kostić, and Svetozar Livada. The basic work on this process is Ester Boserup, *Women's Role in Economic Development* (London: Allen and Unwin, 1970).

30 Davis, p. 181.

31 Miro A. Mihovilović et al., *Žena Izmedju Rada i Porodice: Utjecaj Zaposlenosti Žene na Strukturu i Funkciju Porodice* [Women between Work and Family: The Influence of the Employment of Women on the Structure and Function of the Family] (Zagreb: Institut za Društvena Istraživanja Sveučilišta u Zagrebu, 1975).

32 Alija Silajdžić, "Borba žene za ravnopravnost jedan od uzroka razvoda braka," [The Struggle of Women for Equality—One of the Causes of Divorce] in *Društveni Konflikti i Socijalistički Razvoj Jugoslavije: Referati*, 1. Deo (VI. Naučno Savetovanje, Jugoslovensko Udruženje za Sociologiju i Slovensko Sociološko Društvo, Portorož, February 1972), pp. 205–16.

33 "Grandmother service," that is, the indispensable assistance of retired family members in domestic care of children, food provision, and so on.

34 Mladen Friganović, "Demografski Podaci," [Demographic Data] in Mihovilović et al., pp. 17–32.

35 Ibid.

36 Mihailo V. Popović et al., *Društveni Slojevi i Društvena Svest* [Social Strata and Social Consciousness] (Belgrade: Centar za Sociološka Istraživanja, Instituta Društvenih Nauka, 1977), pp. 143–47, 160–67, 180–84.

37 *Javnoto Mislenje vo S.R. Makedonija 1976: Rezultati od Anketnog Ispituvanja* [Public Opinion in Macedonia, 1976: Results from Survey Research] (Skopje: Institut za Sociološki i Političko-Pravni Istražuvanja pri Univerzitetot "Kiril i Metodij," 1976), pp. 247–49.

38 See Kligman, this volume, on the Romanian case; for Yugoslavia, the writings of journalist Slavenka Drakulić-Ilić are most helpful. For example, Drakulić-Ilić and Rada Iveković, "The Six Mortal Sins of Yugoslav Feminism," in Robin Morgan, ed., *Sisterhood Is Global* (New York: Doubleday, 1984), and Drakulić-Ilić, *Smrtni Grijesi Feminizma* [The Mortal Sins of Feminism] (Zagreb: Znanje, 1984).

39 Nila Kapor-Stanulović and Herbert L. Friedman, "Studies in Choice Behavior in Yugoslavia," in Henry P. David et al., eds., *Abortion in Psychosocial Perspective: Trends in Transnational Research* (New York: Springer, 1978), pp. 119–44. Resistance to sex education in the schools by teachers and parents alike reinforces this. See Aleksandra Beluhan, Milan Benc, Dubravka Štampar, and Pavle Trenc, "Mišlenje Nastavnika o Nekim Pitanjima Spolnog Života," [Teachers' Attitudes on Some Questions about Sex Life], *Žena* 1 (1976): 65–70.

40 Other examples of this argument can be found in Kay Ann Johnson, *Women, the Family, and Peasant Revolution in China* (Chicago: University of Chicago Press, 1983); Gail W. Lapidus, *Women in Soviet Society: Equality, Development, and Social Change* (Berkeley and Los Angeles: University of California Press, 1978); Muriel Nazzari, "The 'Woman Question' in Cuba: An Analysis of Material Constraints on Its Solution," *Signs* 9, no. 2 (Winter 1983): 246–63; and the many writings of Hilda Scott, such as, "Why the Revolution Doesn't Solve Everything: What We Can Learn from the Economics of 'Real' Socialism," in *Women's Studies International Forum* 5, no. 5, (1982): 451–62.

15 Social Services for Women and Childcare Facilities in Eastern Europe

1 The author is grateful to his wife, Professor Seiko Mieczkowski of Eisenhower College of the Rochester Institute of Technology, to Professor Andrzej Brzeski of the University of California at Davis, and to Professor Aleksander Gella of the State University of New York at Buffalo for their helpful comments on an earlier draft of this chapter. For additional information and discussion, see Bogdan Mieczkowski, *Social Services for Women in Eastern Europe* (Charleston, Ill.: Association for the Study of the Nationalities, 1982), pp. iii–iv, 10–50, 119–24.

2 Barbara W. Jancar, *Women under Communism* (Baltimore: Johns Hopkins University Press, 1978), pp. 38–40; see also Alena Heitlinger, *Women and State Socialism: Sex Inequality in the Soviet Union and Czechoslovakia* (Montreal: McGill-Queens University Press, 1979).

3 Maria Ziemska, *Early Child Care in Poland* (London: Gordon and Breach, 1978), p. 58.

4 Milena Srnská, "Employment of Women in the Czechoslovak Socialist Republic," *International Labour Review* (November 1965), p. 407.

5 Ziemska, p. 58.

6 See Henry P. David and Robert J. McIntyre, eds., *Reproductive Behavior: Central and Eastern European Experiences* (New York: Springer, 1981), for a comprehensive review of recent demographic trends in Eastern Europe.

7 *Rocznik Statystyczny* (Warsaw: GUS), 1966, p. 478; 1980, pp. 415, 443; 1983, p. 433.

8 *Statistiches Jahrbuch 1982* (Berlin: Staatsverlag der DDR), pp. 228, 338.

9 See Maria Lakatos, "Les services dans les pays de l'Est et de l'Ouest: La Hongrie," *Revue d'Etudes Comparatives Est-Ouest*, no. 1–2 (1979), pp. 124–32.

10 Alice Hermann and Sandor Komlosi, *Early Child Care in Hungary* (London: Gordon and Breach, 1972), p. 41.

11 Hermann and Komlosi, pp. 55–56.

12 See Norton Dodge, *Women in the Soviet Economy: Their Role in Economic, Scientific, and Technical Development* (Baltimore: Johns Hopkins University Press, 1966), p. 99.

13 See David and McIntyre for a review of measures regulating abortion in Eastern Europe.

14 See Jancar, pp. 124–25, 143–44; and Heitlinger, *Women under State Socialism*; Heitlinger and McIntyre also discuss these issues in their contributions to this volume.

15 Stefan Klonowicz, "The Influence of the Legalization of Abortion on the Demographic Reproduction in Poland, 1956–72," in Magdalena Sokołowska, Jacek Hołówka, and Antonina Ostrowska, eds., *Health, Medicine, Society* (Dordrecht: D. Reidel, 1976), p. 48.

16 Ibid. As numerous analysts, including Alena Heitlinger in her essay in this volume, have pointed out, access to birth control devices has developed slowly in Eastern Europe.

17 See Bogdan Mieczkowski, *Personal and Social Consumption in Eastern Europe: Poland, Czechoslovakia, Hungary, and East Germany* (New York: Praeger, 1975), pp. 24–26; Ziemska, p. 50; and Hermann and Komlosi, pp. 32 and 37.

18 Elżbieta Wallewein, "Opieka zdrowotna nad matką i dzieckiem," *Wiadomości Statystyczne*, no. 5 (1979), p. 23; *Rocznik Statystyczny 1982*, p. 431.

19 Zdzisława Czyżowska, "Polityka socjalna na rzecz dziecka," *Wiadomości Statystyczne*, no. 5 (1979), p. 4.

20 Hermann and Komlosi, pp. 33–34.

21 Reinhard Pohl, ed., *Handbook of the Economy of the German Democratic Republic* (Farnborough: Saxon House, 1980), p. 188.

22 See Hermann and Komlosi, pp. 34–35, and Ziemska, pp. 49–53.

23 *Rocznik Statystyczny*, 1980, p. 35.

24 *Rocznik Statystyczny*, 1969, p. 32; 1980, p. 48.

25 World Health Organization, *World Health Statistics Annual* (Geneva: WHO, 1983).

26 World Health Organization, pp. 16–17.

27 Ziemska, p. 104. As Heitlinger notes in this volume, however, women's actual possibilities to use these facilities are limited by the small number of places available.

28 Czyżowska, p. 4.

29 Herta Kuhrig and Wulfram Speigner, eds., *Zur gesellschaftlichen Stellung der Frau in der DDR* (Leipzig: Verlag für die Frau, 1978), pp. 311–33.

30 See Jancar; Sharon L. Wolchik, "Politics, Ideology, and Equality: The Status of Women in Eastern Europe" (unpublished Ph.D. dissertation, University of Michigan, 1978), and Heitlinger, *Women under State Socialism.*

31 *Rocznik Statystyczny*, 1980, p. 62; 1983, p. 64.

32 Czyżowska, p. 3; Ziemska, p. 24.

33 Pohl, p. 188.

34 David and McIntyre.

35 Hermann and Komlosi, p. 35.

36 Czyżowska, p. 3; Pohl, p. 188. David and McIntyre indicate that these payments are common throughout the region.

37 Pohl, p. 188; David and McIntyre, p. 242.

38 Czyżowska, pp. 3–4; Ziemska, pp. 14–15.

39 Hermann and Komlosi, p. 36.

40 Murray Yanowitch, *Social and Economic Inequality in the Soviet Union: Six Studies* (White Plains, N.Y.: M. E. Sharpe, 1977), pp. 177–78. See Joel Moses, *The Politics of Women and Work in the Soviet Union and the United States* (Berkeley: University of California, Institute of International Studies, Research Series No. 50, 1983), for a review of Soviet measures.

41 Czyżowska, p. 3.

42 Srnská, pp. 405–6. See also Alena Heitlinger, "Pronatalist Population Policies in Czechoslovakia," *Population Studies* 36 (1979): 123–35.

43 Czyżowska, p. 3.

44 Pohl, p. 189; Andrzej Tymowski, *Minimum socjalne: Metodyka i próba określenia* (Warsaw: PWN, 1973), p. 90; Mieczkowski, *Personal and Social Consumption*

in *Eastern Europe*, pp. 36–42.

45 Pohl, p. 192.

46 Radio Free Europe Research, December 4, 1980, p. 23; *Rocznik Statystyczny*, 1980, p. 35.

47 Pohl, p. 195; Laura d'Andrea Tyson, *The Yugoslav Economic System and Its Performance in the 1970's* (Berkeley: Institute of International Studies, University of California, 1980), pp. 53–54.

48 See Mieczkowski, *Social Services for Women*.

49 Organization for Economic Cooperation and Development, "The 1974–1975 Recession and the Employment of Women," in Alice Amsden, ed., *The Economics of Women and Work* (New York: St. Martin's Press, 1980), pp. 360, 385.

50 *Japan Statistical Yearbook* (Tokyo: Prime Minister's Office, Statistics Bureau, 1982), p. 619.

51 There is great variation in this respect among Western countries. Provisions benefiting working mothers are most developed in Scandinavia, but advances also have been made in this respect in other West European countries including France and West Germany. See Sheila B. Kamerman and Alfred J. Kahn, *Child Care, Family Benefits, and Working Parents* (New York: Columbia University Press, 1981), and Sheila B. Kamerman, Alfred J. Kahn, and Paul Kingston, *Maternity Policies and Working Women* (New York: Columbia University Press, 1983), for information on Western Europe and the United States.

52 Alice Cook and Hiroko Hayashi, *Working Women in Japan: Discrimination, Resistance, and Reform* (Ithaca, N.Y.: New York State School of Industrial and Labor Relations, 1980), pp. 18–21; 88–90.

16 Demographic Policy and Sexual Equality: Value Conflicts and Policy Appraisal in Hungary and Romania

1 Alexander Dallin, "Bias and Blunders in American Studies on the USSR," *Slavic Review* 32, no. 3 (September 1973): 560–76.

2 See Robert McIntyre and James Thornton, "Environmental Divergence: Air Pollution in the USSR," *Journal of Environmental Economics and Management* 1, no. 2 (August 1974): 109–20; P. Hanson, "East-West Comparisons and Comparative Economic Systems," *Soviet Studies* 22, no. 3 (1971): 327; Robert McIntyre and James Thornton, "On the Environmental Efficiency of Economic Systems," *Soviet Studies* 30, no. 2 (April 1978): 173–92; and "Urban Design and Energy Utilization: A Comparative Analysis of Soviet Practice," *Journal of Comparative Economics* 2, no. 4 (December 1978): 334–54.

3 An interesting comparative analysis of the interplay between women's work and personal lives in the German Democratic Republic and the United States is provided by Marilyn Rueschemeyer, *Professional Work and Marriage: An East-West Comparison* (New York: St. Martin's Press, 1981). This study is based on detailed interviews with professional women and men in the GDR and the United States. Especially interesting are the reflections on the connections

between public institutional and ideological supports for women as equal work participants in the GDR and the private world of friendship and marriage relationships. The GDR has probably gone further in both institutional and ideological directions than any of the other Eastern European countries.

4 See Irene Diamond, ed., *Families, Politics, and Public Policy: A Feminist Dialogue on Women and the State* (New York: Longman, 1983); Karen Wolk Feinstein, ed., *Working Women and Families* vol. 4, Sage Yearbooks in Women's Policy Studies (Beverly Hills, Calif.: Sage Publications, 1979); and Carolyn Teich Adams and Kathryn Teich Winston, *Mothers at Work: Public Policies in the United States, Sweden, and China* (New York: Longman, 1980), for examples of the voluminous literature on this topic.

5 Robert McIntyre, "Pronatalist Programmes in Eastern Europe," *Soviet Studies* 27, no. 3 (July 1975): 366–80.

6 This causal analysis was not universally accepted by Western observers, some of whom argued that abortion only allowed achievement of family size goals that had changed for some other reason. For an analysis that is consistent with the prevailing Eastern European view and that interprets changes in abortion and contraception availability from the point of view of a broad definition of costs, see Robert McIntyre, "The Effect of Liberalized Abortion Laws in Eastern Europe," in *Research in the Politics of Population*, eds., Richard Clinton and Kenneth Godwin (London: Heath, 1972), pp. 200–201.

7 Hilda Wander, "ZPG Now: The Lessons from Europe," in Thomas Espenshade and William Serow, eds., *The Economic Consequences of Slowing Population Growth* (New York: Academic Press, 1978), pp. 41–69; Jason Finkle and Alison McIntosh, "Policy Responses to Population Stagnation in Developed Societies," in *Social, Economic, and Health Aspects of Low Fertility*, ed. Arthur A. Campbell (Washington, D.C.: USGPO, 1979); and A. Otten, "People Shortage: West European States See Economic Troubles as Birth Rates Decline," *Wall Street Journal*, August 23, 1979, pp. 1 and 28.

8 For detailed discussion of the interrelationships between abortion liberalization, declining fertility, and pronatalist programs, see McIntyre, "Effects of Liberalized Abortion Laws," pp. 183–216.

9 Jerzy Berent, "Causes of Fertility Decline in Eastern Europe and the Soviet Union," *Population Studies* 24, no. 2 (1970): 285–89.

10 András Klinger, "The Impact of Policy Measures Other than Family Planning on Fertility," Research Report No. 18, Demographic Research Institute (Budapest, 1984), pp. 21–28.

11 See *Magyar Közlöny* 18 (October 1973): 774–78; *Demográfia* 17, no. 2 (1974): 269, 275; *Demográfia* 22, no. 1 (1979): 133–36; Klinger, p. 35; and Buda Press, "Demographic Measures," no. 23 (1985), pp. 1–3.

12 *Demográfia* 22, no. 1 (1979): 133–36.

13 Klinger, p. 35. There is anecdotal evidence that earlier experimental programs were not successful.

14 Stephen Coelen and Robert McIntyre, "Econometric Analysis of Pronatalist and Abortion Policies," *Journal of Political Economy* 86, no. 6 (December 1978): 1077–1102, and McIntyre "Pronatalist Programmes," pp. 379.

15 Married women qualify if they are over forty or have at least three living children and have, in addition, undergone at least one "obstetrical event." In addition, women may request termination for medical, eugenic, juridical, and "serious social reasons," including lack of adequate housing, husband's military service, or imprisonment.

16 The biomedical grounds for the argument that abortion poses a threat to health or future fertility are far from clear. To the extent that Hungarian evidence offers support for this view it appears to be the result of an anomalous backwardness in the *method* of inducing abortion in Hungary, principally dilatation and currettage (D&C) rather than vacuum aspiration.

17 Peter Jozan, "Planned Parenthood in Hungary," IPPF *European Regional Information Bulletin* 6, no. 4 (1977): 8, and (supplement) 7, no. 1, (1978): 4–5. For a more detailed discussion of contraception, abortion, sex education, woman's roles, and population policy in Hungary, see Henry P. David and Robert J. McIntyre, *Reproductive Behavior: Central and Eastern European Experience* (New York: Springer, 1981), pp. 248–80.

18 David and McIntyre, p. 179. For a detailed analysis of the Romanian experience, see Michael Teitelbaum, "Fertility Effects of the Abolition of Legal Abortion in Romania," *Population Studies* 26, no. 3 (1972): 405–17; Leon Clark, "Baby Boom by Fiat," *Teaching Notes on Population*, no. 3 (Spring/Winter 1973), pp. 24–39, and David and McIntyre, pp. 176–97.

19 The restrictions on divorce are quite exceptional, involving introduction of a large filing fee and a compulsory six-month or one-year period of trial reconciliation contingent on whether there are children involved. The number of divorces granted fell from 26,000 in 1966 to forty-eight in 1967, with only a modest resurgence during the next few years; see United Nations, *Demographic Yearbook 1968* (1969), pp. 672–73, and *1972* (1973), p. 636.

20 Henry P. David and Nicholas Wright, "Abortion Legislation: The Romanian Experience," *Studies in Family Planning* 2, no. 10 (October 1971): 206. Even after revocation of the general abortion-on-demand system, induced abortions remained available to women who (1) were forty-five years of age or older, (2) were already "supporting" four or more children, or (3) had established medical indication. See David and McIntyre, pp. 186–93.

21 See, for example, William Moskoff, "Sex Discrimination, Commuting, and the Role of Women in Romanian Development," *Slavic Review* 37, no. 3 (September 1978): 440–56; and Mary Ellen Fischer, "The Romanian Communist Party and Its Central Committee: Patterns of Growth and Change," *Southeastern Europe* 6, part 1 (1979): 1–28.

22 See the sources cited in note 4 above for some of these analyses.

23 One Hungarian writer who has dealt directly with the questions of the redefinition of work and home and the interrelationship between household economy and work life is Zsuzsa Ferge, *A Society in the Making: Hungarian Social and Societal Policy, 1945–1975* (White Plains, N.Y.: M. E. Sharpe, 1980), especially pp. 195–273.

24 See the chapters by Siemieńska, Kulcsár, and Volgyes in this book for discussions of these effects in Eastern Europe.

25 Alena Heitlinger, "Marxism, Feminism, and Sex Equality," in Tova Yedlin, ed., *Women in Eastern Europe and the Soviet Union* (New York: Praeger, 1980), pp. 9–20, and *Women and State Socialism: Sex Inequality in the Soviet Union and Czechoslovakia* (Montreal: McGill-Queens University Press, 1979). Other analysts have reached this conclusion as well. See Gail W. Lapidus, *Women in Soviet Society* (Berkeley: University of California Press, 1978), for a similar argument in the Soviet case; see also Barbara W. Jancar, *Women under Communism* (Baltimore: Johns Hopkins University Press, 1978); and Sharon L. Wolchik, "The Status of Women in a Socialist Order: The Case of Czechoslovakia, 1948–1978," *Slavic Review* 38, no. 4 (December 1981): 583–602.

26 Cited in Yedlin, pp. 1–2.

27 Cited by Heitlinger, p. 16.

28 See Hilda Scott, *Does Socialism Liberate Women?* (Boston: Beacon Press, 1974), p. 194, for a discussion of this factor.

29 Ferge, p. 25.

30 Alistair McAuley's review of *Women in Russia*, edited by Dorothy Atkinson, Alexander Dallin, and Gail Warshofsky Lapidus, in *Slavic Review* 38, no. 2 (June 1979): 293.

17 Passage to Motherhood: Personal and Social "Management" of Reproduction in Czechoslovakia in the 1980s

1 Ann Oakley, *Becoming a Mother* (Oxford: Martin Robertson, 1979) and *Women Confined: Toward a Sociology of Childbirth* (Oxford: Martin Robertson, 1980).

2 Research for this paper was supported by a grant from Trent University, which is gratefully acknowledged.

3 J. Presl, "Vývoj spotřeby perorálních steroidních kontraceptiv v ČSR a SSR," *Československá gynekologie* 42, no. 7 (August 1977): 543–44. All these figures were supplied by the Czech author. William D. Mosher, *Contraceptive Utilization in the United States, 1976*, DHHS Publication no. 1981–83, March 1981, indicates that use of the pill among U.S. married couples is even higher.

4 František Havránek, "Antikoncepce a umělé přerušení těhotenství, jejich role při regulaci porodnosti," *Demografie* 20, no. 4 (1978): 356–58.

5 "Koordinační porada o výzkumných úkolech s populační problematikou, Žďáň, February 21–25, 1977," *Demografie* 20, no. 2 (1978): 356–58.

6 See Alena Heitlinger, "Pronatalist Population Policies in Czechoslovakia," *Population Studies* 30, no. 1 (March 1976): 185.

7 See Vladimír Srb, "Šetření plodnosti (1977)," *Demografie* 21, nos. 1, 2, 3, 4 (1979).

8 Zdeňka Kadlecová and Marta Brtníková, "Manželství, rodina a rodičovství ve světle sociálních průzkumů v ČSSR," in Brablcová, ed., *Manželství, rodina, rodičovství* (Prague: Horizont, 1977), p. 112.

9 Srb, p. 304.

10 Zdeňka Kadlecová, ed., *Z průzkumu mezi mladými ženami* (Prague: Organizační a tiskové oddělení ministerstva práce a sociálních věcí ČSR, 1974); Kadlecová

and Brtníková; K. Poradovský, "Názory, postoje a chovanie mládeže vo vztahu k rodičovství," *Československá gynekologie* 44, no. 6 (July 1979): 428–49.

11 Josef Hynie, "Příprava na manželství a rodičovství," in Vlasta Brablcová, ed., *Manželství, rodina, rodičovství* (Prague: Horizont, 1977).

12 Havránek, "Antikoncepce a umělé přerušení těhotenství" and "Možnosti medicíny při regulaci porodnosti," *Populační zprávy*, nos. 1–3 (1979), pp. 51–55.

13 Data on abortion in Czechoslovakia are extensive and reliable. Registrations of pregnancies, requests for abortion, and performed abortions are carefully controlled at both the district and central level. Much of the information available already has been published elsewhere and need not be repeated here. See Hilda Scott, *Does Socialism Liberate Women? Experiences From Eastern Europe* (Boston: Beacon Press, 1974), pp. 141–54; Alena Heitlinger, *Women and State Socialism: Sex Inequality in the Soviet Union and Czechoslovakia* (Montreal: McGill-Queen's University Press, 1979), pp. 186–89.

14 See Heitlinger, *Women and State Socialism*.

15 Vladimír Šalda, "K současné potratovosti v ČSSR," *Populační zprávy*, (1978), pp. 19–24.

16 J. Jeri et al., *Organizace a metodika péče o ženu v* ČSSR *(v oboru porodnictví a gynekologie)* (Prague: Státní zdravotnické nakladatelství, 1961); Václav Laně, *Kapitoly o zdraví a hygieně ženy* (Plzeň: Západočeské nakladatelství, 1967).

17 Havránek, "Antikoncepce a umělé přerušení těhotenství."

18 The "menstrual regulation" method has been used only on an experimental basis with good results at the Institute of Care of Mother and Child in Prague, a research institution run by the Ministry of Health. Havránek and P. Šmeral, "Přerušení ranných stádií těhotenství (regulace menstruace, mini-interrupce) v praxi," *Československá gynekologie* 44, no. 8 (September 1979): 561–66.

19 See Milada Hrdá, "Sociálně právní ochrana ženy v pracovněprávních vztazích a její hmotné zabezpečení v době těhotenství a mateřství," in Brablcová, *Manželství, rodina, rodičovství*; Ladislav Jouza, *Pracovní podmínky žen a mladistvých* (Prague: Práce, 1979); and Vlasta Kvíčalová and Jana Zemanová, *Společenská péče o rodinu a děti. Odpovědi na otázky z nemocenského pojištění pracovníků* (Prague: Práce, 1978).

20 J. Michlíček, "Příspěvek k problematice převádění žen na jinou práci v graviditě a mateřství v praxi obvodního a závodního gynekologa," *Československá gynekologie* 43, no. 5 (June 1978): 397–98.

21 P. Baran, "Vliv zaměstnanosti těhotných žen na výskyt komplikací v průběhu těhotenství," *Československá gynekologie* 45, no. 4 (May 1980): 225–28.

22 See Jaroslav Prokopec, *Zdraví a společnost* (Prague: Avicenum, 1975), p. 65, and Mikuláš Petro, *Cesta k socialistikému zdravotnictví* (Prague: Avicenum, 1980), p. 120.

23 Vladimír Šabata and Zdeňka Fišerová, *Výživa těhotné a kojící ženy* (Prague: Avicenum, 1974), and Stanislav Trča, *Budeme mít děťátko* (Prague: Avicenum, 1979) and *Umění zdravě žít* (Prague: Avicenum, 1980).

24 Stanislav Trča, "Kolik žen přestává v těhotenství kouřit," *Československá gynekologie* 42, no. 10 (December 1977).

25 Glos, "Vliv sportu a tělocviku na trvání porodu," *Československá gynekologie* 43, no. 2 (April 1978): 119–21.
26 Hilary Graham, "Images of Pregnancy in Antenatal Literature," in Robert Dingwald, ed., *Health Care and Health Knowledge* (London: Croom Helm, 1977).
27 I. Havlík et al., "Výsledky psychoprofylaktické přípravy k porodu," *Československá gynekologie* 43, no. 10 (December 1978): 776–79.
28 "Výsledky sociologického průzkumu 'Rodina a děti,'" *Populační zprávy* (1978), pp. 65–78.
29 Stanislav Trča, "Příprava těhotných žen na porod," *Populační zprávy* nos. 1–2 (1978), pp. 38–41.
30 Czechoslovak physicians and state officials are very proud of these figures. See, for example, Prokopec, p. 65, and Petro, p. 122.
31 B. Srp et al., "Intenzivní porodní péče z hlediska současných požadavků," *Československá gynekologie* 43, no. 10 (1978): 756.
32 Ibid., p. 752; and Petro, p. 123.
33 Petro, p. 122; and Štembera, p. 40.
34 V. Suk, "Technizace v porodnictví," *Československá gynekologie* 44, no. 7 (August 1979): 477–80.
35 M. Janovský and E. Procházková, "Některé fyziologické předpoklady úspěšné laktace," *Československá pediatrie* 36, no. 1 (January 1981): 27–29.
36 Josef Švejcar, "Výživa kojence kojením," *Československá pediatrie* 35, no. 10 (October 1980): 550.
37 Dagmar Ouřadová, "Aby se děti nerodily dvakrát (aneb co je to rooming-in)," *Mladá fronta*, June 13, 1981.
38 *Encyklopedie mladé ženy*, p. 634.
39 Ibid.
40 Josef Houštek, "Význam kojení pro zdravý vývoj dítěte," *Populační zprávy*, nos. 1–2 (1978), pp. 42–44.
41 Švejcar, p. 551.
42 Jaroslava Sommerová, "Výroba sušené kojenecké a dětské mléčné výživy v ČSSR," *Populační zprávy* (1978), p. 49.
43 Miroslav Matoušek, *První rok dítěte* (Prague: Avicenum, 1980).
44 Augustín Bárdoš, *Žena = Zdravie + Krása: Sprievodca modernej ženy* (Martin: Osveta, 1978), p. 68.
45 Jiří Dunovský and Marta Zelenková, "Nemanželské děti po třech letech," *Populační zprávy* nos. 1–2 (1977), pp. 101–30.
46 D. Fukalová and R. Uzel, "Motivace k mateřství u svobodných matek," in *Aktuální problémy v porodnictví*, 1976; J. Němcová and J. Langrová, "Domov pro osamělé matky," *Populační zprávy*, nos. 1–2 (1977), pp. 49–52.
47 Jiří Prokopec and Oldřich Mikšík, "Pražský výzkum psychické zátěže zaměstnaných žen-matek," *Demografie* 20, no. 1 (1978).
48 See also V. Srb, "Šetření plodnosti žen v ČSSR (1977)," *Populační zprávy*, nos. 1–2 (1979), pp. 21–28, and M. Schvarzová, "Niektoré poznatky o prognozách v oblasti populačnej klímy v ČSSR z hladiska vydatých ekonomicky činných žien s nezaopatrenými dětmi (výsledky empirického výzkumu)," *Populační*

zprávy, nos. 1–2, (1979).

49 J. Havelka, "Výsledky a úkoly společenské pomoci rodinám s dětmi," *Sociální politika* 15, no. 6, (June 1979).

50 See J. Židovský, "Pomoc a úkoly výzkumu v oblasti péče a ženu matku a novorozence," *Československá gynekologie* 43, no. 7 (August 1978): 485–89.

51 D. Kvíz, "Zamyšlení nad dvaceti lety platnosti zákona č. 68/57 Sb.," *Československá gynekologie* 43, no. 6 (July 1978): 452–53.

52 Petr Víšek, "Výsledky šetření o příjemcích přídavků na děti v roce 1978," *Sociální politika* 5, no. 6 (June 1979): 125.

53 Ivan Lesný, "Plodnost poválečných kohort v ČSR," *Demografie* 20, no. 2 (1978): 106–16.

54 Srb, "Šetření plodnosti," p. 28.

V Women's Voices

Introduction

1 For an essay on this clash between Marxism-Leninism and traditional culture, see Alfred G. Meyer, "Communist Revolutions and Cultural Change," in *Studies in Comparative Communist* 5, no. 4 (Winter 1972): 345–70.

18 Women, Work, and Gender Equality in Poland: Reality and Its Social Perception

1 Magdalena Sokołowska, "Polityka rodzinna w Polsce," *Przegląd Humanistyczny*, nos. 11/12 (1980).

2 *Mały Rocznik Statystyczny* (Warsaw, 1938).

3 Mieczysław Przedpełski, *Struktura zatrudnienia kobiet w Polsce Ludowej* (Warsaw: Panstwowe Wydawnictwo Naukowe, 1975) and R. Wieruszewski, *Równość kobiet i meżczyzn w Polsce Ludowej* (Poznan, 1975).

4 Aleksandra Jasińska and Renata Siemieńska, *Wzory osobowe a powieść radiowa* (Warsaw: OBPO ISP, 1975). Aleksandra Jasińska and Renata Siemieńska, *Wzory osobowe socjalizmu* (Warsaw: Wiedza Powszechna, 1978); Aleksandra Jasińska and Renata Siemieńska, "The Socialist Personality: A Case Study of Poland" *International Journal of Sociology* 13, no. 1 (1983): 3–86.

5 K. Knzychała, *Zatrudnienie kobiet w Polsce Ludowej w Łatach 1955–1974* (Poznan: PWN, 1978).

6 Janina Waluk, *Praca i płaca kobiet w Polsce* (Warsaw: KiW, 1965); Stefania Dzięcielska-Machnikowska and Jolanta Kulpińska, *Awans kobiety* (Łodź: Wydawnictwo Łódźkie, 1966).

7 *Rocznik Statystyczny*, 1980.

8 Dzięcielska-Machnikowska and Kulpińska; J. Piotrowski, *Praca zawodowa kobiety a rodzina* (Warsaw: KiW, 1963); S. Dzięcielska-Machnikowska, ed., *Kobieta w rozwijającym się społeczeństwie socjalistycznym* (Łodz, 1975); and Aleksandra Jasińska and Renata Siemieńska, "Rola rodziny w propagowanym wzorze osobowosci socjalistycznej, a jej miejsce w hierarchii wartosci spol-

eczenstwa polskiego," *Przegląd Humanistyczny*, nos. 11/12 (1980).

9 Correlations between reactions to the two statements were generally lower among women than men and, depending on the socio-occupational category, ranged from .318 to .509 (compared to .04 to .421 for men). These correlations were statistically significant at the .0001 level, with the exception of male blue-collar workers.

10 Krystyna Bursche, *Awans robotników w zakładzie przemysłowym* (Warsaw, 1973); G. C. Coin, *Married Women in the Labor Force: An Economic Analysis* (Chicago: University of Chicago Press, 1969); Marjorie Galenson, *Women and Work: An International Comparison* (Ithaca, N.Y.: New York State School of Industrial and Labor Relations, 1973); Viola Klein, *Britain's Married Women Workers* (London: Routledge & Kegan Paul, 1965); and Adam Sarapata, *O zawodoleniu i niezadowoleniu z pracy* (Warsaw: Instytut Wydawniczy CRZZ, 1977).

11 Waluk; Wieruszewski; and Victor Harold Vroom, *Work and Motivation* (New York: John Wiley and Sons, 1964).

12 The mean value of the difficulties (the question was a closed one) that the respondents were willing to accept as the "price" of promotion was 2.538 for male blue-collar workers and 1.630 for women; 2.373 for male white-collar workers and 2.153 for women; 2.040 for male teachers and .939 for women; 3.000 for male managers and 2.750 for women. (Minimum score = 0; maximum = 6.) Among the six types of drawbacks involved in accepting promotion, greater responsibility and duties met with least resistance. There was least acceptance for complications in the respondent's family life.

13 Magdalena Sokołowska, *Kobieta pracująca* (Warsaw, 1963); Eleanor Emmons Maccoby and Carol Nagy Jacklin, *The Psychology of Sex Differences* (Stanford, Calif.: Stanford University Press, 1974).

14 Renata Siemieńska, "Woman and the Family in Poland," in Eugen Lupri, *The Changing Position of Women in Family and Society: A Cross-National Comparison* (Leiden: E. J. Brill, 1983).

15 K. Miller, "Wpływ modernizacji na ideologie rodziny i równouprawnienie kobiet," *Przegląd Humanistyczny*, 1980.

19 The Rites of Women: Oral Poetry, Ideology, and the Socialization of Peasant Women in Contemporary Romania

This chapter is a revised version of an article by the same title, published in *Journal of American Folklore* 97, no. 384 (1984).

1 Martha E. Gimenez, "Structuralist Marxism on 'The Woman Question,'" in *Science and Society* 42, no. 3 (1978): 301–23. Gimenez observes that "male dominance subsists unchanged as a structural feature of capitalist society in the context of drastic changes in the division of labor between the sexes within and outside the household" and will continue to do so inasmuch as change is relative to structural compatibility with the "maintenance of capitalist relations of production." The contradictions inherent therein pertain to Soviet and East European development as well. See Gail Warshofsky Lapidus, "Sexual Equal-

ity in Soviet Policy: A Developmental Perspective," in *Women in Russia*, edited by Dorothy Atkinson, Alexander Dallin, and Gail Warshofsky Lapidus (Stanford, Calif.: Stanford University Press, 1977), pp. 115–38; and William Moskoff, "Sex Discrimination, Commuting and the Role of Women in Romanian Development," in *Slavic Review* 37, no. 3 (1978), pp. 440–56. Lapidus insightfully underlines the relationship between sexual equality and changes in social structures, values, and authority patterns. Also refer to the chapters and bibliographies included in this volume for additional sources as well as to, for example, Zillah Eisenstein, ed., *Capitalist Patriarchy and the Case for Socialist Feminism* (New York: Monthly Review Press, 1979), and Heidi Hartmann, "Capitalism, Patriarchy, and Job Segregation by Sex," in Anthony Giddens and David Held, *Classes, Power and Conflict* (Berkeley: University of California Press, 1981), pp. 446–69.

2 See Kenneth Jowitt, "An Organizational Approach to the Study of Political Culture in Marxist-Leninist Systems," in *American Political Science Review* 68, no. 3 (1974): 1171–91: William Moskoff, "The Problem of the 'Double Burden' in Romania," in *International Journal of Comparative Society* 23, nos. 1–2: 79–88; and Mihail Cernea, "Macrosocial Change, the Feminization of Agriculture, and Peasant Women's Threefold Economic Role," *Sociologia Ruralis* 18 (1978): 239–50.

3 See Gail Kligman, *Căluş: Symbolic Transformation in Romanian Ritual* (Chicago: University of Chicago Press, 1981). It is beyond the scope of this chapter to review the literature on women in peasant societies. It is as varied as it is immense (e.g., women and development). For the purposes of this chapter, the following related works on the peasant family in Europe are provided; they are meant to be suggestive rather than exhaustive: John Campbell, *Honor, Family, and Patronage* (Oxford: Oxford University Press, 1964); *Appearance and Reality: The Status and Roles of Women in Mediterranean Societies*, special issue of the *Anthropological Quarterly* 40, no. 3 (1967); Jane Schneider, "Of Vigilance and Virgins: Honor, Shame and Access to Resources in Mediterranean Societies," *Ethnology* 10 (1971): 1–24; Peter Laslett, ed., *Household and Family in Past Time* (Cambridge: Cambridge University Press, 1972); Michelle Rosaldo and Louise Lamphere, eds., *Women, Culture, and Society* (Stanford, Calif.: Stanford University Press, 1974); Jack Goody et al., eds., *Family and Inheritance: Rural Society in Western Europe, 1200–1800* (Cambridge: Cambridge University Press, 1976); Ann Cornelisen, *Women of the Shadows* (New York: Vintage Books, 1977); Louise Tilly and Joan Scott, *Women, Work, and Family* (New York: Holt, Rhinehart & Winston, 1978); Jean-Louis Flandrin, *Families in Former Times* (Cambridge: Cambridge University Press, 1979); Stanley Brandes, *Metaphors of Masculinity: Sex and Status in Andalusian Folklore* (Philadelphia: University of Pennsylvania Press, 1980); Barbara Laslett, "Production, Reproduction, and Social Change: The Family in Historical Perspective" in James Short, Jr., ed., *The State of Sociology: Problems and Prospects* (Beverly Hills, Calif.: Sage Publications, 1981), pp. 239–58; Michael Mitterauer and Reinhard Sieder, *The European Family: Patriarchy to Partnership from the Middle Ages to the Present* (Chicago: University of Chicago Press, 1982); Martine Segalen, *Love and Power*

in the Peasant Family (Chicago: University of Chicago Press, 1983); and David Gilmore, ed., *Honor and Shame in the Mediterranean*, forthcoming.

4 See Paul Stahl, *Sociétés Traditionelles Balkaniques* (Paris: Études et Documents Balkaniques, 1979). Also refer to note 3.

5 See Ion Mihaily, *Diplome Maramureşene din Secolul al XIV-lea şi al XV-lea* (Bucharest, 1900); and Radu Popa, *Ţara Maramureşului în Veacul XIV-lea* (Bucharest: ed. Academiei, 1970).

6 Ieud is also vaunted as the "intellectual" village. The oldest written documents in Romania (*Manuscrisul de la Ieud*) were found in the church dating from 1364; the first personal letters purportedly were sent by an Ieudan in 1585. *Manuscrisul de la Ieud* (Bucharest: Editura Academiei Republicii Socialişte România, 1977).

7 A *strigătură*—shouted, rhymed couplet—collected in another village of this region attests to this transformation in conditions:

My, poor Ieud
How it was,
And how it is now!

8 See Daniel Chirot, "Social Change in Communist Romania," in *Social Forces* 57, no. 2 (1978): 457–88; Cernea; and Moskoff.

9 President Ceauşescu recently conceded in *The New York Times*, March 9, 1981, that his government has neglected the development of agriculture in favor of industry. Moreover, a serious component contributing to poor agricultural productivity is the predominantly female composition of agricultural workers (70 percent).

10 See Jowitt; Chirot; and Moskoff. For more extensive historical studies, see Katherine Verdery, *Transylvanian Villagers: Three Centuries of Political, Economic, and Ethnic Change* (Berkeley and Los Angeles: University of California Press, 1983), and, for example, Caroline Humphrey, *Karl Marx Collective: Economy, Society, and Religion in a Siberian Collective* (Cambridge: Cambridge University Press, 1983), and Peter Bell, *Peasants in Socialist Transition: Life in a Collectivized Hungarian Village* (Berkeley and Los Angeles: University of California Press, 1984) for comparative works.

11 See Marcel Mauss, "Une Categorie de l'Esprit Humain: la Notion de Personne, Celle de 'Moi,'" in *Sociologie et Anthropologie* (Paris: Presses Universitaires de France, 1950), pp. 333–63; Nancy Munn, "Symbolism in a Ritual Context: Aspects of Symbolic Action," in John Honigmann, ed., *Handbook of Social and Cultural Anthropology* (New York: Rand McNally, 1974), pp. 579–612; Terence Turner, "Transformation, Hierarchy, and Transcendence: A Reformulation of Van Gennep's Model of the Structure of Rites de Passage," in Sally Moore and Barbara Meyerhoff, eds., *Secular Ritual* (Amsterdam: Van Gorcum, 1977), pp. 53–69; and Sherry Ortner, *Sherpas Through Their Rituals* (Cambridge: Cambridge University Press, 1978). Caroline Humphrey's chapter (see note 10) on "Ritual and Identity" offers an insightful discussion on contemporary ritual as a means to make sense of experience. I highly recommend it, as well as the entire book

12 See Ion Meţoiu, *Spectacolul Nunţiilor* (Bucharest: Comitetul de Stat pentru

cultură şi artă, 1969); Nicolae Cartojan, "Oraţiile de Nuntă," in *Cărţile Populare în Literatura Româneasca* vol. 2 (Bucharest: ed. Enciclopedica Română, 1974), p. 274; and Mihai Pop, *Obiceiuri Tradiţionale Româneşti* (Bucharest: Consiliul culturii şi educaţiei socialiste, 1976), pp. 137–57.

13 This statement acknowledges that the "bride's crying is a ritual imperative" (Pop, p. 152). Requisite "ceremonial weeping" speaks to the fact that the ritual is concerned with social sentiments as opposed to individual feelings. Arthur Radcliffe-Brown, *The Andaman Islanders* (Cambridge: Cambridge University Press, 1964), pp. 116–17, 238–43.

14 See Stahl, p. 27. Regarding the conceptualization of gender and sexuality in different cultures, see Harriet Whitehead and Sherry Ortner, eds., *Sexual Meanings: The Cultural Construction of Gender and Sexuality* (Cambridge: Cambridge University Press, 1981).

15 All *strigături* utilized in this chapter were collected during the winter wedding cycle in Ieud, Maramureş, 1978. Also, texts have been selected from several weddings. Together, they form an "ideal typical" representation of wedding texts.

16 See Tudor Pamfile, *Cerul şi podoabele lui după credinţele poporului român* (Bucharest, 1951), p. 13. The reader may wish to refer also to the Mediterranean "honor and shame" literature, which is extensive. See, for example, Campbell, Schneider, the *Anthropological Quarterly* issue, and Gilmore, cited in note 3.

17 See Stahl, p. 38.

18 Today most girls and women wear aprons woven with wool and mixed fibers. However, for the ritual handshake, only pure woolen aprons are worn, even if they must be borrowed. Regarding wool and prosperity, a game to foretell traits of one's future spouse is played on New Year's Eve by those of marriageable age, male and female. A series of plates cover various symbolic media; it is said that he/she who overturns a plate and finds a clump of wool will marry someone prosperous.

19 To be buried among the flowers is to be buried "unpicked." For a girl, marriage is metaphorically equated with death. Also persons of marriageable age who die are symbolically wed during the funeral. See, in particular, Ion Muşlea, "La mort mariage: une particularité du folklore balcanique," in *Cercetări Etnografice şi de Folclor* (Bucharest: Minerva, 1972), pp. 7–36.

20 See David Rheubottom, p. 233, in "Dowry and Wedding Celebrations in Yugoslav Macedonia," in John L. Comaroff, ed., *The Meaning of Marriage Payments* (New York: Academic Press, 1980), pp. 221–48.

21 Rheubottom, p. 242.

22 Space permits only the most cursory outline of the wedding progression. See Tiberiu Graur, "Predici rituale în structura şi funcţia ceremonialului de nuntă traditională," in *Anuarul Muzeului Etnografic al Transilvaniei* (1976), pp. 283–94; Simon Florian Marian, *Nunta la români* (Bucharest, 1890); and Meţoiu. The basic ceremonial phases, following Van Gennep's classic model, are:

I. Separation: The dance of the groom's flag and of the bride's crown; dressing the bride; the bride and groom respectively asking forgiveness from their parents; the church ceremony.

II. Liminal: Exchanges of bread and *ţuică* (plum brandy) from the wife-givers and vice versa; asking for the bride; selling of the hen.

III. Integration: Bringing of the bride to the groom's home; coming after the bride; undressing the bride.

23 See Turner, p. 54.

24 See Petr Bogatyrev, *The Functions of Folk Costume in Moravian Slovakia* (The Hague: Mouton, 1971), and Denise Pop-Cămpeanu, "Les fonctions signifiantes des costumes populaires roumains," in *Buletinul Bibliotecii Române* 7, no. 11 (1979): 233–78, on the functions of costume with regard to the marking of status changes. For a comparative example of the ritual underscoring of changing social relations between unmarried friends and the "bride," see Kirin Narayan, "Birds on a Branch: Friendship in Kangra (India) Wedding Songs," *Ethnos*, forthcoming. Also, refer to Van Gennep on the structural features of rituals.

25 See also Edward P. Thompson, *Folklore, Anthropology, and Social History* (Sussex: John L. Noyce, 1979), p. 71. It should be noted that the superior status of the groom's family vis-à-vis the bride's is formally marked in the terms of address: *socrii mare* (grand in-laws): *socrii mici* (little in-laws), Stahl, p. 49. Such status differentiation is not uncommon; see Maurice Bloch, *Political Language and Oratory in Traditional Society* (New York: Academic Press, 1975), p. 11.

26 See Claude Lévi-Strauss, *The Elementary Structures of Kinship*, rev. ed. (Boston: Beacon Press, 1969), pp. 52–68.

27 Villages in Maramureş are divided into *susani* (upper part) and *josani* (lower). Upper and lower are reckoned either according to altitude or proximity to the source of the river.

28 Michael Silverstein, among others, has noted the metapragmatic and metasemantic character of formal oratory as being inherent features. Recall that in the bargaining situation the formal church marriage has already occurred. The ritual enacts it, moving participants through complex transformations of status/roles. Silverstein has pointed out that such performances "give structure to the relations among the participants in them because they literally are metaforms of the ordinary" ("Metaforces of Power in Traditional Oratory," p. 12, unpublished manuscript, delivered at University of Chicago, 1981).

29 See Claude Lévi-Strauss, *The Raw and the Cooked*, vol. 1 (New York: Harper Torchbooks, 1970), pp. 336–37.

30 The mother-in-law syndrome is generally characteristic of southeast European peasant societies. See, for example, Irwin Sanders, *Balkan Village* (Lexington, Mass.: Greenwood Press, 1949); Joel Halpern, *A Serbian Village* (New York: Harper Colophon, 1956); Ernestine Friedl, *Vasilika: A Village in Modern Greece* (New York: Holt, Rinehart, and Winston, 1962); Vera St. Erlich, *Family in Transition* (Princeton, N.J.: Princeton University Press, 1966); Eugene Hammel, *Alternative Social Structures and Ritual Relations in the Balkans* (Englewood Cliffs, N.J.: Prentice-Hall, 1968); and Andrei Simić, "Management of the Male Image in Yugoslavia," in *Anthropological Quarterly* 42, no. 2 (1969): 89–101.

31 Auntie is a general term used to address older women, usually married ones.

The term establishes a degree of familiarity although a kin link is not required.

32 See Danielle Musset, *Le Mariage à Moiseni, Roumanie* (Paris: Études et Documents Balkaniques 3, 1981), on the normative importance of the bride's virginity.

33 Ten lei is equal approximately to eighty cents. There are twelve lei to the dollar; singular, leu.

34 Pornographic *strigături* are, in fact, rarely heard in Ieud because they are not well-tolerated by Ieudeni. This is peculiar to Ieud and not characteristic of neighboring villages.

35 It is interesting to note that in respect of conspicuous consumption, the result of socioeconomic change has produced (thus far) a situation similar to that which is representative of capitalist modes of production. The conservative content of the housewife's role within the family is pertinent. Joan Landes, on p. 406, in "Women, Labor, and the Family Life: A Theoretical Perspective," in *Science and Society* 41, no. 4 (1977–78): 386–409, points out that "the family teaches workers to sell their labor power for the sake of consumption which they come to understand as leisure time. It teaches that leisure, not productive activity, gives meaning to life." See also Rayna Rapp, "Family and Class in Contemporary America: Notes Toward an Understanding of Ideology," in *Science and Society* 42, no. 3 (1978): 278–300.

36 William Moskoff, p. 601, in "Pronatalist Policies in Romania," in *Economic Development and Cultural Change* 28, no. 3 (1980): 440–56.

37 Cernea.

38 See Jowitt, pp. 1173–74.

39 See Turner and Munn.

40 Ceauşescu's current pronatalist campaign coincides well with "traditional" peasant values; however, Ceauşescu's "modernization" programs have succeeded in transforming those values. Ieud is more exceptional than it is representative in this regard. (Ieud purportedly had the second highest natality figure in Romania in 1978.) Most urban residents and village dwellers prefer to maximize familial benefits with respect to material gains. This contributes to a declining birthrate. In any event, it is conceivable that the Cultural Committee may attempt to extol the cultural virtues of the Romanian wedding rites as a means to encourage further participation in cultural patriotism: celebrate the heritage through ritual and through childbearing. (The potential disjunction between ritual discourse and actual practice is again evident. The state declares that the population must be increased regardless of the availability of infrastructural resources to facilitate that process.)

41 See Cristel Lane, *The Rites of Rulers: Ritual in Industrial Society—The Soviet Case* (Cambridge: Cambridge University Press, 1981), for a discussion of "socialist" rituals. Also see the special issue of the *Anthropological Quarterly* 56, no. 2 (1983), edited by David Kideckel, "Political Rituals and Symbolism in Eastern Europe," and, again, Caroline Humphrey's chapter on Ritual and Identity, especially pp. 382–401. There is very little in the way of literature on socialist rituals. In Romania the socialist wedding has gained in popularity in urban centers. All marriages, urban and rural, must be recorded in a civil ser-

vice that creates a formal relationship between the couple and the state. Following the civil marriage, wedding participants either proceed to a church for a religious wedding or to a rented hall or restaurant to celebrate. The celebration may include components of "traditional" wedding rites. To date, most people perform both the civil and religious ceremonies. (Sometimes, the civil marriage occurs well in advance of the religious event and wedding celebration.) Interestingly, many urban dwellers return to their natal villages to be married in some variant of the "traditional" wedding. Work constraints are influential in this matter; few people can afford to take three days from work. As mentioned previously, under these circumstances, the ceremonial complexity of the wedding rite decreases while the material exchange aspects increase. For a more comprehensive discussion of life cycle rituals in Transylvania, see my forthcoming book: *Beyond Dracula: Transylvanian Rituals of Life and Death* (Berkeley: University of California Press, forthcoming).

20 The Emancipation of Women in Fact and Fiction: Changing Roles in GDR Society and Literature

1 Alfred G. Meyer, "Marxism and the Women's Movement," in *Women in Russia*, edited by Dorothy Atkinson, Alexander Dallin, and Gail Warshofsky Lapidus (Stanford, Calif.: Stanford University Press, 1977), pp. 84–112.
2 Herta Kuhrig and Wulfram Speigner, "Gleichberechtigung der Frau—Aufgaben und ihre Realisierung in der DDR," in *Wie emanzipiert sind die Frauen in der DDR?* edited by Herta Kuhrig and Wulfram Speigner (Leipzig: Verlag der Frau, 1979), p. 40.
3 *Dokumente aus den Jahren 1945–49* (Berlin, DDR, 1968), p. 179, cited in Jutta Menschik and Evelyn Leopold, *Gretchens rote Schwester: Frauen in der DDR* (Frankfurt am Main: Fischer Taschenbuch Verlag, 1974), p. 13.
4 Kuhrig and Speigner, p. 41.
5 Menschik and Leopold, pp. 14–15.
6 Gabriele Gast, *Die politische Rolle der Frau in der DDR* (Düsseldorf: Bertelsmann Universitätsverlag, 1973), p. 20.
7 Gast, pp. 20–21.
8 Kuhrig and Speigner, p. 41.
9 Gast, pp. 36–37.
10 Menschik and Leopold, pp. 197–98.
11 Gast, p. 65.
12 Women held 32.4 percent of the seats in the Volkskammer in 1982, compared to 30.6 percent in 1970. *Women in the GDR, Statistical Report 1983.*
13 Gast, p. 67; pp. 242 ff.
14 Author collective: M. Allendorf, R. Blaschke, I. Tenske et al., *Women in the GDR* (Dresden: Verlag Zeit im Bild, 1983), p. 12; *Statistical Abstract of the United States*, 1984, p. 872, table 1519.
15 Renate Bridenthal and Claudia Koonz, "Beyond *Kinder, Küche, Kirche*: Weimar Women in Politics and Work," in *Liberating Women's History*, edited by Bernice Carroll (Urbana-Champaign: University of Illinois Press, 1976), p. 310.

16 Heinrich Goralzyk, "Ist die Frau Arbeitskraft schlechthin?" *Neuer Weg* no. 8 (1961), p. 399.
17 Inge Lange, "Die Frau und die technische Revolution," *Einheit* no. 1 (1965), p. 2.
18 Walter Ulbricht, speech to a convention of women's committees, cited in Menschik and Leopold, p. 32.
19 Ibid., p. 200.
20 *Women in the* GDR, p. 162.
21 Ibid., p. 167. Interviews conducted by the author in March and April 1980 indicated that childcare facilities were not being expanded rapidly enough to meet demand and women were experiencing more difficulty in placing children.
22 *Europa Year Book 1979* (London: Europa Publications, 1980), p. 673.
23 Menschik and Leopold, p. 196.
24 Marianne Kayser, Martin Zobel, and Bernhard Metzner, "Zu einigen Aspekten der Reduzierung der Hausarbeit," in Kuhrig and Speigner, p. 310.
25 See, for example, Juliet Mitchell, *Women's Estate* (New York: Pantheon, 1971), for an analysis of contemporary Marxism's failure to recognize or respond adequately to this contradiction.
26 Renate Apitz, Monika Helmecke, Helga Königsdorf, Maria Seidemann, and Charlotte Worgitzky, to name a few, have satirized, criticized, and openly attacked the male-female division of domestic labor in works of fiction printed since 1976. The best-known critic of the domestic status quo in the GDR is Irmtraud Morgner, whose 1983 novel *Amanda* offers witchcraft as a solution to the problem. In a burst of exasperation at the fact that 80 percent of all housework and childcare in the GDR is still performed by women who also have full-time jobs, she comments in a recent interview that the answer to the problem has been known for years: proletarian solidarity in private life. The problem lies, as it has for the past hundred years, in inspiring men to give up their domestic privileges. The interview contains an explicit Marxist analysis of this question. *Weimarer Beiträge* 30, no. 9 (1984): 1500–1502.
27 See for example, Sandra Gilbert and Susan Gubar, *The Madwoman in the Attic: A Study of Women and the Literary Imagination* (New Haven, Conn.: Yale University Press, 1979); Rachel M. Brownstein, *Becoming a Heroine* (New York: Viking, 1982); Carolyn Heilbrun, ed., *The Representation of Women in Fiction* (Baltimore: Johns Hopkins University Press, 1983), among many other works discussing this problem. See also *Signs* and *Feminist Studies* for articles on women writers and feminist criticism.
28 For discussions of the status and image of women under Nazism see, for example: Leila Rupp, "Mother of the Volk: The Image of Women in Nazi Ideology," *Signs* 3, no. 2 (Winter 1977): 362–79; Gisela Bock's forthcoming book on racism and sexism in Nazi Germany, sections reprinted in *Signs* 8, no. 3 (Spring 1983): 400–421. See also Renate Bridenthal et al., *When Biology Became Destiny* (New York: Monthly Review Press, 1984); *Mutterkreuz und Arbeitsbuch, Frauengruppe Faschismusforschung* (Frankfurt am Main: Fischer, 1981); *Der alltägliche Faschismus: Frauen im Dritten Reich*, (Berlin and Bonn:

Verlag J. W. H. Dietz und Nachf., 1981).

29 Silvia Kontos, *Die Partei Kämpft wie ein Mann: Frauenpolitik der KPD in der Weimarer Republik* (Basel: Stroemfeld/Roter Stern, 1979), pp. 172–74.

30 Willi Bredel, "Petra Harms," in *Fünfzig Tage* (Berlin: Neues Leben, 1950).

31 Elfriede Brüning, *Regine Haberkorn* (Halle: Mitteldeutscher Verlag, 1955).

32 Lutz-W. Wolff, "Nachwort," *Frauen in der* DDR (Munich: DTV, 1976), pp. 252 and 260.

33 Brigitte Reimann, *Ankunft im Alltag* (Berlin: Neues Leben, 1961).

34 Christa Wolf, *Der Geteilte Himmel* (Halle: Mitteldeutscher Verlag, 1963).

35 *Women in the* GDR, p. 162.

36 *Dokumente der Berliner Frauenkongress*, p. 33.

37 See Günter de Bruyn, *Buridans Esel* (Halle: Mitteldeutscher Verlag, 1968); Erik Neutsch, "Akte Nora S.," *Die Anderen und ich* (Berlin: Verlag Tribüne, 1974); Dieter Noll, *Kippenberg* (Berlin and Weimar: Aufbau Verlag, 1979); and Benito Wogatzki, *Das Preis des Mädchens* (Berlin: Neues Leben, 1971).

38 Elfriede Brüning, *Partenerinnen* (Halle: Mitteldeutscher Verlag, 1978), pp. 13 and 80.

39 Brigitte Reimann, *Franziska Linkerhand* (Berlin: Neues Leben, 1974).

40 Gerti Tetzner, *Karin W.* (Halle: Mitteldeutscher Verlag, 1974).

41 Christa Wolf, *Nachdenken über Christa T.* (Berlin and Weimar: Aufbau Verlag, 1975).

42 Irmtraud Morgner, *Leben und Abenteuer der Trobadora Beatriz nach Zeugnisse ihrer Spielfrau Laura* (Berlin and Weimar: Aufbau Verlag, 1976).

43 Helga Königsdorf, *Meine ungehörigen Träume* (Berlin and Weimar: Aufbau Verlag, 1978).

44 Brigitte Martin, *Der rote Ballon* (Berlin: Buchverlag der Morgen, 1978).

45 Helga Schubert, *Lauter Leben* (Berlin and Weimar: Aufbau Verlag, 1975).

46 Christine Wolter, *Wie ich meine Unschuld verlor: Erzählungen* (Berlin and Weimar: Aufbau Verlag, 1976) and *Die Hintergrundsperson oder Versuche zu Lieben* (Berlin and Weimar: Aufbau Verlag, 1979).

47 Renate Apitz, *Evastöchter* (Rostock: Hinstorff, 1982) and *Hexenzeit* (Rostock: Hinstorff, 1984).

48 Beate Morgenstern, *Jenseits der Allee* (Berlin: Aufbau, 1979).

49 Maria Seidemann, *Der Tag an dem Sir Henry starb* (Berlin: Eulenspiegel, 1980) and *Nasenflöte* (Berlin: Eulenspiegel, 1983).

50 Angela Krauss, *Das Vergnügen* (Berlin: Aufbau, 1984).

51 For criticism and commentary on recent GDR fiction see *Studies in* GDR *Culture and Society*: Christiane Zehl Romero, "Recent Developments in GDR Literature," vol. 1, pp. 111–26; Charlotte Armster, "Merkwürdiges Beispiel weiblicher Entschlossenheit," vol. 2; Zehl Romero, "Vertreibung aus dem Paradies: Zum neuen Frauenliteratur in der DDR," vol. 3, pp. 71–86; Dorothy Rosenberg, "On beyond Superwomen: The Conflict between Work and Family Roles in GDR Literature," vol. 3, pp. 87–100; Zehl Romero, "Weibliches Schreiben-Christa Wolfs Kassandra," vol. 4, pp. 15–30; Rosenberg, "Another Perspective: Young Women Writers in the GDR," vol. 4, pp. 187–98. Also see Karen Achberger, "GDR Women's Fiction of the 1970's: The Emergence of Feminism within

Socialism," *Central Eastern Europe* 6, no. 2 (1979): 217–31, and *New German Critique* cited above.

52 For an ongoing series of articles on feminist theory and women and literature, see *Signs, Feminist Studies*, and for specifically German perspectives, *New German Critique*, especially Special Issue of Women Writers and Critics, no. 27 (Fall 1983); Sigrid Weigel, "Contemporary German Women's Literature" *New German Critique*, no. 31 (Winter 1984) and no. 32 (Spring 1985); and Judith Stacey, "The New Conservative Feminism," *Feminist Studies* 9, no. 3 (Fall 1983): 559–84.

53 Personal interview with Irmtraud Morgner, May 26, 1980.

Editors
Contributors

Editors

SHARON L. WOLCHIK is Associate Professor of International Affairs and Political Science and a member of the Institute for Sino-Soviet Studies at the George Washington University. She received her Ph.D. in Political Science from the University of Michigan in 1978. She is the coeditor of *Foreign and Domestic Policy in Eastern Europe in the 1980's* (London and New York: Macmillan and St. Martin's Press, 1983) and is the author of articles on the status of women in Eastern Europe, women in politics, national inequality, and the role of specialists and professionals in policy-making in communist states. She is currently completing a book comparing women's roles in communist and noncommunist countries and is continuing her study of policy-making in communist states.

ALFRED G. MEYER has been Professor of Political Science at the University of Michigan since 1966. Born in Germany in 1920, he came to the United States in 1939 and served in the U.S. Army from 1941 to 1945. He received his graduate degrees from Harvard University. He is the author of books on Marxism, communism, Soviet politics, and Soviet foreign policy, and is also the author of a biography of Lily Braun, a German Marxist feminist, recently published by Indiana University Press.

Contributors

MARTHA BOHACHEVSKY-CHOMIAK, a Professor of History at Manhattanville College in Purchase, N.Y., is currently with the National Endowment for the Humanities. She received her Ph.D. from Columbia University in 1968. Her books include *Spring of a Nation: Ukrainians in Eastern Galicia in 1848* (Philadelphia: Schevschenko Scientific Society, 1967), *S. N. Trubetskoi: An Intellectual Among the Intelligentsia in Pre-revolutionary Russia* (Belmont,

Mass.: Nordland, 1976), *A Revolution of the Spirit: Crisis in Value in Russian Thought, 1980–1920* (Newtonville, Mass.: Oriental Research Partners, 1982), and *Feminists Despite Themselves: Women in Ukrainian Community Life, 1884–1939* (Alberta: Alberta University Press, forthcoming). She is a recipient of numerous grants and fellowships, among them the Woodrow Wilson Fellowship, Ford Foundation Fellowship, Founders Fellowship of the American Association of University Women, International Research and Exchanges (IREX) Board Fellowships, and a Fulbright grant.

MARY ELLEN FISCHER is Professor of Government at Skidmore College. She earned her Ph.D. in Political Science at Harvard University in 1974 and has published a number of articles on Romanian politics. Her research has received support from the National Council for Soviet and East European Research, IREX, Council for International Exchange of Scholars (Fulbright-Hayes), and the East Europe Committee of the SSRC and ACLS.

KAREN J. FREEZE is currently a Research Associate at the Harvard Business School. She completed her Ph.D. in East European history at Columbia University in 1974. Her article on Czech immigration appeared in the *Harvard Ethnic Encyclopedia* in 1980. Under grants from the German Marshall Fund and IREX, she spent 1983–84 in Germany and Czechoslovakia doing research on technological innovation in the postwar Czechoslovak textile machine industry and the transfer of technology to the west.

BRUCE GARVER is Professor of History at the University of Nebraska at Omaha and a Fellow of the Graduate Faculty of the University of Nebraska. He is the author of a book, *The Young Czech Party 1874–1901 and the Emergence of the Multi-Party System* (New Haven: Yale University Press, 1978), and various articles on Czechoslovak history. He received a Ph.D. from Yale University in 1971, has twice studied in Czechoslovakia on IREX exchanges, and is now writing about Czech immigrants in the United States.

ALENA HEITLINGER is an Associate Professor of Sociology at Trent University, Peterborough, Ontario. She obtained her B.A. from the University of Kent at Canterbury in 1971 and her Ph.D. from the University of Leicester in 1978. She is the author of *Women and State Socialism* (London and Montreal: Macmillan and McGill-Queen's University Press, 1979) and *Reproduction, Medicine, and the Socialist State* (London and New York: Macmillan and St. Martin's Press, 1985).

BARBARA W. JANCAR received her Ph.D. from Columbia University with a Certificate of the East European Institute. Her publications on the status of women in Eastern Europe include *Women under Communism* (Baltimore: Johns Hopkins University Press, 1978) and articles on women in Yugoslavia. She is currently working on a manuscript on women in the Yugoslav National Liberation Movement as well as on a study of environmental issues in communist states.

GAIL KLIGMAN is currently a visiting Assistant Professor in the Department of Anthropology at the University of California, Berkeley, and a Mellon Research Associate of the Center for Slavic and East European Studies, Berkeley. (She is on leave from the University of Chicago.) She is the author of *Călus: Symbolic Transformation in Romanian Ritual* (Chicago: University of Chicago Press, 1981) and is completing *Beyond Dracula: Transylvanian Rituals of Life and Death* (Berkeley: University of California Press, forthcoming). Future research plans include a project on the politics of culture in Eastern Europe.

JOHN KOLSTI is currently Associate Professor of Slavic Languages and Literatures at the University of Texas. He received his Ph.D. in Slavic Languages and Literatures from Harvard University in 1968. His areas of publication and research are in South Slavic and Albanian oral literature and in Balkan studies.

RÓSZA KULCSÁR graduated from Karl Marx University of Economics in Budapest in 1967 and received her Ph.D. in 1976. Group leader of the Mobility Section of the Social Statistics Department of the Central Statistical Office in Hungary, she has focused her research on intergenerational mobility, women's social mobility in historical perspective in Hungary, and the role of marriage as a channel of social mobility.

ROBERT J. MCINTYRE is Associate Professor of Economics at Bates College in Lewiston, Maine, and previously taught at Bowdoin College and Dartmouth College. He obtained his Ph.D. in Economics from the University of North Carolina at Chapel Hill and has written articles on Soviet environmental policy and performance, pronatalism and abortion policy, and Bulgarian historical demography. He is coauthor with Henry P. David of *Reproductive Behavior: Central and East European Experience* (New York: Springer, 1981) and is currently working on a monograph on the Bulgarian economy and a book on comparative economic systems.

SILVA MEŽNARÍC received a law degree in 1964 and a Ph.D. in Sociology in 1983 in Ljubljana, Yugoslavia. Currently a senior researcher of the Academy of Science and Art in Ljubljana and Professor of Sociology at the University of Ljubljana, she is engaged in a study of the theoretical roots and empirical manifestations of ethnicity in Yugoslavia. A former Fellow of the Woodrow Wilson Center for Scholars, she has published works on migration in Yugoslavia, the division of roles within the family, and Yugoslav workers in Germany.

BOGDAN MIECZKOWSKI, Professor of Economics at Ithaca College, Ithaca, N.Y., received his Ph.D. in Economics from the University of Illinois, Urbana-Champaign, in 1954. He has published five books, including *Social Services for Women in Eastern Europe* (Charleston, Ill.: Association for the Study of Nationalities, 1982), and numerous articles and reviews. His current research is on the problems of bureaucracy and technological change.

DANIEL N. NELSON, who received his Ph.D. in Political Science from the Johns Hopkins University in 1975, is a Professor of Political Science at the University of Kentucky. He is the author of *Democratic Centralism in Romania: A Study of Local Communist Politics* (New York: East European Quarterly, 1980), and editor of and contributor to *Soviet Allies: The Warsaw Pact and the Issue of Reliability* (Boulder, Colo.: Westview Press, 1984), *Communism and the Politics of Inequalities* (Lexington, Mass.: Lexington Books, 1983), *Local Politics in Communist Countries* (Lexington, Ky.: University of Kentucky Press, 1980), *Romania in the 1980s* (Boulder, Colo.: Westview Press, 1981), and *Communist Legislatures in Comparative Perspective* (Albany: State University of New York Press, 1982). He also has published numerous articles in scholarly journals and is currently working on a textbook and reader on East European politics.

MARY E. REED received her Ph.D. in History from the University of California, Berkeley, in 1980 and is now Director of the Latah County (Idaho) Historical Society and an independent historian. Her current projects include environmental and community studies and research on the role of women in western towns and agricultural societies in the United States. Her work on Croatian women was sponsored by IREX and a Fulbright-Hays Research grant in Croatia.

DOROTHY ROSENBERG received her Ph.D. in German Studies from Stanford University in 1977. She is currently Assistant Professor of German at Colby College. Her areas of current research include work and family role models and social change in the literature of the German Democratic Republic (GDR); social activism and domestic responsibilities in the autobiographies of twentieth-century women; and contemporary GDR women writers.

RENATA SIEMIEŃSKA received her Ph.D. in Sociology in 1969 from Jagiellonian University in Cracow and her next scientific degree (habilitation) from the University of Warsaw in 1976. Currently Associate Professor at the Institute of Sociology, University of Warsaw, she is the author of books on life in new towns in Poland, the aspirations of students in higher agricultural schools, personality patterns in socialist society, ethnicity in the United States, and the Polish value system and consumption patterns; she also has published widely on topics related to women's status in Poland. She has been a visiting Professor at the University of Michigan, the University of North Carolina at Greensboro, the Ontario Institute for Studies in Education, and the University of Rome.

IVAN VOLGYES is Visiting Distinguished Professor of Political Science at Rutgers University and Professor of Political Science at the University of Nebraska. He received his Ph.D. from American University in Washington, D.C. He is the author or editor of more than twenty-two books and several scores of articles dealing with Eastern Europe and the USSR. His latest book, *Politics in Eastern Europe*, will be published by Dorsey Press.

SUSAN L. WOODWARD is Associate Professor of Political Science at Yale University. She received her doctorate from Princeton University and writes on comparative socialist development and Yugoslav political economy. She is currently writing a book on unemployment in Yugoslavia and another on Yugoslav education.

Index

Library of Congress Cataloging-in-Publication Data
Main entry under title:
Women, state, and party in Eastern Europe.
(Duke Press policy studies)
Revised and updated papers first presented at the Conference on Changes in the Status of Women in Eastern Europe held at George Washington University, December 4–6, 1981.
Includes index.
1. Women—Europe, Eastern—Congresses. 2. Women in politics—Europe, Eastern—Congresses. 3. Women and socialism—Europe, Eastern—Congresses. 4. Feminism—Europe, Eastern—Congresses. I. Wolchik, Sharon L. II. Meyer, Alfred G. III. Conference on Changes in the Status of Women in Eastern Europe (1981: George Washington University) IV. Series.
HQ1236.5.E85W65 1985 305.4'0947 85-16262
ISBN 0-8223-0660-3
ISBN 0-8223-0659-X (pbk.)